SOGGY RED CONFETTI

A Celebration of a Family Changed by Drug Addition

By Lory A. Harris

Maggie -
Celebrating life +
loving you!
Life is awesome!
Love,
Lory Harris

Soggy Red Confetti
Copyright © 2017 by Lory A. Harris

ISBN: 978-0-9995029-0-7
CBIII Designs, St. Charles, Illinois

Cover design by Ace Silva
Portraits by Stacy Vitallo
Editing by Jennifer Arbaugh

Praise for *Soggy Red Confetti*

Life, as it turns out, is rarely just joy or pain; the two are often inextricably intertwined. It is a rare person who can hold both these realities simultaneously, neither minimizing one nor ignoring the other. Lory Harris is one of these people, and I can think of no one I'd rather journey with down a road marked by colliding sadness and celebration. She writes out of the heartbreak of a mother watching her beloved son self-destruct, and while her story is unique and compelling, I have no doubt you will find your own story on these pages, too. This book is filled with authentic faith and wrestling, poignant hope, and unexpected humor, and I guarantee it will stay with you long after you've read the last word.

STEPHANIE RISCHE
Author of *I Was Blind (Dating), but Now I See*

Soggy Red Confetti is a story about redemption. Lory Harris writes with a bold vulnerability about how her faith in God was challenged and strained through their family's nightmare. This story beautifully illustrates how God goes with us into the darkest places and He is able to fill them with His light. This is a story about the ultimate healing of a family that was bruised and battered, and that kind of healing only comes by God's grace.

JEFF FRAZIER
Senior Pastor of ChapelStreet Church, Geneva, Illinois

I had the great privilege to read *Soggy Red Confetti* by Lory Harris, the mother of a formerly homeless son. In intimate detail, she shares the deep love both parents have for their child, as well as the torturous decisions they were forced to make as his life began to unravel. They had pulled all the proverbial rabbits out their hat seeking services which might allow him to have the life they all had dreamed of. With one poor decision after another, resulting in their own lives being in constant turmoil, they asked their son to leave. Middle of the night manic worries for their son's safety defined their lives: Is he warm? Does he have food? Is he safe? Does he know deep down how much we love him?... Is he alive? It was a long journey, a rough one, but I'm sure you will agree, the destination was worth the effort.

LIZ EAKINS
Executive Director of Lazarus House, St. Charles, Illinois

For my family and fellow travelers.
Let's celebrate!

Author's Note

Sometimes life changes on a dime. Sometimes, rather than thin, that dime resembles a mist-shrouded mountain of unknown height and dimension. Having grown up in the flatlands of the Midwest, I prefer to view rather than climb mountains. Sometimes the choice isn't yours to make.

This book represents truth, at least as it was seared into my memory and then re-assembled several years later. Incomplete journals, random letters and scraps of ancillary data helped to keep the time line accurate. While all the characters within existed, not all are personally or specifically identifiable. In some instances, names, locations and details have been changed and color has been added to flesh out some situations while preserving the outcome. Some events are composites, or might be composites, my memory tending to blur some situations where others seem crystal clear. There is no attempt to deceive or exonerate, especially myself. I am responsible for so many of my own tears.

SECTION ONE
DUSK
December 2002 – November 2003

Excerpts: University Hospital
Emergency Room Record
Sunday, December 8, 2002

18-year-old white male brought to emergency room by Iowa State Campus Security at 2:12 a.m. He has no ID, but states his name is Courtlandt Harris from St. Charles, Illinois, currently a student at Iowa State.

Per officers, patient admits to wandering around campus in only slippers and a blanket. Fellow students were alarmed by both his action and his speech. They contacted Campus Security for assistance. Mr. Harris voluntarily left with Security.

A physical examination shows that Mr. Harris is in good physical health apart from large blisters on both feet, the probable result of walking outside in sub-freezing temperatures with only wet cloth slippers on his feet.

Patient appears to have difficulty staying on topic. His conversations range from paranoia and conspiracy to reincarnation and exaggerated self-importance.

Patient's mother, Lory Harris, called the emergency room, having been advised that Courtlandt had been brought here. Patient was in Australia over Thanksgiving break and has not been able to regulate his sleep since his return. Observed psychotic behavior may be a result of severe sleep deprivation. Toxicology tests also reveal the use of marijuana, with levels high enough to indicate recent use. Reported behaviors may indicate suicidal tendencies.

Patient has agreed to check into the Psych Unit for observation and diagnosis. Mother has been advised to call the Unit around 8 a.m. for an update.

And So, It Begins – Part I **Lory Harris**
December 2002 **St. Charles, Illinois**

My eyes are open, but they can't focus. Is it 11:11 or 1:11? How many vertical lines are electronically swimming on my bedside companion? My brain can't focus, either. Reaching to silence the alarm, I realize it still slumbers. The phone is the disturber of the peace. Phones are not supposed to ring when darkness is complete and the first number on the clock is a "one" - or two, three, four or five, either. Six is suspect, too.

Throwing off the covers, I cross the room in three strides. "Hello?" There is an edge to my voice – both fear and annoyance amplified by the body's natural fight-or-flight reaction. It had better not be a wrong number that dragged me from the warmth of my bed. That would irritate me for the next couple of hours while waiting for my body's chemical reaction to subside.

"Hi, Mom. What are you doing?" It's our youngest son, Court. His words are too rushed, too staccato, and apparently oblivious to the sun's current position. The cold that had been nipping at my toes joins forces with the chill running down my spine. I find myself instantly wishing for that wrong number after all.

"Are you ok?" Not my most eloquent greeting, but perfectly adequate when the clock is sporting three of a kind. My eyes are starting to focus, though my brain is still swimming against the early morning darkness.

Just a week ago, my husband and I returned from the trip of a lifetime: two weeks in Australia and New Zealand visiting our middle son, Corey, who is studying abroad for the semester. Court joined us for the second week during his Thanksgiving break. Since Court's return, though, jet lag is really doing a number on him. He has barely slept since I dropped him back at Iowa State six days ago.

"I miss you, Mom. I want to come home. Will you come pick me up from school for the weekend?" It's Saturday night—well, no, it's Sunday morning. The round trip to and from Ames, Iowa, is 10 hours—20 for me, since I would have to make the trip twice. "I can't sleep. It would really help me to be in my own bed." Timing couldn't be much worse with Christmas approaching and me trying to catch up from vacation. Add to that, I am slated to teach my very first quilting class later today.

In truth, Court made the same request yesterday morning. At that time, we had struck upon a compromise: his grandparents in Grinnell,

Iowa, a mere 30 miles from him, would pick him up from school and drive to a mall roughly halfway between our two locations where I would meet them for the afternoon. After we spent some time together, Court could decide if he wanted to come home or go back to school.

The visit had been odd. Court was disheveled and wild-eyed. All the words made sense, but the trails they led down were a bewildering maze of randomness. "My English Comp paper is due on Tuesday, but every time I work on it, I fall asleep. If only I could sleep. It's okay, I'm almost done and I'm acing that class. What do you think I should write about? Are you sleeping ok? Wish I could borrow some from you." Wandering the mall, Court eyed some plush Iowa State slippers. He was still wearing them a couple of hours later when he opted to head back to school and his paper. Walking him back to Mom and Dad's car, he stepped over piles of snow in the slippers, his shoes carried securely in the bag I handed to my mother. Court had set the bag down and forgotten it three times in 45 minutes. Mom seemed a much more reliable choice to protect the more practical footwear.

Yesterday's shadow floats around the room bringing its own chill to what already feels sub-zero. "How about next weekend? I can come out on Friday and pick you up after your last class to come home for the weekend. Do you think that would work? In the meantime, how about hanging out with a buddy? Is Matt around?"

"Okay, sure, that will work. I'm with Matt right now. I'm using his phone. Mine is in my room, but I'm headed back there now. I think I'll get some sleep. Bye, Mom. I love you!" Even fluffy slippers wouldn't warm me up now. The bed with the down comforter looks inviting but woefully inadequate against the frost rattling my spine.

There is no sound of sleep coming from my husband, Ken, either, so we pass the time discussing the previous day in light of the awakening phone call. Even as I left the mall parking lot yesterday, I was dimly aware that practicality was overshadowing my better judgment, but Court had insisted on heading back to his comp paper. I reasoned he just needed a good night sleep, and that my parents were only 30 minutes away from him, if needed. I can't call them, though, at this insane hour - and to do what, tuck their grandson in? What he needs is a good night's sleep and that's where he's headed. Eventually his body must give up and give in to sleep. I pray that tonight is the night.

From our down-covered cocoon, Ken and I circle the same themes and options several times. It seems to take an eternity, though the clock, running on electricity rather than adrenaline, shows the passage of only another seven minutes. We finally decide I should tuck Court in, long distance style. His phone, apparently taking a powerless nap, goes straight to voice mail without courtesy of a ring. Maybe he hasn't gotten back to his room yet. I leave what I hope is a calm message asking Court to call me – calm words, maybe, but measured with a crisp cadence. I wait a full half hour before calling again, though the clock credits me with only 40% of my effort. Again, there is no answer in Iowa and no disguise for the panic in my voice, either.

Feeling suffocated by the once-welcoming cocoon, I opt for fuzzy-slipper-pacing, the phone in one hand while the other clutches my robe more tightly to my body. It must be the wintery shock that awakens my senses. Court called from Matt's phone, meaning that I now have another link to my son, electronically preserved on my Caller ID. Matt was up half an hour ago, and he's a college student approaching the end of his first semester. Surely, he's still awake, or is fair game to be woken, at least. I pause only long enough to make sure the correct number will be activated by the redial command. Four rings later, Matt's voice speaks with mechanical diction, directing me to leave a message. Panic ill-contained, I comply.

My husband, the voice of reason, insists on letting the redial button rest. My brain might agree, but my finger twitches as it hovers over that slim but quickest link to my son. Every three minutes I pray that the technology gods will bless me with a live voice on the other end: I call Court's phone twice with identical results (sans leaving another message), and then Matt's number. Finally, I am rewarded with a conversation. Matt has the opportunity for only one word, "Hello?" before I start talking.

"I can't get a hold of Court. Would you please go down to his room and have him call me? I want to make sure he's okay."

And So, It Begins – Part II
Matt Wilson

December 2002

Iowa State University
Ames, Iowa

I've known Court a long time. I don't honestly remember when I didn't know him. We grew up a few houses apart in a quiet suburb outside of Chicago. He wasn't my best buddy (that was James) but growing up with a readily available group of boys for a baseball game or snowball fight within a block or two is a good day. I had lots of good days growing up.

Court was a really smart kid. He and another girl, Katie, were in a special math group starting in second grade. While the rest of us pulled out books and pencils, learning techniques and tables, they talked excitedly about long division and geometry. They weren't exactly speaking our language, but we looked longingly at their enthusiasm.

Court also used his smarts to dream up ways to grab attention. Once he put a tack on a classmate's chair. It was effective: Court got his seat changed to the one right outside the principal's office. He spent a lot of time in that unofficially assigned seat throughout that year.

Intense would be another good word for my childhood mate. If you could be on his team for a school project, a good grade was guaranteed, and you wouldn't have to carry the project by yourself to earn it. He could tell a whole group of pre-adolescent boys to stop picking on a kid or he wouldn't be their friend, and they would listen to him. On the flip side, he once took a swing at a girl who was teasing him. She ducked, and he hit her friend square in the nose – warranting more time at his non-classroom desk. I remember a time in high school when he put green pond dye in the retention pond on school property. He earned a special seat then, too, in the school library on a Saturday.

Court and I played competitive soccer together from grade school all the way through high school. By the latter years, though, our friendship revolved almost exclusively around the "pitch." We both paid our dues, climbing the ranks and ending up on varsity. Court was the goalie and I was a mid-fielder. We missed the state playoffs by one game our senior year, putting a disappointing period on the end of our soccer careers. Well, we both played in an intramural league here at Iowa State. That, though, was purely recreational with none of the pressure to perform and no coaches yelling their directions or displeasure.

Besides the occasional soccer game and living in the same dorm, we don't see a lot of each other here at school. He is in pre-vet classes and I spend my spare time in an art studio. His roommate requested a change of address after only three weeks of school amid rumors of some wild behavior, but I stayed out of it. As it has been our entire lives, Court and I are friendly, but we only skirt the edge of friendship. It suits both our personalities.

If Court has always walked on the edge of eccentricity, he has certainly fallen over the edge now. Tonight, I was taking a study break with a couple of friends when Court walked into my room just after midnight. He was talking a hundred miles an hour and pacing back and forth. The words were all coherent, which is more than I can say for his thoughts. He talked about evading some sinister-sounding people by jumping out his dorm room window. He grabbed a phone from someone walking on campus to call the police, but then gave it back without making the call. He couldn't trust the police, I guess – or the phone. When he finally went back to the dorm, he realized his keys were locked in his room. Since his room was up half a flight of stairs, he couldn't enter the same way he had exited—the window sill was beyond his reach. We let him prattle on.

After a while, though, his stream of consciousness got a bit tedious to follow and my mind drifted. It's cold outside, even colder than usual for December in Iowa. There is a dusting of snow on the ground and the ponds around campus are starting to freeze over. Court was wrapped in a blanket, showing his school spirit with some fluffy Iowa State slippers on his feet. His bare legs peeked out from time to time as the blanket swayed in response to his pacing. Curiosity and the need to stem his diatribe got the best of me. "Court, what are you wearing?"

"This," he replied, opening the blanket to confirm that his entire wardrobe had already been visible. From there he launched into a one-sided discussion of Socrates and reincarnation. "I met Socrates, in his tenth incarnation, at the student union just last week. He encouraged me to be content with minimalism to become richest of all! My life on this plane is drawing to a close," he intoned, "as I reach the level of God's omnipotence. Iowa State has nothing to offer me, since my true intelligence is in admitting I know nothing." Have you ever tried to tell someone about a dream you had and the more you fumble for the right words and descriptions, the less plausible the whole thing becomes? That is how it would be to tell you about Court's conversation. The circular logic was dizzying.

At some point, he changed lanes to near-normal and mentioned something about having seen his mother earlier in the day. He wanted to call her, but his phone was locked in his room. I loaned him my phone to make the call. Frankly, I was hoping for some adult intervention. Judging from the incredulous looks on my friends' faces, they were also willing to grasp at any plausible straw.

Of course, I only heard the Iowa side of the conversation, but it didn't seem to be going as I had hoped. I'm not exactly sure what I had expected, to tell the truth. Even if his parents jumped in the car immediately and drove like maniacs, it would still be morning before they would arrive. Court sounded more upbeat than he looked, though my knowledge of his attire might have influenced my perception. In the end, he handed the phone to me and announced he was going back to his room to get some sleep. Having been stunned into silence, we just watched him go.

The next sound heard in the room was our laughter. I wish I could say otherwise, but laughter is a great tension reliever, and we all needed that! Then we reached for the student handbook hoping for words of wisdom. Where in the index do you search for 'crazy dorm mate'? Campus Security seemed to be the catch all, so we called.

A hopeful plan in place, we were just getting ready to go find Court when he appeared at my dorm door. His keys were still locked safely in his room and the window had not stretched any closer to the ground. We told him that Campus Security would be willing to take him to University Hospital, which is only a couple of miles from campus. Court kind of brightened at that. I don't know if he wanted the help or if he even understood the kind of help being offered. Maybe he was just thinking of the previous threat from the mysterious foes that had caused him to jump out his window. Maybe this was something Socrates would want to experience upon being thrust into the 21st century. Whatever the rationale, he left peacefully with the summoned men in uniform.

My phone had rung and been pointedly ignored shortly before Court's departure. Shortly after, it rang again – an Illinois number, and likely, under the circumstances, Court's parents. It was his mother. I've met Mrs. Harris a million times, maybe a million and one. But suddenly, I felt overwhelmingly shy or maybe just exhausted. I didn't offer any of the back story, but told her that Court was acting erratic and that Campus

Security was taking him to University Hospital to be checked out. I'm not sure what I heard coming through the phone line: fear, disbelief, the desire to talk to a doctor who might have concrete information? Our conversation was short. She thanked me for being there to help Court and we ended the connection.

It's shortly after 2 a.m. now, but no matter how tired I feel, my brain is having none of it. It's running in circles like a remote-control car with fresh batteries. I hope he's okay, this friend-ish of mine. But, to be honest, I hope our established boundaries won't be put to a similar test again anytime soon.

Socrates has left the building.

And So, It Begins – Part III — Court Harris
December 2002 — University Hospital, Ames, Iowa

My new location is a hive of activity, and I am at the center, of course. The minions bustle around calibrating and re-calibrating their instruments. I'm not sure if they recognize me or not, disguised as I am in borrowed pajama pants and emblazoned t-shirt. They speak in hushed tones, aware, no doubt, of my recent awakening. A pretty blonde dressed in nondescript fuchsia scrubs studies a chart for several long minutes, her pen gracefully resting against her lips. She appears frozen in time, waiting for a spring thaw that is still months away. Closing my eyes and opening my mind, I focus on freeing her from her predicament, an act of pure benevolence. Within moments, I am rewarded with two taps of the once inert pen on the chart. Simultaneously, I "hear" her birdlike voice chirp of an inaudible "thank you," her pretty lips remaining as perfectly pursed as before. With equally fixed lips, I acknowledge her gratitude, "You are most welcome. Go in peace." She turns and recedes down the hallway, a lighter lilt in her pre-dawn steps. Telepathy is a much more efficient form of communication: not just words, but emotions as well, are exchanged with ultimate clarity. What remains to be perfected are the distances between conversational locations.

My extraction was amazing, a bit heady even. The two uniformed agents who met me at Matt's room escorted me to their waiting vehicle and whisked me away to this undisclosed location. In route, I glanced out the back window a couple of times, but we did not appear to be followed. My chauffeurs performed with absolute deference and respect, holding doors and inquiring continually about my comfort. I should have gotten their badge numbers to express my appreciation to their superiors. I did, however, offer my sincere accolades, multiple times, as they drove back to their assigned post. They were quite professional in all their actions and humbled, I believe, by my gratitude.

My fuchsia friend returns with a middle-aged man who introduces himself using spoken word (much more pedestrian). Though he is obviously well-educated, mentioning his post-graduate degree several times, he is poorly dressed: green scrubs ill-disguised by a white jacket. He, too, is respectful, though he seems to have a foot-fetish or something. At least, he is spending a lot of time examining my lowest extremities. He asks if I would like to spend a day or so at this location; it would not be an imposition. In fact, sleeping facilities have already been prepared in anticipation of my arrival. His hospitality being so accommodating, it's hard to say no to the offer. Pronouncing my feet fit for use, something I could have told him with much less fanfare, he covers them in soft blue tubes of fabric.

As my foot-fetish friend retreats, I use traditional means to ask Fuchsia for another set of tubes. Green, this time, which makes a nice visual contrast as I wrap them around my hands, I am offered a ride in a wheeled chair to transport me to my waiting bed and I see no point in risking the soiling of the softness covering my feet. I ride in warmth and comfort, down a passageway, up an elevator, and through a corridor. We, Fuchsia and I, pause in front of a formidable set of doors, standing resolute at our arrival. "Behavioral Medical Center" touts the sign on the door. What is the world coming to that it is necessary to request appropriate behavior when one receives medical care? Of course, they can count on my complete compliance.

Fuchsia speaks briefly into a box on the wall. Honoring my silent and her spoken requests, the doors swing noiselessly inward, revealing my spacious accommodations for the evening – the well-appointed lounge, complete with a small library and a ping pong table, deserve more than tonight's cursory viewing. The concierge rises from her desk to greet me and shows me to my room.

Dimly lit though it is, my sleeping quarters meet with my approval. What light there is chases after us from the hallway and is joined with diminutive efforts from the two windows on the opposite side of the room. My bed is closer to the exterior light than the interior one. Climbing obediently between the crisp white sheets of my bed, my blue festooned extremities disappear like early spring blossoms under an ill-timed snow. I am indeed thankful for their contributing warmth.

With the hallway door now closed, I turn my face away from the suddenly more persistent brightness offered by the windows. As my eyes adjust to the new level of luminosity, I study the contours of my roommate's face. Weathered and wise, the persistent pull of gravity has added both character and whimsy to his features. His nose is too big, his cheek bones too high. A jagged scar just below his left eye speaks of both strength and endurance. Streaks of grey in his white flowing hair and beard blend with the snowy crispness of sheets and blanket. The whiteness claims all but his nose and eyelids. Even the bushy eyebrows resonate with the relentless march of time. His name is Tom, as the concierge had indicated just before returning to her assigned post. His soft snoring necessitates the delay of formal introductions.

Tom. Naturally we would be selected to share a room together – his wistful yet sage appearance reveals a soul open to more intimate forms of communication. But like ordinary speech, telepathy is not effective with a drowsy soul, and I have been taught to respect my elders. Still, excitement quells my attempts at sleep. Tomorrow the two of us shall have long rambling conversations. I had just never realized that Father Time's first name was Tom.

Down Under — Corey Harris

December 2002 — Gold Coast, Australia

I've been in Australia for the semester and am having a great time. My roommate, John, and I just got back from a week in New Zealand – a vacation to celebrate our academic successes, slender margins notwithstanding. Fortunately, my school in the States only takes pass/fail for studies abroad.

As amazing as Australia is, New Zealand's South Island surpassed it by leaps and bounds. We hiked, we partied, we slept on the beach, we tested the limits of our fear and then pushed beyond. John and I got back today, tired and broke and without a single regret!

Our apartment manager saw our return and waved us down to pass on a message. I guess my parents have been trying to get a hold of me. Not knowing we had taken a side trip, they finally called the complex manager to get word to me. John and I carried our luggage in. I thought I would quiet my stomach's rumbling and have lunch before calling Mom and Dad. Though the cupboards are technically less bare than our wallets, they house only one package of spaghetti. Pasta it is.

Reaching Mom on her cell phone, I offer a quick apology for being out of touch and start to tell her about the trip. Judging by the meager words coming from stateside, it seems she is listening politely, though not completely engaging in the dialogue. I decided to save most of the details for a future conversation and ask how things are back home.

"Court is in the psych ward of the Ames hospital. He has had a psychotic break. We know he has used marijuana recently, and the doctors suspect it may have been laced with embalming fluid or something. He isn't talking – at all. He wanders around the unit, but like it's just his body and the rest of him is nowhere to be found." I am catching Mom's panic through the phone lines. I wish I had held off on my scant lunch; it isn't mixing well with my raising anxiety level.

Embalming fluid? Is that some kind of sick Iowa college prank? Pot is usually such a mellow, joyful high. It's like everything of importance just slows down for closer inspection. But it doesn't stop altogether, which seems like what Mom is describing. And it only lasts for hours, not days.

Court was just here in Australia about a week ago. He stayed with me for a couple of days after Mom and Dad headed back to the States. We had a great time: went to the beach, flirted with girls, had some beers, and smoked some weed. I mean, it was just normal guy stuff - John, Court and me. But he was fine when I dropped him off at the airport.

As if she can hear my thoughts, Mom asks, "How was Court when you were with him? Any problems? You guys didn't smoke any pot, did you?" Why did she have to put it so succinctly? I want to say, "He was fine, and we don't use weed," but I'm not a great liar, and this is my brother's life we are talking about. It's precious little, but maybe this truth will be useful in some way.

"Court and I had a great time when he was here. We did share some weed one night, but it was no big deal and Court was fine when he left here." Who knew that plain pasta could get so churned up in your stomach?

A moment of silence and a sigh makes its way half way around the world. "Okay. I'll pass that info on to the doctors." I think I might have felt better with a verbal rebuke of some sort. As it was, I just feel a world of disappointment standing between us. I can't see how last week's pot factors into what is happening now. There was no embalming fluid in the bowl we shared.

It makes me feel even worse about what I must say next. "Mom, I just had the vacation of my life. I mean, it was awesome! And my money has held out for the whole semester – until now. The only food in the house is a half a box of pasta. I'm broke, and John is more broke than I am, if that's possible. And we still have the second half of the month's rent to pay..."

"It's okay. It's just money, Corey. How much do you need? All I want is you, Colin and Court all home for Christmas. I'll transfer the money to your account tomorrow."

Suddenly, looking out the window at the sunshine and the girls lying by the pool, lorikeets singing in the distance, I realize that's all I want, too – the snow and cold of Chicago, and the warmth of family around the Christmas tree.

"I love you." The words arrive simultaneously on both sides of the world.

Visiting Hours **Cora Swanson**
December 2002 **University Hospital**
Ames, Iowa

I grew up in small-town Iowa. It's a good place to live, where the role of the local newspaper is only to confirm what is already commonly known. News, rumors, and other human anomalies circulate widely, and much more quickly than the Ames Tribune. The same can be said for the college campus news mill, especially when the student population doubles the size of the town nine months of the year. Printed news is a mere formality. As both a resident and a student, I have near-immediate access to all information in this corner of the world, real or touted. So, when my study partner missed our standing date a mere ten days before finals, I consulted my sources to ascertain his whereabouts.

Court and I met the first week of school. Despite our differences, we hit it off immediately and formed our own study group. He is big city to my small town. I am unconventional to his clean cut. For example, he keeps his hair short and stylish. Mine varies wildly in both cut and color, currently shaved on one side and blue on the other. We hit it off right away. I met his girlfriend when she came to visit, and he has met my boyfriend. We aren't likely to double date or anything, but we are well acquainted with each other's lives.

The thought of him sitting by himself at University Hospital in the psych ward hit home. Let's just say that I have been detained before, and I know the feeling of dejection and loneliness. His visiting hours are restrictive, but I managed to work my schedule around them. When I arrived around 8 tonight, Court was sitting with a couple who I presumed, correctly, to be his parents. We had discussed parents over a beer, and he had done a good job of it. His dad fidgeted in a bored kind of way. You could tell he wanted to be elsewhere – *anywhere* else. He's like a farmer wearing a tux at a wedding: it's not that the farmer doesn't want to see his daughter wed, but, he reasons, what do collar stays, cummerbunds and bow ties have to do with marriage? Mrs. Harris, on the other hand, looked battle weary but determined. The scant two visiting hours are likely to be the highlight of her day. My own son is just two, but I understand her mother's heart. There is no where I would rather be than with my child, even if he is someplace I don't want to go.

We shared small talk about the upcoming finals and school in general. Court will be taking incompletes in all his classes and finishing them up next semester. While he doesn't look thrilled at the prospect, it's probably the right decision. Missing the last full week of prep and walking into his exams cold would be a GPA killer.

Mr. Harris excused himself shortly before 9. Mrs. Harris and I left a few minutes later when visiting hours ended. "Thank you so much for coming to visit Court. The doctors think," she said, "that he smoked pot that has been laced with embalming fluid. It caused a psychotic break. Court has mentioned several times that the two of you are friends. I guess I'm just asking you to be a good friend and don't let him smoke pot again. He rarely uses drugs anyway, but I would really appreciate your help. We certainly don't need a repeat of this."

"Absolutely," I stammered, hoping I sounded more convincing than I felt. But I was really thinking, *So, he doesn't tell his mother everything.*

Diagnosis **Ken Harris**
December 2002 **University Hospital**
Ames, Iowa

It's odd making this trip alone. Lory and I drove out together a couple of days ago. The five-hour trip required two: one to drive and the other to make sure eyes didn't close. Our rest that fateful night couldn't really be called sleep; it was more like marking time, waiting until the rest of the world woke so we could get more info. The overnight ER doctor told us specifically to wait until morning before deciding to drive out. It was a relief to hear that Court was physically fine, but a sleep-stopper to hear that they believed our youngest may have attempted suicide, based on his lack of apparel and frostbite to his feet. The drug tests didn't reveal much beyond pot in his system, but you can't test for everything, I guess. Maybe he tried to overdose on something. But the suicide label, though shocking, didn't seem to have much evidence supporting it. However, even if Court had been pronounced fit after a good night's sleep, we would have made the trip anyway, just to lay eyes on him.

By the time we got to the hospital early Sunday afternoon, the psychiatrist had made a thorough examination of Court. Well, it was mostly a visible examination since Court refused to talk. He was wandering around the psych ward wearing a fellow patient's socks – on his hands. He seemed to recognize us when we walked in, but said nothing. He just fixed us with an intense stare, as if that was supposed to mean something. No amount of pleading or reasoning could wrench words from his mouth.

Given the silence their patient had been maintaining, we were on the hook for what answers we could provide the medical staff. Court is a straight A student with a large academic scholarship for his pre-vet major. He has not slept more than a few scattered hours since returning from our Australian vacation a week earlier; the jet lag seemed to be especially hard on him. No, there is no history of mental illness in either of our families. Yes, we knew he had tried pot, but he doesn't use on a regular basis – nor does he use any other drugs.

After all the questions – theirs and ours – one thing was not in doubt: our office would not be opening on time on Monday morning. Lory and I own an architectural design business, CB III Designs, and we are the only two employees. After two weeks of vacation, we were scrambling to catch up. This couldn't have come at a worse time – not that there could possibly be a good time to find your son confined in a mental ward.

University Hospital has a nearby house with rooms for rent to the out-of-town relatives of patients. For $20 per night, we slept in twin beds on opposite sides of a tiny room. At least we pretended to sleep, and our tossing didn't jostle the other awake during a chance moment of successful slumber. With visitation between the hours of 7 and 9 p.m. only, there was ample time to lament the missing nighttime dream state. While everyone in our shared rental was very respectful, daytime sleep was no more prolific. Our minds just wouldn't shut down long enough to allow for sleep.

We made the rounds of local restaurants for meals. I was always hungry, probably because it felt like a brief respite from a world gone literally crazy. Lory's appetite was just the opposite – she ate two or three bites max before pushing the plate away. She excused herself to use the restroom and invariably returned with red-rimmed eyes. I wanted to hold her and draw out the poison that was infecting her soul, but no matter how close or how long, I only succeeded in drawing out more tears. She remained haggard and diminished – fragile.

It took almost 24 hours, but we finally reached our oldest son. Colin recently joined the Marines and is at the School of Infantry in California, or in the military vernacular, SOI. Communication channels are slightly more available than when he was in Boot Camp, but Uncle Sam still dictates the conversation opportunities on an ever-rotating-but-not-consistent time table. Like Corey, Colin is shocked and concerned about his little brother. Maybe Colin is even a bit more concerned, or at least more informed, since his undergrad major was Psychology. It's probably a good thing his employer is so demanding of his time. I know from personal experience that long hours with nothing to do but play the "what-if" game is personal torture.

Late yesterday when I called my mother, she casually mentioned that my dad was prescribed Miltown before he died, back when I was in my teens. Miltown is used for anxiety disorders, and in the 60s and 70s, it was used to treat manic depression. Bingo! The missing link – there *was* some mental illness in my family. As of this morning, Court is diagnosed as bipolar. Not the best news, but there are medications that will allow him to lead a normal life. They made slight changes to the drug cocktail he had been prescribed, and even in the space of a few hours, he is talking more and seems to be coming around.

After two extra days of forced "vacation," I'm headed home and back to work. Lory will stay in Ames in the little rented room and keep watch over Court and his progress. We borrowed a car from her parents so she can get around. If everything goes per plan, I'll be making a return trip this weekend to bring Lory and Court home. In the meantime, there is a lot of work to be done – for all of us, I guess. Mine is of the conventional variety. Lory's and Court's are of the healing variety. All in all, the Christmas season might be looking a bit brighter now than it has looked for the past few days.

And I Quote **Carol Gunter**
December 2002 **University Hospital**
Ames, Iowa

It was the morning of another gnawing day when I first saw those green eyes. I remember because I was eating my breakfast of blandness accompanied by nuggets of pharmaceutical numbness. *Resistance is futile* (The Borg). My pink socks, which he had employed as hand warmers, set off the color of his eyes. "Give me back my socks," I told him. I really didn't care if his hands were cold or not. His attempt to escape my request was blocked by a lady in shapeless scrubs who de-gloved him and handed me my prize. His eyes looked so much more dull without the pink contrast. *Eyes are the window to the soul* (Shakespeare). He looks like a contender to break the residential record I am setting here.

With breakfast finished, time lulled forward to morning group: grab a seat and grapple with the words to impress Scrubs, who is suddenly 30 pounds heavier and male. Attention is focused on the green-eyed newcomer, donning white socks now on his more northern digits. Scrubs introduced us to Court, who offered no acknowledgement or spark of recognition to the world that held him captive. "Court, would you tell us something about yourself?"

As senior member of this exclusive club, it fell to me to rescue the newbie from scrutiny. *"I'd rather regret the things I've done than regret the things I haven't done,"* I quipped (Lucille Ball). Immediately, I knew that this rather clever retort from the famous redhead took the heat off Green-Eyes and shifted it to me. Scrubs wasn't impressed. My record may yet stand…

As it does every day, morning group droned on into lunch and then into afternoon group, spreading five hours across what feels like three weeks' time. But break time and the possibility of ping pong arrived at last. I just needed an opponent. Scrubs, still male but now more athletically built, feigned too much work. Most of my fellow guests were tucked safely away in their rooms, eyes closed, willing time away.

It was then that I caught a deeper flash of green in his eyes. "Court, you want to play ping pong?" Still wordless, he walked over to the table and removed the sock from his right hand. I made haste to request the ball and paddles from Scrubs lest the green fade again. He was good – better than most, and would have likely beaten me with his normal chemical balance. Thirty minutes flew by in three before Scrubs came to gather the paddles and Green-Eyes. "Court, the doctor would like to see you now." I watched as the green receded. *"I glanced seaward – and distinguished nothing except a single green light, minute and far away..."* (F. Scott Fitzgerald).

Predictably, as always in the world within these walls, dinner arrived with spaghetti, salad, bread, a cupcake, and a small blue chaser of sanity to be washed down with water. As expected, and dreaded, the visiting hours of seven to nine arrived right on time. Of the fifteen captives interned here, only three or four can expect a visitor on any given night. Of those, only one will enjoy the visit after the first brief moments of broken monotony. As always, I retreat to the company of my closest companions, who sit jacketed and dusty in the corner that doubles as a library.

That night, new faces entered our realm: a couple – obviously visitors, since those of us with a reserved bed always arrive as singletons. Truth be told, though, the stress on their faces, the water that threatened to leak from their eyes, and the nervous shuffle made them indistinguishable from those of us with assigned pillows. Both in their forties, I guessed, they walked in holding hands. It was difficult to know who was the donor and who the receiver in their transaction of shared strength, but their feigned resolve couldn't fool a trained professional like me.

Their eyes matched: my ping pong partner's and his visiting mother's. They hugged as each set of green orbs dripped on the other's shoulder. Dad, one hand around each of his family members, completed the circuit. When the words started, they were of a predictable nature: "We love you. What happened? We are here to help. How are you feeling?" But, perhaps put off by Court's fingerless gloves, now blue, they did not ask if he was okay. His words were more plentiful, predictable, and insistent than they had been earlier in the day. "I'm sorry. I'm okay now. I want to go home."

A couple of hours later, the family's smattering of conversation ended with a hug, a kiss, and another plea. Court's plea was replaced by his parents' promise to return – same time, same station. It wasn't what he was looking for, of course, but it was the best he could expect: that, and a pillow, and a capsule of forced sleep, followed by another day of sameness in search of saneness.

I would love to say that the next day dawned all bright and shiny. Nope. The same dull December dreariness filled the appointed hours. But the day was not without its highlights. Court wore new hand coverings almost the exact shade of his eyes. Frankly, I think Scrubs was messing with him. How many colors do those footies come in? As the ranking

POW, it was my duty to let Green-Eyes, the ping to my pong, know that no one walks out of here with socks on their hands. Between bites of oatmeal, I made my case. He looked at me skeptically, but at morning group an hour later, I saw for the first time that he needed to clean and cut his fingernails. His silence, though, remained deafening. *Action speaks louder than words but not nearly as often* (Mark Twain). Mark may have a point, but in here, if you don't talk, you will stay. I made a mental note to discuss that with Green-Eyes over breakfast the next day.

Court's Mom and Dad were true to their word, arriving again at 7:02 p.m. Dad looked a bit wearier, but stronger. Mom looked sleepless and melting. How does a person melt? She was certainly smaller, softer, grayer, though by an act of sheer willpower, the tears did not escape. Their conversation varied only by degree. Beyond pleading for release, Green-Eyes had little to say. Mom and Dad seemed relieved to see 10 fidgeting fingers, but did not mention the reduction in footwear from four to two. Dad won't be back for the next torture period. He must return to work. Mom will stay here. If you ask me, Dad craves normalcy and Mom wants her little boy back. They will be lucky if they get either.

I approached breakfast the next morning with my pep talk prepared. But as I chewed my first bite, weighing my words, Court's voice interrupted softly, "Do you practice telepathy?" My startled eyes met his green pleading ones. How could I have forgotten? Why, yes! Just two weeks ago I had a long and rambling conversation with the Pope. We had discussed abuse and forgiveness and the merits of red shoes. How had we left that conversation and why had I not returned? I glanced up at the florescent lights and then back at him. "Yes, of course, but not in here. They block those things," I said with an upward nod. "In here, we have to talk." Ever so slightly, his head nodded acceptance.

And so goes life behind the invisible bars. Eat, boredom, group, boredom, eat, boredom, group, ping pong, eat, torture, sleep. Mom returned every evening to even more forceful demands for release by Green-Eyes. She wasn't in control of that, but she was his only outlet, and he used it liberally. She continued to melt a little more each day, though I doubt he noticed.

I think it was the day before his actual release (though each day blurs into the next without distinction) when I heard Mom and son embroiled in another round of the same conversation.

Green-Eyes: "I'll come home for Christmas break and then come back here in January for second semester. I'll follow all the rules you have set. I just want to come home and be with you more than a couple of hours a day. I won't use weed ever again."

Mom: "I've heard that promise before. What has changed that I should believe it now?"

"Oh, what a tangled web we weave when first we practice to deceive." (Sir Walter Scott).

She stopped and looked at me. I saw again the family resemblance in the windows to their souls. (Shakespeare). She was weary and definitely melting, but there was strength there as well: resolve and the tenacity of a mama bear. And with a nod in my direction, she turned back to her son.

Mom: "What she said! I love you, but why should I believe you now?"

He was caught, but he knew he was loved. And even in his desperation, he also knew he had won. She will fight for him because she believes in him. Her skeptical reply was only for show. She will believe him again, and again, and again. And like the frequent flyer I am, he and I will meet for more games of ping pong. Together we will search for a door that opens and leads back to our own normal.

So, when Scrubs (now slender and female) allowed Court's escape this morning, I didn't say good bye, but rather, "see you later."

Home **Lory Harris**
Christmas 2002 **St. Charles, Illinois**

Merry Christmas – just barely. It's not even 12:30 yet. Ken and the boys helped Santa deposit the gifts at the base of the tree before retreating to other corners of the house – the boys to watch a movie and Ken to visions of sugar plums. More accurately, the boys are having a slumber party in the basement. The movie, abandoned within the first 30 minutes, continues to play on in their sub-consciousnesses. It might not sound like the perfect start to a perfect Christmas, unless you spent the bulk of the month wondering if normal ever really existed.

Corey's issues were easily solved: a little cash in the bank account and a long hop across the pond. He came home with stories from Australia and New Zealand that made me truly grateful for the bliss afforded by the lack of foreknowledge: surf lessons, skydiving for the first time with no tandem instructor, bungee jumping over a mountain pass from a gondola.

It ended up being theatrics that made my heart beat faster for Colin. Remember the famous parenting mantra, "Because I told you so?" Well, apparently, it's borrowed from the military, though our parenting version is a mere toothless shadow compared to that of the Marines. Parents tend to make wild threats that both sides of the equation know will come to naught. But when a jarhead with stripes tells your son to toe the line or their Christmas leave will be spent eating turkey surprise in the chow hall, there is justifiable panic all around. Marines don't prohibit beer, but they also don't tolerate the lingering effects of it during working hours. Colin tucked his toe back onto the southern side of that northerly line and kept it there until he was safely in the air making his way home. Smart boy.

Still, Colin's skirmishes were child's play next to Court's. We had spent the first few hospital days wondering if our son's brain was just so fried that he would never return. Who would lace pot with embalming fluid and why would anyone do that to another human being? Finally, the sun had begun to dawn on our tilted world when we found out that Ken's father had likely been bipolar, judging by the medication he was taking in the early '70s. I guess my scant faith in drug dealers is restored; the pot was just pot and not laced with anything.

From that discovery on, things had changed quickly. Rather than overcoming an individual event, we were now looking at treating a life long illness; this was both the good news and the bad news. At least we had a diagnosis to treat and a course of treatment to employ, rather than playing the waiting-praying-hoping game. I'm still waiting and praying, but I am more hopeful.

It was difficult to find a psychiatrist to take on Court's case here in our neck of the woods. The difficulty was not in the rarity of the diagnosis or the proposed initial course of action – neither of which are unusual in the world of mental illness – but rather the scarcity of such trained medical specialists, which says something about the mental stability in the Chicago 'burbs. Gratefully, God gave us an early Christmas gift. Dr. Orson was highly recommended to us, but his staff reported he was not taking new patients. He personally returned Ken's call and agreed to handle Court's case, and he recommended a psychologist. Thus, we have our team assembled.

With a top-notch medical team and modern pharmaceuticals employed, we are poised to return to our normal life. In addition to the more ordinary miracles of life, there is plenty of reason to praise God and celebrate His Son's birth. There may still be a couple of bumps along the way - after all, Court still has all his classes to complete at Iowa State sometime over the next three months. He will attend Elgin Community College, just up the road, starting in January, so he will be close to medical monitoring of his treatment during this initial phase. I don't think he is thrilled with the prospect, but he has decided not to continue with pre-vet anyway. This change gives him time to find a new life focus.

Every year we choose an ornament for the Christmas tree that represents the previous year, usually just one. This year, though, we have three. There is a Marine in his dress blues in honor of Colin's decision to join the military. Not so coincidently, there is a full-sized set of blues under the tree that he will open later today. I can't wait to see them on him! There is a kiwi bird ornament to commemorate Corey's semester in Australia and the trek that Court, Ken and I took to visit him. Finally, there is an Iowa State football ornament, to celebrate Court's graduation from high school and the next step in his educational process. All three ornaments were purchased in November and waited in anticipation of the tree they would adorn. I wonder what the ornament would have been if we waited until December to choose one? What about this overshadowing month would I want to commemorate from year to year on boughs of green? Nothing, I think, except maybe the gift now hidden by brightly wrapped presents, at the base of our tree: a child in a manger with His parents' loving gaze fixed on His swaddled form.

Thank you, God, for the return of our life as it should be. Happy birthday, Jesus.

Unwelcome Company
February 2003

Court Harris
Iowa State University
Ames, Iowa

I'm frozen. Not just freezing, but totally frozen. I can't move; I won't move. I won't give away my position to anyone or anything lurking about seeking to devour me. I am barely breathing, fearful that the rise and fall of my chest might give me away. But my heart betrays me. It pounds wildly, demanding attention, seeking escape, revealing the true writhing within my frozen body.

I was sleeping, dreaming, I think – I hope. But I was not alone. With razor-sharp claws and talons, my companions of the dark shredded the veil that protected my world from theirs. Was it their world they revealed? Or was it the true authenticity of my own dimension flooding my dreams? Regardless, that world of senses, excluding sight, has overrun my consciousness: at once cold and blistering, void of light yet fearfully jagged, oppressive and simultaneously empty. Their words start as a hiss, lisping softly in my ears, "This is real. You have been chosen, trusted with the truth. This is all life has to offer."

My mind struggles to run from the vision of despair, while my feet are rooted by fear. If I run, will I fall from this precipice into the nothingness of life? Am I standing on a cliff? Am I standing? A mirthless laugh fills me, but it is not my voice. No longer a hiss, but now a reverberating roar, they continue, "You cannot run! You cannot plead ignorance! You cannot un-see the truth that imprisons you! Your only escape is suicide." Terror fills my paralyzed limbs, as my mind runs blindly, far less afraid of the falling than the staying.

Am I alone now? I will not open my eyes for fear the flutter of the delicate lashes will attract attention and bring the beasts back to gnaw on my soul, already mauled and bleeding. I must trust only my ears to see discretely, to discern my world – and discover my companions. I hear breathing, asynchronous with my own, causing my heart to redouble its tell. Probing the sounds still more, I hear the breathing spiral into a moan and then a shift of body mass. Brent, my friend Brent. He has not abandoned me nor been eaten by the demons of the night. Or was it the whimper of his spirit's final release that I heard? My companion's breath, whoever he might be, continues deep and even, compared to my shallow, ragged cycle.

A closer auditory examination reveals scuffling and clearing of the throat, though both are muffled by concrete barrier walls. Perhaps the beasts have left in search of other victims. Have they left a lisping jailer to ensure my complicity? Some indistinct music filtering through multiple barriers sings of hope and goodness - or is it a wicked, deceitful trap? My eyes remain closed, fearful of catching a glimpse of the terrifyingly un-seeable.

My heart, slowing from exhaustion, gives way to messages from other bodily parts. I am painfully reminded of last night's alcoholic intake. The presence of the beer and whisky is being discussed in both my head and my mid-region. My nose, discretely joining the investigation of my circumstances, confirms stale cigarette smoke mingling with the remnants of the sweet bowl of burning leaves Brent and I shared well into the night. So, I have been returned to the dorm room, but who is my companion?

Without warning, there is a rustling and a cough. I can both hear and feel the footfalls as they advance toward me. Waiting for the sinister cackle of a thousand beasts to fill the room, my bed suddenly shakes. Despite my best efforts, my eyes fly open. Struggling to focus on my aggressor, the sudden light renders me as sightless as the total darkness had. The voice is not a rasping hiss, but rather Brent's sleep-laden one. "Isn't your make-up English final at 10? It's quarter to."

Not trusting my voice with a response, I nod and head to the bathroom on shaky legs. I have survived the night, but with a well-warranted fear of ever closing my eyes in sleep again. The dawn has not vanquished my foes. Even in the night's single encounter, I can tell they will return again and again. Sweet dreams are no longer an option.

My Baby Boy **Lory Harris**
February 2003 **St. Charles, Illinois**

Finally, my son is back. Corey is still in Wisconsin finishing his last semester of college. And Colin, deployed to Iraq, is stealing my sleep if his youngest brother hasn't already beaten him to the thievery. Court pulled into the driveway two days ago, returning from a weekend of makeup finals at Iowa State. I was so relieved to see him, having spent the hours leading up to his 1:00 a.m. arrival quelling my panic. Nearly convinced that he was dead in a ditch or wandering around in a cornfield wearing only shoes and a blanket, I was thrilled to hear his car in the driveway and see him walk through the door. It just took another two days before I could ask how the finals went. Well, no, I asked immediately. It took two days before he "returned" so he could, or would, answer. First, we had to endure 48 hours of his mute silence.

While he was in Iowa, we discovered he had not been taking his medication on a regular basis. Those meds are the ticket back to our normal life: no more "telepathic" answers when we ask questions, no more discussion on how microwaves have doomed us all to miserable deaths. I know he needs to get into the habit of taking them, but a habit should be forming by now. When he returned Monday night, or more accurately, Tuesday morning, I was so panicked by his wild-eyed look and complete refusal to talk that I even called his psychologist in the middle of the night. She advised that he was exhibiting signs of either a psychotic episode or the effects of alcohol mixed with drugs, prescription or otherwise. If the latter, Court could quit breathing.

I stayed up until 4:00 a.m. watching his chest rise and fall in the rhythmic pattern of sleep. I don't even remember doing that when Court was a baby. I mean, I remember watching him sleep, that tiny gift of life, the wonder of a miracle entrusted to me. I would marvel at the way the moonlight caught his pudgy cheeks and upturned nose. I would touch his peach-fuzz head, just to make sure that I wasn't dreaming, assuring myself of the authenticity of the blessing. But I don't remember listening and specifically watching his tiny chest rise and fall, making sure that one breath followed another. It's a beautiful sound, the soft intake and exhale of life-giving breath. It has a peaceful rhythm to it that shouts "life" when I quiet myself enough to hear it.

All the anticipation I had of the much-needed conversation in the daylight went unrealized. On rising, if that's what you call it, Court was near catatonic. Still 100% non-verbal, his eyes remained closed all day. Silently, wordlessly, he spent the day crying, doing nothing for himself. I walked him - led him - around the house. I fed him each bite of food, led him to the bathroom. I read books to him as I would a sick preschooler. His psychiatrist advised that hospitalization was an option, but he felt we could handle the situation unless things got worse. Court took the medication he had been missing, and I prayed that with the pharmaceutical assistance my son would return this morning.

There was a marked change in Court when he rose today. Gone were the tears and lethargy. He was happy and very compliant, doing everything asked of him - short of opening his eyes or talking. Again, I guided him around the house and fed him. Today, the tears were all mine, though I tried to shed them privately. With his eyes closed, I guess Court wouldn't have seen them anyway, but it didn't seem right to burden him with my panic and fears.

The reality of bipolar is settling in. How much damage will be done before Court realizes that the chemical imbalance in his head doesn't have to remain? What kind of damage will result: physical, mental, emotional, relational? I have talked to mothers of bipolar children who are now in their forties, still battling that demon, refusing to silence it with the necessary medication on a permanent basis. I see such a long road ahead of us, and I will walk it if I must. But I am terrified. The only way to win is to surrender to the necessary medication. Are you strong enough, Court, to do that?

Around five this evening, Court spoke his first sentence: "Mom, what's wrong with me?" As we talked, his words came easier and after a while he opened his eyes. Half an hour later, he went down to the basement to play pool until dinner was ready. Later this evening, he explained that he was in control the whole time. He had simply been conducting a scientific experiment on the possibility of returning to infanthood, which had been, in his estimation, a total success. I, on the other hand, observed a trapped and tortured soul unable to control the slide into madness.

Lord, give me strength to do what I must and wisdom for the journey. But most of all grant us peace – for Court's mind and my own. What a precious commodity, and how I long for it. But if there is only enough peace for one of us, please grant it to Court. His peace is my peace.

Mailbox Mayhem **Martha Gaines**
March 2003 **St. Charles, Illinois**

I live in a premiere neighborhood of an affluent suburb. My husband and I built this house twenty years ago--no, thirty. Where has the time gone? A hard worker with a great job, this was his dream, and mine, too: a four-bedroom brick house with all the amenities. Our neighbors are good friends. Many have lived here as long, raised families and are now being visited by the grandchildren and even some great grandchildren. The wooded lots offer both habitat for wildlife and privacy from other human inhabitants. It is our own in-town acre oasis – close enough to be in community and spread out enough to enjoy solitude.

We are only forty miles from "the city," and yet a world away. A city dweller might think that we are country folk, but that's not how we view it. Chicago is in our back pocket: when it suits our mood, needs or desire, it is an hour's train ride away. Otherwise, it is a foreign country, one, it seems, too often on the verge of civil war. Here, we lock our doors at night and when we are away, of course. But even when I come home to an unlocked door, I simply enter my home chiding myself for my forgetfulness, never doubting that all my belongings will be as I left them. Except for the tornado siren tested on the first Tuesday of each month, a piercing wail is rare indeed. When it breaks into our quiet subdivision, the Early Neighbor Alert Network will likely pinpoint the exact reason for the ruckus before the sound waves have even dissipated. If not, the small-town newspaper will deposit explanatory details on my doorstep the next morning.

I live here alone now, my children pursuing their own American dreams, and my husband now resting, having realized his. It's lonely sometimes, or at least it has been. In the five years of my forced solitude, I have learned to enjoy my own company and to seek out friends when the quiet starts to overwhelm. It is a good life: comfortable, secure, idyllic even. Or so I believed until a few days ago.

I was watching *Everybody Loves Raymond* in my family room. It's a good way to start the evening, even if I had seen the episode before. It still makes me laugh, albeit a bit longingly for the antics that were a part of *my* life before this house grew in equal and opposite proportion to its number of inhabitants.

Suddenly, with a sense of urgency, my ringing doorbell brought me to my feet and my feet to the front door. My neighbor Brenda was there. I know because I heard her voice over the approaching sound of sirens. I didn't see her as I was looking straight past her to where her husband was throwing a bucket of water on fingers of flames reaching from my mailbox toward the trees above. In short order, sirens drowned out Brenda's actual words, their meaning having been previously punctuated by the now silent doorbell. The neighborhood gawked at flickering red light bouncing off homes and trees, emanating from the general direction of my front yard. Fortunately, the color disturbance came not from the flames, which were quickly extinguished, but from the lights of two fire trucks now blocking the road in both directions. No doubt my neighbors would not need to read about it in the paper. Most were gathered out front having opted for this live performance over a Raymond re-run.

The excitement was over within an hour with only the faint smell of smoke in the air as a reminder. An amateur sort of firebomb had ignited the blaze – some kids' idea of fun, I suppose. But I won't be forgetting to lock my doors any time soon.

I spent the next day buying a mailbox to replace the charred hunk of aluminum that rests on the post in my front yard. I also bought 9-volt batteries to replace the ones in my smoke detectors. Finding someone to install the new mailbox was proving to be a problem, though. My son would do it, of course, but not until he gets back from a family vacation. Until then, I guess I will make a daily trip to the post office.

Yesterday as I prepared my early lunch, the doorbell rang, again, though not with the same urgency it previously exhibited. When I opened the door a young man in his late teens or early twenties stood before me, fidgeting slightly. Behind him was a woman who appears to be his mother, judging by age and facial similarity.

"My name is Court Harris, and this is my mom. We live on the other side of the river," he says. "I was with a group of my friends the other night when we put a fire bomb in your mailbox. I am here to do whatever you judge would be fair to make it up to you. I will pay for the damages, or you may call the police and have me arrested. I'm sorry for what I did, and I want to make it up to you." He looks at me steadily as he says these words. But his eyes are soft, not at all defiant, showing what seems to be a genuinely contrite heart.

"It's a good thing my neighbors were home. If they hadn't seen the flames, it could have started the trees on fire. Even with their quick action, the closest branches are singed. The results could have been horrific!"

"I know. It was so stupid. I'm sorry." His head suddenly seems to bend under extra weight of this knowledge and he examines his shoes. I guess I can't blame him.

I wonder aloud where his friends are. Why is he the only one here to shoulder the blame? But he insists that this is about him and his actions. "I could have stopped them, or at least I could have left and not participated. I knew it was wrong. I know I was wrong. I am here for myself."

Whatever anger I thought I could muster dissipated as I watched his shy eyes meet mine again. In them, I saw my son's eyes when he was that age – not that he had ever caused deliberate damage to someone else's property. But there was a familiar look of remorse that I've seen when good times have doubled back on themselves and sped off in the opposite direction.

"Insurance will pay for the damage. But, I have a new mailbox that needs to be installed after the post is cleaned, repaired and repainted."

"I can do that! I'm good with tools. I'll do it today." There is a spark of possibility in his whole being, like a puppy who thought he was in trouble but is thrown a ball instead. I suppress a smile as I show him my new mailbox, and he assesses the tools he will need to complete the job.

I have hardly completed my lunch when he returns to starts work on the project. He takes care to wash down the post, sand where needed, and repaint it entirely. When he goes to grab the new mailbox, I catch his mother by herself. "Thank you for making him come over to apologize. I appreciate his honesty."

"Oh, this was 100% his idea. I'm just here for moral support. Last night he told me what he had done and insisted on confessing to you. I heard about his offer to be arrested at the same time you did. Thank *you* for not taking him up on it, though I would have allowed it if it came to that." Her eyes are as transparent as his, a genetic trait, I guess. Here is a woman who loves her son but will not keep him a little boy. I'm glad I chose this path over the others offered by my eager handyman.

My fire incident made the newspaper today, and it also mentions another mailbox burning that same evening on the other side of town. I wonder if Court paid a visit, and a return visit, to that house as well. At least his name isn't in the arrest report. While my mailbox installation may not be of a completely professional standard, it does once again receive and dispense posts as it was designed to do. It lists slightly to the left, a reminder of an imperfect world where grace has been given and gratefully received. It is enough.

Standing Room Only — Merry Luehr
March 2003 — St. Charles, Illinois

It's a comfy chair, leather and overstuffed. I've been here often, in the home of my bestie, Lory. But until tonight I've never noticed how comfortable that chair can be. Remembering the sight in my periphery for the past couple of hours has made the chair that much more inviting. Court stood there while the two of us watched a movie. I let him pick the DVD, a poor decision on my part. Monty Python – irreverent British humor, suggestive and inappropriate for a mother's bestie and son to watch together. Still, if the content made me uncomfortable, it was nothing compared to how Court must have been feeling. He looked exhausted, shifting endlessly from one foot to the other in an effort to equalize the pain of standing for so long a period.

Ken and Lory are out of town this weekend, a necessary escape from the crazy that seems to be housed here for an extended stay. They felt comfortable enough with Court's recent demeanor, or perhaps desperate enough despite it, to leave their son home alone for a couple of days. Certainly, they didn't trust him implicitly, a misgiving that has been borne out by the flamingo stance of tonight's movie companion. Perhaps I should suppress my smile, or maybe not – I did let him choose the movie.

The plan had been for me to invite Court over for dinner, to lay prying eyes on him and assess the situation. That part had gone reasonably well; what teenage boy would turn down a free meal? He rode up on his bicycle, claiming to have needed some exercise. The late winter streets are marginally passable on two wheels, and our houses are only a couple of miles apart, so the trip was short. Court wandered around the house, something just short of pacing, but not accepting a seat when offered, either. Still, the conversation fell within the normal range. I chalked the wandering up to nervous energy.

Food and table preparations complete, I invited both Court and my husband, Mike, to the table. Court entered the dinette, glancing at the spread. His eyes widened in an expression that I could not read at the time, and he suddenly announced that he forgot he had a pizza in the oven at home. Mike offered him a ride home, but Court declined. We watched him leave, standing while pedaling to get there more quickly—or so we had surmised. Mike and I ate our meal and then opted for an early evening car ride. A four-mile round trip should be plenty, we decided.

Court's car was in the driveway when we arrived, but no one answered the door. I certainly hoped he wasn't out on his bike in the waning evening light. On a whim, I had Mike take an indirect route back to our house. Rounding the second corner, headlights illuminated our quarry walking in the general direction of his house. "Hop in, Court, we'll give you a ride."

"No, thanks, I'll walk." His demeanor was pleasant enough, though his attire was scant given the direction of the mercury in the post-sunset thermometer.

Mike and I held an entire conversation in a glance. "I'll give you a call later," I said and exited the car to walk with Court back to the house. He was quite talkative—rambling, yet coherent. But when I asked him about the pizza, I received a blank look, as I had suspected.

I went into the house with him and attempted an inconspicuous examination. Everything looked to be in place. I suggested the movie and sunk into this chair while he started the regrettable show. As the opening irreverent scene started, Court returned to stand beside me. "Don't you want to sit down?" I suppose I could have offered him the chair, but apparently, it wouldn't have mattered anyway.

"No, thanks, I have to stand to please the gods." He didn't offer more in the way of explanation, and I wasn't quite sure where to steer the conversation.

"How long have you been standing?"

"Since I got up this morning."

"So, are you going to stand up all night?" He nodded.

Half-way through the movie, he asked if I thought it would be okay if he knelt. I shrugged. His flamingo dance had lost its initial charm. He reached for one of the pillows on the coach. "I don't think they would approve of the pillow, though." Not that I have the inside scoop on what his gods think, but I wanted this to end as quickly as possible. Knees on oak flooring should hasten his admission of defeat. Before the credits rolled, Court silently screamed "uncle" and flopped into bed.

Time to give Mike a call, I guess, and let him know he can likely pick me up in the morning. The guest room is just across the hall from where Court is now snoring. I should be able to hear him if he decides to practice standing again. But somehow, I doubt he will. I think Court learned a valuable lesson about the way God made him: little 'g' gods can make whatever silly requests they will, but big 'g' God sets the rules. Just standing on His promises…

From Iraq to Wisconsin — Ken Harris
March 2003 — St. Charles, Illinois

I spent the day working by myself again. My business partner, my wife, headed to Wisconsin to collect our silent son and bring him home. Court had been visiting his brother Corey at college for the weekend. When he headed out I felt just a bit of stress depart with him on his two-hour drive. At least I didn't have to wait up for a few of nights wondering when he would return and in what condition. I don't think there has been a more nerve-racking week in my life, and that includes the University Hospital week last December.

The whole nation had been watching and waiting to see what would happen in Iraq. Would Saddam Hussein feel the pressure of the U.S. military at his doorstep and back down? Would he be foolish enough to unleash chemical weapons on our troops as it appears he has on his own people? The nation was watching with 6 o'clock-news rapt-attention. In our house, though, the need for news knows no hour. We hang on any and every tidbit the internet offers. It is neither national pride, nor sympathy for the oppressed, nor the price of a barrel of oil that links me to any shred of Iraqi information. All my focus is on one particular Marine who is currently making his home in the desert: our son Colin.

We woke on Thursday morning to the news that airstrikes had commenced on Baghdad. At least we hadn't stayed up late enough on Wednesday to acquire that information. One final night of rest was appreciated, though it is now, of course, a distant memory.

During lunch, neither Lory nor I exercised our vocal chords with sentences longer than a few words, leaving the rest of the verbalization to CNN and CSPAN. I wandered out to the mailbox as she cleaned the kitchen, and there, found the one thing that could distract me from war's oppressive grip: a letter from Colin. Little did I know it would only squeeze me that much tighter.

"03.03.11" it started with military date nomenclature. The letter was written almost two weeks earlier, but it felt fresh and current - tangible proof of life as I started to read. Colin talked of readiness drills to don their "mop suits" (chemical warfare protective clothing), a whole company of warriors watching a movie in the desert heat, each man self-enclosed and sweating profusely. He relayed the challenges of driving an LAV (light armored vehicle) across landscape that literally changes with the wind, hills of sand disappearing only to reform a couple of klicks (kilometers) away. So much of his meaning must be deduced from context or ignored when all else fails. Military vernacular sounds familiar but is really a foreign language. Unintelligible acronyms dot the page, leaving me to feel either ignorant or just terribly out of touch – a feeling with which I am well-acquainted, having raised three sons to their late teens and early twenties.

Lory and I drank in two full pages of information, front and back. Until, that is, our hearts stopped at the last full paragraph. "If for some reason I don't come home, I want an Irish wake. I want everyone to have a beer, many beers, and sit around and tell stories about me and all the things I've done: the good, the bad, and the ugly. I want everyone to remember me as I really am." I had anticipated proof of life, but not this. Not foreshadowing, I prayed. The fear of war renewed its grip, squeezing out the last of my resolve and my first tears of the day.

For the last three days, Lory and I have longed for word from Colin, but knowing that at present, no news is the best news. When the phone rings it mimics our jittery nerves. We approach the Caller ID screen with trepidation. If it spelled out "US Government" or something similar, I'm not sure we would even have the strength to pick up the receiver. Would it be our son on the other end or another uniformed voice with news we couldn't bear? There is, of course, no bank of phones available to the enlisted as our national mission draws them onward in tighter and tighter spirals toward Baghdad. We are left to conjecture about our son's location, driven alternately by hope and fear. It's like an anti-party game, "Where in Iraq is Colin Harris?" Nasiriyah? Basra?

I should have known that today's innocent-looking phone tag would cause our world to crash. "Corey Harris," it read – Wisconsin calling, not Iraq or Washington, DC. Celebrating their youth, Corey and Court had decided to party. Apparently, though not immediately confessed, their definition of party included pot. Court is, once again, entirely mute. Corey is at a loss for what to do next. Lory left almost immediately, medication in hand, to gather our temporary distraction from war. Her best friend, Merry, went with her, since someone had to drive Court's vehicle home: we weren't going to allow our son to share the road with anyone in his current state.

My afternoon has been split between Iraq and Wisconsin, all the while trying to accomplish something in Illinois. Illinois is getting short-changed. Where is Colin? Is he safe? What is he enduring in the name of Operation Iraqi Freedom? What was Corey thinking, letting Court smoke pot? Did he think we were kidding about the way it affects his younger brother? And just how hard is it for Court to pop a couple of life-restoring meds daily? But if this is the life he wants to live, why does he have to do it under my roof? He's over 18, why do I have to keep picking up the pieces?

It's nearly five when Court's truck pulls into the driveway - Lory is driving, of course. I can see them talking as they approach the door – well, I can see Lory talking. I don't see any evidence of reciprocal communication. When Court enters, he is staring down as if each step's placement is of the utmost importance – walking through a field of landmines or something. He's not the one at war. He will see no true danger here, just the anger in my eyes. I imagine his eyes are blank, again.

"He's still not really talking – just a few words, but he took his meds when I gave them to him. I think he will be okay by tomorrow," said the mother, as her gaze lingered on the doorway through which her child had just disappeared.

I don't see the door. I don't see the mother. I see scarlet scud missiles bursting overhead. I see fiery flames of destruction raining down around me. I hear my youngest son's mocking silence. I see my middle son's actions flipping me off. I feel my eldest son's precarious situation and I see those who would do him harm. I feel my wife's distance as she gathers her chicks, leaving me to fend for myself amidst a blaze of glowing embers.

I see red.

And as I describe the color of my world in succinct and boisterous terms, I see my wife turn to me, noticing for the first time since her return that I, too, am a member of this family. Embers are raining down among swirls of smoky ashes.

Dinner is a silent affair. The sun has set, changing the world from vermillion to black, the exact reflection of the mood within these walls.

A New World — Court Harris
March 2003 — St. Charles, Illinois

I was in high school, hanging out with members from the soccer team – which, incidentally, is a great cover. Parents are very trusting in such circumstances. I guess it only takes a couple decades for them to forget their own high school follies. All the better for me. At any rate, my mates were sharing some weed as an ice breaker of sorts, leading to conquest stories of opposing teams and the opposite sex. It wasn't the whole team, mind you, just the enthusiasts among us. We didn't want to split our bowls with the squeamish, casual, or possible snitch. I was just one in a gathering of guys sitting around doing what guys do. Well, I *was*, and then, suddenly, I wasn't.

This time was different. I'm not quite sure if the world slowed or I sped up, but there was a not-so-subtle shift, and I was on the exhilarating side, careening past my teammates. They were moving so slowly that I could have read their lips, could have finished their sentences. But why bother when I was discovering the value of telepathic skills? I could hear their thoughts; I could watch their minds form stories in the continuing game of one-upmanship. I moved quickly and easily to stay on top of the drivel they were drowning in. I could feel myself surpassing, evolving.

It was then, for the first time, that I heard a kind of foreign whispering. The language, crisp yet soothing, wasn't familiar, though it was obviously purposeful and intelligent. I wondered if perhaps one of the guys had caught the same ribbon of consciousness I was riding. But a glance showed each of them as lethargic and dull as before, more so even, their thoughts of sports and girls having slowed to the pace of a tourist struggling to stammer out questions in a foreign tongue.

The whispers, though, flowed around me and through me. It was like a river rushing past, or a wind swirling around. No, not really. In both of those cases, I would be merely an inconsequential impediment along the course. I was neither blocking nor diverting the whispers. Rather, the whispers were rushing and swirling around me. I was their focus, their target. They were the Ones, beckoning me to read their lips, dive into their thoughts, join their world. I could see it all, in ways too sacred for words. I saw the shimmering brightness of their laughter, the broiling murkiness of their anger, the tendrils of their mercy reaching for me, their chosen vessel. I could see it, but I couldn't quite catch hold. I was the foreigner, hoping to hear familiar phrases as the multitude of whisperers beckoned me onward.

I wanted them to slow down, speak separately, to give me the key to gain entrance to their world.

Even as I lunged toward them, I saw the chasm between us widening. They were still reaching, whispering, inviting. But the gravity in my reality of origin was cruel and relentless, dragging me back to a bunch of teenage boys who worship a black and white leather sphere. Slow and dull, they remained mired in and unaware of the bull shit that encased them. I could still hear their thoughts, decipher their motives, but I no longer cared. Theirs was just noise threatening to drown out the whispers. The sun shone greyer here. Blue sky seemed suddenly smog-like, covered by a grimy film. The overwhelming longing for my new next reality gnawed at me, mocking my inability to decipher the language of the whispers. But even in my longing, in this flat, pedestrian world, I clung to the Rosetta Stone, the one foreign phrase I could decipher: *weed*.

The World in 2D
April 2003

Lory Harris
St. Charles, Illinois

Dear Court,

Here we are again. You smoked pot and have retracted into your world of silence. When I ask the small and predictable, though weighty question, "Why?" you hold up two fingers in the 1960s salute to your deepest desire – Peace. You are not alone in wanting peace. We all want it with the longing that God built into the core of humanity. It is a sweet delicate bird that lights in your soul, cooing softly and soothing knotted stomach and racing mind. Peace is a desperate desire, elusive and not consistently sustainable. I know. I have yearned for it, received it, and then seen it fly suddenly and swiftly away.

If you have indeed found peace, though chemically induced and not God-given, then I'm sure it feels good. But, Court, you are to be pitied most among men, because peace is only one of the desires built into us, and not even the greatest at that. Of course, you would probably disagree with me, but your search for peace has left you two-dimensional like this sheet of paper. You can shake and nod your head and shrug your shoulders in your universe of one, but there is no depth to you.

You have given up on companionship, and with it, the blessing of sharing whatever peace you have with the world. You have discarded the opportunity to contribute peace that will outlast the chemical effect of marijuana. Enclosed and cut off from the world, even whatever peace you might fleetingly realize is hoarded and dies a lonely death.

You have given up on joy. You may think you have joy, but the truth is that joy cannot be contained. It bubbles from the core of a person. It needs companionship to make it complete, but you have rejected all others. Whatever joy you may have will bubble for a while. But like an open can of soda, the bubbles will dissipate with no source of renewal. Sad, but true, you cannot maintain joy in your 2-D world. Bubbles are decidedly 3-D.

You have given up on faith – faith in God who created this world and all that is in it. You have hidden yourself beneath a mantle of silence. Your peace, no matter how intense to you, is not at all apparent to anyone else. Faith radiates out, not just to the left and the right, but in all directions at once. Faith, like bubbles of joy, requires a 3-D world.

You have shut the door on hope – hope for a better world and a better life. You have padlocked your hope that was meant to be shared with the world behind the sound-padded walls of your mind. You have treated with distain any hope for healing given through family, friends, and, yes, even medical intervention. You have wrapped yourself so tightly in your new-found peace that hope has been strangled.

But most importantly, you have given up on love. Can you love? Yes! Do you love? Definitely! Can it be reciprocated? That is hard, very hard, though not impossible. I love you with all my being, and I always will. You can count on that! I have had 19 years of growing my love for you. It has been tended, pruned when needed, and watered with tears of both joy and pain. My love for you is not a sapling, dependent on the care and nurture of a gardener. It is, rather, a mighty oak, spreading its branches to shelter those I love the most. But the love of others, as you have seen, can be hard for them to maintain, and in many instances, disappears altogether. Love needs companionship, joy, faith, hope and even peace to grow. But peace alone is not enough, especially a peace so tightly hoarded.

You are like a once mighty tree, now self-pruned to the point of mutilation. There is but one leaf clinging to your few remaining appendages – the leaf of peace. That leaf is paper thin, offering no shelter from the rain, no relief from the scorching sun, and no beauty to behold. It is a sad tree: lonely and foreboding. Silence shrouds your branches where no birds sing. I continue to watch the tree, loving it, hoping for it, and having faith that new growth will fill its branches. I pray that love will return it to its former beauty and spreading peacefulness that benefits all – especially the tree itself.

For all the gifts you have given up on, I pray the Lord will coax you to reach for them again. They are awesome!

Love,
Mom

Northern Hospitality — Sheriff's Officer Brian Fisher
April 2003 — Milwaukee, Wisconsin

I've worked in Milwaukee my entire professional career. Our issues are the same as any large city. We don't make headlines like New York, Los Angeles or our Illinois neighbor, Chicago. We don't often make national headlines, anyway, and that's okay with us. But in large part, the type of local news reported at six o'clock doesn't vary that much from our bigger brothers.

Milwaukee is a beautiful town. Not only do we boast of Lake Michigan's beautiful shoreline, but the Menomonee, Milwaukee and Kinnikinnic Rivers also bisect our borders. In some ways, our water features are very well hidden, especially given their size. A traveler from the South, following Interstate 94, rides an inclining ribbon of concrete for several blocks soaring above the Menomonee River before descending again into the downtown area. The construction marvel carries cars far above Milwaukee terrain so high that even the rooftops disappear. Concrete guard rails leave drivers free to concentrate on driving and on the myriad of exit markers. They will do well to watch carefully when navigating onto I-794, I-94, I-43 or one of the city street exits.

On a typical Monday morning, like today, it is the less attentive drivers that earn my attention. They come in two varieties: the quick who must be slowed, and the overcautious who are mentally reviewing their insurance coverage (auto, health or both) to the detriment of traffic flow. Our concrete spaghetti bowl is at its worst when there is an accident that removes two or more lanes from use. That can extend morning rush hour into mid-day gridlock.

Today's clamber to return to the work week went as smoothly as one can expect, and by 10 a.m. I was returning via the concrete ribbons to complete my other duties at the police station. It's a beautiful spring morning with temperatures well above normal. It might even be hot this afternoon, a welcome respite from the winter.

I saw him just as my radio alerted me to his presence: a man walking along the side of the elevated interstate. I hadn't passed a disabled car, though in this concrete menagerie, it could have been on another spur. Regardless, pedestrians are not allowed on the Interstate for obvious safety reasons. With lights flashing to warn other drivers I pulled up behind the man and stopped. He was young, probably around 20, and completely ignored my presence.

A myriad of possibilities accompanied the young man. Was he injured and in shock for some reason? High? Defiant? Armed? Suicidal? I didn't want to spook him and cause him to run into traffic. Nor was I going to trail him in my squad to the next exit two miles away. Stepping from my squad car, I approached cautiously on foot.

He stopped when ordered, giving me a look that certainly could be viewed as defiant, but he retraced his steps to my car without incident. He would not give his name, why he was walking on the Interstate, where he was going, or, as a matter of fact, any information that would require the use of words. When I asked where he was going, he pointed south, which of course, I had already observed. All other inquiries were met with a shrug, a nod or a shake of the head. Do you have any ID? No. Do you live in the Milwaukee area? No. Do you have family nearby? Hesitation and then a shake of the head. You can't walk here. Will you come with me? A shrug. For safety, I must put handcuffs on you. Another shrug as he extended his arms to me.

It seemed obvious to me that there was no point in taking him to lock up. He didn't appear to be a danger to the public once he was away from the traffic, though I wasn't so sure he wasn't a danger to himself. I took my John Doe over to Milwaukee County Psych Hospital for evaluation. Barring something unforeseen, standard procedure will be a 48-hour hold, at which time there will be a hearing before a judge to determine the next steps.

We hadn't been at the hospital for more than ten or fifteen minutes when we received tentative identification of Mr. Doe. His mother had been calling hospitals looking for him when one of the them recommended she call Milwaukee Psych. She described him perfectly, including clothing, glasses and the tattoo on his back. My silent walker's name is Courtlandt Harris from St. Charles, Illinois, and he has, indeed, had some mental health issues.

I glanced in on mother and son before leaving 30 minutes later. Her conversation seemed to be going about as well as mine had. Actually, mine might have gone better. At least Mr. Harris looked me in the eye and responded minimally. For all her efforts, he is looking straight through her. The only indication that he is even aware of her presence is an unmistakable look of distain when she tries to engage him.

Maybe I'll hear his voice in a couple days when I return for the hearing, which will be held in a room in the lower level of the hospital. Until then, enjoy Milwaukee's hospitality, Mr. Harris.

A Losing Battle — Court Harris
April 2003 — Milwaukee, Wisconsin

Grey – that sums up my whole experience in Milwaukee Psych. The walls are grey, as is the well-worn linoleum under foot. The mood is grey; the food is grey. The windows, which should be allowing in glorious shades of blue and spring green, are muffled by grime and chicken wire, allowing in only a shadow of the world beyond. Even the people are grey, myself included. It is odd how bright shades of pink and blue pharmacology can homogenize a population and render them colorless.

When I arrived here a few weeks or even months ago (I can't keep track), I was working on a record for length of time without opening my mouth. No talking, no eating, no screaming, the latter being the most difficult. For Mr. Guinness' information, I made it to 48 hours. I was working my retail job when the personal challenge commenced. Seeing no reason to lose the first hour of my efforts, I just left – obviously without a word to anyone.

My truck and I wandered around for a while letting the radio fill the silence. Without a single word, I was the master of my whole world. I saw, heard and went per my absolute desires. Eventually I decided to make my way to my brother's apartment in Milwaukee. Unfortunately, Corey was away at a lacrosse tournament, so I took refuge at his friend's next door. While they knew me by sight and allowed me in, they obviously didn't understand or respect my silent communication. They called my mother. She showed up several hours later, panic barely contained and packing pills. Being on record pace for my quest, I did not open my mouth for discussion, and certainly not for chemical alterations! Corey arrived about the same time. He and I went back to his apartment for the night. Mom took a hotel room.

The next morning, I was nearly 24 hours into my pursuit when Mom arrived with the same pills and more pleading. She had taken my car keys the night before, so I couldn't exit the same way I had arrived. But exit I did, at a dead run. After giving mother and brother the slip, I decided to make my way back to Illinois by the only route I knew – the interstate. That, it appears, was my first mistake.

This new residence of mine initially offered me food with a chaser of mind-altering chemicals. I refused both with a defiant shake of the head. My assigned doctor acknowledged that they would not force me to take any medications against my will. Score one for me! By the way, the doctor wore white, in stark contrast to the rest of this habitat. She must use gallons of bleach to hold the infecting grey at bay.

I gave up my quest for a world record on Tuesday. My stomach was insisting, my surroundings were gnawing, and I wanted to impress the judge the next day. Even with the prescribed chemical assistance, I only managed to alleviate one of those three motivators; not an impressive stat. And my one "win" only required something grey masquerading as a sandwich. A second court date was set for this morning. I guess I made a better impression.

Today is Good Friday, and I am casting off this grey shroud and heading for home. Both the judge and the doctor emphasized that if I don't take my meds they will have me arrested and brought back here – something I would certainly like to avoid. Mom, while not successful in springing my release a moment earlier than judicially determined, did manage to secure my continued employment at Home Depot. An impressive feat under the circumstances, especially since I'm only a seasonal employee. Even though the garden center might not be a passion of mine, I can use the cash. At any rate, I'm happy to be leaving the land of the cheese heads, albeit with a new set of mind-altering scripts and the threat of a return visit hanging over my head. But for now, at least, I'm homeward bound, and viewing the world in living color, again.

The Return of Spring — Lory Harris
May 2003 — St. Charles, Illinois

There might not be any better time of year than spring for all the predictable reasons: longer days, warmer weather, color filling the formerly drab and lifeless landscape. I've always liked meteorological spring, but this is outright glorious! It seems like forever since last spring season and I am basking in the light of hope and the colors of possibility.

Born and raised in small towns in Iowa, I remember my agrarian experience: winter snows protect and insulate plant roots and then provide the first reviving waters for spring growth. For the record, winter snow also chaps and bite.

I remember our first record-breaking parenting winter a little over a year ago when we thought we had experiencing a worst-case parental fail. Corey, 20 years old at the time, was caught using a fake ID to buy beer. There were court dates and fines, of course, but they turned out to be the lesser consequences. The Illinois Secretary of State revoked our son's driver's license for a period of time to be determined and, as yet, to be fulfilled. He is now legal to drink, but needs to bum a ride even to buy a beer.

By comparison, though, that was almost inconsequential compared to this latest bitterly cold and endless winter. Starting with the blizzard at University Hospital, ending with another of the Wisconsin variety, and interspersed with multiple attention-getting snow falls, it seemed we were always digging out of something! In God's due time, thankfully, the seasons change. And His timing is perfect, or so I profess to believe.

When Court was first hospitalized, I thought it would be a one-and-done event. I was worried about my son, but honestly, my energy was being expended just to keep myself upright. In retrospect, I guess it was like starting an exercise routine, and like it or not, repetition strengthens. By the time Milwaukee came around, I was a fighting machine. No way was a child of mine going to spend time in a public psych hospital! There was no argument that he needed care, but I could afford better, and I wanted the best for my son.

I was insistent at telling God what He should do – and how and when. God, it seems, was patting me on the head and saying, "It's going to be okay. I've got this one," though I was having none of that. Court's Illinois psychiatrist would not or could not offer more than medical records, which of course, only emphasized my son's need for intervention. I attended the court dates in Wisconsin but was not allowed even to speak on my "adult" son's behalf. Talking to his Milwaukee appointed psychiatrist was pointless. She feigned sympathy, "no one wants their child in Milwaukee Psych," while refusing to do anything to change the situation. In her estimation, their doctors see so much that no one pulls the wool over their eyes – "unlike the guys in private practice." During the day, I would spend as much time with Court as possible: reading to him, talking at him, watching TV with him. When visitation ended, I would go back to my hotel and devise my next round of attack to secure my son's freedom.

All my kicking and screaming went for naught while God worked His plan despite my diligent counter-efforts. Court's meds were changed and have proven very effective now several weeks later. And better yet, he is taking them as prescribed. I think the judge's threat that they would drag him back to Milwaukee if he didn't take them was enough to get Court stable on his meds for the first time since this mess started. In truth, once he crossed state lines, the Wisconsin judicial-hold lost its grip entirely, a fact I did not bother to pass on to my son.

God interceded on behalf of Court, giving him both the medication and motivation he needed. Court's humor and teasing has returned, and his eye to the future is sharpened. I'm not ready to say it's all behind us now – I'll wait another few months before making that pronouncement. But my son seems to have peace in his own skin. His life is his own again. The God of the desperate showed His love and mercy. He granted healing to Court and hope to me. He took what I thought was the worst and made it into something beautiful.

Thank you for answered prayer. Thank you, God, for spring!

Road Trip **Corey Harris**
May 2003 **St. Charles, Illinois**

Four years in college and a diploma to show for it. I got a great education, and I don't refer only my GPA. There were friends and girls and girlfriends, parties and lacrosse and lacrosse parties, a semester in Australia and the eventful return home. I now know that when you are too broke to buy a text book, there are ways to get the required material that do not involve the loss of beer money. I learned about all-nighters of various kinds. And I learned that if the events of Friday night don't end until Saturday afternoon, you'll have a story to tell on Sunday – after getting some sleep.

Much of the book knowledge gained is not currently applicable, though with the number of résumés I am sending out, this can't last forever! Working in the family business all day and then hanging with my parents in the evening is not the graduation gift I was anticipating, but that is where I find myself, especially without the freedom of a driver's license.

Yesterday, Court was working, pulling a double shift to continue stocking after the Home Depot closed. The two of us were planning to hang out once he got home.

Mom and I were talking around 10 p.m. when the phone rang; the Caller ID heralded "Pay Phone." Weird. Those are kind of hard to find anymore. Though apparently, they are still readily available two states away in Nebraska. Court was calling to say he wanted to come home. Mom had a confused look on her face, but told Court that if he was done at work, he could certainly come home. His store is only five miles from the house, a straight shot down Randall Road. Even in heavy traffic, it's not more than a 15-minute drive.

"I quit my job," he said. "Then the radio told me to just keep driving, so I did."

The look on Mom's face was morphing from confused to concerned to the verge of panic. "Where are you and why are you calling from a pay phone? Is your cell phone dead?"

As a matter of fact, his cell phone was DOA at some random mile marker on Interstate 80 where Court had jettisoned it several hours earlier. It had been "talking" to my brother as well, and interrupting the conversation he was having with the radio. Maybe the call home was prompted by Court having grown tired of the radio's banter or maybe it was the radio that cried uncle. For whatever reason, Lincoln, Nebraska, was the end of the line for his drive. He was eight hours from home and wanted to return. No one had even known he was gone.

A very hurried conversation was held between Mom, Dad and me while Court waited on the pay phone. Mom and I would drive to Des Moines, the long half of halfway, and meet Court at my Aunt Ginger's house. Court would stop for a rest every hour or so, find a pay phone and call Mom's cell phone. Mom and I left five minutes later.

I think Mom had settled into a comfortable routine in the weeks since Easter with the expectation of life as it had been before last December. Maybe we all had, though I would judge that each of our memories of "had been" varied. Dad, I think, was looking for a compliant son. Mom was looking for an inspired scholar. I was looking for my brother, my friend, who knew how to take things just to the brink before using his wit to back away. None of our thoughts had included Nebraska.

As we drove, Mom called her sister, letting her know she would have visitors arriving in the wee hours of the morning. Ginger and her husband, Dale, don't do a lot of traveling with their boys being only four and six, so Mom was surprised when no one answered the phone. She left a message apologizing for the late-night intrusion and asking Ginger to call back. Mom called again half an hour later, still apologizing to an answering machine. It wasn't until the third phone call, nearly identical to the first two, that she finally decided her sister wasn't available to offer us housing per our hurried plan.

On the other hand, Court's calls from pay phones came more or less as directed. The variance was likely due to the lack of available pay phones, and to Court's general ignorance when it comes to reading a clock. He has always lived life on his own schedule, a trait that has grown more pronounced over the past six months. You could see Mom's anxiety level raise as each hour mark approached. "What if he changed his mind or the "radio" told him to take another route? We have no way to reach him and no way of knowing where he might go." The ringing of her cell phone, jarring as it might otherwise be in the early morning hours, was quite soothing.

Since the hearing to restore my legal permission to drive is still three weeks away, my primary job was to keep Mom awake in the early morning hours of our trek. It made sense, and was probably the most coherent part of the plan, but it was equally unnecessary. Mom was so wired with worry that sleep was not even a remote possibility. There was no chance of my sleep, either, since the whole car was electrified with emotion. Mom and I talked about anything and everything: my graduation, work, my music preferences, the latest round of job applications, Colin's anticipated return from Iraq, and, of course, Court. It would be more accurate to say that I talked about the various topics while Mom had the uncanny ability to segue back to her sons, concern over myself least of all. She has always worn her worries on her sleeves. Let's just say they are currently covering more than just her arms.

We were probably thirty minutes from Ginger's house when Court called to say he was there. Mom told him to just sit tight. We would find a hotel after we arrived. Good thing it was a Thursday, well, Friday early morning, as Mom would likely have earned a speeding ticket on a more law-enforcement-laden night. We completed the trip more quickly than was strictly legal, only to find Ginger's driveway empty. Court was nowhere to be found. Had we made it all this way only to miss our goal by less than thirty minutes?

A grid search of Des Moines was not a viable possibility. Besides, what if Court had just jumped back on the interstate and headed back to Lincoln – or any other direction? Interstates representing the four points on the compass converge for easy access in Des Moines. As we sat wondering what to do next, Mom's cell phone mercifully rang. Court had grown tired of waiting and had gone to get gas and scout out hotels. He had succeeded on both accounts. We met him at a hotel a few miles away.

It's not often that you walk into a hotel past 3 a.m. without even a reservation. The night clerk seemed to welcome the break during his otherwise tedious hours. He also seemed to like the power he held over us: yes, there was a room, but we must be out by noon. The hotel was full the next night. With wakefulness running on fumes, we would have taken any room at twice the price regardless of check out time.

Court and I took one bed leaving the other for Mom. The two of us were asleep before Mom even got in bed. She woke us a few hours later at 11:30 so we could vacate on schedule. I don't know how much sleep she got, but her red rimmed eyes over dark circles indicated "not much."

Mom insisted I go in Court's car and she would drive her own. I think she wanted the alone time to collect her thoughts, and I know she wasn't ready to trust that Court would head home and only home. I was the trip insurance policy – both ways, come to think of it: once as protection against sleep and the other against unauthorized detours.

Court and I split a pack of cigarettes on the drive home. Never having smoked in her youth, Mom will silently disapprove at first sniff.

Dad, on the other hand, will offer his objection with fanfare and verbosity--the most ardent non-smoker is always a reformed one. My smoking partner and I talked the whole way home, mostly on the same topics that I had participated in the night before, but with a much higher degree of banter. Mom was sure to grill me later regarding the discussions in our car. I've found it's better not to lie to someone to whom you would rather tell the truth. Court wasn't anxious to rehash the previous day. Outside of the oft repeated rant against taking prescriptions that made him feel like someone he didn't recognize and didn't want to be, we stuck to safe subjects.

My less conventional college education was put to good use today: how to muscle through with little sleep. It's Friday night and I'm staying in. Maybe Court and I will play some pool. Or maybe we will rent a movie to watch – our eye lids drooping long before the credits roll up the screen. Tomorrow night, though, I'll go out with friends and laugh about radios and cell phones and vacations in Nebraska. I'll laugh because I don't know what else to do. Here's to education, in whatever forms it presents itself.

Hazard-ous Times — Keith Worthington
June 2003 — Hazard, Kentucky

I've made this trip to the Appalachian area about a dozen times in as many years. On a strictly volunteer basis, I lead a mission trip for the youth in my church, Geneva United Methodist, to the Appalachian Service Project (ASP). The scenery here is beautiful: lush green and, by Illinois standards, mountainous. Yet, each bend in the road, and there are many, attempts to hide the poverty within. Deceased cars and appliances dot front yards of houses, whose state of repair is questionable, as well.

We break into work crews of 4-6 high school and college-aged kids and a couple of adult leaders to repair homes in some of the poorest counties in the country. We have brought as many as eight work crews at a time, though that taxed the limits of successful cat herding. A few years back, we split our efforts over two weeks with two separate groups of volunteers.

The extent of the week's work varies greatly. Some of the houses need minor repairs, while others need structural work that stretches the reaches of our abilities. Fortunately, we have a dedicated group of adult volunteers with a wide range of skill sets. Upon arrival at our assigned center's facilities, frequently a school, the week's projects are distributed between the crews based upon the leaders' confidence level to accomplish the needed tasks, which vary from painting and digging drainage ditches, to insulation and drywall repairs, to plumbing repairs and replacing sagging or damaged floors and roofs. Over the week, the leaders will attempt to direct their youthful crew in completing the prescribed repairs, and more importantly, engage the homeowner and family to show them the love of Christ. It's a tall order, and do-able, though only with God's help.

In addition to the repair projects, there are also assigned tasks around the facility. Thankfully, except for each crew making PBJ or mystery meat sandwiches for their lunches, we are not in charge of meals. That would certainly be more challenging than any of the roofing, deck building or underpinning projects. Those extra tasks range from meal set-up or clean-up, to mopping the center's public areas, to the never popular bathroom scrub downs.

Generally, the school buildings that house us will not hear the laughter of children in September, nor have they for many years previous. The kitchen has been made serviceable for the summer's stream of might-be handymen. Broken windows have been patched well enough to deter both storms and voracious insects. Toilets flush, more-or-less predictably, though they can be temperamental. Water rains from the shower heads, or trickles at least, drawing on the 50-gallon water heater to meet the demands of the 30 to 60 people housed there. In other words, the first work crew returning to the center after a long day's work gets tepid showers. All other showers are hasty of necessity, which is good since the number of shower stalls is not likely to exceed four per gender. Water, especially warm water, is a precious commodity for us, as it is for the permanent residents of our host county. The difference being, of course, that we will return to long hot showers in middle-class suburbia in a week's time.

The trip itself is never the same twice and never dull. With so many teenage missionaries among us, there are the inevitable romantic hook-ups, as well as ill-timed break-ups. During our work week, neither paint nor tar is confined strictly to the intended surfaces. Copious amounts return to Illinois each year, proof of assigned tasks, if not completion of them. Every year, the list of essential items that miss the trip is mind-boggling: prescription drugs, work shoes, sleeping bags. Some things that have made previous trips can also defy explanation: fireworks and pot, to name a couple. The week is bound to bring some injuries: bruises, scrapes, cuts and blisters mostly. Once a metal bar flew through the front window of a van and struck a crew member in the ear. Thankfully, we returned with our full complement of workers, though down one vehicle.

I awoke this morning prior to the traditional 6:30 wakeup call. Surprisingly, I am not the first person awake. There is an empty bed, Court's, I believe, though he may just be in the bathroom, reveling in the rare warm shower. I close my eyes again, in prayer this time, not sleep.

It is Mosey Monday. The theme of the day is not to get a running start on the projects, but to begin to form a relationship with the families on whose houses we will labor throughout the week. The amount of mosey varies greatly, depending on crews and families. If the family has already spent several Mondays moseying, they may be more anxious to reclaim their house, or they might be very social people who enjoy the company. I am just completing prayer for each crew's family when the loud-speaker blares a wake-up song, and a room full of spent adolescent exuberance groans in unison. Hoping to inspire the troops, I dress quickly and head for the bathroom, finding it completely void of other early risers.

Here just outside of Hazard, Kentucky, the center is small and amazingly well-appointed being one of very few year-round ASP centers. I make a quick tour of the facility, wanting to congratulate Court on his punctuality before heading back to shake his compatriots out of their slumber. The kitchen is occupied by our cooks, who have yet to see any teen to twenty-somethings this morning. The gathering room, entry way and front porch are also empty of the younger generation. The grounds appear void of ASP-ers as well; though someone walking in the woods could easily be hidden by the vegetation.

A gnawing concern is growing. Court has had a difficult year, to say the least. While the trip from Illinois to the center is generally a raucous affair, as one would expect with a group of kids on a road trip, Court has been a bit taciturn – rallying at times, but generally withdrawn and a bit sullen. I saw him run up to his mom last night after closing devotions and give her a hug and a kiss, so maybe my concerns are unwarranted. Still, my next stop is to check in with Lory to see if she knows where Court might be.

Lory doesn't look appreciably more awake then the rest of the girls, but while the younger generation of women are primping for a "hard day's work," Lory is already dressed in overalls and a previously paint-splattered t-shirt. Those of us who have been here before, tend to pack the same clothes year after year. I think I recognize her outfit from previous years.

"Have you seen Court?" I ask. "He wasn't in his bed when I woke up and I have not been able to find him."

Her eyes and her mouth gape open in unison. She draws a deep breath and says in a quiet but firmly resolved voice, "I'll find him."

I return to my roust-and-rally duties. Twenty minutes later, we circle up in the front yard for devotions before breakfast. Lory is there, but remains silent. Her eyes are darting from tree to tree in the woods over my shoulder. Breakfast is next, but it is optional, and she doesn't join us. If anyone was previously unaware of the drama on our doorstep, they know long before the dishes are cleared.

Emily, the center director, pulls me aside as I rise to take care of my dirty dishes. "The rear fire escape from the boys' dorm was unlocked and held ajar. It was closed at our final check before the staff turned in last night. We told Court's mother. She seemed to almost expect that kind of news."

Lory is sitting on a bench by the parking lot when I find her. Her back is to me, but I can see she is talking on her cell phone - talking to Ken, I assume. He has been on several ASP adventures, too, though he couldn't make it this year. Respecting her privacy, I return to my duties, getting all the work crews ready to depart.

At the appointed time, everyone moseys to the vans in the spirit of the day. I'm finally able to catch Lory as she, too, makes her way to the van. "You don't have to go if you don't want to. You can stay here."

There is a slight side to side movement of her head, as if even that effort was more than she could bear. "No," she said, "I don't think he will be back today, and someone from staff will be here all day if he does return. But this was planned; Court intended to leave. He will be back; I must believe that. But it won't be today." She greets one of her crew members by draping her arm over his shoulder as they climb into the van. Her movements are mechanical but rallying.

The word of the day may be "mosey," but there will be no dawdling in my prayer life. I will be assailing heaven's gates continually for my friends: mother and child.

Yardwork — Ken Harris
July 2003 — St. Charles, Illinois

When we bought this house seven years ago, Lory and I were in love with the maintenance-free yard. Even at an acre and a third, the grass was minimal owing to the heavy woods that surrounded the house on all sides. Court was in middle school at the time and hated the move. It's not that we moved a great distance from the old neighborhood – it didn't result in a school change and he could still bike back to see his friends. But it was obvious at a glance that there would be no baseball games in the backyard – no soccer, no football. Even the sloping driveway would make basketball difficult once the promised hoop was installed. To make matters worst of all in his eyes, the basement was a walkout. He wouldn't be able to rollerblade there in the winter or play crab soccer against unfinished concrete walls. Our first spring, we also learned that buckthorns are aptly named and can catch and render soccer balls unplayable in as little as one errant kick. It was our turn to be momentarily unhappy with our landscaping and frustrated with sons who insisted on practicing their skills in such benign-appearing but threatening surroundings. I'm not sure that he will care anymore, but the buckthorns are disappearing – along with the scrub trees and eye level weeds. I guess I should thank Court for the motivation – if I ever see him again.

Ever since Court's impromptu Nebraskan joy ride, his mood vacillated by the hour. Clearly the bipolar meds are not doing their job, though most likely the fault is not product, but rather, operator error. Why he won't just take the meds and get back on track is an absolute mystery to me! He can't enjoy what passes for his life – I know I'm not!

Saturday morning when I dropped Lory and Court off at the church to head down to ASP, I was kind of looking forward to a peaceful week to myself. Naturally, I would spend time working for both my clients and Lory's, but this is our slower time of year, so I anticipated a relaxing week. It was with some kind of wicked foreshadowing that I returned home to a message from our bank advising us of Court's over-drafted checking account. I transferred funds to cover my youngest's ill-developed financial prowess. When Lory talked to Court about it, in route to Kentucky, he predictably claimed bank error. There was an error, for sure, but it was mine for not just letting him face the music. We will never see that $200 again.

Lory and I had insisted that Court look for a job since he quit at Home Depot. Supposedly he was offered a job, took the drug test, and is waiting for a start date – but they lost the test results, so he must take it again. Refusing to just hand him cash to tide him over, we are paying him to paint a widow's garage. You would think the garage was of the four-car variety for as long as it is taking him, when it's more of a shed than an automotive shelter. At least it got him out of bed before noon.

Lory called Monday morning to let me know that Court was nowhere to be found. Our first panicked thought was that the depression had finally won out and he would be coming home in a body bag. But as we talked and held each other long distance, we realized it was a planned departure. First, he took both a suitcase and a backpack to ASP, the backpack seeming totally unnecessary – though it proved to be much easier to carry when wandering off in the middle of the night. And on closer inspection, there was little of anything useful packed in the suitcase he left behind at the ASP center; it was just for show. Then there was his request that we process payroll early, so he could have money to take with him on the mission trip, which we did. And finally, there was the "bank error" that fattened his wallet. According to the bank, he cashed a check elsewhere and then withdrew money from the ATM before the check cleared. That's one way to stretch a dollar, at least until it snaps back and slaps you in the face – or, more accurately, my face.

For now, our options seem limited. Lory is convinced that Court just needs a few days to himself and will return by Saturday for the trip home. She won't leave Kentucky before then, at least not without Court. Some friends have volunteered to drive down with me to search the Appalachian hollers for a son who clearly does not want to be found. They don't know how lucky they are that they can't understand why I declined their offer. At least Lory and I agree on the futility of that plan. It has been three days now with just one voice message from Court telling us not to look for him.

Earlier in the week, as I feigned work while totally ignoring the computer, I caught myself staring outside at the tangle of underbrush among the trees. It looked as disheveled and jumbled as my thoughts. I could feel the weedy tentacles choking life out of the delicate wildflowers cowering in their shadows. Despite temperatures in the low 90s and humidity slightly higher, I changed into jeans and a long-sleeved shirt. With saw, shovel, pickaxe and leather gloves, I made my way to the front yard.

My project is not deterred by the mid-summer heatwave, though I am enjoying a beer and air conditioning as the setting sun brings on the blood-thirsty mosquitos. The yard now has a fifty-square foot scrub-and-weed-free zone, which expands more each day. A little piece of my world is behaving and bowing to my will, though it has not given up without a fight. The buckthorns have done their best to deflate my spirit, adding blood to the sweat that plasters my shirt to my body. Despite aching muscles, or maybe because of them, I sleep well at night. Sleep induced by physical exhaustion is so much more restful than that of emotional fatigue. I am looking forward to another night of deep and dreamless slumber.

Fireworks – Part I — Lory Harris
Independence Day 2003 — Hazard, Kentucky

Tomorrow we celebrate the birth of our nation, well, no, the clock corrects me. The fireworks are scheduled for later today – much later. I am exhausted from the week's physical work, but more so from emotional duress. I spend my days in wakeful sleep, counting the hours until I can place my head on my pillow. Then I spend my nights in sleepless nightmares, anxious for the diversion of daylight. For over two hours, I have alternately feigned sleep and stared at the bunk above me. When I judged that the rest of my companions had succumbed to the gentle rock of slumber, I crept silently to the dining room to cry in peace. Well, to cry alone; there is no peace.

There has been just the one proof of life from Court – a voice message on my phone late Monday morning. Our work site, nestled in a holler and well-secluded from the nearest cell phone tower, prevented me from answering my son's call. His message was succinct but momentous. "Mom, I'm fine. Don't come looking for me. I have found the love of my life. He and I are very happy together." I listened to it twice in the van as our crew drove to a gas station at lunch time. I would have listened to it a hundred times more if the cellular grasp was not so fickle. What must my face have revealed to my fellow passengers? Were they unaware, too polite, or was it just too awkward to inquire? Regardless, I was grateful for their silence. My mind was reeling, as it is still.

He's alive! Relief washed over me at the sound of his voice. I breathed the kind of panic-laden exhale that escapes when your skidding vehicle finally responds to brakes applied in desperation, stopping inches from a precipice of unknown depth. But seconds later follows the jarring scrape of metal on metal, and the realization that the mechanics of the following car were not as responsive. "He and I…"

I never saw it coming. Court has always had a girlfriend. In grade school, he announced that he was going to get married and have a daughter named Christina. In junior high, Diana was the object of his first crush. As a freshman in high school, he talked of marrying his girlfriend, Krista. Just after his Iowa hospitalization he proposed to Amanda, who he had been dating for a couple of years. She was still attending high school in Illinois at the time, but was mature enough to know that the time was not right for such a decision. They broke up a month or so later, Court's erratic behavior straining the bonds of young love. The shock of his latest announcement so casually dealt left me not in free fall, suspended on a cushion of disbelief, but rather careening down a mountainside buffeted by rocks and trees, grasping for something to slow my descent.

Is he gay? Has he always been gay? Have I glossed over signs that I should have seen? How will this change our family, challenging again beliefs we thought inviolable? How does one find the love of their life in the scant dozen hours since his departure? The same unanswered questions swim through my consciousness now, days later. I had decided not to pass Court's announcement on to Ken when we talked earlier in the week. I wanted to be with him when he heard the news. I wanted to hold him, clinging to each other, sharing what strength we could jointly muster. But now I want to talk to him, to puzzle through the answerless queries that plague my early morning wakefulness. Instead, I continue my solo wilderness plunge, bloodied and still grasping for an elusive anchor.

With the ghosts of what-should-have-been swirling around, I cry out to God once again. I know too much – have seen too much – to think that He doesn't exist, but how can I believe in a loving God? Whenever I adjust to the pain, feel life start to move again, God makes Himself known with sharp, stabbing, relentless pain. The raw agony drives me to my knees and then prone, face down in the mud.

Is this the kind of adoration You want, God: a stricken subject, begging for the mercy of a terrible, all-powerful king?! Or maybe You aren't the cause of my pain, but rather impotent and unable to help? If you want my life, then take it! Let me die rather than live mired in such pain and heartache. Give me eternal relief from this terror called life. If I'm lucky, grant me a glimpse of Your "plan," or even just blessed nothingness. Just stop the agony!

Then, though relentless tears, I realize that if this is my torture, what must my son be enduring? To run from a family who loves him into the arms of a stranger who offers acceptance that fits a wanton and temporary definition of that word? I understand the deep-seeded desire to define what love is and what love does to meet one's deepest wants. Then again, is my morning rant any different?

Please, God, whatever modicum of love You possess, give it to Court, even if it means grinding my face further into the mud. I will voluntarily lay my face down for even a glimpse of Your love and mercy extended to my child.

I choose to believe in You, but only because the alternative is bleaker than the all-encompassing inky gloom You offer. Don't make me a fool, believing in an all-powerful, caring God who doesn't exist. Grant me a glimpse of Your power and might and LOVE! Let me believe again that they define who You are.

With my fireworks spent and the country's a couple of hours closer, I trudge my weary body back up to my bunk. My eyes close, vision fading from black to same, as a final blurry prayer is offered requesting enough mercy for just three blessed hours of nothingness.

Fireworks – Part II Court Harris
Independence Day 2003 Hazard, Kentucky

Mornings are not necessarily my forte. Given the choice, I generally prefer to wait until the sun has passed its apex before acknowledging its presence. But I woke up early today and life seems to be just exactly what it was destined to be. Today the a.m. side of noon seemed uncharacteristically inviting, so I gave it a try. First order of business: a cigarette. The second is a cup of coffee. The third, a repeat of number one, will require an intermediate step since I just snuffed out the stub of the last of my smokes.

My new roomie, Lucy, is still asleep. At least I don't hear any sounds coming from her bedroom. She could have left, I suppose, but that seems unlikely. We were up late partying last night. Then again, I'm up, so it is possible. Stomach now satisfied with the requisite morning caffeine and lungs processing nicotine, I sit contentedly and survey my new home. The little garden apartment had an unexpectedly available bedroom last week, but the vacancy sign is down now. Everything is coming together just like I was told it would.

I was in a bowling league earlier this summer with my friends Aaron, Jordan and Jordan's girlfriend. That might be one of the things I will miss about Illinois come to think of it. Anyway, I was in a groove: smoking some weed and then going bowling every Tuesday night. The most important part of the night, though, was the open line of communication with the Ones. Though I am making some progress, their language is difficult to master. Not all communication requires verbalization, of course, which is where the bowling comes in. I would ask a perplexing question and receive a reply from the Ones on a frame by frame basis. A strike or a good roll was a yes, while a lower pin count was a no. A five or six meant I needed to rephrase the question. Testing my theory over several weeks, one thing became certain: I should go to ASP and take off from there to hitchhike around with only a backpack – maybe landing in Canada. My ultimate destination had been left a bit ambiguous with a strike, a gutter ball and six in the tenth frame of the last line on that final Tuesday.

I packed lightly for ASP: no work clothes or gloves, just stuff thrown into a duffel to keep up appearances, though I did add a walking stick that fit perfectly – not necessarily a coincidence. My backpack, however, was packed meticulously, including a sizable stash of weed in a hidden compartment, two pipes - just in case - and all the cash I could muster.

Within thirty minutes of leaving the ASP center, I was stopped by local police investigating reports of a hitchhiker threatening cars with a large stick. I was beginning to think my adventure would end in jail after they searched my backpack and found the film canister of weed and my small pipe, my public supply. But I never should have doubted the Ones. The Hazard police dumped the canister and confiscated the pipe, but never found the mother lode. They let me go with a warning, which I heeded: rather than sticking out my thumb, I hid from traffic for the next couple of hours.

Eventually lack of sleep, food and progress won out. I offered my thumb to the next car, and it changed my life. Three guys around my age named Andrew, Kevin and Tom were on their way back from visiting Andrew's boyfriend in some little town east of here. They had tried unsuccessfully to score some pot for their trip home. In gratitude for their vehicular transportation, I offered them herbal transportation, which they graciously accepted.

I'm not sure exactly how, when or why Andrew and I hooked up that night, but we did. I've never thought of myself as gay, but I didn't see any reason not to give it a try, either. Andrew will be headed east later today to break up with his boyfriend there so the two of us can be together.

Until he returns, he convinced Lucy to let me live here. Her apartment, half below ground, isn't dependent on the tilting stairs that lead to the rental above us. If our stairs give way, the worst we will get is a twisted ankle.

Glancing around, I see her purse, a coveted pack of cigarettes revealing itself – not my brand, but tobacco none the less. Still, I am appreciative of the hospitality that has been extended. I have cash, and a convenience store lurks just down the street. Finding my shoes, I decide to go for a walk.

The temperature and humidity in a Kentucky summer appear to be conjoined twins, marching upward together relentlessly through the daylight hours. But at 9:30 a.m., they haven't yet gathered the steam that will condense and drip from various body parts when the clock indicates my usual waking hour. A full pack minus one now rests in my pocket, as I start the return trip to my new abode. I am in a state of perfect contentment, when I hear my mother's voice telling me to look both ways before crossing the street. Honestly, will I ever be rid of her? But being the dutiful son, I look up in time to see a white 15-passenger van approaching from my right. Not only do my feet stop, but my heart stops, as well. The van, a rental with green window paint advertising "ASP" and "Kentucky or Bust," is as easily recognizable as the driver: Keith. He and his crew are off to do their good deed of the day, and fortunately, totally oblivious to this former participant, newly-freed and standing on the side of the road.

Their taillights climb a hill and wind around a corner as my cigarette turns to ash more quickly than normal. By the time I make my way the two blocks back to my subterranean retreat, the new pack has lost another member, but my breathing has finally returned to normal, along with my heart rate. When I rise tomorrow, the vans will be making their way back north. And I'll sleep extra late just to be sure! Until then, I'll definitely look both ways before crossing a street. As an added precaution, I will cross as few as possible.

Man Down – Part I — Aaron Johnsen
July 2003 — Kentucky to Illinois

Court and I didn't go to the same high school, though ironically, his house was closer to my school, Geneva High, than to his, as can happen when living in neighboring towns with indistinguishable, artificial borders. We both go to Geneva United Methodist Church and have been adding live color to Sunday school lessons for some time now. For a couple of years, Mrs. Harris and Mrs. Luehr were our teachers. They were cool, though I couldn't tell you what I learned. At least we kept coming back week after week, so that's something.

It feels like half a lifetime ago, but it has only been a year since I graduated from high school. So, so much has changed – none of it in the direction of last summer's expectations. Court and I have that in common, which is probably why our friendship has grown, despite my parent's misgivings. Of late, they think that Court is a bad influence. That probably means that their opinion of me is overinflated, and of my friend, too harsh. Court has done some bizarre stuff, most of which my parents haven't a clue about, but our times together are as they have always been: what one doesn't think of, the other does. Truth is, we have both been battling depression lately. The world just doesn't make sense anymore – not like it used to. Court and I have long rambling conversations about that. They don't solve anything, but it's nice to abandon the loneliness even if just a few hours at a time.

It was Court's idea that we both come on ASP this year, as we have in the past. What did we have to lose? It's a week spent with friends and away from parental rules. Even though Court's mom would be there, she's pretty laid back. My girlfriend, Addie, has been out of town for a couple weeks and wouldn't be back until we returned from Kentucky. I am still looking for a summer job, which means my parents are spending their time on my back. A week's vacation sounded good to me.

Mrs. Harris came straight to me after Court took off on his midnight adventure. She wanted to know what I knew: not accusing, just fact-finding. After just one glance at the fear in her eyes, I would have told her everything – except I knew nothing. I was duped in the process, too. Looking back, maybe I knew more than I thought I did. Court hated the meds they forced him on, and his parents by extension for their insistence that he take them. He talked about leaving – we both did from time to time. But it never occurred to me that he would leave on foot with only a backpack, and from Hazard, Kentucky, no less. How appropriate is that name! I guess this is as good a place as any to get lost, maybe better than some, but it didn't seem like much of a plan. Ironically, though, I'm a bit jealous. He did it. I, on the other hand, will be woken by my parental alarm clock next Monday morning.

I've spent the week watching Mrs. Harris closely. She went out on the work crew every day, and according to everyone with her, she worked hard and helped anyone who needed it. She might be a bit quieter than usual, but she has never been overly gregarious. Most people wouldn't even notice the change. It really came to my attention during the evening prayer circle. No one is required to pray out loud – you just squeeze the hand of the next person to take a pass. But the adults, wanting to set a good example, almost never take a pass. I don't think Mrs. Harris has prayed out loud since Sunday night. That doesn't mean she isn't praying. I'm sure she is doing that constantly – just not with public words. I would wager she doesn't trust her voice. She seems often on the verge of tears, though I haven't seen any.

I pulled her aside midweek to talk, and we ended up talking less about Court, and more about me and the things I'm going through. It was so good to have someone to talk with who took the time to understand what I was saying. I guess the graduation dreams she had for Court have spiraled out of control, too, so she really can feel my pain. Again, tears threatened, but were denied.

The drive home from Kentucky was a long one – 10 hours including stops. It seems like there was one stop for each of the 23 people in our group – which is not to say I tired of the breaks. Herding everyone back into the vans and arriving at the correct nose count was the hard part, the noses being down one since the start of the week. Court hadn't shown up or contacted anyone since Monday. Mrs. Harris insisted we all head home and leave Court behind. I think that one decision aged her several years overnight. Up until then, she kept insisting that Court would join us on the return trip. I wasn't in her van on the way home, but when I asked friends who were, they said she slept the whole way. Now, I'm a teenager, and I can sleep, but that's impressive! Either she hasn't slept all week, or she just didn't want to face the world. I frequently cope with my misbehaving life the same way.

We arrived back at the church to the usual bedlam: spouses and children or parents and siblings greeting the returning missionaries. There is always a lot of laughter and talking and hugging. Keith runs around making sure everything is unloaded from the vans and stowed in the church or sent home as appropriate. The extra hands make for lots of disorganization, but quick work. I looked for Mrs. Harris mid-way through the process, and saw her getting in the car with Mr. Harris. It's not like either of them to leave before everything is done, but under the circumstances, no one blamed them, either. I wanted to run to the car and give her a hug, but the backup lights warned me off as the car was shifted into gear. It was my turn for a quick silent prayer before the celebration of the returned swept me away again.

I wonder what Court is doing – and where. I wonder if the freedom he feels lives up to what we imagined. I wonder if I could be brave enough to find out for myself. I wonder…

Man Down – Part II — Lory Harris
July 2003 — St. Charles, Illinois

I was so certain all week that Court would return with us – it was the only thing I felt truly positive about. A relative of one of our ASP crew members lives in Hazard, the largest population concentration in the area. I grew up in a town about that size - 5,000 - and know well that strangers on the doorstep are noteworthy gossip fodder. After a couple of inquiries, not only could Adrienne tell us a young male hitchhiker had been picked up by some locals, but she could give us the address where he was staying, too. A couple of days ago, another leader and I drove over, walked up rickety stairs to a second-floor apartment and knocked on the door. I thought maybe I heard someone inside, but the noise might have been coming from the residents of the garden apartment below. At any rate, the door remained closed and we left empty handed. Maybe it was the fear of success only to be followed by rejection, but I opted not to go back to the apartment again. What would I do if I found Court and he refused to listen to reason or even just listen?

Everyone from the ASP center went to the fireworks last night, along with what seemed to be the rest of the county and at least half of each collar county. While everyone was watching the sky and cheering, I was scanning the crowd and hoping. Surely Court would be there, and just as surely, he would make a sheepish return wanting a ride home the next morning. For all the success realized, I could have been looking for him in the sky among the flashing array. Still, I held tightly to my last vestige of hope: he walked away from the ASP center (and me) in the middle of the night, and he could return the same way. He could have, but he didn't.

There is an unwritten ASP van rule: the adults get the front seats. The driver, of course, must be over 25 to pilot the rental. But the second adult, the one charged with keeping the driver caffeinated and alert, automatically rides shotgun, unless they abdicate. All I wanted to do was to be magically transported away from the pain visited upon me in Kentucky. I relinquished my duties and my prime perch, opting to bury my face in my pillow, feigning sleep, and crying the whole way home. Well, when we stopped, which was far too frequently, I had to "wake up" and join the frivolity. I doubt my red rimmed eyes were too convincing.

Ken met our returning group at the church parking lot where the two of us clung to each other as I dampened his shoulder. Suddenly I didn't care who saw my tears or what they thought. I just wanted to go home, though, of course, that was akin to entering the lion's den by the back door rather than the front. Court's room was there, in total disarrayed, as usual, and yet completely empty: the perfect reflection of my own emotions.

Once home, I told Ken the rest of the story a tenderly as possible, letting him listen to Court's message for himself. I hadn't wanted him to be alone with the shock of the revelation as I had been. I wanted to give him the comfort and support I had lacked. He didn't see it that way, though. Ken was furious that I had kept Court's revelation a secret, not deeming him worthy of the handling the truth. Nothing I said in my defense mattered and I guess I can't blame him for his reaction. After all, I have had a week to assimilate my son's new identity, or start the process, at least. Ken is at the raw beginning and feeling duped by both his son and his wife. I did the only thing I could think to do: I cried some more.

After eating dinner, both bites, and cleaning the kitchen, I grabbed my cell phone and took my tears for a walk. The sun was still up, but the neighbors were all hiding inside, evading both the heat and the mosquitos. Wandering the subdivision aimlessly, I ended up at the local grade school. Suddenly feeling too weary and too wary to make it home, I sought some comfort at the swing set, allowing the plastic seat to support my weight as I rocked from the heavy metal chains.

I needed someone to talk to, and neither Ken nor God were listening, so from my schoolyard cradle, I called my best friend, Merry. "Of all the people that could have picked Court up in the middle of the night, why did God allow them to be gay? Couldn't He have arranged for a grandparent-type who would have brought him back to the center? In the space of one week, will I lose my son and my husband? Is that what God grants to those who try to remain faithful?"

Merry's response wasn't what I expected. "Lory, what do you want from God?" But I had a ready answer. In the mail that day was an envelope addressed to our middle son, Corey, the response to his formal request to regain permission to drive again. We had been told, in classic legal lethargy, to anticipate a provisional license, at best. Corey, however, wasn't home to open the envelope and receive the expected non-information.

"I want," I spat back, "for God to show that He is even vaguely aware that the Harrises exist! I want that letter to restore Corey's driver's license without limitation."

Unspoken but equally true, I wanted Merry to jump on my bandwagon: to rally against God's lack of evidential love – to take my side, two on one against the author of the universe. A true friend, though, will tell you not what you want, but what you really need to hear: "Oh, Lory, God doesn't work that way." Quite frankly, I'm getting pretty accustomed to the way God doesn't work. On the other hand, at least my rage had dried my tears, so it wasn't a total loss. Our conversation wrapped up quickly after that. How many times can you say the same thing, and what good does it do anyway?

As I started to wander back to the house, absolute despair overtook my whole being. It wasn't the mosquitos whose numbers were growing exponentially in an effort to block my path. They wouldn't get much blood out of me anyway, as my heart, shattered into a million pieces of soggy red confetti, was no longer capable of pumping anything remotely life-giving through my veins. I have never felt such misery, not at any time in this surreal year. All I wanted to do was cry, and the one thing I could not do - was cry. It really is possible to run out of tears. And impossible as that might seem, it just leaves you that much more destitute and wanting.

That Way **Merry Luehr**
July 2003 **St. Charles, Illinois**

I didn't get much sleep last night, though I'm sure our household collected more Zs than the Harrises'. I just kept thinking maybe I share the blame for their sleeplessness - this round, at least. Lory called me from Kentucky last week in a state of emotional shock after Court's message. Of course, I wanted to be a good friend to my best friend and help her process the revelation, but the initial burst of information had apparently destroyed the pathways between my reason and speech. When she said she wasn't going to tell Ken until she got home, I agreed with her. It sounded right at the time, but I should have seen the storm on the horizon.

Ken and I may as well be twins. We didn't know that growing up. In fact, we didn't know each other at all in our youth, though we both lived in the Chicago 'burbs. In an ironic quirk of fate, my husband, Mike, and Lory are also twins. The four of us met about 6 years ago at a couples' Bible study. Mike signed the two of us up. I came in tow, a bit reluctantly. It had been Ken's idea for the two of them to join, so I guess we aren't quite identical. But his outgoing, irreverent wit matches mine, as does his propensity toward occasional fiery outbursts. Lory and Mike, on the other hand, are the epitome of 'still waters run deep.' It wasn't long before we were "couple dating": dinners, concerts, a glass of wine on random Saturday afternoons. Eventually we formalized the relationship with joint vacations and the right to walk into each other's houses unannounced.

I should have felt Ken's impending betrayal and warned Lory against it from the start, but my brain had bogged down at Court's announcement, "He and I are very happy together." Whatever twinges of awakening I might have felt after that were numbed while watching my best friend's world spin recklessly out of the realm of possible. Everyone was just trying to remain upright, myself included.

Last night I found a better posture: on my knees. Even during my fitful sleep, I was praying, aided by the Spirit's groans as promised in Romans 8:26. I wanted to call Lory first thing when I got up this morning. I wanted to use my uncensored access to their house and give her a hug. But I was hoping everyone was still sleeping there, and secondly, all privileges have their limits. Today was likely not the time to test those boundaries.

As it turns out, I didn't have to wait long before she called me. "Merry, yesterday was the worst day of my life. I don't think I could or would live through it again. In one way, though, it was also the best day of my life." She went on tell me that when she got home from her neighborhood wanderings, the argument that had paused while she walked, picked up where it had left off. There was no resolution between Lory and Ken, but rather, each of them ran out of ways to say the same thing.

After a few moments where the conversation was carried by the TV, Ken told Lory of his news during her absence. He had reached Corey on the phone and asked for permission to open the official letter that had been delivered. Corey's lawyer had previously told him that if his request for a full license was accepted, he should immediately buy a lottery ticket, because he would be the luckiest person on the planet. Expectations set low, Corey agreed to the revelation of next round of hoop jumping and legal expenses.

"It's over, Merry. Corey's license has been fully reinstated." It was one of those rare times when any words of my own absolutely refused to form. "It was," she continued, "like God reached down and gave me a hug - me, specifically me. It was exactly what I demanded of Him, and He gave it to me. I buried my head in my hands, and I wanted to cry, but no tears would come. So, I just leaned in and let God hold me. Yesterday was still the worst day of my life. Even God's gift of the exact miracle I demanded does not change that. But there is an asterisk on the calendar as well. It is a day I will never forget."

When our conversation ended, I found myself on my knees, and once again relying on the Spirit's groans to complete my sentences. "Thank you, God," I started, before wonder interrupted gratitude. For the life of me, I couldn't figure out what words should come next. I have never been so ecstatic to be 100% wrong. Apparently, sometimes God does work exactly "that way."

Degrees of Separation – Part I — Ken Harris

July 2003 — St. Charles, Illinois

It has been over a week now since Court left on his Kentucky vacation. Though he is never far from my mind, there are also some daily reminders of his absence. First, his room is clean, thanks to Lory. It's a pleasure to walk up the stairs and see the floor in there – so unfamiliar, but welcome. And while my wife puts things in order inside, I have also made progress outside. Our front yard now sports an area 50′ by 200′ that is free of underbrush and weeds, and the area continues to grow a little each day.

I made considerable progress the first couple of days Lory was home. I needed something to join me in my pain, and buckthorns seemed a good victim. They got their licks in, but slow as the going has been, I am winning. The physical labor continues to be a great sleep aid, a welcome bonus. After the sun goes down and the mosquitos steal more blood than the prickly plants had, I have been doing some research on the internet about what to grow in the newly cleared space. Even without the underbrush, the area will still be in deep shade owing to the trees towering above. Hostas seem to be a distinct possibility, and there is a huge number of varieties, many of which, I believe, are destined for our yard.

In October of this year, Lory and I will have known each other for a quarter of a century. And in a little less than a year, we will celebrate our 25th anniversary. We have been married longer than we were single, and we would like to stay that way. So, by mutual, non-verbal consent, we are moving forward and leaving the Kentucky should-have-would-have-could-have-been conversations behind us.

Our next steps are as baffling as the previous ones. There are just no guidelines for what to do when your child purposely disappears in the Appalachian Mountains. It seems every month the medical experts change Court's prescriptions, the ones that might or might not be effective if ingested. Those meds run us about $1000 per month – after insurance. It's just one of the joys of self-employment and the lack of group health care.

Legally, of course, Court is an adult, and being mentally ill is not a crime. How much responsibility do we have to dictate his life, and how much right do we have to force him to acquiesce to the vacillating medical collective? I want my son back – the one who graduated at the top of his high school class and went away to college to become a veterinarian. But once again, my desires are not a factored into the possible outcomes.

Yesterday, after collecting the various professional opinions, we finally decided to have Court listed on the national registry of missing persons. That process was both easier and more gut-wrenching than I expected. Surprisingly, within an hour of completing the process, we received a phone call from a Hazard, Kentucky, payphone, which had to be a coincidence. Nothing can possibly work that quickly! The conversation was short, owing to the lack of permitted response time. "Tell Mom to quit looking for me. I'm home. I love you. Goodbye." The connection was broken before I could utter even a word of acknowledgement.

This morning, less than 24 hours after initiating the process, we had Court removed from the national registry. It's not like we are throwing in the towel. We couldn't even if we wanted to; the towel isn't ours. But we are still hoping to win a war, which will require far more than a bit of cloth used after bathing. In what I hope will be a sign of things to come, Lory and I made the decision together and agreed almost immediately.

Court's fate is, again, as it probably always has been, in his own hands. It's a waiting game now. You would think that eight months has been wait enough, but apparently not. Who will be on the other end of the phone next time it rings: Court, the police, a hospital, a morgue? Each one seems more likely than the previous. How ironically appropriate that his "home" is now in Hazard. Whatever attraction holds you there, Court, I pray for the best for you. We love you, too, and this home is still waiting for you, if and when you decide to return.

Degrees of Separation – Part II Schley Brandt
July 2003 St. Charles, Illinois

My name is Schley, and I'm a quilter. When I started quilting 30 years ago, that was a bigger distinction than it is now. Now there are good, accessible, quilt shops in most areas of the country. Back then, I had to open my own store just to have somewhere to shop. When I moved to the Atlanta area several years later, I started a quilt guild to join with other like-minded women. There is just something about taking perfectly good fabric, cutting it into little pieces and sewing it back together again that calms the savage beast and feeds the soul. It begs the world to come see the inner artist. It beckons me to acknowledge and celebrate that artist in myself and in others.

Quilters are a special breed. On her way to a quilt show, a quilter may be dressed to the nines - with or without some quilted clothing. Or she may be dressed down in jeans and a sweat shirt – with or without a pithy quilting slogan on it. But she will be wearing practical shoes, even if they don't match her outfit. Shoes are the key, and they will not hold her back. She has miles to walk to see the quilts, shop the vendors, and listen to lectures by artists whose work she admires. The quilter celebrates heritage with log cabin blocks, flying geese, and feathered stars, but she seeks to put a new and unique stamp on the traditional, as well. The log cabins twist, the geese dip and soar, and the stars twinkle in colors that would have crossed great-grandma's eyes.

Quilters are generous. We will freely give time, talents and templates to another in need. If our own fabric will perfectly fill the missing place in another's project, we will happily donate to their art in progress. Advice is dispensed across the board, though maybe more frequently by the chronologically advanced. Quilting age is measured not in years of breathing, but in hours of quilting time - a measure of mistakes made and the conquered "now-what" factor. The quilter's rule of thumb is: if you can't fix it, feature it. It has its application for non-quilters and for life in general, too.

Speaking to non-quilters: we love to share our creations. We can't keep them all for ourselves. That would be like the *Princess and the Pea* – no one needs that many layers aside from establishing royal lineage. But, you generally can't get on the gift list just by asking, we must offer. We are trusting you with our art, our life-blood, a piece of our soul. It is not a blanket (try Walmart) or a thick, fluffy comforter (next to the blankets at

Walmart). Nor is it a delicate flower: use it! Quilts are made with love and made to be loved. There is no higher compliment than coming back to me a decade down the road with a quilt loved back to the pieces from which it was created. That will, indeed, make my heart sing!

Is it any wonder, then, that when I moved to Chicago I first found a quilt store, then a quilt guild, and then formed a quilting bee? The bee is the highest rung on the quilting social ladder - the top of the pyramid. The six generous women in my bee gather every other week, sharing it all: fabric, advice, food, laughter, tears, stories, wishes and fears, what-if's and used-to be's, brags and dreams. We talk about it all over the hum of the sewing machines or the quiet of hand sewing. I may not know their bra sizes, but we have certainly discussed the relative differences on more than one occasion. We have also discussed religion and politics - and couldn't agree less, but it doesn't hinder our friendship. These women know me in ways I would be embarrassed to admit to anyone else. And I trust them with that information implicitly. Generous souls.

Children, of course, are a major topic of conversation. When Lory first joined our bee, we discovered that our children already knew each other. My daughter, Jennifer, and Court had a class together their freshman year of high school. It was mutual respect that held their friendship, loosely but permanently. Good partners in a group project, they would each pull their weight and then some. Both would describe themselves as shy, painfully so, but no one would have guessed Court's self-assessment. His introvert nature was pushed down until it popped out as wit and humor – cutting at times, but especially hilarious for others who could keep up with his stream of logic. He alternated between teacher's pet and class clown, depending, I suppose, on his respect for the teacher and interest in the subject at hand. And he was a jock – first string soccer goalie at his grade level. All told, he could have been a member of the "in" crowd, but he wasn't. He hung out down a rung or two on the social ladder. Maybe it was his self-perceived shyness that held him back, but I don't think he aspired to the top. Court was a good kid – the kind any mom would be proud to point to as her own. And Lory was proud and pointing.

As their high school careers ended, Jennifer made plans to attend Columbia College. Court was headed to Iowa State. Both were practically invited guests at their respective schools, thanks to impressive lists of scholarships and grants. Neither attended the other's graduation party. They weren't that close, or maybe Jennifer had already witnessed the change that the rest of us had missed. Humor and history have a way of hiding what hindsight makes more obvious. But no one, least of all Ken and Lory, saw the storms on the horizon. It wasn't until the thunder boomed and the lightning struck in unison during Court's freshman year at college that they snapped awake to the horrors of their son's situation.

I remember that day, or more accurately the email that brought news of that day. Lory sent it to each of us in the quilting bee from Court's email address. Conventional wisdom is useless for responding to the information that a friend's child is in a mental hospital with vacillating diagnosis. I didn't want to respond to his email address not knowing if he had access to it. We discussed it at length in our bee, but we were all stunned into inaction. It is a testament to our friendship that after one mention of the hurt she felt at our silence, Lory let it drop. It is a mistake none of us will ever make again. Sometime later, she told me her philosophy on such delicate topics: it's okay to ask a person in crisis how things are going. Ask, and then take their lead. If they don't want to talk about it, they will put you off with a non-answer. But they might just be waiting for someone to care enough to inquire, and the flood gates will open. Then just listen. There are no easy answers, nor are any expected, but the act of caring enough to ask and then enough to listen, is a gift that soothes a threadbare soul.

It's been eight months now since the storm broke loose, and it is still a drenching downpour. Court is somewhere, presumably in Kentucky, but who really knows for sure?

It's Lory's turn to host bee, which entails opening the door and making lunch. I thought she might cancel, but I imagine she would like a diversion or a piece of "normal" somewhere in her life. I'm glad she didn't ask to switch dates with someone. Any of us would have done it in a heartbeat, but I'm afraid then she wouldn't have come. She needs to feel our love as much as we need to love on her. Hers isn't the only heart breaking over her youngest son, though the crack in mine does not compare to the chasm in hers.

Bee day starts the night before. The project de jour needs to be portable enough to transport the needed components, and not so complex that conversation will become difficult to follow or detrimental to the quilt. It goes without saying that anyone in the group will give whatever they brought to cover a forgotten item, though some items are more difficult to share. For example, one should always remember to bring the pattern for the quilt you are working on <u>and</u> the foot pedal to your sewing machine.

Of course, if you forget an irreplaceable key something-or-other, you can always help someone else with their project. Any day of quilting is a good day, even if it involves the dreaded un-sewing. On those days when female banter causes copious amounts of un-sewing, the ripping of stitches will be greeted with knowing laughter and a helping hand. No one ever forgets their seam ripper, which means there will be six at the ready. Again, generous souls.

Over the course of the morning, Lory fills us in on the scant information they have about Court. The words come out almost flat, like they had been rehearsed, and maybe they were. Or maybe the heart and soul need to shut down at some point to be recharged for the next demands. Though she probably didn't expect any words, we all struggled with just what to say. How do you react when a friend tells you their child has dropped off the grid? How do you reassure someone when no one believes it will be okay any time soon, if ever?

Lunch was light, and the conversation turned to follow suit. Lory was talked out, and whatever words of comfort we could cobble together had been offered. We talked of local gossip, weather and movies, colors and cuts (quilts, not hair). Dishes were cleared and sewing machines took up their background hum again. In deference to our hostess, we steered clear of bragging on our own children. Generous souls.

Toward mid-afternoon, our numbers began to dwindle as other obligations reclaimed priority. So, it was that when the phone rang, only Lory and I remained to hear Ken call from the adjoining room that it was a Kentucky area code on Caller ID. Tension registered as she reached for the extension. "Hi, Court! How are...," and then silence as she listened intently to the voice on the other end of the line. The conversation went on for some time, if indeed it could be called a "conversation." No more words were issued from the Illinois end of the connection, the only sound in the room being the ragged breathing of my friend attempting to cry silently and meeting with minimal success. After what seemed an eternity, but was probably not more than two minutes, she replaced the phone and sat again.

Head down, in a voice broken by sobs and gasps for air, she recounted the one-sided conversation. "He said just to shut up and listen and he would let us respond when he was done talking. He said to 'call off the dogs,' that he wasn't crazy and didn't need the police checking up on him. He said he trusted Ken and Colin, and maybe Corey, but he hates me, and he never wants to see me again. He said I have lied to him his whole life and manipulated him and I would never get another chance. He said he would call back with further directions for Ken and Colin, but he would never speak to me again. And then he just hung up."

At some point during the recitation, Ken had entered the room to comfort his wife. He was ashen and obviously shaken, but she was crying the tears for them both. They held each other, as I sat in awkward silence, not wanting to intrude on their private pain, and unable to find a graceful exit. She seemed to draw strength from him, the tears slowing and breathing becoming easier. "He didn't mean it," he comforted her. A sad smile crossed her lips briefly to thank him for the attempt. "I'm glad he is back in touch with one of us," was her reply. There was a hug, a tender kiss, and a nod letting him know she would be okay before Ken returned to his office.

What could I say? I'm sorry…it's not true…he loves you…at least he's alive… As it turned out, it wasn't even my turn to talk. "Court knows that I know that he doesn't mean it," she volunteered. "He and I have always had a close relationship and this change nothing. The hardest part is knowing how much pain he must be in to lash out like that. He said it to hurt me, but he hasn't succeeded. I am hurt with him but not by him." The tears were flowing again, but there was strength in the alignment of her shoulders and the set of her jaw. There was little for me to say – a hug and a co-mingling of tears. Her love held strong, her resolve fortified. Generous soul.

A Pastor's Visit **Pastor Bill Obalil**
July 2003 **Geneva United Methodist Church**
St. Charles, Illinois

Monday– my day off. In theory, I have Saturday off, too, if my sermon is complete (rarely), and there isn't a wedding...or a funeral... or a meeting to attend. Monday's are a more predictable day of rest, though family crisis never consults the calendar.

So far today, the weather is beautiful, perfect for a bike ride. The phone hasn't rung, and emails replies can wait. It's shaping up to be a great day off, except for the nagging thought that started yesterday during worship and refuses to be silenced even after a night's sleep.

Like many sanctuaries on Sunday morning, the pews are filled in a predictable way. There is no formal seating chart, to my knowledge, but from my perch at the front, I can take attendance at a glance. If a different face is sitting in the Ellis's spot, it means a new family has joined us. If the newbies become regulars, they may cause a slight shift in another's vantage point. But frequently the next week things settle back to usual. It's not a matter of ruffled feathers; we are all just creatures of habit. My unease this day is because Ken and Lory's spot has been occupied by squatters the past two Sundays.

When they weren't in their self-assigned places the day after the return from ASP, I wasn't surprised. I noticed and worried, but wasn't sure what to make of it. In an average year, ASP both exhilarates and drains the crew, especially the adults. I'm used to missing most of them the next Sunday. In a normal year, that is, without the trauma of this specific trip. Keith had called to let me know about Court's disappearance the morning it happened. Our staff have been praying diligently for the Harris family ever since. My associate pastor, Melissa, volunteered to visit Ken and Lory early last week. Having been on several ASP trips with the Harrises, she seemed like a good emissary for our community of believers. Her visit was, as expected, tearful and heart-wrenching, but not without God's grace and mercy. No one expected a quick fix, but Ken and Lory seemed to be hanging on to each other and to God, something you can't necessarily count on. Often in a family crisis, one or both of those touchstones are discarded.

I'm not sure if I expected to see them back in their pews yesterday or not. To tell the truth, I'm not sure which would be healthier. If they attended out of duty, knuckles white from swallowed anger and anxiety over quizzical looks or prying questions, God's offering of grace and mercy might be blocked, anyway. And yet, if they came, they would be opening themselves to the genuine love and care of our faith community, which I trust God would use in a powerful way. But God can also use mournful solitude as a salve for the wounded. I trust God will always find us and meet us, wherever our pain chases us to hide.

The urgent question for me is, *what is the role God is assigning to me in this devastation?* As if I didn't know. I'm the pastor. It is quite literally "my job," and much more, my calling, to go to them, to be present in all their agony, to represent the presence of God that no one can completely portray, and to offer what comfort I can – or what comfort God is able to convey through me. Show up; I'm clear about that. But I'm not so clear about what then. Just what is it that I can say that will make a difference? I'm weary and fed up with the shallow platitudes and puny Christian pieties that are so often spoken in the face of indescribable pain. My mother died when I was a senior in high school, and I was infuriated with inadequate elixirs that trivialized my grief. I think they're designed to comfort the speakers, not the suffering. I was intent not to inflict that additional pain and insult.

I must depend on the Holy Spirit to come alongside me, guide me and provide the needed words – if, indeed, words are needed. That is, of course, God's promise, and I count on God keeping it. Otherwise I'd find lots of good reasons to procrastinate on showing up. It seems people expect us pastors to have the right things to say in these moments. As much as nature abhors a vacuum, people seem to abhor silence even more. Oh, how people squirm when there are more than a few moments of wordlessness in worship. Recognizing all this does not make me immune to the temptation of filling the silence with jabber, like Job's so-called friends did in the Old Testament. They encouraged Job to challenge and blame God, but it wasn't the salve he needed. Nor is it likely to be the one that will heal the Harris household. Sometimes it is best to be mute – excruciating, but best. Before I get in the car, I pray long and intently for the Holy Spirit to ride with me. And I coach myself: "Don't just say something; sit there."

I received a polite greeting when I arrived at the Harrises. They were neither surprised nor exactly expecting my appearance. Both were working, which Ken continued to do after offering apologies and citing a fast-approaching deadline. Lory and I went to sit on the deck in the relative cool of the morning. She brought me up to date on the situation, which had, if possible, deteriorated some more. It seems to me that more than being hurt *by* Court's rejection, Lory is hurting *for* Court. It wasn't anger I saw in her eyes, but longing – the same kind of longing that I have seen in the eyes of a woman who has miscarried, or a parent coming to grips with their child's terminal cancer diagnosis. It is a longing for what could have been, what *should* have been, and an acknowledgement that life has just irrevocably changed.

Our conversation probably lasted 20-30 minutes. I wrapped it up with a pastoral prayer – both obligatory and deeply desired - and a time when I find myself most in need of the Holy Spirit's intervention. I know how to pray in public at the drop of a hat. I'm not sure what power those prayers carry, but to me, they sound composed. Now, sitting with Lory, I am aware that what needs to be prayed struggles to find my words. Were it not for the Spirit's intervention, my prayers might be only a smattering of beige starting with "Dear Lord" and ending with "In Jesus name, Amen." I am not able to judge my success on this occasion, nor will I try. But, boy, do I want God to show up!

"I hope to see you in church soon. God's people want to come along side you and love you and hold you up." It was only the briefest glimpse before her gaze rested on the deck board nearest my toes, but it was there. Her look of longing had been replaced by a depth of doubt and disbelief, and even fear. When she looked up again, her emotions were cloaked.

"Thank you for coming by. I really appreciate all you and Melissa have done. I mean that most sincerely! Please don't stop praying for us. The journey is so long, longer than I thought possible." There was finality to her words: not the slamming of a door, but the gentle click as it is eased closed, the lock already set.

On Sundays, I will be checking the seating chart, as I always do, with conscious focus on the Harrises' spot. And mentally, I will be holding the pew for them. But more so, I will be lifting them up in prayer: for mercy, for grace, for healing, for endurance, for relief, for a miracle, for God's glory. Those pleas murmured silently within my heart, will be rich and vivid, indeed, with no hint of beige to be found.

Kentucky Hospitality — Court Harris
July 2003 — Backroads of Kentucky

Andrew left last Friday, promising to break up with his boyfriend and get some money he was owed. When he returned a day or so later, we were to have started our life together. I waited with anticipation for his return all weekend.

On Monday morning, my anxious restlessness got the better of me. Using the last of my cash for a pack of cigarettes, I just started walking. Of course, I extended my thumb on those rare occasions when a vehicle chose to share my road. But I've learned over time that cars seldom recognize that digit as the sign of distress it is. Unfortunately, there were no truckers in need of a few miles of friendly conversation on those back roads.

Even before noon, the heat rising off the pavement made my whole world shimmer with a surreal translucency like viewing the countryside through a plastic shower curtain. Eventually, my undulating black ribbon of road brought me into a small town. It was early afternoon and I hadn't eaten all day, had little more to drink, and was starting to think this might be my final resting place when I was rewarded by the kindness of strangers. First, I was granted a cup of Sprite – glorious sugar-water of the gods! A block later, another citizen responded to my request for food with a five-dollar bill. Feeling my soul, legs and blood sugar revived by the soda, I now had a decision to make: food or cigarettes. Not up to the debate, I opted for a candy bar and a pack of smokes.

The afternoon heat took its toll on my temporarily revived legs, though they kept trudging on as if on automatic pilot. I wanted to pull out my cell phone and call someone, except there was no cell service in those hollers – there never was. And anyway, Andrew had admired my new phone, so I let him borrow it. I would get it back from him later.

The angle of the sun confirmed the fast-approaching dinner hour that my stomach had been insisting upon for quite some time. Not that it mattered, really. There was no food available - to beg, borrow or steal. For all I knew, I had been walking in circles the whole day and Hazard would be around the next corner, which was a cheery thought. Why had I embarked on this walk-about anyway?

My mind paid dull attention to a rusting pickup truck parked on the side of the road with a similarly paint-challenged mailbox listing in its direction. It was one of those rare pockmarks of humanity that had decorated my route occasionally throughout the day. Lengthy weeds surrounding all four wheels, gave no indication of actual life. The thought of sleeping in the cab was just beginning to form in my mind when a voice startled me. "You look hungry. Would you like to join us for dinner?"

I thought the heat was starting to affect my ears as it had my eyes until I found the source of my solidified relief: an older man was waving at me from the porch of a little cabin partially obscured by overgrown bushes and trees dripping with kudzu. My legs carried me with purposeful steps toward the promised meal even while my mind was trying to process this amazing turn of fortunes. "This is my grandson, Levi. Levi, show our guest the creek around back while we get dinner finished up."

Levi was the perfect host, chattering as quickly as his southern drawl would allow, pointing out places of interest in the big, wide, wonderful world of an 8-year-old. The redhead and I raced leaves down the flowing waters, using sticks to release them from ensnarling eddies. His freckled face smiled up at me as I studied footprints cast in the muddy banks. The coolness of the water and the warmth of human companionship rejuvenated me in ways that even the Sprite could not match.

The call to wash up for dinner reminded me, again, of just how hungry I really was. It was tempting to grab a roll from the table even before I sat down, but I resisted out of respect for the kindness of my benefactors. Grace was offered, perhaps too long for my heightened digestive awareness, but appropriately said. There was a stew (beef, I think), a salad, and the bread, of course. As I swallowed each bite, another one poised on my fork, I made sure to exclaim how wonderful it was and how thankful I was for their invitation. I ate my fill, and maybe a portion of Levi's, too. At least he couldn't stop his little boy giggles when I served up my third helping, though it was at his grandparents' insistence. "Where are you headed?"

"I'm trying to hitchhike to Chicago," I replied. "That's where my folks are."

"There's not much traffic in these parts, as I'm sure you already know. We can set up a tent for you to sleep in the front yard, if you like. Tomorrow I'll drive you to the main highway where you are more likely to catch a ride."

If they had offered me a room at the Ritz Carlton, I wouldn't have slept better than I did that night. The trio of physical exhaustion, a full belly and the kindness of strangers is probably the best sleep-aid ever. I woke the next morning to the smell of bacon, accompanied by pancakes and a stout cup of coffee that chased away any remaining cobwebs.

The promised ride to the highway took nearly an hour. It would have taken me another day's walk, assuming I didn't take a wrong turn along the way or pass out due to dehydration. The gratitude I felt as I waved goodbye to my saviors brought me to the verge of tears, but a truck was approaching, so I stuck out my thumb. Wonder of wonders, I saw his brake lights glow red as he passed. Running a little to cover the ground between my thumb and my new patron, I just couldn't contain a smile. "Thank you" was the word of the day, and I was going to make good use of it.

A Fare to the 'Burbs — "Winks" Winkelman

July 2003 — Chicago, Illinois

He wasn't the kind of fare I care to see hailing me down: young, unkempt, male. He had the look of a hitchhiker, which I have been, so I'm not holding that against him. But I give rides for a fee in this vehicle, and he certainly didn't look like a man of means. With the day's weather being so unseasonably pleasant, my fares had been scant. The average business man was already safely riding the rails home and any real income action wouldn't start for another few hours when the dinner crowd brought their full bellies and alcohol-induced cleverness to the curbs. I had time if he had cash.

He slid into the backseat, and before the door was even closed, we hit our first stumbling block. "I need a ride to the suburbs, to St. Charles."

"Man," I said, "I can't get a return fare from there. You are going to have to pay for my return trip. That will be $80 – in cash – up front."

"Well, here's the thing," he continued. I've been at this job too long; my initial wariness had been warranted. "I don't have any cash, but I'm going home to see my parents. I'm running late, and they are anxious for me to get there. They will pay you when you drop me off. How about $90?" Assuming anyone would be on the other end with actual cash, he had me leaning.

Our negotiations continued to proof-of-parents. It turned out he couldn't call them since he lost his cell phone. Perhaps against my better judgment, I loaned him mine. Either my night's work was looking up, or I had wasted ten minutes when I should have been trolling for actual income. I certainly didn't want to drive 40 miles each direction on a promise and end up with only an empty gas tank.

"Hi, Mom. I'm coming home. I'm in Chicago right now. I've been on the road for two days, and I really don't want to sleep at a homeless shelter for the night. I found a cab driver who will bring me home, but he needs $100 in cash when we get there. Will you do that for me?"

Gaunt as he was, he hadn't impressed me as overly up-tight or stressed, but the transformation his face undertook in the next few moments was unmistakable. I hadn't consciously noticed his shallow breathing until he emitted a long steady exhale. He shoulders softened as he leaned back against the seat for the first time. His brows lost their furrowed edge and an ever so slight smile found his lips. I motioned for the phone to confirm the funds commitment and the address. I all but had

$100 in my pocket, and at worst, I had the number of a co-conspirator stored in my phone.

Negotiations complete, we headed to the western sticks. We chatted for a while, my fare and me. He was returning from Kentucky, walking and hitchhiking the whole way. He hadn't been home in a while and was looking forward to some home cooking and a good night's sleep in his own bed. There were the typical "Chicago" talking points: the weather, road construction and the Cubs verses the Sox. After what seemed forever, he told me to take the Randall Road exit and head south.

Shortly after following those directions, I noticed that our conversation had turned one-sided, in my direction. Glancing in the rear-view mirror, I saw him resting against and looking out the window. The image reflected in the glass showed the creases in his forehead had returned, cancelling whatever glimmer of a smile had once found its way to his eyes. I wasn't sure if I should be concerned for him or worried about my payday – either seemed equally precarious. Our only words for the last ten minutes of the drive were his directions as to where to turn.

Even in the dark, it was easy to see that we weren't in Chicago any more. Of course, in Chicago it is never completely dark owing to all the streetlights and headlights, as well as the offerings from the many windows. Even in just these few westward miles, the suburban night multiplied the stars exponentially. The houses are bigger, the lawns more spacious, the traffic lights more scantly spaced. Suburbia is indeed a foreign country to me, a city boy. The sounds of traffic are replaced with the voices of what must be the world's largest insects!

We pulled into a drive of a house with two, two-car garages and a door in between that seemed to go to an office of some kind. Silhouetted in the doorway was a woman who was obviously watching for us. The doors opened simultaneously: hers and the rear door of my cab. They met half way and embraced, mother and returning son.

I was starting to feel a bit uncomfortable, almost voyeuristic, when they finally seemed to remember I was still there. She pulled six (not five!) twenties from her pocket and handed them me with a thank you. I graciously accepted 150% of my initial fare demand and put the car into reverse.

It isn't the longest ride or the biggest fare I've ever received, but it was unique. I'm happy to be headed back to my world where you don't have to be worried about being eaten by a six-legged carnivorous cockroach, but I'm happy to have delivered a country boy back to his world. Now, if I can just catch a fare as I enter the city, I could to go home early tonight!

Weary Worship — Lory Harris
July 2003 — Geneva, Illinois

My timing was a little off this morning. I didn't want to be rude and walk into church late, but I really didn't want to smile at complete strangers and pretend that life is good, either. Five minutes early – I guess I can pretend to be enthralled by the prelude. Fortunately, I don't know many people here at First Baptist Church of Geneva[1], so maybe I can get by with just a nod and a smile – the latter being the more difficult part.

Maybe I should have just stayed home, but I need to be here. More specifically, I need to be somewhere that God might show up and extend some comfort. Church seems to offer at least minimal hope along those lines. I can't go back to Geneva United Methodist Church – how could I? I can't bear the thought of the knowing looks and whispered conversations. "There is Lory. She taught Sunday school, spoke in front of the church, and was a Stephen's Minister leader. I guess she should have focused more attention at home. Did you hear that her son disappeared at ASP?" What makes it worse is that it is all so well deserved. I was buying into my own PR, thinking I was doing it all right: the perfect wife, mother and Christian. But it's not supported by the evidence.

Walking down the side aisle, I find a deserted pew and hope to claim it as my own. One of the few people I know, Claudia, is a couple rows in front of me. A friend for years, she knows what is happening in my life. I am sure she will offer a hug if she notices me here, but I hope she didn't want an update. I can't do that without ending up with rivers of mascara running down my face.

It was so good to see Court on Wednesday night. When he stepped from the cab, none of the 'whys' mattered anymore. He was home! Former harsh words were set aside. There were things to work through, of course, but there would be time. Well, I assume there would be time. But by Thursday afternoon he was gone, again, headed back to Kentucky… and Andrew.

Am I supposed to be thrilled that Court has found his life's dream while mine lays trampled in the mud? Will I be able to accept Andrew if it comes to that? Can I ever forgive him for this earthquake that is shaking the foundation of our family? No, it isn't Andrew that requires forgiveness. At most, he is just the sign post of a change we didn't see coming. Can I forgive God? I know He's the one that we beg forgiveness

---

[1] First Baptist Church of Geneva is now known as ChapelStreet Church

of, but if He is so all powerful and loving, why does He dangle my heart's desire in my face only to pull it away when I dare to reach for it? I am lost in a desert, overwrought and crawling to water only to come up with sand, the shimmering mirage giving way to futile reality.

Once again, the options granted by my son are as impotent as my prayers. The only allowable contribution Ken and I could agree upon was a bus ticket back to Kentucky. The thought of Court hitchhiking across three states a second time was unbearable. Odd, isn't it, that all of the 'whys' cast aside so quickly during my son's presence now matter once again? Virtually all of them are still unanswered, maybe even unanswerable.

A subtle shift in the musical flow and a shuffling of feet awakened me to the start of the service. Obediently, I stand with the rest of the assembled to sing the opening praise song. The tune is familiar, but the words projected on the screen are illegible. Listening to the voices around me, I realized no one else is having vision problems. Even if I could have made out the words, under water as they appear, my voice is not reliable enough to sing. I had promised myself I would not cry in church today. But a mere thirty seconds into the service, I have broken my own vow. At this rate, I will never meet anyone in this congregation. They are all busy trying to respect the privacy of the unstable lady with black lines running down her face. My sole Kleenex is struggling to keep up.

There is a brief pause before the tune changes. The new one, though, did not require any reading. The words form in my brain in perfect timing with the instruments.

Here I am to worship.
Here I am to bow down.
Here I am to say that you're my God.

The tears wouldn't stop, and I don't dare to trust my voice, but there is the slightest hint of an eternal arm around my shoulders. In a world gyrating noisily and radically out of control, this is something I can grasp. I made the decision, the choice, to be here this morning; *I am.* To claim God is a matter of my will; *I do.* To bow to His wishes is my desire; *I will try.*

As the service progresses, the flow of my tears, too, wanes. By the time the benediction is given, I am once again viewing my surroundings though dry eyes. Tucking my well-used Kleenex into my pocket for appropriate disposal, I think I will bring the whole box next week, just in case.

Hitchhiking **Court Harris**
July 2003 **Kentucky to Florida**

When I left home less than a month ago, I was headed to Canada via Kentucky. It may not be the most direct route geographically, but I was following the directive I was given. When I went back to Illinois a week ago, I just knew I couldn't stay. I needed to get back to Andrew, except that when I did, he took off to visit his boyfriend, again. You couldn't call it a lover's quarrel; we didn't fight. He was still working on ending that relationship. I needed time to think, which I do best with my thumb extended. Not wanting to get lost on the back roads of Kentucky again, I pointed myself in the opposite direction. With considerably more traveling success, I ended up here, in Florida.

One of my first transports was a luxury liner of a semi. The driver was friendly enough and happy for the companionship, I think. His idea of conversation, though, was pretty one sided: either the radio or my monolog. His replies were both sparse and monosyllabic. After a few hours, his longest verbal string offered me the chance to nap in the top bunk of the cab. Apparently, he had decided he preferred the radio to my banter. At least he didn't put me out on the side of the road. Admittedly, sleep sounded like a good way to pass the miles. However, in addition to the radio, my mute friend employed liberal use of the air conditioner to keep himself alert. I wonder if he heard my teeth chattering. When we parted company several hours later, the southern blast furnace that greeted me was a welcome change - for the first five minutes.

Perhaps I should be grateful for those hours of frozen non-sleep. So much of the time, the only cooling breeze I felt was from vehicles passing me by without as much as a backward glance. Even just a few hours standing on the side of the interstate in the southern summer humidity took its toll.

At one point, my ride let me off at a truck stop advertising hot showers and food. After hustling a little food, I made my way to the shower area. Still penniless, I caught a shower's door as its previous inhabitant exited. The luxury of warm running water and a bar of soap cannot be overrated.

That clean feeling didn't last long, though. As I exited the shower room, I was met by two men demanding restitution for the stolen water. When I explained that my ride had promised to pay for my shower and would be along shortly, they insisted upon meeting my benefactor. While being escorted to the parking lot for that meet and greet, I took off running – straight toward an eight-foot-tall chain-link fence. One advantage of dining at the table of human kindness is the resulting physique which allowed me to slide through a hole under the fence at something close to a dead run. Shower security, having received their meals more conventionally, were not able to follow. I had beaten the soap and water thievery rap, though my fence limbo left me muddy again.

I'm not sure if I have arrived at my final destination or not. I hope not. The accommodations are sparse, to say the most: no air conditioning, no running water, and a concrete pillow. I'm living in the stairwell at an apartment complex. My fellow tenants are of the understanding that my girlfriend kicked me out and I have nowhere else to go. At least the latter is true. Given another day or so, my neighbors are likely to employ the same directive as my fictitious former Florida love interest.

Maybe I should call Andrew. I know his number, of course, since he has my cell phone. When we are apart, I long for his love and acceptance. But when I'm with him, he is constantly leaving to end his perpetual relationship. The road, as inhospitable as it can be, is less confusing; it just is what it is and makes no promises otherwise.

I'm not quite hungry enough to commit a crime worthy of jail time, but the thought has crossed my mind. I need a plan that doesn't include my thumb or Florida…or Kentucky.

Nightmares — Lory Harris
July 2003 — St. Charles, Illinois

My eyes snap open, fumbling to make sense of the inky blackness surrounding me. The paths of tracer bullets are no longer visible, and the sounds of battle are fading. Not wanting to give away my position, I lay motionless, eyes dart from side to side, stretching to see around corners without pivoting my neck. I am not alone; I hear the slow steady breathing of another in stark contrast to the heaving of my own chest. Adjusting to the darkness, I see a fan dangling from the ceiling and the dim outline of a window framing a starless night. A slow realization forms in my mind: I am home, and I am safe. I continue my statue-like demeanor, just in case.

What would Freud have to say about my dreams? I am rarely a participant in the night terrors, nor are those whom I love. But over the past few weeks they have revealed every horror known to mankind: murder, rape, mutilation, natural disasters leading to an unnatural existence. I don't need anyone to analyze the source of my doomed sleep patterns that started in Kentucky and have intensified ever since. Colin is home from Iraq, so even the images of war are not centered on his current well-being. Court's feet reside on native soil, as well, but it's not his feet I worry about.

Sleep is no longer an attractive alternative for dismissing a few hours of being. Nor is wandering an empty house, but it seems preferable in the early hours of this day. My war-torn mind and I creep silently off into the consuming darkness.

I might have to regrettably agree with Freud about one thing: it all comes back to family. This family could not be more split, albeit evenly, on the appropriate actions to be taken regarding our youngest member. The alternatives are either tough love or loving him back into the fold. The common denominator, of course, is love. But how do we keep from being torn apart by the love that should be binding us?

There is the camp that believes Court, an adult, departed of his own accord and needs to find his own way unless or until he decides to return as a full and functioning member of this family and of society at large. Then there is the other half of us, willing to grasp at whatever it takes to bring our youngest home and restore him to his rightful place in this family. Both sides believe we need to stand firm in our endeavors, a united front. But split as we are, "united" seems an insurmountable hurdle. How can we know that Court's call from Florida yesterday with his request to return home wasn't exactly the start of a path to redemption? And how could I ever deny my child the opportunity for a new start? How could I leave him homeless and hungry and in need of the basics of life when he reaches back to us?

Every moment of every day I am thinking of you, Court. Even in tonight's waking panic, my thoughts were already on you. A bus now carries you home from Florida. With Western Union's assistance, I have supplied you with a ticket and some cash for food on the journey.

It occurs to me how much effort and will power it must take for you to make this trip. You have 24 hours of travel and many stops along the way to consider where the bus is taking you. How will you be received? How has our family changed irrevocably by your actions over the past three weeks? Will there be forgiveness? Understanding? Will love be greater than hurt? What happens next? Where do the psychologists and psychiatrists fit into your return? Does each mile bring you a new doubt, a new question, a reason to reconsider your homecoming?

I thought I was afraid of what your homecoming would bring, but now I'm afraid it won't happen at all! That would be worse, much worse. Not to see you and hold you and make you feel loved. That thought breaks my heart all over again. Now I can't remember why I was so anxious about your return. There are issues, of course, that we must address – to trust and move forward again. The hard work is far from over, but we must work though it as a family, united by the one thing we all profess – love.

But the first work is yours, Court, and yours alone. The work to return, to stay on the bus that carries you here - to family and the work of being a family and the love and forgiveness that comes with family. The latter we must work on together. For now, I just pray for your strength to complete the journey home. I love you, Son!

On Crying — Merry Luehr
September 2003 — St. Charles, Illinois

Tears: those rivulets of water collecting in your eyes and eventually giving way as gravity pulls them down your cheeks, the byproduct of great pain - physical or emotional. That's what I saw last Sunday afternoon when I answered my door. I wasn't expecting anyone when the doorbell beckoned, but I was happy to see my bestie standing there. Happy, but for the trail of tears she brought with her.

I hate to see Lory cry. It's not that I wish she would just buck up and dry up; I'm happy to provide a shoulder for her to cry on, and I'm honored that she will. She is not a crier, or at least, she wasn't until this year. At the end of a sappy-movie double date, our husbands and I would dive for the Kleenex box while hers would be the only dry eyes in the bunch. We teased that she is just hard-hearted, though we know better than that. She could never understand why we would cry for actors reading a script. We couldn't understand why she didn't. And now, fortune has reversed. She can dampen my shoulder all she wants; I'll dampen hers *and* provide the Kleenex. She isn't living in Hollywood, and she can't flip to the last page to see how it all ends, either.

Her request was straightforward and simple: "I need a hug." I pulled her inside and wrapped my arms around her. Sometimes words, when mixed with water, refuse to form coherently. Sometimes a person knows it's better not to attempt speech at all. Lory just cried, and I joined her. Eventually, her breathing became less ragged. I imagine her tears were subsiding as well, though her head seemed to lack the strength to lift itself.

As much as I would have liked to offer advice, to solve the problem or at least ease her pain, I knew that was not within my power. No amount of words, mine or anyone's, could banish the hurt. It will take time, the strength of an army, more tears, and a whole lot of prayer, if indeed that will be enough. Though I had given her all she requested - a hug - I still felt the need to break the gathering silence now that the tears are mostly spent. "You aren't crazy. This really is as bad as you think it is. I'm sorry, and I'm always here for you, whatever you need." The silence fell again, though more comfortably this time, as we leaned into each other and I prayed silently for my bestie.

Eventually, she straightened and stood. "Thank you," she said, a look of exhaustion tinged with relief in her drying eyes. "Thank you for not quoting Romans 8:28 to me. If I hear one more time how 'all things work together for good for those that love the Lord,' I'm going to scream. If this is God's idea of good, then He is a sadistic monster." Though I'm rarely at a lack of words, no adequate response was forming. Well, lots of responses were vying for air space, but none of them would say more than another embrace. I let my arms do the talking. She left a couple of minutes later. We never even made it past the foyer, and she never explained the day's crisis.

Today, as I gathered with other Bible study participants, a sea of dry eyes glanced my direction and then politely away. My tears were flooding my own collar, and my Kleenex supply was woefully inadequate. Perhaps I should have left then and shed the remainder of my tears privately. But like the river that flowed from my eyes, I felt powerless to enact my own will. I couldn't make myself leave any more than I could make the tears stop. Even when we broke into our small groups after the initial group lecture, I still lacked the ability to do anything more than shuffle down to my assigned group location. In that more intimate setting, I hoped I could stanch the flow and request prayers for my friend. But after another fifteen minutes, like Lory was as she stood in my foyer, I knew my words are too watery to be coherent. I just sat and continued to cry.

I'm not sure why I was crying. That is, I know what I was crying about, but I'm not sure why the tears continue to flow in unending waves. Nothing has changed in the past two days in the Harris household – for the better or for the worse. When I talked with Lory last night, she seemed to be holding up. We know each other intimately enough to know when the other is feigning wellness. She started her week with a breakdown and has clawed her way back to ground level. "Ground level" might not be good, or necessarily stable, but it is coping, and that's enough for the moment. I can only pray that every tear I shed spares Lory an equal number of them. That thought is enough to keep me 'happily' crying for the remainder of the hour.

As the designated study time winds down, so do my tears. Concerned members gather around, offering assistance, comfort and pray on my behalf. Finally, my voice steadies, allowing me to direct their prayers toward my bestie and her family.

Lord, grant her Your mercy and tender grace. Let her feel Your loving embrace. And grant me the wisdom to point her to You. Amen.

Coffee Shop Talk
September 2003

Pastor Jeff Frazier
First Baptist Church
Geneva, Illinois

I'm a bit of a coffee fanatic. As a youth pastor in a large church, the caffeine comes in handy at times, but it's more than that. It's my drink of connection, and it crosses generational lines. Teenagers are willing to discuss life over a cup of my favorite beverage, and their parents will invite me into their houses for a cup of Joe, as well. Not that I drink it to be politically correct; I just love the stuff!

My left hand is impervious to heat since I must keep the other one available for the traditional ministerial handshake. Other than Sunday morning, you will generally see me wandering around with a Starbucks cup. It's not that I abstain from coffee on Sundays, but I've already had my morning quota by the time the congregation gathers.

While the younger generation finds it off-putting to come to a pastor's office to discuss issues in their lives, a coffee establishment does not hold the same stigma. I am constantly on guard to protect the privacy of our conversations, but certain times of day generally allow for a private discussion in a corner of our choosing. I'm in a secluded corner of Starbucks now, with an empty cup and an empty chair across the table from me.

Several weeks ago, Ken Harris asked if I would meet with his son, to maybe give Court some guidance with issues he is facing. Court did not come up through the youth program at our church, so I didn't know him, but I agreed. We have met once now, and he was 10 minutes late then. I'm two cups into this meeting and still solo. I don't think my caffeine partner is going to make an appearance.

From the first time I met Court, it was obvious that he was checking a box to get his dad off his back. He didn't want to talk with me – or anyone else who might think they were going to offer him advice or counsel, especially on faith issues. He was, however, willing to play "shock the pastor," and he gave it his best shot. He started off telling me about hitching a ride from three guys and then, entering a gay relationship with one of them, his life's one true love, as he described it. I've been a pastor long enough to be largely shock-proof. My previous experience didn't let me down that day.

Court's issues seemed to me to be less about his sexual identity and more about just identity. He lost who he always had been: student, athlete, middle-class suburbanite growing up in a stable family. Maybe he just discarded those labels, trading them in for something new. He just wasn't sure what their replacement should be: free spirit, philosopher, contrarian, discoverer of the next "new world?" I can't help but think he is a prime candidate to be abused. I don't think he would disagree with that, but sadly, I think he either doesn't care or believes it is deserved.

He told me he was not interested in the church's life-is-good-lobotomy. Of all the misnomers about Christianity, that one might be the most subscribed to and the least related to reality. Christ *promised* us trouble in this life in His words recorded in John 16:33. With one exception, all his original disciples died gruesome deaths because of their faith. How did the popular belief that Christians get to lead charmed lives get morphed so far from reality? If that were true, who wouldn't want a piece of that pie? Churches would overflow every week. Court wasn't really interest in that dialog, either.

I'll leave a message on his cell and continue to follow up, but I'm not overly hopeful that another meeting will be arranged. It took two weeks of phone tag to schedule this non-meeting. He will be in my prayers for safety and God's intervention, but that might be the most I can do at present.

Trick or Treat — Court Harris
October 2003 — St. Charles, Illinois

I was feeling good when I got home from class this morning. Our English Comp assignment is to write about a personal experience. It feels good to put into words some of the events leading up to my initial psych hospital incarceration. There is a logical order to those events, an order that I couldn't make either my parents or the doctors understand at the time. Now, with a little perspective of my own and an audience that isn't squelching my thoughts and jumping to judgment, events and rational are beginning to un-jumble. It's like retrieving a length of string that was thrown into a drawer. How does it get so knotted? You find one end of the string and wind it around and through the ensnaring tangles, knowing that each loop it passes through will create another tangle further down the line which will require an equal amount of tactical endeavor to free. Eventually, though, the reward is a rational, ordered string of logic – pure, simple and undeniable.

Mom and Dad insisted I take classes at Elgin Community College in order to keep me on their health insurance policy. This is stop gap; the exact timing of my stop is yet to be determined. But if they won't pay for me to go back to Iowa State, at least this absolves me of finding a full-time job flipping burgers or something. And I am enjoying the comp class.

I'm a little relieved to see that Mom and Dad aren't home when I arrive. I don't feel like having the same snippet of conversation that transpires every day. Funny, though, that it replays in my head even without their input: "Hey, how was class?" "Fine, nothing special." "Do you want to join us for lunch?" "No, not hungry. I'll grab something later." Knowing I have the house to myself always restores my appetite. I head directly to the fridge. Rummaging through the left-over offerings, I settle on lasagna and dish up a healthy serving. While I don't trust the molecular changes a microwave makes to food, my stomach's demands win out over my brain's caution. Having had my food radiated my whole life, it's probably too late to save myself, anyway.

Sitting at the table, with a steaming pile of cheesy goodness in front of me, I notice a new addition to the table. My mom is a chocolate fanatic – milk chocolate only - and she will share, but only by way of diminishing her guilt, I think, or maybe strategically spreading a few calories. Here, just in time for Halloween, is a bowl full of black and orange foil wrapped chocolates right alongside the salt and pepper shakers. As always, there will be enough leftover chocolate in the house after the 31st, when trick-or-treaters don't show up at our door. Their numbers in this dead-end subdivision never reach the level of Mom's chocolate preparations. The bowl, I suppose, is filled with the good stuff, never destined for deposit in a plastic pumpkin or a pillowcase pulling double duty. It won't survive the week at any rate.

My lasagna is temporarily forgotten as I grab a foil-wrapped piece of sugary smoothness. While I am a chocolate fan, it's the foil wrapping that had grabbed my attention. This time last year I was selling similar looking chocolates at Iowa State, but they were most decidedly *not* my mother's variety.

I first tried smoking pot my junior year in high school. When I was a senior, I had the program down. I could smoke all I wanted, still get straight A's, and start on the varsity soccer team. Once, a friend and I decided to get high before school every day for a week. We met before our first class, shared a bowl and went about our business in a totally chill frame of mind. If any of the teachers had suspicions, they checked them at the door. We never got caught. When I went to Iowa State on the better part of a full ride scholarship, I decided to turn over a new leaf and stop using. For one thing, I didn't have any connections to buy. That seemed just as well since my pre-vet curriculum was destined to keep me busy.

I met Cora during freshman orientation the first week of school. Each of us was involved in a steady relationship, so there was nothing romantic about it, but we hit it off as friends right away. We got to know each other during midnight study sessions, that sometimes included greasy burgers, soggy fries and beer to satisfy the munchies. High school seemed a logical topic, and that conversation can't be had without a laugh about the adventures of flying high while staying under the radar. Turns out she had a source, her boyfriend. In short order, we would share a bowl of weed; just a couple of college kids doing what they do. No harm, no foul.

There are several bonding factors between most college students: professors, parties and poverty. Besides supplying us with reasons to stay up all hours of the night to complete even the most routine assignments, professors also gave us endless fodder for late-night discussions. Parties go without saying, and were frequently the cause of the last-minute, all-night rush to complete the demands of the professors. It's a vicious circle. While I wasn't completely broke, I had lost my ready access to the Bank of Mom and Dad. Lucrative employment with flexible hours had a lot of appeal, so I sold "chocolate" on "consignment."

Cora's boyfriend would front me a sizable quantity of individual "chocolates" wrapped in orange and black foil wrappers, so appropriate for those early fall months. He had his own secret ingredient for the confections – magical, even: mushrooms. It might not have been the best candy you ever tasted, but no one ever complained about taste the next day. As little as the foil wrapper contained, I always advised newbies to start with half a piece (not that they always listened).

I came up with a sure sales pitch that was effective for moving the product: I would let the user test drive the goods. The obvious flaw to the plan was the "trip" factor, which could last for eight hours, during which time I had to keep track of my consumer in order to collect on the contract. Doing homework while watching someone else enjoy my chocolates violated the fraternal party bond. We tripped together, and I didn't limit myself to half a chocolate either.

Those foil-covered nuggets provided quite the education during that semester. I had what could have been a successful cottage industry or more accurately a dorm industry. Every payment due my supplier was made on time and in full; I never tested those limits. Of course, I didn't realize much in the way of profits, either, since I was ingesting as much – or more - than I sold. I may not have alleviated my poverty, but I had everything I wanted, including multiple "vacations" a week. In so many ways, the universe opened its arms to me, showing me marvels the professors never thought to explore, much less teach. The minutia was magnified, revealing wonders that surpassed modern medicine. I viewed in and through my hand, beyond the ability of an x-ray or MRI, unlocking chemical wonders not subject to scrutiny in the lab. The larger world was also made clear and concise, reducing it to rational, attainable order – for eight hours at a time anyway. I demonstrated a viable solution to homelessness with just a blanket and a pair of slippers during the Midwestern winter. That was the same night that the universe introduced me to the world of psychiatric "care." It wasn't a bad trip at the time, but it sure did change my trajectory – for the worse.

The sound of the garage door opening calls me back from my reverie to the lasagna, which has cooled off enough to eat in quick bites. Mom and Dad join me in the kitchen. "Hey, how was class? We missed you for lunch, but I see you managed to find something to eat."

"Yeah, I just got home. Nice chocolates, Mom. I think I'll have some for dessert." Pretending to grab a couple, I replace the one I had in my hand. She isn't paying attention anyway. I put my empty plate in the sink and grab my keys. I'm headed out – in search of chocolate.

Radio Rants **Lory Harris**
November 2003 **St. Charles, Illinois**

In the car, again. Such is life in the 'burbs. Mass transportation is pretty much limited to the train into Chicago, which we use on those rare occasions when the crush of humanity seems appealing. But getting around in the land of sprawled housing and businesses is difficult without a car. My VW Bug, affectionately known as BuBu, does not frequently engender requests to ride along and never by more than one person. No one wants the backseat for obvious reasons.

Today I'm running errands, at least that is the stated purpose, and I will come home lugging bags to prove it. Working out of my house and with my husband, sometimes I just crave alone time, and the car is good for that. Generally, I listen to the radio, hoping it will drown out the arguments raging in my head: Should I? Should he? How can I? How can he expect? Why doesn't he? The "I" is self-explanatory. The "he" could describe any one of the other four family members, and it rotates through all of them. But usually it describes the two currently living under the roof with me: Court or Ken.

Today, though, no matter how loud the volume, my thoughts are screaming louder than the radio can drown out. Willing myself to silence, the words of the song from the Christian radio station break into my consciousness. I recognize the song immediately, having heard it often enough to sing along without even realizing I know the words, thanks to the repetitious on-air play of Third Day.

You are so good to me
You heal my broken heart
You are my Father in heaven…[2]

The low, guttural growl of wounded animal, fractures my self-imposed stillness of thought. With clarity and focus that has been conspicuously absent in my life of late, I crank the radio's volume hard left, proof positive of both the wound and the animal. Third Day, now silenced, can listen to me for a change! "God? So good? That's a fantasy God, not the God I know!"

"You want me to talk to you, O Master of the universe?" the distain exits my lips like projectile vomiting. It cannot be stopped or slowed or altered in any way. "Where are You when Court is refusing his

---

[2] Third Day. "You are so Good to Me," written by Don Chaffer, Ben Pasley, and Robin Pasley. *Offerings II: All I Have to Give*. Essential Records (2003).

medication and using his own instead? Where are You when he walks out of yet another job? Where are You when Ken and I turn on each other, clawing out the other's eyes and slashing their heart with surgical precision?"

I suppose it's a good thing that the cool fall weather keeps the car windows closed. At least other drivers can't hear the enraged lady screaming in her car. It must be obvious that I'm not singing along to the radio, face contorted with anger and venom flying from my lips. "You are a sadistic monster! Either You are ineffective or uncaring or just downright cruel!"

I can hear a still small voice calling me back from the edge, telling me that screaming insults at the One who created the heavens and earth is as effective as an insect caught on flypaper thinking his demands for release will be honored. And like the fly, even if God did pluck me from this predicament, I would most certainly be forced to leave behind most, if not all, my appendages. The tears are flowing now joining rivers of endless pain and anger plainly written on my face.

I suppose it is a sin, maybe even of the unforgivable variety, to give voice to such obscenities. But then, if God really is God, He already knows what I think of Him. The act of screaming the words is more an admission to myself than a surprise to God. For a year, I have steadfastly forced my lips to praise that deity in the storm. The crashing waves have not subsided, or even just held steady. They are relentless, increasing both in frequency and magnitude. I am drowning, even as the pounding wracks my body and rips at the foundation of who I thought I was. The God of my former fantasy is showing Himself for who He is: impersonal, unfeeling, malicious, and, yes, sadistic.

Words spent, the tears continue in heaving sobs. I feel my age, my spiritual age, and realize I am but a toddler, somewhere in the terrible twos. I want my way, and I rage against my Parent who does not honor my demands. He must see the pain that forces my words to the surface. If He is indeed a just God, He has already forgiven me. And if not, then I am already damned to Hell, and this life is just a foretaste of what is to come.

Say you're sorry, whispers something from deep inside. *Ask His forgiveness.* It must be a remnant of pure child-like faith murmuring in my soul. I know I should, and maybe I even want to do it. But in a fit of maturity, I know it would be a lie. I'm not sorry for what I said; I don't take it back. Maybe it's not true, but it is an honest cry from a hurting soul.

In my mind's eye, I can see the toddler years with my own sons. It could be any one of the three of them, their small form thrown against the floor, screaming and pounding their fists. I would gather them to me trying to calm them, only to be rewarded with their kicks and an emphatic 'I hate you!' As much as their words reflected their heart at that moment in time, they were also secure in my love for them. They were never in danger of losing that love, no matter how many times they exclaimed the opposite feeling toward me.

And therein lies my hope, my only hope. If God really is the perfect Father, He will endure my tantrum. He will wrap His arms around me and let me kick and scream and empty myself of my infantile wrath. He will love me still, love undiminished, love washed by my own tears. If only He is who I have believed, who I need Him to be.

SECTION TWO
GATHERING DARKNESS
November 2003 – August 2005

Kane County Offense/Incident Report

December 9, 2003

Charge or Incident: Theft over $300.00
Victim's Name: Harris, Kenzie B.
Suspect: Harris, Courtlandt B.
Witness: None
Narrative:

Upon arrival R/O [reporting officer] spoke with Ken Harris, father of Courtlandt Harris. Ken advised R/O the following. On today's date Ken received a statement on his bank account with several unknown charges. Upon contacting the bank, they advised several of the withdrawals were made in St. Charles. Ken advised his son Courtlandt took his truck on 112903 and drove to San Diego, where Courtlandt's brother lives. Further, Ken advised he confirmed this matter by speaking to Courtlandt via telephone and advised him to have the truck back by Sunday 121403. Ken advised if Courtlandt did not have the vehicle back by 121403 he would pursue charges.

Ken advised R/O while reporting the stolen ATM card to the bank authorities; a transaction was attempted again, in San Diego around 2 p.m. Ken advised the transaction was declined. Ken reported he suspects Courtlandt due to him not taking his medications for being bipolar and suspects him to be abusing alcohol and cannabis. Ken provided R/O with a copy of the statement he received and a copy of the Card Loss Claim form, filed on today's date. Ken advised R/O he doesn't think Courtlandt is aware they have reported the card stolen and he is the suspect. Ken further advised R/O he suspects Courtlandt further, due to his wife advising, prior to Courtlandt leaving, she noticed her credit cards were re-arranged in her billfold and she questioned Courtlandt who was standing next to it at the time. Ken advised they did not see Courtlandt take the card.

Ken further advised Courtlandt is aware that if he does not return the truck by 121403, Sunday, it would be reported to police. Ken further advised complaints would be signed and would call the Sheriff's Office when and if Courtlandt returned home. R/O advised Ken a report would be taken and forwarded to investigation.

Holiday Travels – Part I — Lory Harris
Thanksgiving 2003 — St. Charles, Illinois

Today is Thanksgiving, my favorite holiday. It's a day all about the people I love - there is no room for commercialism. How can you profit from thankfulness? Well, unless you work for Butterball. Or if you make those French-fried onions that go on top of the green bean casserole - does anyone eat those the rest of the year? Olfactory senses are stimulated by the smells of homemade pumpkin pies cooling on the counter and turkey cooking in the oven mingled with the scent of cooked onions and sage still lingering from the stuffing preparation. The kitchen windows are fogged from the boiling water that will render potatoes mash-able. As guests arrive, nearly every pot and pan we own will be in some state of use or after-use, crowding the counters, drawing attention away from the house that was my brand of spotless just yesterday.

Of course, everyone congregates in the kitchen, which is large enough most days. But by mid-afternoon, getting a stick of butter from the fridge will require a request stated loudly enough to draw the attention of the body parked closest to that appliance. Appetizers are mixed in among meal preparation items, everyone reaching and talking and eating. Sweet cacophony!

Attendance is not optional, either. Everyone is expected, and "everyone" can stretch to mean anyone - extended family and friends - who wants to come. All of them are welcome! But in my motherly vernacular, "everyone" means Colin, Corey, Court, Ken and me. Therefore, despite the turkey and fixings and a crowded kitchen, today will not really be "Thanksgiving." Colin is on base on the East Coast, low enough man on the totem pole that he has to remain for guard duty. Corey, on the West Coast, will be heading to his retail job extra early on Black Friday. Up until last night, I had been planning - recklessly hoping - that Court would join us. But the randomness of Court's actions is one of the few things we can still count on.

Let me back up a bit. A week ago, Court disappeared in the middle of the night. I have the perfect view of the driveway from my desk in the office. So, on rising, his empty parking spot drew my attention. I went down to check his bed only to find it in the same state of un-use. Trying to keep my tone calm and collected, I left a voice mail on Court's long-overdue cell phone replacement asking him to call home. Of course, he didn't call, but I wasn't all that calm and collected either. Several hours later, motivated by guilt, compassion, or just to keep me from leaving another voice message, he called to let us know he was staying in the city with a couple of Corey's friends, Jake and Josh.

I guess I assumed Jake and Josh would tire quickly enough of the "younger brother" flopping on their couch, mooching their food, and smoking pot. On second thought, Corey's friends may not be far enough removed from the college scene to think those actions are anything out of the ordinary. But, as it turned out, Court was garnering attention for a reason that really matters to guys in their twenties: he was frightening their female visitors. I'm not exactly sure what he was doing to frighten them, the lingering adolescent code of silence still largely intact. But yesterday Jake called asking for help in removing their squatter, our son.

There is this ill-conceived, but widely accepted notion that your parenting job is done when you send the last kid off to college. That one was shattered for us almost a year ago, but we still didn't expect the parental learning curve to be so steep at this point in our lives. We have spent months calling psychiatrists and psychologists, with a stack of bills to show for it, but little-to-no change in Court's behavior. A couple of days ago, shedding what remained of my shredded pride, I put on the cloak of humility and called Darlene Marcusson, the director of the local homeless shelter. Ken advocates changing Court's mailing address to Lazarus House; I will not allow it. But I am hoping that Darlene can offer some practical advice. Though I certainly wouldn't say I know her, we have met a couple of times. She has quite the reputation, and well-deserved. Anyone who can single-handedly wake this sleepy little 'burb to the homeless problem within its borders and open a shelter (that unfortunately is consistently full), is a force to be reckoned with and a resource to be tapped.

Darlene listened with matter-of-fact sympathy and understanding. She has heard it all before. There is no silver bullet cure, nor did we expect one. But she felt it was an opportunity to force Court to get the medical attention he needs. Darlene's advice was to contact the Chicago Police Department (CPD) for their assistance in transporting Court to the closest hospital with mental health services for evaluation. On the plus side, it would be an in-state hospital, unlike the previous two in Iowa and Wisconsin. Ken went to work coordinating with CPD and Jake.

By late afternoon, plans in place, we made the hour-long drive to Jake's apartment. Both of us were lost in thought, both of us hoping that Court would go quietly to the hospital and both of us expecting that

Court's Thanksgiving turkey would be of the institutional variety. How could they not keep him for evaluation? In the past few months he has quit several jobs, claiming management did not appreciate him or utilize him properly. We are frequent flyers at the ER for suicide attempts, though so far, the pills and non-vital cuts that Court has subjected himself to have seemed unlikely to result in death. But now, some sort of threat to girls here in the city is serious enough that one of them is considering filing for an order of protection. Added to Court's diagnosis and non-compliance with taking his meds, another hospital stay seemed a foregone conclusion.

Court seemed surprised to see us, looking through pupils far too dilated for the room's lighting. If he was surprised to see the police officers walking in soon after, he didn't show it. The officers, obviously well-trained and expecting a volatile situation, asked Court what was in his pockets (cigarettes) and to remove anything that they "wouldn't want to find on him." There was nothing. They patted him down, removed his lighter and put him in cuffs. We followed them to the paddy wagon and waited while the officers lit a cigarette for Court before taking off for the hospital. We followed, grateful for how smoothly things were going so far. As it turned out, we shouldn't have been so grateful.

Court, maybe more coherent than we have experienced lately, was reportedly quite charming in handcuffs, a cigarette dangling from his mouth. In the ten-minute drive to the hospital, he told the officers all about his over-protective parents who wanted to keep him under their thumbs. He must have painted a masterpiece of suburbanites who just couldn't handle their free-thinking child—and he wasn't yet done with his paint brush. The psych evaluation produced a painting of the same image on a different canvas. In the end, the doctor felt there were perfectly reasonable explanations for everything: the offended girl had just misunderstood Court's intentions; of course, he was taking his meds; he no longer had suicidal thoughts despite recent self-inflicted injuries; there were perfectly logical reasons for leaving his previous employers and that wasn't a crime at any rate.

We saw Court briefly – long enough for him to say he was staying in the city, though it wouldn't be with Jake. Our truck, the one he uses, that is, was nowhere to be seen on the streets around Jake's apartment. Apparently, he had dropped it off several miles away in a parking garage. The logic of it all escaped us, as usual, but we got the keys from him. After locating the vehicle (a feat unto itself) and paying the fees (seemingly half the value of our prize), we made our way home. We got here about one o'clock this morning. I was ready to collapse from the exhaustion brought on by emotional drain. Ready, that is, until I hit the pillow and the silence started screaming at me again. Where is he tonight? Where does one sleep in the city in November when friends' doors are closed and bolted? Where would he be for Thanksgiving? How could the doctors so completely and quickly dismiss the truth of the life he was living? What would we tell the relatives when they arrived for their fill of turkey and thankfulness? And what was there to be thankful for anyway…

So here I am, elbow deep in Thanksgiving preparations. All the traditional dishes will be represented, though none of them sound appealing to me this year. I don't want to talk with anyone or even be with anyone. At least I currently have the kitchen to myself. If Ken wanders through and catches me crying, I can claim it's caused by chopping raw onions. I will drain all possible tears this morning, allowing me to feign thankfulness later this afternoon. I hate this holiday.

Holiday Travels – Part II — Court Harris
Thanksgiving 2003 — Northern Illinois

They surprised me a bit this week, my parents, but just a bit. Showing up with the cops was a new trick in their arsenal – ineffective, of course, but novel. They think they can out-smart me, fools that they are. What were they expecting me to do, go crazy and attack a cop? Maybe get me arrested for possession – lock me away so they never had to think about me again? They just think their brand of crazy is better than mine. Well, I have been watching theirs for a lifetime. I can fluently regurgitate their saneness. I vomited it out all over the cops and the doctors. And they, equally idiotic, sucked it up, nodding their heads as I pulled the strings. I walked free, and the bill gets sent to the 'burbs. Score another point for me! I even got them to pay the parking fees for the truck.

There were a couple of hiccups in my evening, though. First, Jake and Josh wouldn't answer the door. I went over to Kristen's apartment to talk to her about the whole order of protection thing. It was probably close to midnight by the time I walked over there, though the lights were still on. When I knocked on the door, the apartment went black. I knocked again until she shouted through the door that she would call the cops if I didn't leave. Having already conquered CPD earlier in the evening, another round with them sounded boring. I was getting cold and hungry and sober – not my favorite combination. With plenty of cash, thanks to the ATM card, I just wanted my truck, which was now 40 miles west of my location.

When I was a kid, the whole family would watch *How the Grinch Stole Christmas* every December. There is that one part when the Grinch is dressed up as 'Santy Claus' going down the chimney and gets wedged in. The voice over says something about 'he got stuck a time or two, but only for a moment.' I was formulating a plan for 'How the Son Stole Thanksgiving,' and had the same kind of dilemma, but only for a moment or two. I started walking to the train station. The walk kept me warm as I made my way through the wee morning hours in the city. I love this city! If only it was further away from the parents.

It was mid-morning by the time my circuitous route brought me to the train station. Using my best puppy dog eyes (yes, they can be heard over the phone), I called Mom to apologize for the previous night and ask if I might come home for Thanksgiving. She immediately offered to pay for a train ticket if I didn't have $5. She clearly doesn't know about the ATM card. Remember when Cindy-Lou Who caught 'Santy Claus' shoving the Christmas tree up the chimney and the Grinch lied about how he was going to fix a broken light at his North Pole shop and then bring it back? I took another page from the story and told Mom how I had pled with the ticket agent. "I told him," I explained to her, "that all I want is to be with my family for Thanksgiving, but my wallet was stolen. The agent took pity and gave me the ticket." Mom bought it: hook, line and sinker. I, on the other hand, obtained a ticket in the usual way and made my way home to a great meal and my truck.

Mom was so thrilled to have me home, she started making plans for me to find a job and get back on track. She also got the hugs and kisses she so desperately longed for. Hopefully it will hold her over for a while. Dad was appropriately leery of my overnight change of heart. I did my best imitation of loving-son and stuffed myself with turkey and all the fixings. Eventually the dishes were done, and the leftovers were wedged into the fridge in just such a way as to allow the door to close. Knowing that I was reaching the end of both my patience and my acting abilities, I excused myself to the porch to smoke cigarettes (something not allowed in the house) and wait for the lights to go out. Honestly, weren't the old folks tired after their trip to the city yesterday and all the preparations and tryptophan today? When the darkened house finally signaled the time for escape, I grabbed the truck keys and headed for freedom.

As much as I love the city, I couldn't go to Chicago. It was too close and too easily accessible, as my parents proved yesterday. But there are other cities, even ones with better winter weather. I hit the ATM again, maxing out the daily limit. The fastest way out of town would be an interstate. The closest interstate is 88. The speed limit is higher headed west on 88 toward Iowa, rather than east which would take me back into the city. I-88 west it was, with a full belly, full tank of gas and full wallet. Freedom.

Desperate Options
December 2003

Darlene Marcusson
Lazarus House
St. Charles, Illinois

It's a small office, carved out of the space that is Lazarus House. Really, it's too bad such an office is needed. We could fit two or three more sets of bunk beds in this space, providing people with a more permanent place to lay their heads away from the cold December winds. But there needs to be a place for confidential conversations. Where else would we put the mounds of paper: stacks of incoming mail, program research in various states of assimilation, community resources, grant applications and confidential guest information? There is a lock on the door, of course, but just the thought of shuffling through all that paper is likely deterrent enough to keep most people at bay.

A little over six years ago, God gave me a dream – an assignment, really, to open a year-round homeless shelter in affluent, suburban St. Charles. Against all odds, the city council and then the whole town got behind the idea. Our first donation came from a ten-year-old girl's birthday money, then the gift of this space from the Free Methodist Church, and a Boy Scout Eagle project helping to prepare the space for our first guests. I am forever awed and humbled by the way God has orchestrated His shelter, using a middle-aged mom with a willing heart. It would be easy to give into my doubts and the scope of the project if I did not keep my eyes on the size of my God.

I need to settle into my studies to become a licensed substance abuse counselor, but decide first to return a phone call from a local mom with a child in crisis. Lory has called before for advice. I'm sure placing the call itself was difficult enough - admitting to a family problem and reaching out for help. Too many of the well-kept houses in our town also have well-kept secrets shaking their very foundations and are hoping that no one will notice. When Lory answers the phone, the story comes quickly, though occasionally halted as she checks her emotions enough to continue speaking. Court disappeared Thanksgiving night and finally surfaced at his brother's place in San Diego. He took the car without permission, stole their ATM card and withdrew over $2000 from their bank account. Court has been diagnosed with bipolar and is non-compliant with meds. He's been hospitalized twice in psych hospitals over the past year. In high school, he was the top of his class, but is currently on the verge of flunking out of community college. It is a frantic litany that I have heard too often, and it breaks my heart every time.

I can hear the flow of information starting to slow as Lory talks about Court's classes. "It's too late for him to drop them, and if he doesn't pass them, he will be kicked out. And if he is no longer a full-time student, he isn't eligible for our health insurance," she laments.

"And then what?" I replied.

"His meds are already costing us $1000/month WITH insurance. Not that he always takes them. And what if he is hospitalized again? We won't be able to pay it."

"He is an adult. He can pay his own bills."

"He's going to end up on the streets or dead. He keeps running away, if a 19-year-old *can* run away. And he refuses any help to get his life back under control," Lory continued. She ran through the extenuating circumstances like a woman coming to grips with an unending bad dream. It is, of course, just that: a nightmare that defies sunrise. She is not in need of platitudes, or even a Kleenex, as much as she needs a new plan of action. Her son needs a new direction, as well. He needs accountability to something bigger than himself, accountability that she cannot demand now that he is legally an adult.

"He has clearly committed a felony by taking money from your bank account. I suggest you file charges against him and get him into the Kane County drug court…" I begin.

Lory cuts me off mid-sentence. "He is bipolar; he's not an addict!"

"If there were a mental health court, I would recommend that, but there isn't. The drug court is the next best option. They can order him to take meds. They can force him into treatment, for both mental and drug related issues, and they will even pay for it. But to get into drug court, he must plead guilty to the felony charge. Judgment will be suspended while he goes through the program. He will meet with the judge once a week and be drug tested three times a week. If he comes up dirty, he may be put in jail for a week or more to think about it. The program lasts two years. If he graduates, the charges will be dropped from his record."

There was a dumbstruck silence on the other end of the phone, with only the audible and irregular breathing of someone whose tears were falling to let me know she was still there. "I'm not a doctor, and I don't even play one on TV," I said, hoping she heard all the compassion I feel for her. "I can't tell you what to do, but that is my best suggestion. You can keep doing what you are doing, but are you making progress?"

When she answered, her voice revealed all the fear one would expect. "How can I put my son in jail? What if he doesn't make it through the program and ends up in prison? You are strong, you have brass kahunas. I'm not. I can't."

"The future offers no guarantees, and no one can make this decision for you. If you believe that your current path offers Court his best chance, then you should continue as you have been. If you need another course of action, I recommend the drug court. There is a local group of moms of addicts called Hearts of Hope. They meet once a week for mutual support and education, and to pray for their children. I will send you information if you are interested."

Our conversation lingered only a bit longer, with few spoken words reaching this direction through the phone. But in the silence, I heard a strengthened resolve. I could feel the slight breeze caused by the wings of hope taking flight. At least I prayed it was so as I hung up the phone.

Brass kahunas. I'm not sure if I should laugh or cry. I grew up in a tough neighborhood, sometimes falling asleep to the sound of gunfire. I had escaped to the 'burbs, only to find out that being poor is not necessarily defined by one's bank account. All too frequently it is the soul's resources that define poverty. Me? Strong? Would she laugh to see me cowering at the Father's throne, begging to know what comes next and afraid of what the answer might be? No doubt she would identify with my internal debates on what road to take and my hesitation even after a course has been set. Self-generated strength is little more than an illusion, or maybe delusion is the word. Perhaps weakness is really our only true strength; weakness searching for strength in the only One who truly possesses it and freely gives.

Father, bless my friend. Calm her heart, guide her thoughts. And hold her child in Your tender care. In their weaknesses, may Your strength show through. Amen.

California Dreaming — Corey Harris
December 2003 — San Diego, California

A year and a half ago, San Diego was where the Chargers played football and the Padres played baseball. In my world, it meant little else. I had never been there and had only a vague Mid-Western idea of the city. Then my older brother, Colin, went to boot camp there. When I came out for his graduation, the city burst onto my radar: beaches, uninhibited women, perfect weather, perfect life. I still had a year of college to go in the frozen Northland of Wisconsin – well, a semester in Wisconsin and one studying abroad in Australia – but San Diego was on my short list thereafter. If you must work for a living the rest of your life, you should at least like the climate, I reasoned.

So, a few months after I graduated from college, I moved to this city. I knew no one, had no job or place to live, and was not going to return home with my tail between my legs. I was so sure of my decision until it came time to say goodbye. I wasn't expecting the mixed emotions as I drove west with all my earthly possessions in my car and life savings of $500 in my pocket. But my family is a part of the "charmed ones" where everything always works out. Court was back from Kentucky. Life was back on track. So why did I have that nagging feeling that maybe I should have stayed when I said goodbye to Court? Partying wasn't foreign to me, and never really caused me any real pain, aside from the occasional hangover. I reasoned Court must be going through the same thing.

I've been here three and a half months now. My two roommates and I live in a little house on a bluff. A strong wind or a big rain would likely relocate our rental, making the trip to the mail box a long upward climb. But it's affordable between my job selling cell phones in a mall kiosk and a couple of credit cards that are approaching their maximum life spans. Good thing my commissions are starting to kick in.

If there is one thing I miss in San Diego, though, it would be family. My dad may be one of the most competitive people you will ever meet, and I inherited that from him. He's demanding--both of himself and of the world. I inherited that from him, too, or at least the part about the demands I place on myself. Since it is a well-known fact that opposites attract, my mom, by definition, is just that - opposite. Mom is, well, more nurturing, I guess. But she's the one to take charge and right the world when things go awry with us boys. That's when her inner bulldog comes out. Funny, though, as resourceful as she can be, she is also kind of clueless. I remember the morning she came into my room my senior year in high school. She said I smelled like a camp fire. I told her about how one of my friends had a big bon fire the night before. Mom never smoked weed growing up, which I find hard to believe, but likely true. She never had any idea what kind of fire my friends and I had played with the previous evening.

Colin is on the opposite coast now, at Camp Lejeune in North Carolina, when he's not deployed. He was changed when he got back from Iraq earlier this year: more chiseled in body, mind and soul. I admire him for what he has done, and continues to do. It seems to fit him. But I also hope he won't make a return trip to Iraq, for the sake of family sanity. When he is deployed, you can just feel the stress-o-meter climb for everyone.

One would expect that Colin and I would be very close, born only 11 ½ months apart. And we are close. We share a brotherly love – not the Philadelphia kind, but the real kind between siblings. Sometimes we are best of buds and sometimes we tease each other to the point of open wounds. Court and Colin are also close, sharing a common techie interest. When they start speaking that language, I just leave. They actually want to know more about how computers work than just where the on/off switch is – go figure. They are Star Trekkies, too, and would always out vote me to watch endless episodes after school. I complained the whole time, but I never left. No way would I give up my good spot on the couch just to avoid seeing pointy Vulcan ears!

Court and I are close for other reasons. For one thing, we both played competitive soccer, starting at an age when the biggest competition was who got the extra oranges and drink box at half-time. Eventually, we both became goalies, which might say something about our personalities, as well. A goalie can stand around on the field the whole game, waiting for a five-second opportunity to become hero or goat. We have each spent time on both sides of that great divide. Also, growing up, our best friends were brothers: Jake (my friend) and Jordan (Court's). I guess you could say we "double dated," or more accurately, double troubled: baseball in the backyard, soccer in the basement, always one more scheme to change the world or torment the opposing duo.

A few of weeks ago, I was working at the mall kiosk, enjoying the sunshine and an abundance of flirty females, when Court called to let me know he was in the area. It's not that I was expecting him, but it made sense to me that he would want to start his life over again in San Diego. I had, after all. He always loved to drive, and apparently half a continent was not at all daunting to him. Besides, I had heard the story of home life from both sides, and both agreed that things weren't going all that well. Mom and Dad were at odds with how to deal with Court but in agreement that nothing seemed to be working. Court was at odds with Mom and Dad, just wanting to get out from under their thumbs. I was probably closer to Court's camp overall. Really, Mom and Dad have no idea what life is like now. They think they have all the answers, but obviously, it's not working out all that well. As a contemporary and brother, I figured I could show him the way--to whatever extent he needed assistance, that is. I love my brother, and I sincerely thought I could help him out, so I left work early to meet him and give him the tour of my topographically challenged house.

My roommates were cool with the idea of Court living here for a while. Marcus is an over-the-top kind of guy. He used to be a druggy, but now his addiction is Jesus. No disrespect to God's son, but Marcus goes about religion with the fervency of an addict looking for his next hit. It's intense. I like that about him...and not. A couple of months ago, he met this cute, little, naïve blonde named Jill, selling magazines subscriptions door to door. She had left a boyfriend and son in Louisiana and landed here. Marcus invited her back to the house to live with us, "as Jesus would have done." We all took her in – our group good deed. A few days later, Marcus stayed up late with her talking and led her to Jesus. He was so ecstatic! The next morning, he came in and woke me up, a different kind of frenzy in his voice. Jill had died in her sleep. It was my first experience with a dead body, and with explaining a corpse to the police. Maybe we watch too many cop shows, but three twenty-somethings in a run-down house with dead girl seemed reason enough to panic. Had we known about the bag of brightly colored pills in her purse, we would have panicked that much more. Fortunately, not everything you see on TV reflects life. A murder investigation did not ensue. Her death was ruled an overdose.

Maybe Marcus thought Court was another 'Jill' – a lost soul to be led to Christ. He did his best with long rambling conversations late into the night. Court was up to the challenge, debating in an endless game of give and take without really giving an inch. Marcus and Court are evenly matched, just on opposite ends of the addiction continuum.

My roommate, Lisa, on the other hand, is the mom of the house, low-key and calming. She knows how to party, but somehow nothing ever gets away from her; she is always in control of herself, and usually the rest of us, too. She is level-headed and certainly not impulsive. Well, except once, a couple of days after Jill's death, when Lisa made a trip to the local animal shelter. Just like that, Jazz came to live with us. He is a gangly adolescent mutt, the best kind of canine. We had to pool our money for the puppy basics, like a collar, leash, vet and food, but Jazz has love in abundance. That and pizza scraps – what more could a dog want?

Looking back, I think Lisa saw through Court the quickest. She knew he didn't want a new start, but rather, a flophouse. I'm sure she would have preferred to feed the pizza scraps to Jazz rather than Court, but she kept that to herself. I wonder how long she could have maintained her silence.

As for me, my personality bounces between my two roommates. I like to live in the practical, but occasional walks on the wild side are just too tempting to pass up. That wild side joined Court in some chemical experimentation while he was here. I kept it recreational; Court was obviously making it a way of life.

The practical side of me knew that Court needed to call home and let Mom and Dad know where he was here. They had called several times asking if I had heard anything from Court. You could hear an escalating panic in each call, not that I blame them. It had been a week since Court had taken off in the middle of the night. They were starting to resign themselves the worst kind of phone call imaginable to a parent, but I had to stay loyal to Court. I was encouraging him to call home, but I wasn't going to do it for him.

Well, a week ago, I *did* make that the call, after Court agreed. He didn't want to bear the wrath that would be climbing through the phone to greet him; he is no fool. Neither am I, but practically speaking, someone had to show some mercy to Mom and Dad – and it was becoming obvious that Court would not be staying here indefinitely, either. His welcome had already become threadbare. Besides the evening debates with Marcus, Court's days entailed either getting high or getting the necessary product to get high. There was no indication that he would look for a job or even help around the house. Outside of keeping Jazz company, he did nothing remotely useful.

When I got Mom and Dad on the phone, you could hear the desperation in their voices when they asked if I had heard anything from Court. When I told them he was here, you could feel the tension release even halfway across the country, which was a good thing for them. I wish they hadn't asked the second question, "How long has he been there?" Knowing what their reaction would be, it crossed my mind to shorten the time since Court's arrival, but I didn't.

With the energy of a spring that has been compressed and then released, their reaction shot through the phone lines. I could almost feel the fingers of their misdirected anger wrapping around my neck. "He's been there a week and you are just telling us now?!" I really don't blame them for their reaction, and I'm not sure my rationale really mattered, but as I stumbled through my prepared explanation, it gave them time to let the relief wash over them – Court was alive and within eyesight of someone who loves him. I may never understand my parents, but I can relate to their anxiety and the way it releases explosively. I remember the relief I felt just two days into Court's disappearance when he called me at work to announce his arrival in San Diego. It was angering and then good to know he was still breathing.

Apparently, Mom and Dad had not been sitting idly by wringing their hands and waiting for Court to re-appear. They had a plan, and they had leverage. Court's truck was his due to usage only; the title does not bear his name. Mom and Dad had not given him permission to take their property out of the state. Court was given one week to return the vehicle or Mom and Dad would press charges and have him arrested. They also had bank surveillance video of Court using Mom's ATM card, one more reason for arrest. A police report had been filed and the arrest warrant was only briefly on hold. He could return the truck and the money and then leave home if he wanted; he could return the truck and stay at home if he followed the rules and went into counseling immediately; or he could stay in California and be arrested.

Honestly, if Dad had single-handedly orchestrated this scenario, Mom might have been able to stay his hand. All of us boys knew to approach Mom first; she has a soft touch and is willing stand in the gap for us. But we also knew when you lost Mom, you had crossed a line that could not be retraced. Court has his options, but he looks destined for an orange jumpsuit if he doesn't watch his steps. I don't think my brother is convinced they will follow through. The next day, he unveiled his plan for helping with the rent: he would start dealing drugs out of our house. Thus, began the forced preparation for him to leave San Diego and drive back to Illinois to face the music.

When he left this morning, it was not a fond farewell; more of a three-fingered salute and I'm not sure all three fingers were extended on either of our hands. My precariously-perched abode is a little more run down now, a little older and sadder somehow, though my roommates are breathing a bit easier. I love my brother, but I am not his parent. Maybe Mom and Dad aren't doing it right. Will they really have their own son arrested? But I won't be as harsh in my judgment of their actions hereafter. Dad's strict determination and Mom's absolute protectionism have galvanized. The object of their aim is Court's well-being. It's a long shot, but it's worth a shot.

Jazz eagerly jumps in the car for a trip to dog beach. He will play with other dogs at the ocean's edge as I walk barefoot in the warm Southern California sand. The sound of the surf, the smell of the salt air: I love San Diego. On the short drive to the ocean, reruns of the past couple of weeks and my hopes for the future swirl in my brain: I love my family. What if Court never makes it back to Illinois? What if he heads north or south instead of east? What if I am the last family member he ever sees? Can Mom and Dad hold it together – really be united in their resolve? Will Colin keep his boots on U.S. soil?

Jazz tumbles out of the backseat and bounds toward the ocean. Moments later, he returns, his tail wagging, a wet and wildly happy puppy with a stick in his mouth. I wish I could throw my cares as easily as the stick now flying through the air. But just like the stick, my concerns return over and over again. I love you, bro. Drive east. People really do love you there.

Parenting Choices — Sheriff's Officer Tyler Blake
December 2003 — Geneva, Illinois

I grew up believing the stereotype of a cop's life: chasing the bad guys through the streets and ending up at the donut shop. That scenario doesn't exist in Mayberry, CSI any city, or here in the Chicago collar counties. Well, there is the occasional chase, but given the square miles under our care, the mode of transportation will more likely be vehicular than biped. And, of course, there are donuts to be found, but given the hours and tedium at work that follow the sleep-interrupted nights at home with two toddlers, I'm more interested in coffee than sugar.

I would be a fool to take parenting lessons from the ones we serve and protect – at least the ones whose doors I tend to knock on. In fact, I tend to get a bit jaded – do any kids make it through unscathed? And how can parents be so clueless? Of course, I'm still taller than both my kids combined, and outweigh their total poundage by a factor of four. But I'm taking notes on what *not* to do.

A couple of weeks ago, I got a call from a father who wanted to charge his son with auto theft. Apparently, the son took off in the middle of the night with the vehicle that they allow the son to use exclusively. That's tough to swallow felony charges in that situation – parent holds legal title, but child has functional ownership. However, this son also took their ATM card and stole over $2000 from their bank account. Basic parenting observation: keep your PIN to yourself.

Okay, clearly there are problems on that home-front, which unfortunately is not something new or unusual. Unlike *Law and Order* where there are always staff resources to track down the seemingly routine which inevitably blossoms into something bigger, I don't have either the time or team to locate a child gone missing in a vehicle that he considers his own. Even the cash theft, which would be easy to verify, might not be worth my time. All too often, parents use the Sherriff's office as a tool to get their way – a threat with muscle. Then they get cold feet as the court date approaches and drop the charges. They might temporarily gain the upper hand at home, but I lose valuable time that could have been better spent.

After explaining the thefts to me, the father's first questions are about the drug court. Even if these charges make it to court, my job is to arrest and assist with the prosecution. Drug court is on the sentencing end of things, which is just past my area of involvement. I'm not without influence, but it is beyond my control.

I have yet to decide how I feel about the drug court. To enter the drug court system, there must be a felony charge involving or relating to drugs in some fashion – not necessarily selling or using, but maybe robbery to get money to fuel a drug habit. After pleading guilty, sentencing is suspended for at least two years while the defendant goes through the program. Successful completion and the charges are dropped. Unsuccessful and the pretenses are dropped – prison sentences are imposed. I've seen success stories in the first three years of the program. And I've seen addicts and criminals doing what they do best – playing the system only to disappear when it's time to face the music. Who knows which side of the line this kid could fall on? But just playing the odds, I would say the latter, given his current disappearing act. That assumes the parents' resolve stays active long enough to get to the initial plea.

The program itself involves drug tests three times a week and meeting with the judge once a week. Miss a test or a meeting, and you go to jail to think about it for a week or a month or until the judge thinks you have gotten the message. Dirty "drop" and unless you are really good when talking to a judge who specializes in sifting through addicts' BS, you will see how you look dressed in orange, the length of time TBD and at the judge's discretion.

The father, Mr. Harris, has done his homework. He knows about the drug court and the program his son would be required to follow. The son's drug of choice is marijuana. I'm not 100% convinced that is even a "drug." But then, maybe that makes him a good candidate for the program – before he moves on to heroin, cocaine or meth. I played heavily on the "no guarantee the boy will get into the program" and emphasize that he must plead guilty first. The dad's resolve seems unshaken.

Today, Mr. Harris came in to sign the complaint and review the bank tapes showing his son taking cash from the ATM. There is certainly enough evidence to warrant charges. A conviction should be a slam dunk. When Mr. Harris leaves, his jaw is still set. I believe he will follow through on the charges, but there is a certain sadness in his eyes that intensified during our meeting. His son, Courtlandt, is reportedly driving the car home today, and should be back by Monday. If he isn't, Mr. Harris would like to proceed with an arrest warrant for the stolen vehicle. If the suspect has returned by Monday, Mr. Harris will call to set an appointment to bring his son to my office for questioning.

This is just one more file for me. Hopefully it will remain relatively thin, allowing me to force it into the already burgeoning filing cabinet. This is not the kind of case that will keep me up at night. I am confident that the offender will be punished to the extent of the victim's resolve. The harm to society is minimal, at least to date. So why is it that at day's end, as my little ones wrap their arms around my legs, that my mind flashes back to the image of Mr. Harris walking from my office? His exiting frame seemed smaller than when he had arrived - shoulders rounded, back bent by the weight of what he saw on that security camera tape. Just a boy taking money from a machine designed to dispense it. Just a dream, 20 years in the making, destroyed by those silent images. I am relatively new to paternal dreams of happy, healthy, successful progeny. Young as those dreams may be, they are well formed and well rooted. I cannot fathom the pain of having them torn from my heart. Bending low, I kiss the tousled heads of my dream-makers. I breathe in the sweetness of toddlerhood: peanut butter mixed with jelly, matched by baby shampoo and the faint whiff of a not-entirely-dry diaper. I will never allow my dreams to be shattered, I tell myself with fierce resolve, I just won't. And the giggles of my diminutive duo add their agreement to my decision.

Friendly Skies — Sally Mills
December 2003 — American Airlines Call Center

When I tell people that I work for an airline, they get that typical dream-like jealous look. 'Oh, you get to fly free.' There are perks, of course, as there are with every job, but most of those perks sound better than they are. Generally, my wings are clipped. I can't see any airplanes from where I sit. I can't even see a window.

A newcomer would need a map to find my desk. It's not that it's tucked away in obscurity, but rather, it is hidden in the middle of sameness: *Where's Waldo* meets big business. I'm four rows down, seventh cubicle on the left. To one side of me is a seven by seven plot of office space decorated like an ESPN shrine. Its master, my coworker, was a college football player, though the name of his alma mater doesn't stick with me – somewhere with an affinity for the color red. He certainly is a big guy - just a different shape of big than in the glory pictures that peek between the footballs, baseball hats and assorted jock tchotchkes lining his cubicle. Across the way, the exact same-sized real estate is housed by the cat lady. She has everything but a live feline surrounding her. If you count the fine layer of fur that she transfers back and forth between her clothes and her chair, though, most of a real cat does live there. My favorite neighbor might be "The Nose." It's not that she wears too much perfume – if she wears any at all, I haven't noticed. No, she specializes in bringing the great olfactory of the outdoors to work with her in spray bottles. The identifiable scents aren't so bad: pine forest, spring flowers, pumpkin pie and apple harvest. It's the ones with the creative names that make me wish for a head cold: morning dew, clean linen, full moon over the ocean. Sometimes driving to work, I smell "moss by star light" on my coat, and make an unscheduled stop at the dry cleaners.

Like most jobs, mine would be so much easier if it weren't for the customers. I like helping people and solving problems. But since I was promoted, becoming the next rung up on the escalation scale, the calls entail less solution and more placating. All of us, airline professionals and the flying public alike, are still getting used to this post 9/11 reality. Some things are simply beyond our corporate control. Reduced or free flight coupons may help dissipate anger and frustration, but sometimes it seems nothing less than their own jet will make a person happy. You win some, you lose some. You wait until you are sure the phone connection is severed to say all the things that you had held back with great personal effort.

The first call of the day involves lost luggage and a very dissatisfied frequent flyer. Twenty minutes later and with 25,000 miles added to his account, my first round of muttering commences. With all his flying miles (and they were considerable), he has previously never had lost luggage. Some odds you can't beat forever. As the day wears on, the calls blend and blur. In some ways, they are like the cubicle farm where I reside 40 hours a week: individual yet indistinct. An especially caustic voice may stick with me through my shift and into the evening. But generally, the voices, the issues, the resolutions, blur into time segments that could only be recalled by playing the endless recordings that are meticulously retained. And who would want to do that without cause?

There is one call today, however, that I continue to replay as I make my way home. The caller was not irate, but pleading. There was no lost luggage, but a found son. There was no expectation of pre-9/11 flight regulations, but a desperate search for a needed loophole. Today I did some of my best work, and tonight I pray that it was enough.

As always, I identified myself when starting the conversation. His reply took me a bit by surprise. "Thank you, Sally, for your assistance. I really need some help flying my son home from Las Vegas to Chicago." Obviously, there was some yet-to-be-revealed reason that this phone call was escalated. So far it sounded like a job for online reservations. What followed was a completely transparent conversation with no attempt to disguise or sugar-coat the situation. No anger or frustration, but a palpable undertone of desperate need searching for a solution.

"My name is Ken. My son, Court, is 19 and has been diagnosed with bipolar. We need to fly him home as soon as possible, but he doesn't have any ID," he continues.

"Can you FedEx some form of identification to him? He could have the ID by Monday or Tuesday at the latest. Would you like to look at flight information?" I still wasn't sure of the real issue. Had he forgotten his license at home? Maybe he didn't have a license. There was a momentary pause in the conversation, but only long enough for Ken to take a deep breath and maybe gather some courage.

The situation started to take shape out as he continues. Court stole their truck and left on Thanksgiving night. For some time, they had no idea where he was or even *if* he was. He finally surfaced at his brother's house in California. In the meantime, they discovered the theft of a considerable sum of money from their bank account. It took a few days, but Ken and his wife finally convinced their son to return the truck to avoid being arrested. He will still face charges for the stolen money. I suppose I didn't need any of that information, but it did set the stage for me – made me care about the characters. So yesterday, Court left California to head back to Illinois. He made it just into Nevada when he ran out of gas. Intending to go back to get the truck later, he locked his keys, phone and wallet in the vehicle and hitchhiked to Las Vegas, arriving sometime yesterday. Penniless, for sure, and probably tired and hungry, he had gone to a church for help. There they gave him some food, a phone to call home, and after the call, they agreed to give him a place to sleep and a ride to the airport for the 8 a.m. flight.

"The banks are closed here, so we can't get his passport out of our safety deposit box until Monday to use for identification. His actions are unpredictable, at best. We are afraid if we leave him in Las Vegas for the weekend, he will disappear again. We don't care about the truck or the money. We just want to get him home and get him the help he needs."

Now I understood why this call was kicked up the rung to me. An unkempt young man, traveling alone, without identification or luggage - in this post 9/11 world, he would be lighting up just about every warning signal possible. "Do you have any form of identification you can fax to him – any kind of official document with his picture on it?"

"The only official document we have is his birth certificate. The only thing we have with his picture on it is his eighth-grade traveling soccer ID. Obviously, neither is the kind of official document you are asking about." There was a calm but intense urgency in his voice that touched me again. I don't have a son, but if I did, I, too, would move heaven and earth to get him home.

In the end, I told Ken to fax the soccer ID while I confirmed the reservation for Court and notate his file. "He will be able to get on the plane," I heard myself promise. "He will go through intense security screening at the airport, so he should be there very early. But he *will* get on the plane." Why did I think I can make promises for the TSA – on behalf of American Airlines – on a recorded line, none the less? "Will you be picking him up at O'Hare?"

"My wife will."

"When she gets to the airport, have her go to the ticket agent with the flight information. I have noted in the file that she can get a special pass to go back to the gate to meet him." At least I had not over-stepped my authority on this promise, that is, if Court makes it on the plane in the first place.

As his thanks and praise filtered through the phone line, the sound of relief was obvious – mixed with exhaustion that is only experienced when a must-do anxiety-rush expires.

Looking back, now, at the end of my day, I feel the exhaustion pulling at the edges of my mind as well. It is unlikely I will ever know how this chapter ends, let alone the story. Will he get on the plane? Will a father's efforts to get his son help be successful? You win some, you lose some. I wish this was the type of call that could have been resolved with the addition of 25,000 frequent flyer miles. I have done all I can, and will never know if it was enough. But I desperately want this one to end up in the win column.

Brown Angel **Lory Harris**
Christmas 2003 **St. Charles, Illinois**

Christmas, again – or maybe I should say, finally. It has been the longest year, every day seeming a month long. Last Christmas I remember thinking that with the diagnosis and the prescriptions our life would go back to normal. I was just so grateful that Court was out of the hospital and everyone was home for Christmas. I thought Christmas 2002 would be just a minor blip on the radar. Apparently, the radar is broken altogether.

The moon lends just enough light to the room and my sleep-deprived eyes are now well adjusted to the 2 a.m. luminosity, having stared at the bedroom ceiling for the past half hour. I've moved downstairs to sit and stare at the unlit Christmas tree. Packages are piled around, Santa's hopeful contribution to the cheer of the day. I think briefly of plugging in the lights, but there is something appropriate about the silent lights on this silent night. The mood was set even before I descended the steps searching for a glimpse of the Christ Child's spirit. I pull my robe more tightly around me and wish I had grabbed my slippers.

Thankfulness is the way to start, I guess: *Thank you, God, for Court's return from California. Thank you that he was not successful in his latest overdose attempt and that he is finally taking his prescriptions. And thank you that he is home with us for Christmas. Those are solid thanks.* From there, the slippery slope grabs hold, pulling me downward in a predictable fashion: *Make him continue to take his meds and end this nightmare. Make love be enough to pull us through. Give me the resolve to carry through with the drug court charges. Make the drug court work.* And as always, the prayers of thanksgiving dissolve into another kind of *give*: *Give me back my son. Give me peace. Give me sleep in the wee hours of the morning. Give me back my LIFE!* At some point, I just stop and stare at the tree again. This "Sweet Hour of Prayer" is just a repetitive, whiny rant.

This year's ornament, a wooden Norfolk Terrier to commemorate our new puppy, doesn't represent our year at all, though Cabo might disagree with a growl. Maybe we should have put a map of the United States on the tree, or an empty gas tank (physically and metaphorically speaking), or a *Sleepless in Seattle* DVD. Or perhaps something shattered or a pair of handcuffs? No, in years to come I'll prefer to look back and remember puppy antics and kisses. Maybe we chose correctly after all.

The moonlight catches the shape of an angel, dressed in topaz colored glass, my birthstone. It was the first Christmas gift Court bought for me with his own money so many years ago. We had been shopping together when he snuck off for a moment or two, returning with a small bag in his hands and a smile from ear to ear. That little brown angel might not be classically beautiful, unless, that is, you received it as I did: from the hands of that little boy so anxious to give his perfect gift.

Jumbled images of my son crowd forward in my mind vying for attention: the 9-pound, 2-ounce newborn announcing his presence; the starting soccer goalie on the varsity team; the T-ball player legging out a home run (aided by a misjudged fly ball and three throwing errors); the two-year old offering his blanket for comfort to curb my tears of frustration; the teenager standing outside of Iowa State with a mixed look of excitement and anxiety as I left him at college last year. Not just images, but feelings crept up, as well: the pit in my stomach when he didn't make the junior high soccer team he expected; the pride when he graduated 7th of 700 in his high school class; the new-found dread I now have whenever he leaves for an evening; and the fear he won't return.

Then, earlier this month, there was the overwhelming relief when he stepped off the airplane at O'Hare International Airport. Of course, the airline can't tell you if someone gets on a plane; we tried that avenue. So, I stood, waiting at the gate, not wanting to take my eyes off the ramp for fear of missing him. The initial burst of deplaning passengers gave way to a steady but orderly stream. With every gap in the off-loading line of travelers I started an early panic. What if he didn't leave Las Vegas at all? What would we do then – wait and wonder some more? Or would we have a warrant issued for his arrest? Finally, he was there - beautiful, in a brown-angel kind of way. He was disheveled: scruffy beard, clothes hanging on his thinning frame. His eyes were downcast, almost shy. But then he looked up and saw me weaving through the crowd toward him. Is it my imagination or did his eyes look less chemically altered than normal?

Throwing my arms open to wrap him in an embrace, Court transformed into a weary passenger dropping his bags to receive an overdue welcome – though, of course, he has no physical bags to drop. Everything remains safely locked in an abandoned, gas-less truck somewhere in the desert. Still, Court's demeanor reminded me a little of Colin when he returned from Iraq, dropping his pack for a welcome home embrace. Of course, Colin had been risking his life in service to country. Court's life is certainly at risk, but his enemy is within.

We talked about safe subjects: Christmas preparations, Colin's upcoming leave, Corey's plans for a California Christmas with friends. The police are not able to find the truck. We will file an insurance claim later in the week. But overall, I am the shy one. There are so many things I want to ask, but I hold back, telling myself Court needs his privacy. The truth is, though, that I'm afraid of the answers. *Why did you steal from us? You are an adult; if you want to leave home, you certainly can. Why sneak off in the middle of the night? Why would you want to live this life? Why won't you take the prescriptions? Why? Why? Why?*

It's now been two weeks since Court's return home. The renewed drug use and suicide attempt over the week that followed his return did nothing to answer the questions, nor did Ken's attempts to demand information or any coddling on my part. Court's actions earned him another stay at a psych hospital: his third, each in a different state, and all within the last 12 months. The doctors' educated answers sounded the same in Illinois as the ones from their Iowa and Wisconsin counterparts – solutions without the bite to become reality. The prescription – that is, the order to take the already-prescribed medications – is as effective as gumming a raw apple to satisfy hunger. You hold the solution in your hand, but until you get it into your stomach, it is no answer at all.

Since Court was released about 12 hours ago, at least we won't be spending Christmas behind the locked doors of a psych unit. We can pretend that everything is just fine in the comforts of our own home. Just like every other Christmas, we will open gifts, have a couple of laughs and too much food. But this won't be like any other Christmas. First, Corey is in California - the first Christmas we have not all gathered together. And then there is the court date casting a dark shadow over the festivities. On January 12th, Court will enter his guilty plea and hope to be assigned to the drug court.

I'm not sure if it is better to have my mind dart forward or back. Honestly, it doesn't matter since I am developing quite the talent for doing both at once. It is a silent night, a holy night – and a wholly holey fortnight to come.

Merry Christmas.

Unexpected Friendships
Christmas 2003

Sean Woodman
Linden Oaks Psych Hospital
Naperville, Illinois

Christmas morning. If I didn't open my eyes, I could still plan my dash down the stairs to see the tree buried behind colorful boxes tied with ribbons and bows. I could pretend the stockings are straining on their hooks and the caramel rolls are fastened to a red and green plate with sticky, sugary glue. Instead, when I finally lift my lids, I see white. Not the white of a snowman standing guard or of frozen ammunition waiting to be formed, but institutional white: ceilings, walls, bedding, curtains. And with each blink of my eyes, the white fades to grey, then to black as I close them, again, and beg for more sleep.

My family will show up later today, I suppose, for a sham of a celebration. The truth is they chose this venue, so I'm not feeling sorry for them. They forced me here against my will. My world was loping on at its usual dismal pace. The more tinsel that was hung, the duller my world became. The more bells that rang, the more the din of uselessness sounded. The more gatherings I attended, the more alone I became. It's like I alone am the donor for all the joy the world is singing of, and with each chorus, my lifeblood is weakened and left wanting.

Admittedly, I can spin out of control. It's like pulling the plug from a full sink of water. As you watch at first, not much happens. A closer look will reveal that the water level is going down. Maybe there is a little gurgling sound, but nothing alarming. This is the ignorance stage for the observer. However, if you are the water, as I am, you can feel the relentless pull of the drain, even as light still fills your vision. Next the water starts to visibly swirl down the drain. The casual observer may not even notice the forming vortex, but the water does. There is no foothold to stop the spin. And worse yet, it is not only out of sync with the rest of the world, but counter clockwise to those staring dumbly on. At this point, the water has already silently passed the point of no return. The rest of the world does not even think to react until the final inches of water are being sucked down the drain. By then, a full vortex has formed, a tornado of the soul disappearing into a living sewer. Now the family takes notice. They reach with clumsy hands to stop the inevitable as the water slips effortlessly between their fingers. The crystal-clear liquid swirls away from their futile attempts, leaving behind their bloody hands. All that is left of me is the thin film of water clinging to the sides of the sink, threatened equally by heat, cold, and the passage of time.

Still, yesterday I had things under control--organically, even. Mushrooms are both my life and my savior, down to earth and covered in shit. They counteract the suffocating vortex with a whirlpool of their own, clockwise this time, pulling me out of the grasp of the sewer, lifting me up into the world of possibility. The tinsel and the bells combine, singing of brightness and hope. My two spinning sides - equal and opposite - hold me in a state of normal. Crisis averted. Until, that is, the family imposes their belated solution in a desperate attempt to make up for missed signs.

They forced me here, along with men in blue carrying nightsticks and guns. They have forced their stopper into the drain in their desperate effort to calm the vortex - too little, too late. Their solution is anything but organic. Even as I rationally explained this to them, the straps cut into my arms and legs. Their whiteness along with those of the gurney sheets threatened to bleach my world of all color and beauty. My equilateral spinning was forced to a sudden stop, causing the rest of the world to gyrate wildly by way of compensation. Even with my eyes closed, I could feel the world whirling around me.

Just like yesterday, I must eventually open my eyes lest I give my captors cause for additional pharmacology. The grey-white surrounds me, shrouding me in its monotony. The truth is I am uncomfortable with both the extremes of happy and of sad, but I dread the middle as well. In the middle is the wasteland of nothingness. The middle-class may be an economic term, but it is a psychological one as well. It is safe and predictable – manageable and managed. It is the dirty grey of late winter snow – tired and cold, attempting to stave off spring. I am the first tender shoots of green, waiting for my chance to poke through and radiate contrast in this world.

I swing my legs over the side of the bed, summoning the strength to play the middle-class game of conformity, when I see a flash of green hopefulness in the gritty landscape. Poking out from under the water pitcher on my bedside table is the corner of a page from a magazine. Written on it is the best Christmas present I will receive: Court Harris 630-555-9534. This is akin to contraband in this place, the sharing of contact information, though it happens all the time. Our captors don't want the crazies to gather outside their watchful eyes.

It was not the carefully and forcefully dispensed drugs that slowed my spinning world yesterday. It was Court. In the hour we had together, we bypassed talk of sports and girls and even partying and drugs. We lamented the vortex leading to the depths of depression. We explored the psycho-socio-economic class system and our struggle to realize our upper-class birthright. A strong friendship has been formed which will not be thwarted by the rules of this establishment.

I place this first green of spring in my pocket to keep it safe and warm, protected from the winter frost that surrounds me in this whiteness. Court and I are kindred spirits connected in this place of disconnect. Christmas is looking merrier after all.

Loving Coffee
January 2004

Pastor Jeff Frazier
First Baptist Church
Geneva, Illinois

This time of year, my beloved coffee is the most versatile of brews and I'm taking full advantage of its offerings. First, any measure of warmth in this Chicago winter is appreciated, especially one that is easily transportable and able to warm both hands and body. Not only are January days short and gloomy, but the brightness of Christmas is over with all its fervor. Caffeine is my most reliable dietary supplement for life's reentry after the frenzied events of the previous month. Programs, services, and parties reached a fevered pitch in the church as everyone rushed to the manger to glimpse God incarnate. I just hope we all paused long enough to really see the miracle of the season.

Tipping my head back to glean the last drops of this particular cup, though, I realize its purpose is several months overdue. I pray it was worth the wait – not for the sake of my warmth or comfort, but for Court's. Watching him now, walking to his car, he looks older and less self-assured than his bravado indicated just a few minutes ago. Is he hunched against the wind or bending under the burden he will not release?

He no longer carries the cocky, self-assured swagger that dominated our last meeting four months ago. In less than a week, he will face a judge who will decide his fate for the next few years at a minimum. It weighs heavily on him, of course, and predictably makes him re-evaluate his definition of love. How can parents, whose over-arching purpose is to love and protect, willfully condemn him to the possibility of prison? There is no doubt that both sides of the transaction feel the turmoil. One side cannot fathom how love could conjure such depravity, and the other side is crushed that for the sake of love, they must.

Court is certainly intelligent; his intellect, it seems, sometimes standing in the way of common sense. He spoke freely of his life with drugs, still playing shock-the-pastor, of course. But just as loudly, Court's words declared a complete indifference to his own life. He knows how harmful his actions have been to his body, his relationships, and his life. On occasion, I think, he would like to pull himself back from self-imposed brink, to become the person he is expected to be, the one he sometimes expects of himself. But more frequently, he reaches the conclusion that apathy is the only logical path to follow. Good will never be good enough, happiness is fleeting and more readily experienced when high. If God is love, then neither are reliable and therefore neither are desirable.

He hasn't heard from Andrew, his former lover, since late last summer, and then only when Court reached out to him. While Court maintains that he is still gay, the forcefulness of that conviction seems shaky. There have been no others: no dates, no affairs, no interests. His idea of love found its embodiment in Andrew, who made no demands of him and expected nothing in return. However, what he received was also nothing – an even trade. Love does, of course, make demands of us, and as we allow it to transform us, we find a better self in return. Life lived entirely on our own terms, bowing to no one and nothing, gives what should be expected: a reciprocated emptiness.

It really is all about love. Our souls long for love that is not just a kiss or a hug or any other physical intimacy. Our hearts long for someone to accept us without demand for change. Yet when we really love another, flawed as we are, we inevitably want more for them than they may want for themselves. By polishing their souls, our own reflection becomes clearer in the process. Ironically, though, intent on the other, genuine love barely sees the change in ourselves.

At its core, love does not sit idyllically by the babbling brook luxuriating in the confidence of one beautiful day following another. Certainly, there will be such days, and they should be enjoyed for the respite they offer. But we must also beware of the potential for everything from mosquitos to slippery stones to flash floods. Our wariness is not so much for self-preservation as it is to protect the object of our genuine affection.

Love is not benign; it is demanding. I know it sounds preacher-ish, and forgive me since I am, but God didn't wait along the shoreline in the shade of a favored tree for us to come to Him. He sent His Son in pursuit, to show us the true extent of what love can be. Even when we rejected His extravagance, He did not return to His repose, but offered His only child's life as atonement, bridging what had been an impassable chasm between us.

It is only in giving all that we receive our heart's desire, but how hard it is to let go of ounces of self with hopes for, and in favor of, another. I suspect that Ken and Lory could preach that sermon right now, except that the script is not yet complete. Their contribution to the ultimate ending is a hope and a prayer. Flimsy and fragile as they seem, it is the "everything" they must offer in the name of loving their son. Regardless of results, that "everything" is exactly what God demands and what Court needs most of all. Oh, for faith to trust that the Overseer of such a precious, costly gift will carry it to the intended receiver – and that the receiver will indeed receive.

The January bite in the air as I exit Starbucks is held inexplicably at bay by the warmth radiating from within – a warmth that cannot be explained by mere coffee.

Hold them closely, Lord – close to You and close to each other. Steady their feet on slippery stones and hold the flood waters back from their crossing.

Removing Justice's Blindfold — Judge Dennis Fordham

January 2004 — **Kane County Courthouse, Geneva, Illinois**

The day starts cold but clear – crisp is the word to describe this Midwestern January morning. I had to enjoy the beauty of the day in the short walk into the courthouse since most of my day will be spent in my windowless courtroom hearing arraignment charges read and taking the response of those standing before my bench.

On these days, there is always an interesting mix of humanity spanning the full spectrum of socio-economic classes. The accused come in various shades of dressed-for-the-occasion. There will be suits: some tailored, some borrowed. Many of the men will wear ties: some with ease like every other day of their lives, others unconsciously slipping their finger between their neck and the implement of torture that is constricting their windpipe. Many of the women will stand a little taller than they might on a normal Monday, the result of 3- and 4-inch heels. Frankly, I've always wondered how they can stand at all in those shoes. I prefer my torture of the necktie variety.

Each defendant will be requested to reply to the standard question of guilt or innocence. Of course, in our court system, it is rarely that black and white. We play by well-defined and centuries-old rules. The steps are well-orchestrated, though not universally known. For most, the attorney – paid or appointed - will act as coach, guiding his clients in the steps of this initial dance. Some of the accused will attempt these first steps themselves. Most can succeed at this level, but when the dance progresses to the waltz and then the rumba over the next weeks, months or years, they are rarely as successful. Today, we will keep the steps concise and predictable.

I've lived in this community most of my life, and I practiced law here before I became a judge. I know most of the attorneys, on a professional level, at least. But the county is large and well-populated, meaning that generally, I don't know the accused as the opening dance commences. On occasion, like today, when a case is called, a familiar face steps to my bench. In truth, I don't recognize the young man who stands with his attorney before me. There is a familiarity, of course, but only of the run of the mill variety: eyes downcast, his neck constrained with an unaccustomed length of borrowed silk, his weight shifting slightly from foot to foot, hands dug deep into pockets to keep fidgeting fingers out of sight. This marks neither guilt nor innocence—rather, an encounter with the unfamiliar and uncontrollable.

Courtlandt Harris is accused of felony theft over $300. Harris is a common name, but in the first row of the gallery, I see his parents who were friends and former legal clients of mine in the years before I became a judge. Ken and Lory look up at me and offer a slight nod of acknowledgement as the bailiff reads the charges for their son to answer. I met the Harrises at a young married group in church. The young man standing before me was maybe two-years-old back then. Just more proof that time doesn't really march as much as it tiptoes past when we aren't looking.

Even as I wonder about the facts in question, I know I will not offer judgment. "I must recuse myself from this case, as I know the defendant's parents, Ken and Lory Harris, who are in the courtroom." I can feel the heaviness of their hearts, and it causes mine to be similarly weighted.

"Judge," starts Court's attorney, "we understand your position. We are seeking to transfer this case to the drug court. Perhaps you can direct that this case be heard there." Transferring this case to drug court does not constitute a judgment on my part. It merely moves the case to another judge, which is necessary at any rate since I cannot hear this case.

It sounds trite, but I love the law and I believe in it. It's not a perfect system – how can it be with imperfect people involved? But the rule of law is one of the hallmarks of civility, in my opinion. I think the law is at its best when the punishment fits the crime. I once sentenced a man convicted of cruelty to animals to the maximum sentence plus a community service requirement to assist with the disposal of roadkill on our county roads.

I think the drug court is a solid step toward reconciling crime and punishment. It is housed just a couple of doors down from my courtroom, presided over by Judge Doyle, whose dedication is unquestioned. He is here for endless hours every week, accommodating the working hours of those under his charge who must also find time to meet with him one-on-one each week. His probation officers are on perpetual call, going all over the county to track down and arrest those who don't appear for their thrice-weekly drug test. They also spend time getting to really know the ones who faithfully wait in the courtroom for their weekly conference.

A lot of resources are poured into those addicts in an effort to keep them out of prison and productively engaged in society. There are plenty of success stories; several classes of graduates have emerged from this relatively new judicial experiment. But there are failures as well. The jury is still out, so as to speak, on the program.

"This case is transferred to the courtroom of Judge Doyle for arraignment. Please work with the bailiff to schedule a court date. And good luck to you all." Judge Doyle will make the decision on the merits of the case and whether drug court is an appropriate possibility for young Mr. Harris.

There was the slightest nod, again, from Ken. As a parent myself, it's hard to fathom that this was the outcome they prayed for. I don't see the same kind of pained relief on their son's face. There are certainly some difficult years coming for this family regardless of what happens in the rescheduled arraignment.

They say that justice is blind, and I hope it is. But I am not. When I remove my robes, I see the pleading face of my friends, asking me for the unthinkable – not to free their child, but to lock him into the judicial system. I see the hidden fright of that child, now a man, longing for freedom. I pray for freedom, for all of them. For Ken and Lory: freedom from this terror that is gripping their hearts and their family. For Court: freedom from the alleged drugs that are robbing his life. May Justice, in her blindness, see this family through to wholeness again.

Handing off the Reins — Lory Harris

January 2004 — Kane County Courthouse, Geneva, Illinois

This courtroom door is a few steps closer to the elevators, but otherwise this could be the same room we waited in earlier this week. The building itself is less than a decade old. The courtrooms are adequate in size. The furnishings are dark wood, like all courtrooms seem to be, but with a modern bent. The bailiff reminds me of a uniformed librarian, his head swiveling to glare in whatever direction his ears have detected sound. No talking, no cell phones, no books allowed, and the judge has yet to enter the room.

Ken sits beside me, his back firmly pressed against the wooden bench that comprises our temporary residence. Indeed, with his jaw set and his shoulders back, he may well have become part of the furniture. I see his ram-rod stiff resolve, so unlike my own melting demeanor, and I wonder how. How can he so matter-of-factly watch his son stand there with the attorney, waiting for the judge? Maybe it's just one the many divisions of labor in every marriage: his culinary skills keep our bellies full, I restore post-preparation order to the kitchen. He maintains the house, I manage the magical dressers that are continually stocked with clean clothes. He draws the line in the sand, I puddle across it. It's not that he needs to cry; I do enough of that for both of us. But sometimes I need him to cry for my sake, not his. I need to know that his fears run as deep - that his prayers come from his toes and are tossed heaven-ward before they crash back to earth under their own weight. I need to know that he at least occasionally glimpses our nine-pound, dark headed, bundle-of-joy baby boy when he looks at Court.

I wonder, again, how we came to this. How is it that filing felony theft charges against our son and then paying for his attorney to make sure he pleads guilty is our best option? A river of tears has flowed while contemplating this step. Yet, here we are, and with a tenuous amount of resolve. It's not so much that I think this will work to restore our son, but more that nothing else has. Each step we have taken has been more and more desperate, and less and less effective. We are not able to make Court take the meds that would restore our perfect life, or to make him quit the self-medication that causes him to spiral downward. He flunked out of the local community college last semester. He is personable enough to get jobs, but too narcissistic to keep one.

My mental meandering is halted by the bailiff's directive to stand. Again, I think that some part to the wooden bench must have fused with Ken's being. He stands as commanded, his back ridged and straight, jaw set and eyes watching the entrance of the black-robed adjudicator who will become a staple of conversation around our dinner table. When the order to sit is decreed, all in the sparsely populated room comply.

Before a child is born, much time and consideration go into choosing his name--actually, two names, the winner being decided by the doctor's gender pronouncement. You roll them around in your mind, then try them on for size by speaking them out loud. After Court's birth, we proudly told everyone the full name – Courtlandt Bryn Harris – before adding that we would call him Court. Ironically, though, to hear his name read in court - "in the case verses Courtlandt Bryn Harris" - gives the name a heavy, almost muddy sound. I feel myself melting involuntarily and grabbing for my husband's wooden hand. With the kind of transfer that marriage fosters best, his hand melts a little, and mine draws strength and rigidity.

Even having gained 140 pounds since his start in this world, Court looks small. In the pomp and circumstance of a courtroom, my Court appears to be shrinking like Alice in Wonderland. Something in me wants to scream, 'No, come back!' But the rest of me is all too aware that he won't return voluntarily. That is why we are here: to drag him back by force of law.

Judge Doyle certainly fits the part: tall and broad, military-like clean cut, and just enough grey around the temples to perfect the air of authority. His raised desk, black robe, and his own personal uniformed librarian complete the look. After the charges are read, the judge starts the questioning: Do you understand that you must plead guilty to get into the drug court? Do you understand that if you do not follow the rules set out in the drug court, you will go to prison? How were drugs involved in this crime? How often do you use drugs? Do you want to stop using drugs?

Court looks small and contrite. I, of course, believe every bit of body language and vocalization that comes from him. I always do, which probably makes me the biggest fool in the room. I would say I'm happy to be the fool, but the truth is, I'm miserable. Loving, trusting, foolish, and miserable. I want his life back so much that I will it onto him. I simply cannot conceive that he wants to continue the life he is living.

"Are you high now?" Judge Doyle isn't beating around the bush.

"No, sir," answers my diminutive child.

"When is the last time you used?"

"It has been a few weeks."

"This gentleman, Randy, will be your probation officer. He will be escorting you down a flight of stairs for a drug test as soon as we finish up here. Will those results show that you haven't used in a few weeks?"

"Well, maybe it's closer to a week."

"Are those your parents sitting there?"

"Yes, sir."

"Do you see what you are doing to them? You stole from them and yet, here they are, because they love you. Did they pay for your attorney?"

"Yes, sir."

Questions, largely rhetorical, continue to be lobbed from the bench. The short answers, generally the same two words, return from Court to the court. In the end, this game concludes with a question and the same two-word answer.

"Do you plead guilty to the charges of felony theft in excess of $300 and wish to enter the drug court program?"

"Yes, sir."

"Your plea is accepted, and judgment is suspended subject to the following conditions. You will not use drugs or alcohol of any kind. You will submit to drug testing three times a week. You will meet with me once a week. You will comply with any other orders entered by this court concerning your health or treatment. Upon successful completion of this program for a period of not less than two years, the charges against you will be dropped. If you do not complete the program, judgment will be entered against you and you will be sentenced to prison. I will see you in my chambers next Thursday for our first meeting. Randy, please escort Mr. Harris downstairs for his first drug test."

Should I feel relieved? This is the desired outcome. Or should I just hold my breath for a period of not less than two years? What if Court balks at the rules set out for him? Will he end up being whisked off to prison? Have we just sealed an unthinkable fate for our child?

"Mr. and Mrs. Harris, as you already know, addiction is a disease that affects the whole family. I also encourage you to get the help you need. There is a dedicated group of parents of addicts called Hearts of Hope. The bailiff will give you their brochure with their contact information and meeting times. I highly recommend talking with them for your own benefit during this time of your lives. You may also call me if you have any questions or if there is any way we can assist you. We share a common goal: to see your son free from drugs and functioning in society. May God bless your family."

Bless. Is that what this is called? I remove my hand from Ken's only long enough to put on my coat. In just those brief seconds, I feel the borrowed rigidity drain from me. Not even the below freezing weather outside will keep me from melting without that marital transference. But I am resolved, at least, to wait until I get home before melting completely. Grabbing Ken's hand again, I look back at the courtroom. This will be Court's new home away from home and, hopefully, our savior. God bless Judge Doyle, too, whatever that might mean.

Accompanying Misery
February 2004

Lea Minalga
Hearts of Hope
Geneva, Illinois

Mondays come around on a regular basis around here, and with them come familiar faces I am honored to call friends and warriors. We gather for an hour of prayer to a common God and against a common enemy. I count it a blessing and a necessity. The gathered few of us, all women, share a common mother's heart--the unrelenting love for our children. In that, we are like every other mother the world over. It is the reason we gather that sets us apart: each of us has a child who longs for a high more than our hug. Their first love, addiction, trumps friends, family, comfort and even food. It took me years to recognize that I had been so demoted in my son's eyes. That doesn't mean I must accept it as a permanent shift.

They say misery loves company. There is truth to that, and I suppose it factors into our Monday gathering. But there is also strength in numbers, even in small numbers. Jesus said, "Where two or three are gathered in my name, there am I with them." Now that is strength! There is a joyful sadness when a new mom joins our group: sadness that another family has been gripped by this scourge of drugs, and joy that a mother desires to reach the ultimate Healer along with us. But having lived this heartache for several years now, if it would save others, I would pray to be the only one. If only…

There is one good thing about living in chronic crisis: a refined and defined focus on life. The decisions you must make are more daunting, but more clear-cut, too. The everyday clutter of life fades into non-existence. A little while ago, I was really struggling. My son Justin had relapsed and was in jail, likely headed to prison. As I tried to make one of those daunting decisions that really wasn't mine to make, I got a call from a neighbor who was having a bad day and needed someone's ear. Knowing that exact feeling all too well, I put aside my own pity party to join hers. She went on to tell me how horrible her day was: the hose on her washing machine had sprung a leak. Did I sound disinterested, incredulous? I mean, I like my washer, too, but the degree to which it functions – or not – does not define my day.

In our group on Monday nights, we are all stripped bare. Our children are on our minds and our emotions on our sleeves. We share knowing laughter and heartfelt tears. No matter how often it is told or who the teller is, a story is always the same and yet, always new. There is a new woman in our group tonight. Lory's son, Court, has recently entered the drug court program. Her fears, though newer and rawer, mirror those of the rest of us. Court is bipolar, non-compliant with medication, and a marijuana addict. The drug can be alcohol, pot, heroin or cocaine - or jelly beans, for all that matters. Anything that hijacks a life and drives it to destruction is an addiction. Pot has brought Court to the same fate that heroin brought Justin: into the legal system, standing with one foot in reality, while the other dangles over the abyss of Hell's pit.

Yet, we are not without hope, though at times its remnants are difficult to detect. When we gather from week to week, seeking God's help, mercy and strength, we are rewarded with renewed hope flowing straight from the throne of the Creator of the universe. One of my favorite verses is Psalm 20:7: "Some trust in chariots and some in horses, but we trust in the name of the Lord our God" (NIV). And so, we shall.

Judgment Pronounced — Lory Harris
March 2004 — St. Charles, Illinois

Court is hanging out with Sean again today. Frankly, I like Sean. He's personable, respectful, funny and artistic. He does the most random sketches that just make me smile. In fact, he gave me a page of them. Someday I hope to create a quilt centered on one or more of them. They are fun in a total nonsense way, and they make me wonder what he was using when he drew them – beyond the obvious paper and pencil, of course.

Court and Sean's friendship was initiated at last Christmas' psych hospital stay. I don't even know what Sean's diagnosis is, not that it matters; both have abused drugs. But if Sean uses again, he might end up back in a psych hospital for a week. If Court does, he will end up in jail. I never sleep well when the two of them are together.

The other day, I asked Court why he doesn't call his other friends to hang out. Most of them are away at college, as he succinctly points out, which is true. Most, but not all. Jim is going to the local community college, and Ben is back after deciding that college wasn't for him. Aaron is around, too, though he is having a tough time right now. Maybe he's not such a good influence for Court.

That's when it strikes me: ours is the family being cautioned against at dinner tables around the local communities. How many times have I hosted that conversation? How many times have I passed judgment on a kid because of his actions, painting the family with the same brush by extension? It's a small enough town with a small enough newspaper and a huge gossip mill. There is hardly a way to avoid hearing the dirt when a dust storm roars through. Being the dust storm itself – now that's another experience altogether.

From time to time, I meet up with other parents from Court's youth and high school soccer teams, parents we have spent countless weekends with over the past ten years or so. It's not the questions they ask that tell me they are "in the know," it's the ones that hang heavy and unspoken. "How is Colin?" the other parents ask. "Is he deployed right now?" "I hear Corey is in California. You will never get him home from there! What is he doing now?" They even inquire about Ken and me to avoid weightier topics. "How is your business going? I'm sure you are staying busy in this economy." We can engage in small talk for 10 minutes or so and the one topic that will not be broached is Court. He, of course, is our most direct connection, and the elephant in the room they politely and pointedly ignore.

They would probably like to hear the dirt – more grist for the rumor mill. At least they could have confirmation of all the wild rumors they have heard. Maybe they are just trying to be kind by not broaching the subject and the private turmoil that appears to have gone public. For my part, I just want them to acknowledge my son with a simple, "How is Court?" He lives! He is real! I love him! But an equal part of me doesn't want to be a sideshow attraction – gawked at, and then the subject of an adult game of telephone. In the end, I guess I am as conflicted as they likely are. I don't mention my youngest son's name, either.

In my prayers, I beg for mercy to make this stop! But in my heart, I know I deserve it and more. As a parent I have spent years, decades even, being arrogant and condescending. Oh, no one would say that about me. I kept it well hidden, smugly stowed away to protect my public image. I wanted the other parents to think of me as kind and caring, and I think I am – a part of me, at least. But the other part, the deeper part, believed that if they just parented as I did, their children would be as perfect as mine. If they made a point of having family meals, made church a part of their life, knew their children's friends, were involved in their kids' activities, gave them enough stuff (but not too much), made their kids get jobs to learn responsibility… All that might even look like a formula for success. I certainly trusted it would be. And that was my sin: assuming I did it all right and earned the perfect life, and that anyone with problems was obviously skipping steps somewhere.

I didn't just skip steps, I fell right through them! I lay crumpled and dazed, staring at the world from a completely different vantage point. I struggle to make sense of what I see, of this role reversal. The weight of judgment is upon me--fellow parents' judgment, yes. But even more crushing is my own well-deserved judgment. *What could I have done differently? What should I have done? What does it matter now?* I was trusted with a tiny baby boy, a bundle of personality and possibility, and I have failed him. I am buried in condemnation and pinned down by the knowing looks of my peers.

And what of the child – what of my son? Because he is precariously perched over a precipice of unfathomable depth, is he unworthy of friendship? Are his only friends to be others of ill-repute, leaving the lame to carry the lame? Is he damaged beyond the allowances of polite society due to mental health and drug use? And just how polite is society to expel him at a time when acceptance could pull him back from the edge? Who am I to make such demands? I, who have judged and discouraged so many friendships on behalf of my sons? That question I can answer; I know who I am. I am Guilty.

Bars None **Court Harris**
May 2004 **St. Charles, Illinois**

The bars are so widely spaced that generally I don't even notice them. But I can't take a step without them countering my every move. They surround my bed when I lie down. They follow me to the bathroom, to the refrigerator, to work. Perhaps it is the watchful eyes of my parents, but the bars close more tightly, almost visibly and solidly, at the dinner table. It is then that the cage ensnares me most – there and at the courthouse: once a week to see his eminence and three times a week to pee in a bottle.

I pace back and forth along the barred boundary, the space seeming smaller with each lap. I am like a lion caged at Brookfield Zoo: a once proud and noble king now manacled and mocked by clueless hoards. They call it "educational," bringing "awareness" to the masses. "They" are sadists tenuously displaying their superiority for the sake of their own egos. Like the lion, I turn my back on the gawking crowd and walk through the opening from my indoor cell to my outdoor cell. The bars travel with me.

I am safe from the eyes of my keepers here, temporarily at least. They fear fire and so are repulsed by the smoke from my cigarette. Curling before my eyes in this wind protected corner of my cage, these burning leaves satisfy the desire of my lungs, but leave the soul that much emptier – longing for a bowl of transporting smoke to fill my being.

The whispers of the Ones call to me, pleading for me to escape this anti-world to the security of their bright and superior reality. Their voices rise and fall, bending and blending. Their dance is both verbal and visual, with luminosity that shows this world for what is it – or rather, what it isn't. The smoke filling my lungs isn't real. The bars don't exist. The love that my parents profess is just a projection of who they purport to be. They are not my creators. I am not of this world, or even in it.

The only "real" thing here is the gravity that drags me back with each attempted escape. Who controls the force that drags my soul from its true longing? Whoever it is, they are not all powerful, and certainly not as powerful as the Ones. After all, the Ones devised an organic porthole that quite literally grows like a weed, *is* a weed, my salvation. The desperation of this anti-world is written on the face of Judge Doyle and his lackey, Randy. They test, they measure, they squash my freedoms. Their rule by intimidation cannot continue – will not continue.

Though it has been sometime since I attained the real world, the whispers of the Ones are still distinct and now more directive. *Great success is found in great sacrifice.* My cigarette smoke dances momentarily on the breeze, forming letters like those of a skywriter: *no bars* and then *weed.* Even as the words drift upward, returning to their creators, I hear their promise, their plea, their longing for me to prove myself. The Ones hold the true power in the real world, and they can pull the strings in this anti-world.

I have been robbed by fear – fear of this un-real world that my senses have been fooled into seeing and touching. My imprisoning bars were built by the non-existent. I have been a fool to conform to rules more fleeting than the smoke exhaled from my lungs after the final drag on my cigarette.

Tomorrow, the Ones and I will walk together into Judge Doyle's throne room. We will expose his puppet power for what it is. The Ones, with a nonchalant flick of their wrists, will cause Judge Doyle to wink at my "infraction," if, indeed, he notices at all.

Great reward – to soar above and reach the real again. I grab my keys, heading for my car in search of salvation. I have lived by the rules according to Doyle for too long. The world of possibilities is calling to me so clearly. Everything is finally falling into place.

Long Distance Phone Call Mother's Day 2004

Lory Harris
St. Charles, Illinois

With numbers large enough to be read by the legally blind, my alarm clock mocked me. "12:36!" it shouted. When it displays that number twice more, I mused, this day will mercifully be over. The start of a VERY long day. Happy Mother's Day to me.

I didn't always dread Mother's Day. For long stretches of time I looked forward to it. I remember as a kid taking all my hard-earned money – all coins since paper money represented an unattainable fortune – and walking down to the local five-and-dime store. In a room past the racks of candy were shelves of the most beautiful items imaginable. I studied them endlessly, wanting to get just the right gift. The winner was a handkerchief, edged in pink. In the center were the big letter "H" and a picture of a hen. "H" had absolutely no bearing on my family name at that time. I just had a certain affinity for that letter because it looked like a ladder, making it easy to identify. I couldn't wait to see my mom's reaction when I gave her the treasure. Funny, though, I don't remember her response at all. What I remember is years later, when my mother gave that cloth back to me to use as a rag for cleaning my flute. By then, I was old enough to know that a hanky with a hen on it was not the prize it first seemed, but I was not quite of an age to avoid disappointment when it came back into my possession so unceremoniously. Still, my earliest Mother's Day memory brought a smile to my face as the clock ticked over to 12:40.

Then there was my first Mother's Day as a mom. A squirmy seven-month-old, Colin had huge brown eyes and the beginning of dark curly locks. I'm sure I received the requisite first Mother's Day cards and a gift to commemorate the occasion. But what I remember is both the pride in my son and the weight of responsibility. I held him closely, showering him with kisses, even as his brother-to-be kicked out a Morse code-like message in my again expanding belly. Being a mom was the greatest thing I had ever experienced. Every day was a gift as far as I was concerned, though some of the nights were long indeed.

In years to follow, there were painted handprints pressed on various items and lumps of clay decorated in rainbows of love, all of which still live tucked away in the basement. There were IOUs for picking up toys and making beds and doing the dishes, and homemade cards signed with professions of unending love. One year, three little boys tip-toed into our bedroom carrying a cookie sheet masquerading as a breakfast tray. That afternoon, I did laundry – all the bedding – and found it well worth every errant drop of juice and soggy Cheerio.

This year, though, Mother's Day has been destined for disappointment for quite some time. It will be my first Mother's Day without laying eyes and kisses on each of my offspring. Corey is still in California, a beautiful bouquet of flowers sent as a substitute for his presence. There will also be a phone call, I'm sure – I'm counting on it.

A call from Colin could at least partially rescue the day, but he is currently deployed in Haiti to counter the Aristide uprising. Despite his best efforts, a call from him could be a pipedream. Temporary assignment in temporary shelter means long lines at a short bank of phones – assuming his unit is not otherwise engaged in the business at hand. The Marines do not recognize Mother's Day as an official holiday. It was bound to happen sooner or later – babies blue become boys become men. I understand that. I believe I could have gracefully tipped my hat to the relentless march of time if it hadn't been for Thursday.

We were just settling into the first few months of drug court. Initially, I just couldn't help but confirm with Court that he made his thrice weekly drug tests. I was even starting to trust the process and limit my inquiry to a couple times a week rather than daily. Every Thursday, Court would go over to the courthouse to wait in a queue for his meeting with Judge Doyle.

To say that drug court had brought our life back to the normal we longed for would probably be an overstatement. It was more like the meds after Court's initial hospital stay: they brought us back from the brink of the cliff, but not much further. Still, it was early in the process, and Ken and I were willing to give it time, not that our willingness was really a factor since we had abdicated that responsibility to the judicial system. The die had been cast and there was no grabbing it back. All three of us, Court included, understood the process; it had been memorized by heart and taken to heart, or so I thought until I saw the Caller ID that evening.

"KANE CO CORR" read the display in big block letters across the screen. *Maybe Court is just calling from the courthouse since use of cell phones is prohibited there,* I reasoned. But the courthouse is called the Kane County Judicial Center. Being across town from the correctional institute, the courthouse and the jail presumably have different phone numbers. Sure, Court was later than usual for dinner, but the judge frequently gets backed up on Thursdays, so it was no cause for concern. The whole line of reasoning revealed a hallmark of being me: the heart doesn't believe the head when it states the obvious. I picked up the phone with a tenuous "Hello?" hoping to hear Court's greeting in return. Instead, a mechanical voice informed me that I had a collect call from an inmate at the Kane County Correctional Institution. Would I like to accept exorbitant charges for a call initiated less than five miles away from a person I may or may not want to acknowledge? It's hard to know exactly what to do when your heart, now located in your toes, is directing your head. Apparently, I managed to press the correct number on the phone since after some clicking sounds I was rewarded with Court's voice.

"Hi, Mom. I'm sorry. I was with some friends last night who were smoking pot in the car. I guess I got enough of it in my system and blew the drop. The judge just wasn't listening when I tried to explain. I'm in jail at least until next week when I see the judge. Would you go pick up my car from the courthouse parking lot?" I'm sure he said more in that three minute/ten-dollar phone call. I'm sure I said something, too. But the heart only remembers so much of what the ears hear – and my heart pretty much stopped listening after "jail." The thought of my son behind bars conjures images of the horrors portrayed by Hollywood. *Dear God, protect my son!*

I've cried endless hours over the last few days, and I've made all the excuses when the topic couldn't be sidestepped. But oddly enough, I've also slept well the past couple of nights. I know where he is. I know he is safe. I know there will not be a police car in my driveway the rest of the week. And best of all, I know he is sober and taking the meds I dropped off at the jail on Friday.

As 12:36 made its second appearance of the day, I found myself fidgeting and unable to concentrate on anything. It was too early to leave for our two o'clock appointment to see Court, though we dare not be late. Appointments are only 15 minutes long and this one represented the only face time I have with any of my children on this hollow, hallowed day. As much as I dreaded the prospect, I longed for it, too.

The next hour found us waiting in the crowded lobby of the Kane County Correctional Institute. I was not the only mother celebrating "her day" in this concrete habitat. The benches were filled with women and baby carriers and the coats of women who were chasing rambunctious toddlers. I was too old, too white and too well dressed to be there. And, yet, I was exactly like every other woman there: I love someone who is dressed in orange, who would not be giving me flowers or dinner out or even a peck on the cheek.

In honor of the day and thanks to KANE CO CORR, 2:00 was postponed by 25 minutes. I watched the toddlers eating their snacks while kicking the bench. I wished I was two again: bored, yes, but oblivious, too. The moms of the little ones were clearly wishing for an appropriate celebration of their status that did not include this venue. So was I. When names were finally called again, the little one-sided families disappeared into designated cubicles to celebrate Mother's Day.

When our name was called, Ken and I were shown to our own little four-foot-by-four-foot party room furnished with two institutional-grey-colored chairs. The upper half of the center wall allowed a view into the other side of the upside-down world. Looking through the chicken-wire-pattern encased in glass, I saw an identical space, minus one chair. The matching phones on either side of the walls, both without keypads, had performed their duty for the last century, or so it seemed.

The door in the other half of the room opened, breaking up the drab grey with a splash of brilliant cautionary orange. Shirt, pants, socks and slippers, all matching and ill-fitting, stepped the pace and a half to the solitary chair and reached for the phone. I, too, grabbed for the receiver, ignoring the fleeting question of how many toddlers have spoken into this handset today and what gifts they may have left there. The cord was short, making it necessary to hug the corresponding wall to speak into it. Ken and I knocked our heads together in an awkward effort to share the single communication link.

"How are you?" It might have sounded like a casual greeting, but it wasn't. It carried the weight of the world with it, or the weight of my heart at least. It meant: are you safe? Are you sane? Are you afraid? Are movie portrayals of jail accurate? His answer left as much to conjecture as the question had, "I'm okay."

"Court, wish your mom a happy Mother's Day," insisted my phone-mate.

I think I saw was a flash of guilt in his green eyes just before he lowered them from view. "I'm sorry. I forgot today is Mother's Day. I love you, Mom, and I'm really sorry I'm here and you have to see me like this. It will never happen again." When he looked up again, his eyes glistened with threatening tears. It is all the Mother's Day gift I will get from him, and it is enough.

We moved on to small talk about his brothers, about the weather, about his retrieved car, about work. My partner's head eventually abandoned his side of the handset, leaving me more room to hug the wall and continue the conversation, still devoid of meaningful content. There would be a time for pointed questions and serious discussion. But it would wait until Thursday and the absence of orange behind chicken wire glass.

Fifteen minutes ended appropriately, the small talk having reduced to the point of miniscule. I watched as the other side of the room faded back to the grey from which it came. It was my time for glistening eyes and my best attempt at keeping them unspilled. Happy Mother's Day to me.

Margarita Friday — Merry Luehr
June 2004 — St. Charles, Illinois

I'm not sure exactly when the tradition started – it has been a few years, but it is a sacred one, indeed. My mom's condo association has an underused pool that I would frequent on occasion. I generally had the place to myself, especially on a weekday afternoon. I guess I must have asked Lory if she wanted to join me on a random Friday a few years ago. Neither my bestie nor I are all that anxious to be on the receiving end of swimsuit scrutiny. But we trust each other implicitly, so it wasn't such a big step. Every Friday in the summer we don our suits and talk or not, eat or not, share airspace and friendship – absolutely! Mind you, when we go "swimming," no one swims. Well, maybe an unannounced, random "guest" in our pool, but as I said, that's rare.

Two years ago, we found the perfect raft – a double with attached inflatable pillows at opposite ends. It made it easy to talk and float in comfort – and admire each other's pedicure. Last year's addition to the weekly tradition gave it the official name, Margarita Friday. We bring two small thermoses, one for ice and one for margaritas, two metal cups for a nod to the '60s, and bendy straws. The bendy straws keep us from straining our necks when taking a sip. It sounds decadent or alcoholic. The truth is even if one person drank *all* the margaritas, she would be hard pressed to get drunk. It's just the taste of friendship in the summer: the perfect tradition with my bestie.

Some topics are always on our discussion table: husbands, children, and meanderings about God. But the hot topic for the day may also be an article in *People* magazine or something in the news or a story from 'when I was a kid.' Nothing is taboo, out-of-bounds, or too embarrassing; we are, after all, floating around together being seen in swimsuits.

Last year's mainstay conversation was Court and the resulting periphery. Hmmm, maybe that's why we added the margaritas. That topic continued through the winter and finds itself on the raft with us again this year. Lory thought it would be over by now, that we would be referring to it in past tense. I have had a little more experience with mental illness, and frankly, with drugs, too. As much as I hoped her expectation was correct, I was pretty sure there would be a longevity factor. Now if we just knew what that factor was, it might make the intervening time more bearable.

When we met at the pool today, we were destined for more Court talk--actually, Court *and* court. My job, I knew, would be ears and shoulder. After Court's visit with the judge yesterday, the judge had asked Lory to take Court to the emergency room for a psych evaluation. They didn't keep him, which might be a good thing. Some things seem clearly 'bad,' but the 'good' side often seems a bit blurrier. In my experience with God's ways, even what we define as 'bad' is not that clear cut. But it is so all-consuming that the 'good' in it is hard to see up close. Perspective needs time before the true side can be determined.

"His drop levels were rising as compared to previous drug tests, in contrast to the way the body should be eliminating the remnants of pot. He told the judge it was because he was in a car with his friends who were smoking. We've heard that before. But he also claims to be drinking bleach, so he can develop an immunity to it in case someone tries to poison him. That's when the judge called me. Court and I sat there in the emergency room for hours. He was obviously not dying, placing us low on their priority scale. We had so much to talk about and absolutely nothing to say. I started out concerned and ended up just plain angry by the end. I was kind of hoping they would put him in the psych unit, so I could go home and just forget about it for a while."

On the surface, it sounds like Lory and I should be a bit horrified here, and maybe we should. But the truth is that if Court was really interested in suicide, he sure wasn't good at it. And for a smart kid, he could certainly be dumb! It's not the first ER trip for ingesting obviously toxic liquids. About a year ago, Ken and Lory were out of town when Court called to say that he had been drinking Raid bug spray. Apparently, he was spraying it into the cap and then drinking it. I ended up with ER duty that day. Again, it was obviously not a life-threatening situation. I did have to suppress a smile, though, when he complained that every time he burped, it tasted like Raid. Like I said, smart kid…

"After just sitting in the hospital for a couple of hours, it occurred to me that it was all a big lie to keep from going to jail again. He probably didn't even have any bleach, so I called Ken to have him check. There was an almost full bottle of bleach in Court's car, though that doesn't prove anything." It's kind of unusual to hear Lory talk like that. She usually defends Court. Sometimes I try to subtly point out the errors in her thinking. But I'm a mom, too, and sometimes a mom's heart must come to conclusions on its own. I guess her heart was doing just that.

Today was clear--warm, but not so hot that we might be tempted to get into the water. It was a perfect Margarita Friday. It seemed that every topic that was brought up by either of us always segued back to Court. I would say something about my daughter and Lory would comment on how Court's brothers felt about him. She would talk about work and I would ask if Court found a job yet. Even a *People* magazine article would end up in a discussion of drugs and guess who. After a while, we lapsed into a comfortable silence while we each mulled over the current events.

Well, that's what I was doing when I realized that I was fighting back tears. When I looked over at Lory, it was apparent that if she was engaged in the same battle, she was losing. A steady trickle ran from the corners of her eyes, her sunglasses doing nothing to stop the flow down the side of her face, dampening her hair. While maintaining our wordless communication, I grabbed her hand and gave it a squeeze. Her shoulders relaxed and sagged a little, and she gave a quick, sad smile – a thank you, of sorts. I, too, surrendered to the tears, thankful on one more level for the general underuse of this pool.

There are a lot of ways to measure friendship. Sometimes Lory and I measure it in salt – around the edge of a margarita glass, in sweat and in shared tears. Today was, indeed, a salty day.

On Phones that Ring
June 2004

Gordon Packard
Father of Lory Harris
Grinnell, Iowa

Having been a pastor for over 35 years, I've had a ring side seat to much joy and heartbreak. There have been hundreds of baby baptisms, maybe thousands. Splashing water on tiny peach-fuzz-sprouting heads as parents pledge to honor God in and through their child's life is a true gift of the calling. Presiding over the funeral of a now waxen-faced infant returning too soon to her Maker, is sorrow exceeded only by that of her family's. At other times, there is a painful kind of joy at the death of a parishioner, whose life well lived now receives higher reward. There are hospital beds and graduation parties, professions of faith and tirades of God-focused anger. There is a sad inverse symmetry between marriage counseling and divorce recovery. My phone may ring day or night. The daytime calls are not necessarily trustworthy, though the nighttime ones always are: a phone ringing in the dark is always a bad thing. A pastor must keep the balance on both sides of the scale lest he succumb to his own depression, or worse, irrelevant Pollyannaism with those he is charged to shepherd.

That balancing act is in addition to the one that we all manage: our own lives and families, hopes, dreams and disappointments. In an odd juxtaposition, as I minister, I manage it largely without a pastor of my own to share the burden. In the United Methodist Church, the pastor of pastors is the District Superintendent, who is also my immediate supervisor – so not exactly at arm's length.

Earlier in our life together, my wife and I held each other and prayed when our youngest son was born with a lung defect that threatened to take his life. And we praised God when he returned to us whole after a thirty-minute visit to the other side. Years later, I held my daughter Ginger as she mourned the death of her daughter, born too early even to draw her first breath. God has an almost capricious logic, or more accurately, I suppose, a higher plan that eludes the grasp of mere mortals. Being a pastor does not absolve me of the "whys" of life that never seem to receive a response. I, too, struggle and must convince myself to be satisfied with faith in the One who is in control.

Illnesses, death and divorce have touched our family, as have great joys: graduations, marriages, the births of our five children and eleven grandchildren. It has been a good life, a real life, a less-than-hoped-for yet more-than-deserved life. Next month we will all gather for a celebration of family: the fiftieth anniversary of the "I do's" spoken by my wife, Karen, and I. Well, the actual day is tomorrow, but the family gathering will be over the 4th of July weekend. Apart from Colin, whose Haitian deployment end-date is still ill-defined, all our children, their spouses and the grandchildren will be here. Just the anticipation of this joyful gathering makes any "whys" irrelevant, at least for the moment.

When the phone rang, it was odd to see Ken and Lory's number on Caller ID. The timing today is a bit random especially considering the upcoming occasions for conversation: our anniversary and Father's Day this Sunday. The randomness of the call from any of our other children would have been only a pleasant bonus, but between Colin's deployment and Court's, um-m, life, there is a bit of angst despite the daytime hour.

We exchanged the standard greetings: How are you? How's Mom? How's the weather? But there is a perfunctory clip in Lory's voice that heightens my sense of dread. I wish I had been wrong.

"It looks like Colin's unit will be state-side in time for him to come for the anniversary party, though he doesn't know yet if he will have the time off." The sad edge to her voice screams 'worse news to come.' She doesn't keep me in suspense for long.

"Court failed another drop. He is in jail for at least a month now. I guess our Father's Day will be a repeat of Mother's Day." I couldn't tell if she had bucked herself up for this conversation, was crying silently on her end of the connection, or had grown completely numb to the perpetual state of drama. My overwhelming parental desire to kiss-it-and-make-it-all-better was thwarted by distance, not that I think it would have worked at any rate. It's just one of those fairy tales that we all like to hang onto.

"I could ask the judge to release Court for the anniversary party. He might consider it. But I don't want to send Court the wrong message. He needs to feel the full consequences of his actions. Of course, Ken, Corey and I will still be there." Maybe she is settling into this new life she finds herself mired in, after all.

My heart was heavy as I offered my confirmation of her assessment. "No, he needs to stay where he is. Don't petition to have him released for that weekend." I am silently surprised by my disappointment now taking flight. Our children live far flung: one each in Iowa, Missouri, Illinois, New York and Texas. The kids are quick to tell me it's my fault that they were not afraid to move away. After all, my job caused the family to be uprooted every three or four years. They are used to packing up and pulling up stakes. Thus, rare are the times we can get everyone together at one time. This would have been one of the few, and the first in several years. I think I had convinced myself that Colin would be there, and the circle would be complete for one fine weekend. Now, regardless of Colin's presence, we will still be short of the whole.

The conversation wrapped up quickly after another couple of attempts to discuss "safe" topics. No one really had their heart in the periphery anymore. I hope she feels the electronic hug I am sending her, but cradling a phone is not the same as cradling a child. We are both acutely aware of that right now.

My least favorite four-letter word is only three letters long – W-H-Y. It taunts me in the daylight as it, no doubt, will in the darkness tonight. *Why now? Why mental illness? Why will he not take the medication that would restore our fun-loving grandson? Why is there no healing despite fervent prayer?* The interminable, unanswerable question: *Why*? And the closest I can come to an answer is another question: *Why not?*

Eliminating Risk
June 2004

Court Harris
Kane County Correctional Institute
Geneva, Illinois

It's hard to say what woke me. It's not exactly quiet here, but the sounds are so muffled, indistinct, that they just fade into the background. The faint sunlight creeping through the small dingy window in the cell can't compete with the constant florescent glare of the lights over the guard's desk in the center of this Risk cellblock. The concrete shelf that forms my bed is ill-disguised by the thin pad they call a mattress. I've been in jail before. I've been in *this* jail before. But this is inhuman, medieval. I would like to just rollover and go back to sleep, but dressed as I am – or rather, am not – modesty has been detached from reality. A long, quilted tunic is my only item of clothing; it also doubles as my blanket. Suicide watch makes me regret again my lack of previous success in that endeavor.

The last time I told the judge about drinking bleach, I was sentenced to an afternoon of boredom in an emergency room accompanied by Mom. It was well worth the confession, and one of the few times I ever told him the truth. After another moment of truth designed to escape punishment for a bowl of weed, I find myself in jail for a month starting with this psych eval. The shrink, however, won't be back until Monday to start my 24-hour evaluation. Do I really need any more proof that this "reality" isn't real? Only in dreams – only in nightmares - can a 24-hour hold include an entire weekend.

Breakfast arrived, delivered by a fellow inmate who had been promoted to trustee status. Setting the tray on the metal desk, he turned my direction with an odd kind of smile on his face. "Thanks, man," I mumbled as my hands pull down on my designer tunic, making sure it hasn't ridden up and hoping that the Velcro closures at my shoulders will do their job. There are three seating choices – four if you count the floor, which I don't. There is the bed with its concrete box spring and non-existent mattress, the toilet, and a metal stool. All are in close proximity to each other, all are clearly visible to the ever-present guard, and none offer any comfort. Not wanting any negative marks on the eval, I choose the stool. The contents of the tray will hardly have to change form to pass through my system for deposit in one of my other seating choices, if you know what I mean. I spend some time contemplating just how hungry I am before eating a couple of bites. Turns out I'm not that hungry after all.

I shuffle back to "bed" hoping to make the hours disappear. When I look at the central clock several hours later, I see the big hand has only made a three-quarter trip around the dial; the small hand is virtually refusing to budge at all. I'm hoping it is in the same state of disrepair as the rest of this bunker. The guard, however, seems to revere the time piece - not a good sign. If I wasn't crazy before, I will be by the time the shrink comes visiting on Monday.

Pacing was the next order of the day. Three walls are concrete, the fourth being glass – well, clear-ish in a grubby-kind-of-scratched-up way. When I dare to get my head up close enough to the "glass," I can glimpse parts of three more cells like this one, though it's impossible to say from this angle if they are inhabited or not. I make several more laps around my cell. The clock laughs at me, moving just enough to taunt me, but not enough to register meaningful time.

I've been here less than 24 hours, but I have come to a profound decision: I will not EVER return. The Ones don't seem to be doing their part to keep me out of jail. Maybe I just don't have as firm a command of their language as I thought. Or maybe this is a test to prove I can rise to their level. There are two options: quit the weed or commit suicide as they have directed and join them in their realm.

It's a little odd that I couldn't make breakfast go down this morning since I will ingest almost anything in a suicide attempt: bleach, Raid, a fist full of pills. I can swallow anything. Then I can just sleep and wake up with the Ones. But when I contemplate a method more swift and sure - a knife to the throat, a brick wall with the car – I just can't. There would be no turning back from that, no time to change my mind. Maybe this world is real? What if my parents really do love me? What if the Sunday morning talk of Hell has merit? What if I fail the test of the Ones and am banished? Banished to where – or what? On the other hand, I can't just abandon the Ones and their organic porthole that brings me into their realm. Glancing at the dreaded clock again, I am pleased to accept the gift of the Ones. The clock has miraculously jumped ahead three hours, making up for stalled time.

My thoughts are interrupted by muffled yelling and pounding from the next cell. Standing in just the right location and pressing my head against the glass wall, I see the source of the sound. At least one other cell houses another man fighting both boredom and insanity. A middle-aged black man is lying on the floor, his feet pounding the cell door to test the strength of the imprisoning glass, announcing each test with a shout. His efforts, of course, arouse the attention of others, as well. Four guards arrive for a closer inspection, one pushing a wheelchair. The banging ends long before the yelling does. The shouts, in fact, continue for some time after the foursome walks back across the front of my cell, sans wheelchair, but with satisfied looks on their faces.

A delayed lunch arrives, compliments of the same trustee, along with a little something extra: a love note. *"Look me up when you get out of here. I'm sure we will be the best of friends. Razor"* I am NEVER coming back here again, I remind myself once more. There must be a third option, and, in fact, a possibility occurs to me. The implement of my imprisonment, the one who is quite literally narc-ing on me, is a drug test manufactured by Alby or Albia or something like that. What if the Ones are leading me to themselves along another avenue that eludes Judge Doyle's detection? A little research on the internet, and I should be able to determine which drugs my urine will reveal, and more importantly, which it won't. It may be a month before I can put my plan into effect, but it is also the sanity saver that will bring me through this incarceration.

Two more hours have passed in fairly quick succession when a guard arrives, announcing my opportunity for a shower. As I am led from my cell, I glance to my right to view my now noiseless neighbor. He is slack-jawed, resting in his newly installed "easy" chair, though there really isn't anything easy about it. The wheelchair, aided by wide canvas straps, holds him in an embrace he cannot reject. His sleep, whether from exhaustion or chemical bidding, has restored order to this risk/suicide block.

As the water washes over me under the watchful guard's eyes, I promise myself again: I am NEVER coming back here.

Oranges, Burritos and a Handshake

Rick Rogers
July 2004
Kane County Correctional Institution
Geneva, Illinois

It has been a few years since I looked forward to summer. I'm nineteen and I hate summer vacation. I'm not necessarily all that fond of the school year, but it is way better than summer break. I wear orange all summer, every summer. I hate orange, too. I was 16 when my life changed forever. I was 17 when summers changed. There was the briefest sense of relief before the start of that summer when I found out the dress code would not be for full years at a time. Only summers – what a relief! That feeling has long since melted into dread and drudgery.

Sixteen. I remember sixteen. When I think about it, which I do constantly, I almost forget the thrill of scoring a soccer goal, celebrating with my buddies, full of the exuberance and testosterone of adolescence. The feeling of being a success, a hero, a friend, one of the guys, has been all but eradicated from my memory. There were girls, too, of course, official and unofficial cheerleaders, especially in the soccer focused town where I live. The girls are still there, I guess, nine months of the year. But what steady girlfriend wants summers off? Summer, or the lack of it, changes everything.

Ah, Kane County Correctional, my subterranean-bomb-shelter home away from home. There must have been a sale on concrete and a public official in the excavation business when this place was built. Once inside, the only way I can tell it is summer is from snippets of conversations between the guards complaining about the heat. The few windows are too high and dingy to allow an accurate view of the world. My mom comes to visit me wearing a sleeveless shirt and shorts. I shuffle into the visitation booth wearing orange scrubs over long underwear, with color-coordinated slippers and two pair of socks. Cold is the color of my day, every day, unless the air conditioning breaks. Then, with caged tempers flaring, the day turns to a macho-tinted shade of blood red. This jail is so overcrowded that inmates whose next court date is weeks away are bussed out to jails in other counties for warehousing. I've avoided that so far this year. Some of the other facilities are nicer, which is an odd adjective to use for a jail, but true. The problem is that it might be an hour or more away, which severely cuts down on visitors – one of my few bright spots in a dreary summer. That and it forces you to re-establish your identity among your compatriots.

I'm not afraid to introduce myself to my fellow inmates. The most conventional way would be with a handshake; it's also the rarest. It is reserved for those you met previously in sunnier locations, or maybe someone you lost track of from last year's subterranean get away. We don't, after all, exchange addresses or Christmas cards. You might also introduce yourself over a game of chess or cards. Those are one of the few times a cross-cultural meeting might not involve your hands, and I don't mean the illusive handshake. This place is more segregated than the Deep South during slavery. There are the Vice Lords (blacks), the Gangster Disciples (Mexicans), and the minority (whites). We cluster appropriately.

The mornings find us all moved to the common area, where space is segregated by color. The TV channel is chosen by majority insistence or by the guards when the din is too indiscernible. Our uniformed keepers control the dials. With any luck, you can score two chairs and fashion them into a bed of sorts to pass the hours. Of course, it's the same kind of luck that makes your lottery ticket the power ball winner.

I'm getting good at spades, though chess will never be my game. Again, it passes the time, and there is some satisfaction in beating a couple of Vice Lords or Gangster Disciples in a game. It is a far less painful beating than others I have been involved in, win or lose. The more serious games are complete with a wager, mostly for bread crusts, oranges or sugar packets. Newbies are always invited to play "serious" games. The spoils are stored in a water bottle, near a source of heat, and used to make hooch. The only heat source option is one of the high dingy windows, which must then be plausibly shaded to protect the water bottles from the guard's eyes. Personally, I take a pass on that rock gut.

There are occasions when the natural order of the cell is tested, or maybe more accurately, flaunted. Earlier this summer, a skinny little black punk decided to talk smack in my direction as he walked past. The decision to introduce myself took some thought. First, skinny doesn't mean weak. Some of those wiry guys can take you down without breaking a sweat. And then you must judge the location of the guards and the relative distance to the one location on the block that isn't in their sight line, the bathroom nook. There were approximately ten seconds to make the decision to meet the kid or not. I put my hand out to him after only three seconds, wanting to keep the element of surprise on my side. Let's just say we didn't shake hands; it was more of a "fist bump." It earned both of us two days in the risk cells. But he looked a whole lot worse when we returned to the block than I did. Certainly, no handshakes were offered, and no further smack talk, either.

As my summer reality goes, though, I would rate this one higher than usual at a negative two, the scale running from negative ten to zero. Basically, it's true that misery loves company, and it was a surprise to greet a newbie with a handshake. Court and I didn't know each other well on the outside. He's a year older than me, and in high school, a year can be a huge chasm. We also went to cross town high schools – natural rivals. But we both played soccer, so our paths had crossed many times at soccer camps and even on the field of battle. On the outside, we would be friendly competitors. Here we are just friends in orange.

He has been here for almost a month thanks to the drug court, weed being his drug of choice. I've tried it, of course, but prefer the easier to procure beer, or maybe its big brothers of a stronger variety. Either way, who am I to judge? We talk about soccer, and especially soccer coaches. Now that is a great topic of conversation to pass the time! We have played the sport from our earliest memory. Our fathers and earliest coaches spent their youth playing baseball or basketball; they learned soccer from a book. It is safe to say that if the coach didn't have a foreign accent, his players know more about soccer than he does. We talk about various teammates and whether or not they should have been starters. We replay our rivaled games, play by play, still disagreeing on various calls by the ref.

After losing a few obligatory oranges and sugar packets to the other side, Court and I settle into making jailhouse burritos. First, you save the plastic bag from your sandwich at lunch. They don't sell those things through the commissary. But that is where you get Fritos or Doritos and beef jerky. You smash up the chips and break up the jerky, putting them in the plastic bag with a bit of the hottest water available. The concoction is rolled up in the baggy and put under your mattress to keep its form and to solidify. It probably says something about the quality of the food that we look forward to this delicacy. Sometimes it was hard to wait the required half-hour before burrito time.

Court will be headed to rehab in the next day or two. I guess his mother worked on the judge to get it all set up, and even agreed to pay for it if the drug court wouldn't. Court is anxious, of course, to escape this place. I don't know that he fully realizes that rehab is just a prison without bars, though the beds might be marginally better. Selfishly, I wish he would just stay here. It's likely to do him as much good as rehab, at any rate. If the hooch wasn't so vile, I would drink a toast to his future and to mine, whatever they might hold.

I want to be sixteen again. No, I want to skip sixteen altogether. In my mind, sixteen is all contained in one day – one exhilarating, celebratory, awful, never-ending day. I want to jump from fifteen to seventeen. Would that be enough, or would I just drag my bad luck along with me? And just in case, I sure wouldn't want to jump to eighteen! Imagine if I had been a legal adult at the time of the accident! The rules change on your eighteenth birthday, especially when you mix driving and alcohol. I can't undo the fact that my life changed forever at sixteen. I wish I could change the fact that another life ended that same day. I wish it was September and I could lie to myself and to those around me, pretending that I live a normal life more than just nine months at a time.

So, with my second handshake of the summer, I'll say, "Goodbye, buddy." *Maybe I'll catch you again next year.*

Family Rehab **Dr. Greg Mikels**
July 2004 **Community Hospital Drug Treatment Center**
Arlington Heights, Illinois

It is well documented that the brain does not move from adolescent to adult at midnight on the 18th anniversary of one's birth. This is certainly a case where legislation does not reflect reality. The brain is just not fully developed until around age 25. I believe the years between 15 and 25 are disproportionately hazardous in our society. Adult-like bodies and societal expectations give a decade full of choices and options that these brains are not adequately prepared to process. The false sense of invulnerability, the stuff of legends and heroes, has left many families asking the unanswerable "Why?" while staring at the dash on a headstone that separates too few years.

Compounding the problem is the far too frequent introduction of mind-altering substances to the still-forming brain. From alcohol to pot to harder varieties, they tax and alter that indispensable organ in ways that will never see full recovery. The same can happen to a fully formed brain, of course. But it is the adolescent brain whose development is arrested and often irreparably stunted.

Did you notice you hit on my passion in my life? I could talk forever, trying to educate and awaken society to the epidemic at our doorstep. No, it's not just standing at our door knocking, but an ever present and messy house guest. We owe our youth more than what they have the capacity to demand of themselves. I'm not sure when or how my passion started for the adolescent addict, but I could talk for days on the plight of our sons and daughters that has altered my life, both personally and professionally. I have witnessed honors students becoming drop outs, compliant children turning to menacing monsters, bright futures being snuffed out in a moment of mind-altered frenzy. I have stood at graveside asking my own unanswerable "Why?" *Why could I not save this child? What more could I, should I, have done?* On the other hand, I have attended high school and even college graduations of those who were once labeled lost causes. I have witnessed life regenerating where hopelessness had been the hallmark. I have seen hope, and willed it to those who needed it more than I.

As a society, we want a cure – a pill that heals, medical magic to make the problem disappear. At the heart, I think addiction is just that: self-prescribed medication to cure what ails you. It might be physical pain we try to dull, but more often, especially with our youth, it is emotional pain that has seized the developing brain. The pain is real, to be sure, but in years to come, the same brain will have coping mechanisms to move forward without being consumed. Alcohol and/or drugs become the way to dull the emotional pain with which the brain does not want to cope. Eventually, the chemistry of a brain changes to demand the external anesthesia. Just how much time that change takes may be genetically determined. This is when the self-imposed remedy crosses over to disease. Not all my colleagues agree with me, but I believe that like diabetes or heart disease or AIDS, addiction is a disease. It's a chronic and can be managed, but never cured.

Like other diseases, addiction has cycles of relapse and remission. Some would say that addiction is a matter of the will: only the weak cannot overcome. If that were true, how would you explain high-level, driven and successful executives with secreted addictions?

Frequently, diseases have both hereditary and lifestyle factors. For example, adult-onset diabetes has a strong genetic component, but is also caused by poor life style choices like lack of exercise and an unhealthy diet. Lung cancer, again with a genetic predisposition, can be hastened by the individual's choice to smoke. In neither of these cases would the doctor tell you that you were a bad person to have contracted the disease or that you should just try harder to get rid of it. In both cases, the progression of the disease may be arrested and managed, but not cured. Like diabetes or cancer, the slate is never wiped clean with addiction; there is always a danger of relapse. Another sad commonality: a chronic disease left untreated will lead to death.

Early in my professional career, I worked in traditional substance abuse rehab facilities. It was there that I first saw how inadequate that model is for younger and younger addicts. Let's be honest, the track record of rehab isn't all that impressive. Approximately 30% of addicts go to a rehab facility more than once. I wish that meant that 70% of those attending had recovered. But meaningful statistics are not available, given the wide range of variables in the equation: the drug of choice (DOC), the age at first use, the length of time before first help was sought, friend and family support or lack thereof, family history of addiction. It's a 3D equation that defies traditional mathematical analysis. I guess it always is when it involves human decisions and desires. We are not as rational as we would like to believe.

The problem with rehab facilities is that they lock up a group of people with one over-arching commonality: life-altering addiction. The patients compare notes. Not all the gathered have come voluntarily, or at least not with recovery on their minds. Some come to placate family or to avoid jail time. Especially in the winter months, many come for food and a warm place to sleep out of the elements. There is certainly an exchange of ideas and information happening, but not all of it is centered on recovery. Worse yet is when the self-proclaimed, invincible, adolescent brain absorbs the skewed boasting of older addicts. Too often youth interprets survival stories as exciting and challenging – possible and even desirable.

This is where the program here at Community Hospital is different. Our rehab is only open to those 20 and under. We provide tutoring for students while in attendance, allowing them to continue with their school work. There are family programs five times a week that parents must commit to attending before their child will be accepted into the program. It is imperative that the whole family recovers for their son or daughter to have the best shot at their own recovery.

I hate to say it, but sometimes the parents are the biggest stumbling block to their child's recovery. They want their teen to quit using, but they, themselves, drink daily in front of them. Mom and Dad rationalize their behavior because they need to relax, and, after all, they aren't addicts themselves. Children never respond well to double standards. Sometimes the problem goes so much deeper, even to sabotage. We have a new policy that forbids food from being brought in after some brownies laced with pot were delivered to the unit.

About a month ago, a mother called asking about our program. Her son, Court, is twenty, which is the very top of our allowable age limit. He is in a drug court program, which would theoretically pay for the cost of a rehab program. However, due to the nature of our program, it is approximately ten times more expensive than the court would agree to pay. When Court's family's private health insurance denied the pre-admission benefit request, the family agreed to pay everything the court did not cover, half on admission and half on release. It sounded like a family who was really focused on their child's recovery.

Court came into our program fresh out of 30 days in jail and, presumably, 30 days into sobriety – albeit forced sobriety, but chemically dry, at least. He is a bright and outgoing kid, his biggest complaint being that he is of age but not allowed to smoke cigarettes on our campus. I won't get into how I feel about that addiction, except to say that an addiction is an addiction is an addiction. And each one generally feeds another.

The parents, especially the mother, dutifully attend the family programs. I was hopeful for all of them, but today, a classic parental blunder occurred. During the two hours of visitation, Court and the mother left our campus in her car. Maybe it was to allow Court to smoke a few cigarettes. He didn't ingest anything harder; his drug test on return was negative. Court said he just hadn't driven a car in almost two months and wanted to feel the freedom of the road. Most likely, his mother wanted to earn some points with her son and didn't see the harm since she would supervise the jaunt. But it did undermine our authority here. It showed that she is willing to bend the rules for her child. She took on the favored role while we continued to play the bad guys. She blurred the lines between yes and no, acceptable and unacceptable.

If I know one thing about an addict's brain, I know that it revels in blurry distinctions. The fertile soil of ambiguity is ripe with possibility and potential excuses. Recovery is a family project. All too frequently, relapse is as well. Given Court's age, we won't see him in our program again. I hope the family survives long enough to be part of the 30% that gets a rehab refresher course.

Tropical Holiday — Ken Harris

Christmas 2004 — St. Thomas, U.S. Virgin Islands

Even without opening my eyes, I can feel how foreign this holiday will be. A light sheet covers me, all other blankets and covers having made their way to the floor last night. The hum of the fan overhead is doing its job circulating the humid air throughout the room. And the crash of the ocean waves against the cliffs brings a satisfied smile to my face. This will be a Christmas unlike any other, and mercifully, nothing like the past two. I rollover to greet my wife with a Christmas kiss and find her observing the unending motion of the ceiling fan. "Merry Christmas," we both say as we roll into each other's arms, leaving two-thirds of the king-sized bed unoccupied.

Corey and Court are at the other end of this rental. They, too, can hear the beating of the Caribbean waves--if they are awake, that is. But we won't celebrate the holiday until Colin's military leave allows his arrival tomorrow, meaning the brothers aren't likely to glimpse the sun until it is perched well overhead.

There is no Christmas tree this year, though Lory brought some non-breakable ornaments from home to hang from the potted palm tree in our rented living room. We also purchased an ornament, painted with a beach scene and offering seasonal greetings from St. Thomas. Next year it will have more traditional branches to decorate.

Two Christmases ago, Lory and I tenderly convinced each other that things would be okay. Sometime between then and the next December, the tenderness turned contentious. The only thing we agreed on was that we agreed on nothing. Well, we agreed on nothing related to Court, and he filled our world allowing room for little else. I wanted him to earn his own way; she "loaned" him money. She forgave his blatantly disrespectful attitude while I stewed in it. I demanded he take his meds; she cajoled. Our talk is still guarded and even awkward at times, but the last six months have brought more agreements, or at least less disagreements.

It seems that all Court needed was drug court and 60 days of forced sobriety to rejoin the world. The conflict we have engaged in since his release from jail/rehab has been centered more on our lack of trust than his actual behavior. Last spring, he slid Lory's car sideways into a curb, folding the front wheel under at a 90-degree angle. Oh, and the time he totaled his own car when he drove into a ditch. Our insurance company loves us. But there has also been his return to school at nearby North Central College, and the Dean's list the first trimester. He has gotten into the debate club and has a job delivering pizzas. If he would just quit smoking cigarettes it would help my allergies. Maybe in 2005…

There will be other changes next year as well--in fact, a big one is coming in just two weeks. Our first daughter will join the family when Colin marries Jen. Colin was home last summer when the two met through a mutual friend. They have been dating long-distance ever since and will tie the knot on January 8th. We would prefer they waited a big longer before the marriage, but we have no room to talk. Lory and I were engaged a week after we met and married less than eight months later. For over a quarter century, we have greeted the morning from a joint venue. If we can weather the last two years, we can do anything, and we shall.

Shortly after the wedding, Colin will ship out to Iraq for another deployment. So, next year won't be stress-free, but by comparison, it will be a vacation – less the rhythm of the ocean. In addition to the smell of tropical flowers and salt air, there is now hope – the first wind we have caught of it in so long. I am breathing deeply with thankfulness. Merry Christmas!

Wedding Celebration — Lory Harris
January 2005 — St. Charles, Illinois

I have never been a late sleeper. Well, at least I haven't been since I became a mother over 24 years ago. I'm sure I didn't give up late mornings easily, but by the time Colin was joined by Corey a mere eleven and a half months later, sleeping-in was a distant memory. Now when I sleep until seven, I feel like I've won the lottery! Even over the past couple of years when middle-of-the-night sleep was scarce, I still got up early. There is a certain peacefulness to a quiet house and a newborn day. It doesn't last long, but it does come around on a regular basis.

Today, the sounds of sleep are all around, as are the bodies engaged in slumber. All the bedroom doors are closed, as is the basement door. For some reason, Colin is sleeping on the floor in the family room. His best man has claimed the couch, leaving me to wonder who is in Colin's room. All the twenty-somethings went out for a drink after the rehearsal dinner last night. Who knows what time they returned, but I'm sure the first digit on the clock was not a one. Last night, for likely the last time ever, all my sons slept under the home roof. There is a touch of bittersweet there, but only a touch. Today is a day of celebration. Today I gain a daughter!

As the morning lingers on, various doors open and pour forth a goodly portion of those who will claim the groom's side of the church this afternoon. My mom, sister and I braid ourselves around other bodies inconveniently parked and waiting for food. My nephews wind their way through the kitchen, their pace faster and their movements less predictable than the rest of us – their bellies steadily filling with each round trip.

Within a few of hours, the rousted and assembled groom's side of the wedding party has devastated the kitchen and eliminated all traces of hot water. They emerge with youthful good looks and humor as they head for the church. My eyes rest on the groom, as does my heart. He is busy reliving stories of the earliest hours of his wedding day with those who witnessed the back-story. "See you at the church, Ma," he calls over his shoulder as the inside joke and jokesters carry their laughter toward their cars. The next time I see the crew, at the church, their laughter is less raucous and more nervous. Whatever their opinions are of the institution of marriage, the groomsmen are all aware of marital gravity. It may not weigh them down, but it does get their attention.

At the back of the church, Ken does his best to pin the corsage on my dress, but in the end, I opt for help from one of the assembled women. Those flowers will be viewed for years in pictures scattered through many houses. Flowers securely and artfully attached, it is Court who escorts me down the aisle to my designated seat in the front. His tux is well fitted to his rebounded frame. That is the image I treasure, rather than those of the past couple of years.

Making my way toward the front of the church, arm in arm with my former wayward child, I see the pastor who officiated at my wedding more than a quarter century earlier. My father stands ready to officiate again at this marriage. A woman is supposed to let her emotions leak out her eyes. But I'm not a crier, at least not for happy occasions, even with all that has gone before. But, for the first time in all the wedding preparation, 'water-proof mascara' enters my mind. It's too late now. There is little time to contemplate my makeup before a line of tux-wearing men file into the sanctuary, led by Colin and including both of his brothers, Court having stealthily joined the procession. As strains of tradition come from the organ, the assembled rise and turn for their first glimpse of the bride. She is beautiful, her shining eyes locked on the one who will escort her on the return trip down the aisle.

The traditional giving of the bride is followed by a Scripture reading from 1 Corinthians 13, an iconic chapter on love. The next order of the service is a musical duet on the hammered dulcimer by our friend (and world champion player) Bill Robinson and his protégée, Court. I have heard the song before, and it is flawless as ever, each note sustaining and blending with those before and after. The dulcimers have been positioned at the front right of the sanctuary, making an easy transition for Court from groomsman to performer. From my position in the front row, I have the perfect view of all three of my sons. They are clean shaven, meticulously dressed, and standing united. Who would have guessed at that possibility this time last year? As I watch and listen, a lump of pure joy and wonder forms in my throat. The last reverberating notes waft through the room just before my mascara would have been put to the test. As much as I don't want black lines running down my face, I wish a few tears would have fallen just so people would know how truly happy I am on this amazing day. They will have to judge me by my smile, I guess. The mascara remains intact. As a friend of mine is fond of saying, the wedding went off with a hitch: Colin and Jen are legally joined.

The reception starts an hour from now with an open bar. Fortunately, Court will not be able to drink since he is two months shy of twenty-one. Alcohol wouldn't stay in the system long enough to be detected at his next drug court drop, since the body eliminates it within several hours. But that, of course, says nothing about what drinking would do to his psyche, which is of greater, though less quantifiable, concern than the drug test. You can tell I have spent some time thinking about this. There are still days when I question Court's sobriety, but there have been no more jail visits, so I am left to assume the best. On this day of all days, I will cast aside the specter of the drug court and Court's history with it.

You always hear how the wedding is the bride's day or maybe the couple's day. But today I learn it is the parents' day, as well. It is a graduation in a way that the end of high school or even college was not. It is a line of demarcation, a passage from parent to peer. My baby boy, my first born, has left. He has pledged himself to a woman of his choosing. My vow is to honor his departure even while including this new family in our family. A new balancing act has begun, and I look forward to marking this passage with a gathering of so many that I hold most dear. God's blessings to you, Mr. & Mrs. Colin Harris. Let's celebrate!

Phones that Ring in the Night — Lory Harris

February 2005 — Hermosa Beach, California

Even though the location is perfect, the room is still overpriced. The bed dominates the space, leaving only a pathway between it and the walls or dresser. The bathroom has all the key components, which make it quite serviceable if not spacious. There is a light layer of sand on the carpet, which is the charm of the hotel and the reason for the price: we are staying on the beach. What more can you ask for in Southern California?

Ken and I are in Hermosa Beach to visit Corey. Staying at his place is not an option since he quite literally lives in a one-car garage. Besides the overhead garage door which doesn't get opened, there are only two other doors in his apartment: one to the exterior and one to the bath area (which is barely serviceable and not large enough to be called a room). Even the space affectionately called a closet is just a hanging rod off to one side. There aren't even doors on the kitchen cabinets, which is only fair since the "kitchen" is just a countertop attached to one of the walls, complete with a microwave, mini fridge and an equally proportioned sink. He isn't on the beach, but only one block away. I'm not sure how he can afford to live here (or why), but he seems happy and it gives us a great location and excuse to sneak away for a long weekend.

It would be nice to stay longer, but when Ken and I are both gone, our business is shut down. There isn't even a breathing body left behind to answer the phone – the answering machine informs clients of our Tuesday return to business as usual. Court is watching the house and the dog in our absence. There is some angst that comes with that arrangement, but things seem to be going well for him at present. We decided to put aside our well-establish and well-reinforced paranoia and take the chance.

After the Friday morning flight, we caught a cab to the hotel and spent time walking along the beach while waiting for Corey to get off work. Wandering through the shops along the Strand, we discovered we are a generation too old for most of their offerings. It was fun to return the next day with Corey and buy some things for him, though. The food has been simply amazing – most of it having been of the picked-fresh or recently-lived-in-water variety. There is no reason to come to the coast and eat beef, pork or chicken. Corey introduced us to fish tacos at a hole-in-the-wall grill by the water. I will never, ever be able to eat Midwestern fish tacos again! We met some of his friends and his dog, Jazz, who now lives with his former roommate, Lisa, also in Hermosa Beach. Lisa's house has many doors, one of which opens almost directly onto Dog Beach. Jazz is living the life!

I never sleep well the first night away from home. Maybe it's just the unfamiliar that keeps me awake: odd noises that fester, an unconforming pillow, ill-tempered temperature controls. Similarly, I never sleep well the night before we leave, either, for fear of forgetting to pack a key item, or worse, oversleeping and missing the flight. The second night away from home is my favorite. After two day's inadequate sleep, increased activity, a big meal and a little wine, I sleep like a rock. Well, I did last night, until the phone rang.

Speaking as someone of the generation who grew up exclusively with landlines, there is something about a cell phone I really like: the way it is always with you. There is also something I really hate: the way it is always with you. At two a.m., I was reminded of the latter.

"Hi, Mom, how's the trip?" It was Court, speaking with that all-too-familiar, uncomfortable edge to his voice.

"What's wrong? Are you ok?" Always the mom.

"Yeah, I just had some really bad dreams. You always said I could call." He had me there. Ken groaned, rolled over and attempted to go back to sleep. In our luxurious accommodations and dressed as I am, the bathroom was the farthest I could go to assist with his effort. It wasn't far enough; there were three wide awake Harrises now.

Court went on to explain his dream in detail, which as always, defied human understanding or even vocabulary. I listened for quite some time, interjecting words that I hoped would be comforting, but it all just seemed so irrational. Of course, dreams are always that way, but most of us wake up with hearts racing and tell ourselves the obvious: 'It's just a dream.'

"Court, are you using?"

The silence on the other end spoke as loudly as the words that followed. "Yes. A friend gave me some magic mushrooms and I thought I would try them. I'll never do that again."

Our conversation continued awhile longer and concluded with me praying with Court before we hung up. Lying in the dark, my heart felt as hollow as that prayer had sounded in my ears. *Are we back to square one again? Will he be headed to jail next week?* Somewhere, someone was sleeping, but it wasn't me. I doubted it was Ken, either, but there is an unwritten marital code that required the stifling of conversation when the other is feigning sleep. I respected the code. At some point, exhaustion must have overtaken worry; I don't remember falling asleep.

The sun is now bright and the ocean calm. Looking out the window at the beauty of the day, it is impossible to think there is no God. Remembering the conversation of a few scant hours ago, I wonder where He is – certainly not in Illinois.

My phone rings again as we get ready to head to breakfast. It is Court apologizing for the early morning wake up call. "I'm sorry to worry you. I'm fine, really! Please don't call the drug court. I'll take care of it, and it really was just a one-time thing. Believe me; I have no interest in ever using 'shrooms again after last night!"

Ken and I walk along the beach, taking the long route to breakfast. It seems likely to us that we will be visiting Court in jail again soon, a prospect that brings many dark emotions to a head: anger, frustration, disappointment, resignation. In the end, we make the conscious decision to trust the system and let the chips fall where they may. Neither of us is familiar with mushrooms or how long they remain in one's system. If it is a one-time occurrence, maybe he will get away with it. But if it is a pattern of use, he will eventually have a dirty drop and end up at Kane County Correctional, again. We threw our lot in with the court system, and we will leave it there, for better or worse.

Breakfast is more of the same fresh food eaten outdoors with the sound of the waves and the warmth of the sun. The food just doesn't taste as good this morning, or maybe I'm not acknowledging what the taste buds are conveying. Corey weighs in with agreement that the courts will do what needs to be done. We just need to sit back and let it happen. Court's second trimester of college is nearly complete. Will the judge let him stay in class rather than sending him to jail? Will he recommend an alternative--weekend jail, maybe? Is it really a one-and-done usage? How frightened must my son have been to call in the middle of the night to reach a sympathetic ear - the ear belonging to the same ones who got him into the drug court initially? So many thoughts swirl through my consciousness, but no answers.

Again, I must resign myself to waiting while I sweep up the pieces of the fragile trust that now lay shattered at my feet. And I can pray. One seems every bit as fruitless as the other.

Bail Bond Card
February 2005

Ruby Garcia
Kane County Correctional Institution
Geneva, Illinois

We didn't meet in jail, but Lory and I have certainly bonded over orange. We both love addicts: she her son, and me my brother Will. Even though we are a generation apart chronologically, we are sisters at heart, and being in jail together has forged an unbreakable friendship. We don't wear the orange; in fact, we would not be allowed entrance if we did. The guards want us to stand out from the sea of florescent in case of emergency. We don't buck the system.

Every other Thursday, we meet at the back door of the jail, ring the door bell, identify ourselves, and wait. Generally, the wait is only a few minutes before a uniformed guard opens the door, wands us down, checks our supplies, takes our car keys for safekeeping and leads us to the classroom to wait again, this time for a group of inmates to be gathered. Sometimes that outside wait will extend for thirty minutes or more before the door opens. If it stretches much longer than that, we will likely leave without ever stepping inside. Neither the material we have prepared, nor our expectant students are on the top of the priority list for the jail staff. That is another rule we don't complain about, even if it means standing in rain or bitter cold for forty-five minutes before being told the class is cancelled. A guard's job is hard enough without putting up with complaining volunteers.

Volunteer status can be cancelled at a moment's notice for far less than grumbling, like bringing in papers with staples, a paper clip, a ballpoint pen, or gum. The "guests" of the said establishment have ample time, spurred on by boredom and desire, to turn any bit of errant metal into a projectile or weapon. Even a pencil longer than 4 inches or with an eraser attached by a metal band is considered contraband. We bring boxes of the golf-course style pencils, 4" long and eraser-less, which we freely give to our class attendees. They can also purchase the same pencils through the jail commissary, but free is more attractive, and, who knows, it might even boost our class attendance. Oh, and gum, though not a deadly projectile, can be used to jam locks. Clearly, Lory and I are not smart enough to wear orange. Explanations were necessary for us to understand the reasons for the rules.

The class we teach is called Life Skills and was started by Darlene Marcusson, the director of the local homeless shelter, Lazarus House. I think the class's title is ingenious. I'm not sure what skills the attendees expect to learn, but once they are locked in the classroom with us, we attempt to teach them ones that are sadly lacking in this population: you are responsible for your own actions and associations, but equally, past errors do not have to define who you are or who you will be. And most importantly, Jesus Christ loves and accepts you as you are, and He is not bound by the bars that now confine. There is no reason to be shy about the skills we are offering; we have a captive audience – pun intended. They might or might not come back next week when either Lea from Hearts of Hope or Darlene will further expound. But on Thursday night, we are the only diversion option available. The faces change from time to time, which is the nature of a jail, but there is some overall continuity to our attendees, as well. We have a steady following.

The saddest part is when a familiar face resurfaces after several months, always apologetic that they are back after a respite during which they wore anything *but* orange. It happens too frequently. I guess it could make me wonder if there is any point to our Thursday night efforts. Well, I *do* ask that question of myself nearly every time I drive to the jail. Raised in the suburbs, never having had any interest in drugs, I never had cause to see law enforcement as anything other than an arm of protection. My walk on the wild side has pretty much been limited to jaywalking. What can I possibly say that will make a difference in here? That is a huge question since there is no curriculum. Lory and I just talk briefly a couple of hours ahead of time in hopes of divine inspiration. Thankfully, God tends to honor our heart's desire over our preparation. A Bible verse, a quote, or even a cartoon might form for basis for an evening's conversation, as well as a news story or quote from a book we were reading. I remember one class when no one was saying anything. It was dreadful. We just told them that if there was nothing to talk about we would let the guards know the class was done. That sparked lots of conversation and it turned into a productive evening. God always comes through, though sometimes His entrance is not as expected.

Tonight's session was another example of that. Seventeen men and the two of us filled the room with lively conversation. There was a new guy named Terron, a cocky black kid, maybe 19 years old. The rest of the group was comprised mostly of regulars who were aware of the skills to be discussed. Terron had an opinion, too, and was happy to share. "Jesus," he said, "is like a bail bond card. So, when I get to heaven, I'm just going to pull that card out. God has to love me and let me in." The other guys were doing their best to point out the error in his theology. Yes, Jesus is like a bail bond card, but that doesn't mean you can do whatever you want, for as long as you want, until you die. Terron was enjoying the spotlight and the debate. There was something about the swagger and the smirk on his face that made me like him, even though I knew the kind of fire he was playing with.

Lory and I let the conversation go where it would. Frankly, we didn't have a whole lot of input to offer since the analogies being tossed around were straining the limits of our familiarity. We both have a vague idea of what a bail bond card is, but absolutely no knowledge of how it might be most effectively employed. It felt like an hour later, though it probably wasn't more than a few minutes, when Lory spoke up. "So, let's say that Jesus is a bail bond card and you are facing the Judge. He looks at you and says, 'Guilty.' You point to Jesus and say, 'No, look, I have a bail bond card.' How well will your get-out-of-jail-free card work when you have already been declared guilty? You needed to use the card when you first got into trouble. It is useless to you once the judgment has been pronounced."

Terron's mouth opened, but when nothing came out, he closed it again. There were some notes of agreement from the rest of the assembled before the conversation found its legs and moved on. Surprisingly, though, it moved on without Terron. He spent the rest of the session silently looking down at the table in front of him. All his bravado was replaced by what I believe was a whisper to his heart. *Come to Me,* the Trinity beckoned to a formerly cocky, now quieted soul.

As we walked back to our cars tonight, Lory confessed that she was at a complete loss for words during that discussion when suddenly the fully formed response popped into her head. With far less confidence than her voice had indicated, she let the Lord's words flow through her. Who knows where Terron will take this new revelation? But one thing is certain: for one brief moment, he heard the truth and his thirsty soul drank it in. And that, above all else, is why I will be back here in two weeks, wondering, again, if I have anything to offer. Honestly, I don't, but when God shows up (and He does), He has plenty to offer the willing. Count me in.

Winter Road Races – Part I **Sean Woodman**
February 2005 **Winfield, Illinois**

Winter is dragging on and on and on. That is probably one of the saddest things about the early part of my third decade of life: the joy of winter is waning. I have already created my winter's quota of snowmen, or more accurately, snowman. There is no anticipation of snow days, those being reserved for children and their teachers. There have been days this month that gave me hope of spring: bright blue skies with temperatures and hope rising. January's snow is hiding, ducking beneath a grimy, salty, grey film that disguises the white. It is ugly, to be sure, but a good ugly like a gosling or baby swan – ugly destined to grow into beautiful once spring finally arrives. Then there are days like today when the fledgling hope is dashed with a mid-day glance out the window. The grey film on the tired snow is covered with an icy layer, encasing and stifling all hope.

It occurs to me that my life is in perfect sync with the season. It all looked so hopeful: I'm back in school and in my own apartment. My residence is just a stone's throw from my parents' house, which is a very good thing when funds are scarce--as they frequently are. Their refrigerator stays magically stocked. Mine doesn't. There have even been some blue-sky days, when I dare to hope that I will stay away from the drugs, finish school, and live the life everyone else seems to want for me. Well, drugs kind of wink in and out of my life: their color-enhancing allure alternates with my white knuckled resistance. Occasionally I choose to relax my grip, letting the blood flow back into my fingertips.

Then, just last week, my own personal ice storm raged. One of my best buds died of an overdose. In the surreal haze of wake and funeral, my knuckles were white indeed. For years, we had gotten high together on the drug of the day while beating our chests and talking of girls, cars and sports. The high was more satisfying than the conversation. In fact, my need for "real" conversation is insatiable when I am high, which only serves to highlight the distinct lack of it. Now when I close my eyes, I see my friend forever frozen in clothes he never would have chosen to wear. I see his waxy face drained of youth's bravado and destiny and, well, life. More than a drink, more than a high, more than answers themselves, I need a philosophical discussion that extends beyond "Can you believe it? Bummer" or, "We don't want this to happen to you" or the oft spouted lie, "He looks so natural, so peaceful."

I turned to the one place I know I can get a true intellectual discussion that is not thinly disguised as a lecture: I called Court. Our shared desire to dive deep was apparent the night we met in the psych hospital, and it has continued throughout our friendship. So today, he came over immediately, which is to say, as soon as he was awake enough to get dressed and drive the 15 slippery miles here. He was skipping class today, anyway. We were both 100% sober as the conversation started, and we got right down to a deep conversation about life and death. What does it mean? Where does it go? Who determines destiny? Each topic brought us happily to another rabbit-trail that eventually twisted back upon itself. It wasn't circular logic at all, more like completing a link in a chain and then forging the next.

I don't really remember when the mushrooms joined the conversation; they were just the next logical step to more complete communication and higher-level philosophy. 'Shrooms taste like the dirt from which they spring. Sometimes I bake them into food to hide the taste, but our conversation wouldn't slow for that. Court just eats them in their base state, so I did as well. Between us, there were no leftovers, Court leading the way. It is amazing the amount he can ingest in a sitting. He used to favor weed, but that is easily detected at his drug court drops. After some research on his part, he found out the test they use doesn't detect 'shrooms. In rehab lingo, with which we have both had substantial experience, his drug of choice (DOC) switched from marijuana to magic mushrooms which are, after all, both compliments of Mother Nature.

Our discussion was fascinating, productive, soothing to my ragged soul. It all made perfect sense. I don't remember the specifics (I never do), but I remember the peace, the fulfillment, the intellectual satisfaction. Gazing out the window, I saw the most beautiful sight. It was like living in a crystal world. Even with just the scant sun's rays peeking through the clouds, the world was alive with rainbows of clear, icy brilliance. Feeling the pull of the beauty, we opted for a motorized mode of transportation that would allow us to experience more, and at a pace in keeping with our heightened senses.

Ice was still the order of the day on the roads, which was fine with both of us. The dance of the light drew us on, chasing the bedazzled horizon at faster and faster speeds. While it might not look like a high-performance vehicle, Court was one with his Hyundai. Occasionally cars would attempt to block our path, though their efforts were futile. With a slight turn of his wrist, Court simply veered around them, sometimes sliding sideways toward the opposite ditch before the tires would grab the road and right us again. I have never experienced anything so pure, so peaceful, so secure. We knew we were perfectly safe traveling through the crystal scenery.

After 10 or 15 minutes, we decided to return to my apartment in hopes of finding something to eat, or to my parents' house, if needed. As Court slowed to make a U-turn, four police cars came up behind us with sirens blaring. Their red lights flashing on the crystal background turned the ice to fire, an all-in-all fascinating study in duality. Being responsible citizens, we pulled over to allow them to pass. But they didn't pass. Rather, in quick succession, their numbers doubled. Emerging from the eight squad cars where an equal number of men dressed in blue, each holding their shiny side-arms for our closer examination. Per their shouted directions, Court and I stepped from the car with our hands in the requested up-stretched position.

It is my longstanding rule to say as little as possible to anyone in an official looking uniform, and by "little," I mean nothing at all. So, I was surprised to hear myself scream, "Stop it! You're going to hurt him!" as Court's head slammed repeatedly against the hood of the car. Court wasn't offering any resistance, which would have been difficult between the handcuffs and the six officers surrounding him. The other two uniforms led me away to one of the squads, pushing my head down to keep me from hitting the door frame. Why were they worried about my head and so reckless with Court's?

It must have been the slam of the door against my left side that jarred my senses and reminded me of my code of silence leaving the ensuing conversation very one-sided – theirs. In the end, having no charges fitting the vehicle's passenger, they dropped me back at my apartment. I tried to reach Court by phone, but was sent immediately to voice mail. I left a message that was sufficiently vague enough to get a call back from my friend without raising true-blue-eyebrows if they were the next to turn on the phone.

Sitting now in darkness, I am coming to a couple of realizations. First, I'm still hungry and my kitchen holds as much as Mother Hubbard's did. Even my rumbling stomach cannot make my feet move toward the magical food dispenser that is at my parents' house a couple of miles away. I will stand in solidarity with my friend. I bet he's hungry, too. And secondly, with shades drawn and lights off, the dark is encapsulating and even comforting. It is when I close my eyes that I catch, again, the flash of green in Court's eyes as his head bobs sideways, keeping time with a steady thump of bone on metal. I see red flames dancing on the ice-covered landscape, and force my eyes open again. Winter is showing its true colors. Spring's hope is conspicuously absent.

Winter Road Races – Part II — Court Harris
February 2005 — Western Chicago Suburbs, Illinois

There is nothing better than a full tank of gas. Well, there is, but in the realm of life's simple pleasures, it ranks right up there with sleeping until mid-afternoon and puppy kisses. A full tank of gas is an invitation to explore the world: hundreds of miles of possibilities, radio blaring, cigarette glowing. It matters not to me if I pilot alone or with a navigator, that is, as long as the navigator acknowledges my lead. Sean is an excellent navigator. He sounded really upset at his friend's death, so I made sure I have this simple pleasure available in case he wanted to partake. I used Mom and Dad's gas card to fill the tank.

Sean and I start our conversation from common ground and with mutual respect. We are both looking for answers that our peers deem inconsequential or just uninteresting. Our parents, who seem to think they have all the answers, won't acknowledge there are still unanswerable questions – or at least unanswered ones. The first question of childhood remains: why? Why do people suffer? Why do people cause suffering for others? If God is all powerful and all knowing, why does He allow it? Why do those who profess to love you only hurl hurt? Why does the government feel the need to micromanage my body? Why does sunlight hide fear while darkness throws a spotlight on it? Why does death's door swing open for some who do not will it and remain closed for others who would welcome it?

When I was in junior high, I spent a quiet afternoon thinking about eternity. What does it mean? Where does it go? How long is forever? And for just a split second, I saw it; I saw the absolute endlessness of infinity. That glimpse of the un-seeable frightens me still. I understand cycles: sleep-wake; winter-summer; even love-hate. But when life becomes death, does that rocking rhythm stop as well? How does one cope with the endless reaching for the unreachable? Sean's friend is traveling that road now. I bet he has more questions and less answers than he did last week. I know from my prior glimpse that the answers are at the end, and the end is never in sight. That, my friend, is eternity.

As Sean and I grapple with the infinite, it is only natural to sharpen our mental capacity with 'shrooms. Their ability to clarify a blurry world has proven more and more useful in recent months, for both Sean and me. In time, our conversation leads to the path of peace we were searching for, though we may never be able to recreate that path again. We take our euphoria on the road, compliments of the burgeoning gas tank.

An addendum to the pleasure of today's full tank of gas: an uncluttered roadway. Intermittent freezing rain is keeping amateurs locked in the cocoon of their existence while we examine miles of carefree splendor. At times, the car's wheels vainly attempt to escape my control, but they never have a chance. At a time of my choosing, I allow the speedometer to drop below 90, at least long enough to purposefully head the wheels in the opposite direction.

Instead of beginning our examination of the westerly side of the road, our way is blocked by men in blue, brandishing weapons and spraying foam from their mouths as they shout commands. It is difficult to understand their directions, as my attention is drawn instead to the sound of my head bouncing against the hood of my car. Eventually, when the ringing in my ears subsides, their next step almost makes me laugh: a puppy with a sensitive nose will search my car. I could save the taxpayers some money here – I never leave drugs in my car. I buy and consume what I need at any given time. No need to allow my favorite PO, Randy, to search my car and find something I accidentally forgot. Ironically, I do try to save them the expense of a drug test when I tell them I'm in drug court and being tested three times a week, but they waste taxpayer dollars, anyway. I don't bother to tell them that their standard issue test does not reveal 'shrooms.

I spent the night cuffed to a bench in the police department feigning sleep, actual sleep being an impossibility given my current chemical composition. I hoped that closed eyes would inhibit conversation, which turned out to be a largely successful plan.

At the morning shift change, they have no choice but to send me on my way with four tickets: one for failure to yield and one for each of the three speed zones I passed through. They do not offer me a ride to my car, which has been impounded at another location. Without enough cash in my wallet for a cab, I am forced to walk the 15 miles back to my dorm. Of course, I could have called someone to pick me up, but the numbers I need are stored in my cell phone which is locked in my car. There is no way I'm going to call my parents for a ride, and theirs is the only number I can remember. It is a brisk walk to say the least, but the cold keeps me awake, since I departed the station at just the time I would have been able to fall asleep.

Tomorrow I'll hire an attorney to give me a hand. Can you really speed three times in one traffic stop? Fortunately, the tips are good for pizza delivery. I'm going to need them. Today, though, I'll take a nap and then track down my car. Tonight, I'll have a story to tell, and to counter any skeptics, written proof scribbled in adrenaline-laden legal hieroglyphics.

Birthday Cheer — Court Harris
March 2005 — Naperville, Illinois

The bar is just down the hill about a half mile from my dorm. There are other students here that I recognize by sight, though not by name. Technically, I could spend a week or more in jail just for being here if my Parole Officer, Randy, were to waltz in the door. But I'm 40 minutes from his domain, and willing to take the chance. In the scheme of things, this is a low risk flaunting of the drug court rules. I've done worse and still avoided Kane County's finest concrete mattresses for almost a year. By my 22nd birthday I should be free to walk into any bar and have a drink – even with Randy. Yeah, like I would ever do that!

The funny thing is that I am here by my mother's invitation. She is aware of the rules I live under and doesn't seem to mind being a co-conspirator in breaking them. Mom and Dad met up with Colin and Corey on their 21st birthdays to buy them a drink. It's not like it was the first drink for any of their sons – not even my first "legal" drink, which was at 12:01 this morning. But it's a ceremony of sorts or a rite of passage, I guess, and Mom didn't want me to miss out on it.

Mom and Dad used to let us have a shot glass of wine once a month in our youth. The taste was bitter and jarring, but it made us feel grown up, so we sipped away. They thought they were teaching us to drink responsibly. They did end up teaching us to drink, I'll give them that, though to be honest, it was a skill we all would have acquired anyway. All three of us boys have had brushes with authority figures centered around alcohol and similar substances, though I suppose mine have been most epic. At least my brothers never got to experience group showers under the watchless eyes of guards.

Mom arrives just a couple of minutes behind me and we find a table in the corner. I take the chair that gives me a good view of the entrance. There is a bit of necessary paranoia built into the drug court system that one would be a fool to ignore. As unlikely as I am to see Randy, I would certainly want to see him before he sees me. I order a beer and she gets a margarita. Mom isn't a beer drinker, having missed some part of her college education, I guess. She isn't a big drinker at all, which probably contributes to her naiveté. To tell the truth, it's a little bit endearing.

The talk is light and upbeat. She tells some baby stories about me. The doctor thought I might be born on February 29th, but I waited almost another two weeks to make my appearance. When I was two, I called my Nana "Apple," getting my fruit names mixed up: banana vs apple. In similar fashion, we walk through my childhood with classic family stories: Jordan and I baiting a rabbit trap with carrots (we tired of the wait before the bunnies appeared); getting lost on the ski slopes in Winter Park and then thankfully being spotted by Dad from the chair lift because of my neon orange gloves; having my name known by the administration in every school I've ever attended, though not necessarily for my educational prowess.

I wouldn't mind another beer, and her drink is empty, too. But she doesn't want to push our luck, or rather, my luck. She winds up with how much she loves me and is so proud of me – that I am making it through drug court, not using and getting such great grades in college. She might not be quite as complimentary of the grades when they arrive a couple of weeks from now. They aren't the Dean's List material they were the first trimester. I won't correct any assumptions she has made about my drug intake. After all, it was my parents who got me into this program. No need to test those waters again.

All in all, it was a nice gesture, and informative in its own way. Mom has made it clear she doesn't want me to use drugs, but she also doesn't respect the drug court's view on liquor – her shades of grey in a world of black and white. Can she really blame me if my band of grey is a bit taller and wider than hers?

She drives me back up the hill to my dorm where a party will commence in short order to honor the 21st anniversary of the day of my birth. Happy Birthday to me. It's going to be a good one!

Head Cold
May 2005

Court Harris
Kane County Courthouse
Geneva, Illinois

Another Thursday night means another visit with the judge, albeit a different judge. There was been a changing of the guard in the drug court, which was quite the news at the time: charges were made of favoritism based on gender and capricious jailhouse stays, regarding both cause and length. Maybe so, but what it really means is this new judge uses jail as a punishment much more sparingly, which works for me.

I am getting more and more bold with the loopholes I employ, and enjoying some new freedoms. I discovered the mushroom dodge several months ago, and have made good use of it. They don't test for it, and I take full advantage of that! Ironically, while sitting in this court room waiting to see the judge whose job it is to make sure I don't use, I heard that ecstasy doesn't stay in your system very long. Friday night use will not betray you in Monday's drop. It might make for a nice change of pace to celebrate the weekend. I've heard that cocaine has the same kind of shelf life in your system, a theory that I had hoped to prove at tonight's drop.

Last Friday I tried cocaine for the first time. I will admit to being disappointed; the high just wasn't that good. Of course, who knows how pure the stuff was, most likely cut with something, anything, that could be crushed into white powder. At any rate, I am currently on a naturally-produced high, waiting to play the part of dutiful recovering addict for the judge. The first time through a loophole brings almost as big an adrenaline rush as the high produced by the drug itself.

The new judge is not nearly the imposing figure that Judge Doyle was. Judge Mueller is average height and build, younger, and without the swagger of his predecessor. Oh, he has attitude; I think that comes with the robe – or maybe it's infused in the gavel. But drug court seems much more like a job to him, whereas for Doyle it was a 'mission from God.' Either way, I've altered my life only slightly and still avoided jail. I've managed about 150 clean drops while using the whole time. Who's the one with swagger now!

When I finally sit face to face with the Judge Mueller, my swagger goes the way of Doyle's when it was announced he would be replaced: it drips down my body and puddles at my feet. "Your drop came back slightly positive for hydrocodone. Go sit over by the bailiff while I consider what to do about this." I wonder if he sees the soggy trail of footprints as I join the brown-clad, humorless court official. I receive a severe glance from my appointed monitor, which fortunately doesn't linger long. I've accepted by now that there is no telepathic communication, and for once, I'm really relieved rather than frustrated by that insight. If he could hear my racing thoughts, I would be doomed to wearing orange pajamas tonight!

As much as I would like to just take some deep calming breaths, I don't want to take the chance of tipping my hat to my babysitter. I guess the fact that I have made that realization means that I am still in control. My heart starts to slow, and my mind engages. Hydrocodone – NOT cocaine. I knew there was something wrong with that high. And only "slightly positive." I think I can work with this.

By the time I am called back into the presence of his highness, I have a plan and a story...and hopefully contrite, sympathetic puppy-dog-eyes to match. "I had a really bad cold over the weekend. Saturday night it got so bad I couldn't sleep, so I asked my RA for some cold medicine. All he had was his own prescription cough medicine, so I had a dose of that. I bought my own over the counter stuff the next day, but I guess his was strong. I never thought to ask before I took it."

"I should throw you in jail just for being so stupid! You should never use anyone else's prescription!" Mueller pauses for dramatic effect, but I'm sure I've won the round. Hard to tell if it's the plausibility of the lie or the eyes or a combination of the two, but orange is fading from my sight like the morning sky as the sun rises. And it's looking like a fine day, indeed, despite the actual 8:00 p.m. descending darkness. "If you ever do that again, I'll let you consider your own stupidity from a jail cell. Am I clear?"

Apparently, my reply matched the manufactured canine quality in my eyes, and I left the courtroom a free man. I didn't have to fake my relief when I walked out the door; that was real. I did have to contain the self-congratulatory fist-pump until I got in my car. No need to raise suspicion or tempt fate. Tomorrow is another drop. As much as I would like to celebrate my victory, I think I'll wait until after I pee in the cup. Then I'll stick with the tried and true without fear of failure next week.

Camaraderie of the Heart — Lory Harris

August 2005 — Kane County Correctional Institution
Geneva, Illinois

It is the second time she has read this speech – well, the second time to an audience, that is. I'm sure there was a mirror in her recent past that heard it many times and watched the tears roll down her cheeks. The first official audience of a hundred or so, for whom the speech was written, was family and friends. She might have cried then (I wasn't close enough to see), but her voice didn't carry the expected tremor. It was strong and clear, the strength of a strong woman.

This crowd of ten would not exactly be termed "friends." Some, in fact, are meeting us for the first time. Yet in many ways, this was always the intended audience. Her voice is softer in this more intimate setting--tender, though still clear. There are tears, but they have not spilled over, not yet, anyway. Where the first crowd was dressed in drab, somber colors, this group is dressed entirely in orange. They will not be sending a card later, or even offering a hug or handshake at the end of the appointed hour. There would probably be no more heartfelt interaction of the day, but since physical contact in this setting is considered a security risk, it is strictly forbidden.

I didn't think Ruby would even come to the jail to teach our Life Skills class with me so soon after her brother's death. Tonight, she not only came, but came on a mission of truth and compassion to turn tragedy into hope. A woman with a broken heart and a vision: is there anything more powerful?

"I had a birthday this week," she started. "It was one of the hardest days of my life. I thought there would be family gathering with balloons and cake and laughter. My family did gather, but for a funeral, instead." As she unfolds a single sheet of well-creased paper, with slightly unsteady hands, she continues. "This is the eulogy I read for my brother Will who died six days ago."

> "Will was a sweet compassionate soul. He was a loving brother, son and father. Will had an easy laugh, was quick to help, a loyal friend and an artistic spirit. He was a follower of Christ, always reaching his hand out to help anyone in need. That is how I will remember my brother. He also had a disease. It does not define who he was, but it did rob him of his life at the age of 24. Will died of a heroin overdose, three days before my birthday."

The tears are flowing, and her voice breaks at times. But her words carry in the otherwise respectful silence of the room. Every man hangs on every word as she continues, knowing what she will say even before hearing it for the first time. If they aren't addicts themselves, they know addicts and are veterans of too many such funerals. I saw no tears rolling down their cheeks, but every man's eyes had changed, clearly affected by the words of a woman they barely know but love and respect for her tenacious compassion. Their eyes, softer now, signal an unguarded entrance to their hearts and souls.

When she finishes, Ruby refolds the page, laying it on the table in front of her, but her fingers never lose contact with that tangible piece of her brother that is still within her grasp. "I asked him once," she continues unscripted, "what his addiction was like. 'It's like breathing,' he responded. 'You just have to do it.'" There are acknowledging nods around the room, and more than one head dips just the once and remains downcast, the eyes of self-reflection hidden from the rest of the room.

"I take great comfort knowing that I will see Will again someday in heaven. He was a believer, though his demons still haunted him. But for now, the pain of his absence is overwhelming. My parents wander the halls of blame, escaping occasionally to a room draped in longing and remorse. His daughter will grow up without her father's loving embrace. She will search ever-aging photographs to match her eyes to his. But she will never hear for herself the reflection of his laughter in hers. Over time no doubt, this ache will lessen, but this wound will never heal."

It is doubtful that anyone in that room has escaped the lash marks of drugs upon their lives. Certainly, I haven't, and Ruby is the current focus of that whip. All of us have been required to don orange, or have loved someone who did, or both. All of us have attended funerals that have caused our hearts to drip in tandem with our tears: too young, too senseless, too avoidable, too predictable.

It is certainly a heavy gathering, but heavy in a golden brick kind of way. It was a precious connection of humanity. There was no "them and us," "jail and free," or "right and wrong." Class and race and station distinctions fade away, leaving only that something of great value that is the anchor of who we all are: children. God's children. We gather, weighed down by our inability to control or alter or understand, and bound by our mutual determination to shoulder the other's pain. I hope our group, gathering and allowing our scars to become evident, produces a salve for

Ruby's soul, for all our souls, that just might lessen the pain and hasten the healing.

The evening ends as it began, with Ruby and me being escorted back to "our" world. We embrace as I attempt words of condolence. The words, though heartfelt, feel obligatory. At the same time, my thoughts are turning inward. Though chronologically the eldest, I was the most junior member at the gathering of this evening's elect. Will's was my first such funeral, but likely not my last. With slightly less than three years of experience under my belt, I am frequently brought up short by my naiveté. What right have I to assume I will never fumble over the words on a tear-stained sheet of paper that attempt to sum up the life of one I love? Do I assume to pray the right words in the right order and with enough fervency or frequency to avoid an aching heart like the one that will forever beat in Ruby's chest? Who am I to demand avoidance of the fate so many others suffer?

The drive home feels stifling in a way that the air conditioner cannot rectify. I want to hug my son, impressing on him the reality of the fire with which he flirts. Court attended Will's funeral with me, though judging from his slouched and bored demeanor, it did not have the same effect on him.

Lord, spare my son. But if it is not to be, don't leave me! Don't make me walk that road alone.

SECTION THREE

MIDNIGHT

August 2005 – June 2006

HOMEOWNER INSURANCE CLAIM REPORT
September 6, 2005

Homeowner statement:

Twenty-one-year-old bipolar son was left home alone while parents were on vacation. In "manic" rage, he caused all damage to the house as listed below. The son has now been kicked out of the house and will not be allowed to return.

Description of damage:

1. Hot tub motor burned out. Filter system not working. (Bags of softener salt were added to water).
2. Holes burned in deck boards, affecting approximately six boards.
3. Tempered glass on oven door shattered. Hinge bent. Door will not close. Repair likely.
4. Microwave oven door hinge bent. Door will not close. Repair unlikely, replacement needed.
5. Oil poured across carpet in lower level family room and bedroom. Cannot be cleaned.
6. Seven holes in drywall in lower level bedroom walls.
7. The word "DIE" is carved into the house to garage metal insulated door. In addition, there are 6 slices/stabs to the door. Door is still serviceable.
8. Two computers rendered incapable of booting up.

Adjuster recommendation:

Computers are for home business use. Valued at $3,000. Deny coverage on homeowner policy. Additional claim approximately $7,000 less deductible of $1,000. Except that the son has now been kicked out of the house, the claim should be denied. However, no claims have been submitted by homeowner in 15 years since policy was issued. Recommend paying claim.

FLAG POLICY - DO NOT pay any additional claims arising from vandalism by son without a police report.

Front Porch Theology — Lory Harris

August 2005 — St. Charles, Illinois

It was a beautiful late summer night, and I spent it with one of the people I love most in the entire world. We discussed matters of the soul, side by side and heart to heart - and I failed, again. How is it possible to be such a failure at the one thing that matters most to me – the one thing I must get right?

It started after dinner when Court ambled off to the front porch, his belly full and his lungs screaming for equal time. One of our few rules that Court generally follows is no smoking in the house. Even that adherence comes with his proverbial middle finger extended – he tosses his butts into the flower gardens that Ken so faithfully and lovingly tends. Score one for us: no smoke indoors. Score two for Court: he still smokes, *and* his father ends up cleaning up after him. I let out a sigh; it's just not my battle. When I try to jump in on Ken's side, it's half-hearted, and everyone knows it. I am just battle weary. My words are carried away by the wind as surely and quickly as the visible breath Court is exhaling.

Sliding my back down the wall, I sit on the cool concrete porch beside my son. A wooden bench that would comfortably hold both of us is just four feet further down the way. The only ones who use that more appropriate seating area have eight legs and have staked their claim with strands of silver. Even here, on the concrete, we may be visited by eight-legged creatures, but perhaps they won't drop down our backs, disrupting or cancelling our conversation.

"How's it going?" an inauspicious start if ever I offered one. Why is it that I never know how, or even if, I should start a conversation with Court? I'm afraid to intrude and terrified to just let life take its course. It would seem I would want to disrupt the path has been rushing undeniably and steadily downhill for an eternity now. I'm just never sure if I will slow the descent or give it a hearty push along the way. Court glances my direction, takes a deep drag on his cigarette and shrugs his shoulders. I take that as a good sign. At least his anger doesn't give me a sharp shove in the back. It's funny how my definition of "good" has changed. My words and my intentions stagger forward, simultaneously hoping for the best and bracing for impact.

"Thank you for going to Will's funeral; it meant a lot to me. For such a sad occasion, I'm surprised by how hopeful it was." We are both staring out into the front yard, watching fireflies dance to the sound of cicadas, but my peripheral vision is fixed on my son. I see him glance in my direction and the roll of his eyes, but he says nothing, so I continue. "The pastor was talking about each of us having a set number of days, and those were Will's. We can choose what to do with our days, but God determines how many we get. Will could have died in a car accident or had cancer or slipping the bathtub instead of the overdose. What really matters, though, is that during his days, he surrendered his life to Christ. He is now healed and living life more fully than we can imagine."

It isn't just a glance this time. He turns his whole head in my direction. "You believe that?" It's not a friendly request for confirmation, but an incredulous challenge to my very sanity.

My eyes meet his demanding ones, and suddenly everything I want to say jumbles up like a twenty-car pileup on the tollway during a morning commute. On the other side of the median I can see the open road, but I can't get there. Try as I will, I can only stumble out of my car, with no chance of catching the driver going the opposite direction as he steps on the accelerator. I don't remember ever *not* believing in God. I accepted Christ as my Savior when I was in second grade. I can't be a hypocrite and stop now, just because life is hard. That's the simple truth my words try to convey. But no matter how many times I stop and start again, his look of disbelief never wavers, except maybe to intensify.

I am still trying to align my words with my thoughts when Court's accusation slaps me across the face. "You think I'm going to Hell, don't you!"

My answer is given with confidence that is both immediate and instinctual, "No, I don't. I know God loves you." The jumble of thoughts suddenly aligns with clarity, but I bar all the qualifiers to my words. Instead, I ask him to wait while I go to get something for him.

A few days ago, I stumbled across the Bible I used then I was Court's age. *The Way* it says on the cover in bold 1970s graphics. It seems I've always written in my Bible, though it probably started with this very book. The inside covers and margins contain my adolescent insights on random verses, prayers for God's intervention in apparently gut-wrenching but long forgotten issues, autograph-styled well-wishes from fellow Christian friends, even doodles decorating pithy '70s sayings that once seemed so profound. Tucked in the pages are scraps of paper: notes from friends, song lyrics, articles torn from magazines or papers or church bulletins. Part holy word and part diary, I hand the book to my son, hoping he will be curious enough to open the pages and read the living words contained in it – not mine, but God's.

Taking the odd and unexpected gift, his thumb feathers through the worn pages. "Thanks, Mom," he says without even a glint of enthusiasm. "I'm going to meet up with a friend. Will you put this inside for me?" And he is gone, the Bible back in my hands and the dying glow of a cigarette partially illuminating the underside of a hydrangea.

Of all my faults (and there are many), lying is not among them. I may stop short of full-disclosure or say nothing at all, but the words I do say will be true. So, no, I don't believe he is going to Hell. But it is a belief specifically adopted of a desire to soothe my ragged soul. It is the product of 3:00 a.m. Bible searches in hopes of comfort that will hasten sleep. What I've found, in part, is a possible loophole, and I cling to it, willing my interpretation upon Heaven.

John credits Jesus with saying that He gives eternal life, and no one will snatch us away from His hand. Since Court accepted Christ when he was in middle school, I take that to mean his place in Heaven is assured. But then, when Matthew records the Parable of the Sower, it seems like it is possible to fall away – to wither and die even after "receiving the Word." I could debate endlessly on this topic, with myself and with other Christians. Like so many things in Christendom, there is not universal agreement.

And like so many well-meaning and sincere Christians, I have decided to settle the debate in my own mind by believing the comfortable: once saved, always saved. I truly have no doubt that God is more faithful to us than we are to Him. I'm just not 100% confident how far that extends. If you accept Christ and then later willfully reject Him, does He let you have your own way? It is that doubt that casts a shadow over my newly settled belief. In other words, I'm not as confident as I would like to be. In the end, of course, truth is true whether you believe it or not. But self-preservation demands I either believe my version of this truth or dive into despair, a nearby destination regardless.

The embers have faded to black, though the smell of tobacco still lingers. Before Ken and I leave on our East Coast vacation tomorrow, I will check on Court to glimpse his sleeping form. Perhaps I'll even step carefully into his room, maneuvering between piles of clothing, books, and discarded refuse to quietly kiss the forehead of my baby boy. Even if he wakes, will he open his eyes and mumble a farewell? Or will his eyes remain closed and his breathing steady, willing me to leave him, shoving me away with prickly indifference? How can I possibly fail him so miserably, so consistently, so completely?

I set *The Way* on his bed, blocking his head from his pillow. That, a prayer, and a hope-turned-shaky-belief are all I have. *Lord, let them be enough.*

The Distance Between Us — Ken Harris

August 2005 — Boston, Massachusetts

It is a vacation we had talked of taking for decades. I would finally show Lory where I was born. Almost thirty years of marriage and my Midwestern-born wife had never been to the Boston area! Mind you, there isn't much of my family still in the area - one aunt, her husband and their son, but it was still a homecoming of sorts. Even after so many years, there was a familiar feel in the narrow streets lined with a mixture of national history and modern life.

"It's not too much further," I said, the *further* sounding like *fa-thah* as the accent washes over me, coating my tongue. Slipping back into the dialect so easily after decades in the Midwest both surprises and pleases me. Like singing along with the radio to a song that you hadn't heard since high school days, I join the musical East Coast game of hide and seek: r's appear and disappear in that certain ordered way. I also earn an odd look from Lory, her Midwestern diction hearing dissonance in the tune. But it feels good – familiar – so unlike what passes for life back home.

It is, of course, ill-advised to be here. Well, not "here" so much, but anywhere that is not home where Court teeters on the edge of sanity. When we made the reservations, his stability seemed to be returning. But if there is anything predictable in his personality, it is that as our departure time for a trip approaches, his slide into irrational behavior leads the way. This trip has been cancelled and rescheduled once. And in the back of my mind, Prudence whispers it should have been twice. But our Martha's Vineyard destination a couple of days from now was purchased at a charity auction and will expire in a couple of weeks. We decided, in one of our rare agreements on anything Court related, to remove the safety net, letting him crash, if he must. In short, our desperation won out over our rationality. So far so good, though it has only been about 6 hours since we left the house. He probably isn't even out of bed yet.

It's not just that. Running our own architectural design business brings its own share of stress. It's been an overnight success story (22 years in the making), and we have ridden the booming real estate market like a cowboy on a bucking bronco. The work is good: pay and flexibility. It's also filled with multiple customers all wanting something yesterday. They drop their crisis in our laps and inquire daily as to the progress of the miracle to be performed. I tell them I can't get it done that quickly, but 3:00 a.m. invariably brings worries that deny sleep and I make my way to the computer in our office downstairs, performing miracles for a fee. It's not 'overnight' success; it's 'middle-of-the-night' success.

Here's a laugh: the name of the business is CB III Designs. It's named after our sons: Colin Bryce, Corey Burke, and Courtlandt Bryn. The original name of the company was CB II Designs, which dates the start accurately since Court is now 21. At Christmas, we frequently tag our sons' gifts with a simple CB1, CB2, or CB3 – kind of a family short hand. Last month, Court demanded that the company either pay him royalties for the unauthorized use of his "name" in our business or he would sue us and shut us down. Yeah, as if we didn't name both him and the business – before he even drew his first breath! And now, having given into that memory, Prudence isn't whispering anymore. She's tapping me on the shoulder, demanding my attention.

Oh, stop it! I tell her. *Slip into the dialect, relax, and enjoy the feeling of "home." We are here, and Court is there. And, I suppose, all we really gave up was our figment of control. Just enjoy a week with Lory in a place that must be simpler than the one the plane brought us from: beautiful architecture, beautiful days, blessed distance between here and the craze that rules our lives. Let him try to sue us – I'd like to see the attorney that would take that on.*

If we aren't careful, though, he could take down our marriage. It's a delicate balancing act. You know what they say about mama bear protecting her cub? Well, it's all true. She will claw and scratch your eyes out if you say a negative word about her precious baby. *She* can complain about Court, but you run a risk even agreeing with her. At least it's best not to agree too heartily. She won't let him fail, and even when he does, she has an excuse in her back pocket to cover his sins. There is a word for that - it's called enabling. Lory spells it L-O-V-E. She always was a lousy speller.

Now, Prudence, hussy that she is, delivers the first jab to the side of the head. It comes in the form of a ringing cell phone. With each insistent ring, the feeling of dread rises. What could have happened in less than a day? Maybe the average person would expect casual conversation or a reservation reminder. But, of late, paranoia is the hallmark of our family. And judging by Lory's reaction to the caller on the other end, I am again reminded that it isn't paranoia if you're right.

"No, thank you for calling. I appreciate it. I'll try to give him a call and find out what's going on, and I'll call you back. Thanks, again, for letting us know." Whatever tension had dissipated in the skies between Chicago and Boston just returned with a vengeance. It's the neighbors - not that they are complaining; they are genuinely concerned. Apparently, every door and window in our house is open and multiple streams of loud music are bursting forth. They can't possibly understand what's happening at the Harris household – who can? But it can't be hidden, either – there are too many police cars in the driveway for that. In our dead-end subdivision, cars of the black and white variety don't just happen through. Private pain is never as private as one might hope. I grip the steering wheel of the car (it's not a *cah* anymore) and simultaneously reject the idea (not *ah-dear*) of returning to the airport. It's not the music of New England in my head any longer - fingers on a chalkboard, maybe, or the screech of tires just before impact - but not music.

Lory calls Court's cell phone, the home phone, and the business phone. Each call ends with a cheery voice telling her to leave a message. Well, maybe not exactly cheery, but clearly brighter than the mood on the Boston end of the phone. Should we leave Court to complete his failure on his own or should we rush in like the cavalry – again – picking up pieces, dispensing pharmaceutical nuggets of sanity and demanding obedience? And will my vote even register? Not likely.

Lory makes one more phone call, this time to her best friend, Merry. Tears are flowing now, as she details the scant information she has about the happenings on our street. Merry will send her husband, Mike, over to check on Court and the house. At least that postpones the "what next" decision long enough to have lunch. On the bright side, the bill will be light. No one is really that hungry anymore.

The hotel is quaint, old and architecturally significant, overlooking Newbury Street. It's my kind of room – our kind, being one of the few things we have always agreed upon. It has old world charm with modern conveniences: the ceilings are higher than the room is wide, the bed dominates the floor space, and the bathroom looks like an afterthought (of course, judging by the age of the building, the bathroom *was* an afterthought). We sit on the bed, husband and wife, both attempting to will the tension out of our shoulders and banish the concerns from front and center of our minds. We stare at the TV; we stare out the window; we stare without seeing, our minds racing too fast to allow additional sensory input, until cell phone interrupts, once again.

Court, sounding more lucid than previous reports of the day would indicate, has all the answers. "It was a beautiful day and the house needed airing. I just wanted to hear the music as I sat outside. I'll keep it down if the neighbors are complaining. Don't worry, everything is fine.

How is Boston? Enjoy the trip. Love you…" Boston does not believe the party line from the Midwest. If possible, Lory would jump through the phone and rescue him – again. I, on the other hand, would prefer to kick Court out of the house and rescue our once happy existence, instead. But we have already done a dozen rounds on that. "CB3" may be a lost cause, but kicking him out will not lead back to the bliss of yesteryear, either. We are at an impasse and our marriage teeters in the balance. "We decided to let him fail if he must," I remind her. And with a slight nod of her head, the decision is upheld. We will not run to the rescue, like first responders to a burning building. Let the building burn if it must – metaphorically speaking, of course…

Dinner is at a trendy sidewalk bistro near the hotel. The food and wine get five stars, as does the charm and slight pretentiousness of the location and staff. My date doesn't quite measure up, but she's trying. There is small talk about the city, hotel and food, and some people-watching observations, but even as she professes to love her meal, she picks at it – forcing down a few bites. We call it the Court Diet – her appetite follows his downward spiral. If the past is any indication, on our return home, she will be 3-5 pounds lighter. I, on the other hand, will likely find every pound that she loses. Stress beats on each of us in different ways.

We take a longer than necessary route back to the hotel, breathing in the early fall air. The sun bids us to turn away from the long shadows it casts and instead wander in the warmth of the colors as it exits, stage west. The charm of these once-familiar streets against the backdrop of reds and oranges serves to soothe my soul. Returning to the hotel, our mutual silence shouts of the need to comfort and be comforted. With little more noise, my wife and I make love. It is a nod to the normal, a point of agreement, an escape, however temporary, from the worries and what-ifs hailing from Illinois. Later, as I drift off, I know we will keep alternating watch over the fears that have followed us. She will take the first watch, as she always does, and I won't fight her for it.

The next morning dawns cool and crisp - promising even. The first order of the day is breakfast, which she will order but not eat. Her cell phone is at the ready, but it won't ring--at least not yet. And she can't call for an update, either. The time zone difference exacerbates Court's late morning rising. It will be hours at best before she can glean anything from his tone of voice. We both know the actual words must be discounted. They rarely reflect reality.

After breakfast, we walk the sparsely populated streets of the city, in the no-man's land between commuter rush and the shopping/sight-seeing throngs. Armed with a camera and a love of architecture the way it used to be, we take turns pointing out details of interest. Eye candy is everywhere: a round, brick turret suspended on the side of a building, wooden trim around windows accented by vibrant-but-appropriate paint colors, stone arches around curved doors, Trinity Church and its reflection in the Prudential Building – historic and modern peacefully co-existing. Our moods are maybe lighter than they have a right to be. There are others checking in on our house and youngest son. Maybe this will be a vacation after all.

"Did you see that brick detail above the window?" I say as I snap a picture.

"They don't build parapet walls like that anymore," Lory responds.

"Look at all the steps wrapping about that building. Guess no one was disabled back then." My eyes are darting around, soaking up details while my camera catches them digitally. It takes me a moment to realize that my companion isn't playing the pointing game with me anymore. She is still looking steadily at the steps, which, frankly, are one of the least interesting items receiving comment to date.

Following the gaze of her eyes, I see the object of her attention. It isn't the stairs, or brick and mortar, or colonial detailing. A black man, maybe 40 years old, is sitting on the stairs. It isn't cold out, but he is wrapped in a long black trench coat, the collar pulled up around his neck and chin. I guess it was a bit chilly last night. Two bags lean against him, one on each side – all his worldly possessions, no doubt. If there is such a thing as a stereotypical homeless person, he has taken up residence on the stairs that I so casually pointed out just moments before. It's hard to tell if he is watching us as intently as Lory is watching him, but the embarrassing thought of being caught looking makes me divert my eyes.

A gentle touch to her shoulder breaks her trance. When she turns to face me, our eyes meet. In that moment before she diverts her gaze, I see the pain there. Her soul, having been scraped raw, breaks open and bleeds with just the slightest bump. The one on the stairs is the wrong race, wrong age, wrong geographic location even. Court, how can you possibly follow us so effectively and constantly? When she looks back up at me, it is obvious she has made a hasty effort to hide the jolt her soul has endured. After almost 30 years of marriage, the last three punctuated by Court-induced-trauma, I willingly join her ruse. We walk on with less exuberance than before, and decidedly do *not* talk about the elephant that has just joined our parade.

Lunch is preceded by a quick call home. Everything is fine if Court's words are to be believed, which of course, they are not. He is working on our computers to make them faster. Now I'm ready to jump through the phone line, not to rescue, but to throttle him. "Don't touch my computer!"

"No, Dad, I'm just working on Mom's computer."

"Don't touch her computer, either!" Thank God, we have complete backups. But just the thought of him messing with our livelihood makes my appetite approach Lory's. If not for the bar bill, lunch would have been downright reasonable.

The rest of the afternoon we wander as tourists should. We take a tour of Trinity Church, enjoying both the architecture and history of the building. Much of it is being renovated, but despite the scaffolding, the original grace is evident. It will truly be a thing of beauty when the construction is complete. We make our way to the Boston Commons, wandering the grounds. From its humble beginnings as a horse pasture it has become a beacon of nature's glory and blessed peacefulness. There is a tethered hot air balloon ride that Lory would like to try. I like to keep my feet on solid ground, thank you very much. She decides the long line isn't worth the wait.

By the time dinner rolls around, we have walked ourselves out and welcome the chance to just sit, sip wine, and order a good meal. I guess we have talked ourselves out, as well; dinner is a quiet affair. We aren't so relaxed that we can fall asleep on the spot, but we have done a good job of tiring ourselves out, so sleep should come easily when the time is right. Reds and oranges outline the skyline - lipstick kisses from the departing solar goddess. It has been a better than usual day with no major drama to report.

Back in the room, I plop on the bed and reach for the TV remote. The day has been almost completely devoid of sports information and updates, in this, the climax of baseball's playoff races and the dawn of the football season. All I know is what I've gleaned from a waiter or casual conversation. It's time to get the full story. My mind just barely registers that Lory is standing looking out the window. It is a nice view, though if I were her, I would sit and rest my feet. Baseball highlights give way to football and then golf and a smattering of lesser sports. When the ticker at the bottom of the screen starts to cycle through a second time, I glance over again at Lory. She is still guarding the window with her back to me. "Is everything okay?" I ask, knowing and dreading the answer.

"Did you see him?" she replies, not really an answer to my question. "Did you see the homeless guy on the steps?"

"Lory, there is nothing you can do about him. He will be okay, and he is not Court." I hope that isn't a lie on each count, and I hope she will believe it regardless. I'm not sure she even hears my response.

"He has a mother, too. Do you think she wonders where her son is? Does she cry for him in the middle of the night? Would she trade places with him if only she could? Does time ease the pain, or do you just learn to live with a new normal? Does he ever think of his mother and remember how much she loves him? Does he remember when she sang him to sleep, or when she held his hand crossing the street?"

With an internal sigh, I turn off the TV. I don't know how to make her pain go away, and it both saddens and infuriates me. Putting my hands on her shaking shoulders, I lead her over to sit on the bed. Her tears dampen my shoulder as I hold her as tenderly as I know how. But I can only hold her so closely when I am in Boston. She is much *fa-thah* away. She is in Illinois.

Redecorating **Lory Harris**
September 2005 **St. Charles, Illinois**

I love a vacation as much as the next guy. Maybe more since I work out of my house and never really get away from it otherwise. But there is a certain amount of stress associated with taking a trip. First you must work like a madman to get ready to leave, and when you get back, there will be more of the same to catch up on what you missed. It is important to savor the actual days between the two stress sessions. A good vacation is when you don't pack stress on top of your suitcase forcing you to kill and eat it for the first few days of your escape - and equally, when you don't find it lurking in the bottom of your bag when re-packing to return. Of course, all of that assumes that there will be some days between the two assaults when the tension leaves your neck and your gut. In these modern times, those middle days are more likely to occur in a backwoods location that does not offer cellular service. Apparently, all of Massachusetts is cell accessible.

Each time the phone rang, it was followed by the same discussion: should we head home early? What will we be going home to? Will the house be standing? Will he be alive to greet us when we get there? What could we do even if we were there? Ken and I got so proficient at this conversation that by the end of the week it was reduced to just the look as our eyes met, or a squeeze of the hand. In truth, we always stopped after the first question, never having the nerve or the crystal ball to answer the rest. And that single answer, "we will stay," became our mantra far past the point of logic.

From Court: "Your computer is going to work so much faster when I get done with it."

"Our computers are fine. Please use your own computer."

From Mike, Merry's husband: "There is glass all over the kitchen floor and he has scratched something in the garage service door."

"No problem. We will clean it up when we get back and re-paint the door."

From Court: "Is it really 2:00 a.m.? But I just needed to talk to you, Mom, and you said I could call any time. I just wanted to say I love you."

"I love you, too. Is something wrong? No? Okay, good."

From Mike, again: "I caught him pouring gas on the deck and trying to light it. Fortunately, the gas can was virtually empty, and the deck was wet."

"Thanks, would you please sneak the .22 from the house? We will get it back from you later."

Court, again: "Did you know in Australia they use salt instead of chlorine in their pools and hot tubs?"

"Court, don't mess with the hot tub! It wasn't designed for salt water."

Thinking over the list of bizarre that has somehow passed for normal makes me want to hurry home and assure myself that it is okay – life will go on. But Ken and I wordlessly lie to each other with our smiles as we hold hands, walking toward to our waiting transport. We will be in control again once we get home. Surely our fears and imaginations have magnified the snippets of information we have received. The upcoming holiday weekend will allow us ample time to right our world. With almost no effort at all, I start to believe my own prognostication. I breathe deep and enjoy the first few stress-free moments this vacation offers – ironically, it's the trip home.

The limo from the Chicago airport is more expensive, but more reliable than having Court pick us up. Besides, we didn't want to leave him the keys to our cars, don't want to squeeze into his car, and don't think we could survive his driving. I wish these last few miles of the journey were more relaxing given the competent driver and luxury vehicle. But as home approaches, we are just grateful for the vehicle's stiff suspension that keeps the tires moving forward even as the weight of the world rests here in the backseat. So much for stress-free moments.

The first thing I notice as we swing onto our street is the distinct lack of flashing lights – always a good sign and not one we necessarily take for granted. Next, we notice, in quick succession, that the house looks just like we left it and Court's car is in the driveway. With a cautious but hopeful sigh of relief, I go through the garage to the service door. With a glance into the kitchen, my rising optimism drops to zero. Admittedly, it was a short drop.

The door to the microwave is giving way to gravity. The bottom hinge is doing the work of two, the upper half having lost its battle with a greater force. The crunch under my feet draws my attention to the oven across the room. The unnatural twist of the door reveals a hole in the tempered glass. Droplets of its former window are splayed across the floor like a thousand diamonds, or more appropriately, like an equal number of frozen tears. Would I feel better if a stranger had broken into the house - a random act of violence? *Things,* I tell myself, *just things. People are more important than things* - my new mantra.

I hear the door open and close behind me, indicating Ken has paid and dispatched the limo driver. "What is this?!" Ken is getting his first look at the kitchen, or so I thought. I turn to offer comments, well, excuses, for the microwave and oven door. But his eyes are riveted to the inside of the service door. Being so focused on the "remodeled" kitchen, I don't remember even closing the door when I came in. But looking back, I see something protruding from the door at about eye level. "What is that?" I ask, walking back to the door to see for myself. Ken answers by pulling a steak knife out of the metal door. The door itself has been slashed many times, the final resting place for the knife being just above the eight-inch-high letters D-I-E that have been scratched into the door.

Sometimes it seems the mouth engages before the brain, as is made apparent by my first question, "Does that mean that Court wants to die?"

"Or that he wants to kill us." Ken's response has done the same amount of processing.

What I am filtering is, "I would have assumed metal doors were tougher than a steak knife." But Ken takes my words to mean, "Don't mess with my baby." He turns away from the kitchen, toward the office to check on his more obedient child, the business. I crunch my way across the kitchen on the way to Court's bedroom. It is time he rose to face the world, but first I want to lay eyes on his breathing body and wrap my arms around him.

The rec room in the walk-out basement, just outside of Court's room, is a mess, but only of the teenage variety. There are empty potato chip bags, dirty dishes, partial and empty beverage containers scattered around the room. Sodas are partials. The wine and beer bottles are empties. There is a lecture here – about the mess, about respect, about zeroing out our supply of wine – but there won't be much heart in it after the kitchen and door discussions.

With a courtesy and cautionary knock, I open the door to the windowless room where Court sleeps. Even with the lack of light, the mess is unbelievable - that much hasn't changed in a week. But the walls appear to have writing all over them, punctuated with fist-sized holes in the drywall. When his older brother Corey occupied this room, we patched the drywall to hide the holes left by his ill-advised indoor lacrosse practice. If not so irritating, those would have been almost funny. I wish these had a funny side. I doubt that the writing on the wall will supply the levity either. Breathing ensured and rousting accomplished, I return to the kitchen to await Court's company and commentary.

The words that tumble from his lips are predictable: 'I'm sorry…I love you…I'll clean it all up…I'll pay for it.' I believe more of the commentary than Ken does, but only marginally so, which is to say: I wholly believe number two, wish I could believe number one, will demand number three, and suppress a laugh at number four. The storage closet containing the broom and dustpan are right beside the 'die' door. Maybe he noticed the removal of the steak knife. It's hard to say, since after a quick glance his eyes go straight to the ground and I'm left looking at the top of his head.

Ken decides to join our conversation. "I've been working on the computers for the last half hour and neither of them will boot up. You need to get in there and undo whatever you did to them! You are messing with our livelihood!" Ken isn't interested in his son's statements, one through four, or any other number for that matter. Court disappears into the office with Ken, making more promises. We are hoping he can keep at least the one regarding getting the computers to boot properly. I am left with the broom and dustpan in the room full of frozen tears.

Having captured as many tears as I can find in the kitchen, I turn to start a careful inspection of the rest of the house. Living room and dining room get the all clear and a sigh of relief. Needing to escape and having nowhere to go, Ken eventually leaves Court with the non-functioning computers and makes his way to the backyard.

The family room doesn't bear any obvious scars. I cross to the TV and turn it on. It springs to life with the precision of a week prior. I am ready to pronounce the room unscathed and move on when I notice that someone is missing. There is a crèche that occupies the hearth all year long. Well, now, most of a crèche; the baby Jesus is nowhere to be seen. *People are more important than things,* I repeat to myself. At worst, a trip to Hallmark will again supply Mary with someone upon whom to fix her gaze. I pause long enough to look out the back window where Ken is inspecting the hot tub and picking up empty plastic bags from water softener salt. He sees me watching him and picks up another item for my wordless inspection. It's the Bible I gave Court before leaving for Boston. A gust of wind blows charred pages from the still intact binding.

The need for escape wells within me, and is commingled with maybe the first completely sane thought I have had since walking into the house: nowhere is far enough away. I could go to the other side of the world, but I would have to take myself with me. The heart within me beats for my son, and I am doomed to travel with that telling reminder pounding in my chest. There is no escape.

Turning from the charred Word that represents my greatest solace, I go to check on another babe in a manger, this one in the front foyer. Like His fireplace hearth counterpart, He stays out all year long. This one, though, is not of the Hallmark variety. It was hand-carved and painted in Italy. He, His holy family, and various guests at His birth, are an extravagant and precious symbol to me of all things good. His bed is also viewed by a doting, loving mother and a protective, wondering father. His bed only, that is, because, once again, the manger is empty. The curly haired child with outstretched arms is conspicuously absent. *It's a thing. People are more important than things. The actual Christ Child is still on His throne.*

How do I explain to anyone the knife now lodged in my heart? It's not the door, newly adorned with the word "die." It isn't the pile of frozen tears now deposited in the trash. It's more than a Hallmark figure or the pages of a book. It's more than the exquisitely hand-carved figure of a baby kidnapped from His mother's awestruck gaze. I hold no illusions that Court is a practicing believer in the One who (barely) holds me together on this treacherous broken road. But I had been confident in Court's love and hopeful of his respect. And this he knows, above all else: I love him, and I love God. The order of the two is indistinguishable. With a wave of the hand, I can forgive all else. But it takes a conscious act, an effort of love, to forgive Court's total rejection of who I am at my very core.

Walking into the office where he stares at computer code on a bright blue background, I ask the only questions that really matters to me. "Where is baby Jesus?" This time, his eyes meet mine, and in them, is recognition of the depth of my hurt. He jumps up from the chair, "I'll find Him," and he scampers off. I want to believe that, too, but the fact that he isn't sure where to look doesn't give me much hope. The look in his eyes, though, and the immediate response, offer some salve to my wounds. Maybe he does love me (number two) and maybe he really does have some remorse (number one). Maybe he really does wish he could clean up this mess (number three).

Dinner, prepared and eaten mostly in silence, is followed by an evening where only the TV attempts conversation. Ken and I escape to bed early. All the pent-up conversation of the evening vomits out as soon as our door closes.

"Why is he still in our house?!"

"Where else would he go? It's a holiday weekend. He has agreed to go back to out-patient therapy on Tuesday. We can hang on until then."

"He has destroyed our house, taken down our business, and wants us dead!"

"I think 'die' refers to himself, given the many times he has tried to commit suicide. He would never harm us."

"I don't believe that!" Ken hands me a bag for my inspection. Inside are all our kitchen knives. I am repulsed by the sight of them, angered that he feels we need this measure of security, and flooded with relief, all at the same time. We do another couple trips around the dance floor, moving to different music and neither of us altering our steps in the least. Ultimately, we turn our backs, one to the other, and I settle into my pillows for a night of making sure the digital clock doesn't skip any numbers.

How could I kick Court out? Our friends, Ann and Bill, did that with their son, and he died alone in a homeless shelter. I couldn't live with myself if that happened. There must be another way. If Court would only take the medications. It's not really his fault; it's a chemical imbalance.

Like our earlier dance steps, my prayers follow the same circular pattern. *Please be with Court. Please guide me in what to do next. Please change Ken's mind. Help us to agree on something.* (Sidebar to self: quit obsessing. Pray about something else.) *Please keep Colin safe in Iraq. Where is he now? What is he doing? Please surround my son with your protection. And Corey, too; be with him in California. All my sons. Lord, don't make me go through losing a child. Help me to know what to do next. Help Ken and me to agree on something. Be with Court; ease his pain. Help us make it to Tuesday.* (Quit obsessing) *Thank you, God, for safe travel home…that the house is still standing…that we have good computer backups…that Court is alive. Please help me to know what to say to Court to make the difference. Bring someone else alongside to guide him. Make him decide to take his meds…*

At some point the clock does skip a few numbers, though not nearly enough. As if the whole universe is conspiring against my sleep, there is a loud creaking sound in the hallway. I sit up with a start. "Court?"

Missteps and Miracles – Part I
September 2005

Ginny Hanson
First Baptist Church
Geneva, Illinois

When you are retired, holiday weekends don't really have the same feel as before, but the last official days of summer carry a sweetness all their own. The sun climbs out of bed a little later than it had been, as do I. Coffee is brewing, and a light breakfast is on the table for my husband and me. We say a short prayer of thanks for the food and for the day. Church is still an hour away. Breakfast is a comfortable affair, with light talk about the stuff of life and comments on the newsprint scattered on and around the table. After cleaning up the dishes, there isn't enough time to do my Bible study lesson, but I can pull out the list of prayer requests to lift up the other women in my group. The older I get, the more confidence I have in the faithfulness of the Lord. He has brought me through so many crises, real and imagined. It is good to rest in this rocking chair, physically and metaphorically, and better still to pray for younger women bearing a familiar haggard look as they daily attempt to harness their challenges and concerns. The demands of children, spouses, these modern times and the desire to do it all conspire against them.

At church, the sermon continues the theme of my day. *Thank you, Lord, for life.* In the lightness of the day, there is so much to be thankful for, the list would draw out forever. The benediction bids us to go into the world, sharing the grace of the Lord. It is with this confidence that I turn to Lory, a fellow Bible study member, who was seated behind me during the service. "How is your son?" We have been praying for Colin during his tour of duty in Iraq. Although he is in a war zone, I don't expect it to be a sensitive topic. If something serious had happened, there would have been an announcement from the pulpit, and would she really have been just sitting in church? So, when she burst into tears, it took me by surprise. They weren't the tears that leak from the eyes despite best efforts. No, these tears started at the toes and gushed out in choking sobs. Like an old-fashioned water pump from the days of my youth, her shoulders rose and fell, bringing the water up and out in an almost constant stream. I was almost a bit embarrassed for her, and I was certainly caught off guard, but I was also determined to offer what love and comfort I could.

With words spilling over at a pace that matched the tears, she said, "I kicked him out at two o'clock this morning. He came up to our bedroom insisting that he had proof there were ghosts in the house. I followed him down to his room, where he pointed to a trail of chainsaw oil running from his bedroom throughout the rec room and ending at the patio door. Oil was smeared on the glass door – something was written in the oil. The only word I could make out was 'die.' The work of the ghosts, he insisted."

The service had been lightly attended, normal for a holiday weekend, especially when the weather is so gorgeous. It was to be expected that the sanctuary would empty out quickly, but people exited more quickly on our side than the other. It's hard for men to know how to handle a crying woman. It's hard for women to know how to handle a sobbing one, too. Pastor Roger must have seen us, not difficult in our near-isolation, and, bless him, he joined us to offer his learned and well-practiced assistance.

Lory backtracked only briefly, enough to let Roger know that she had kicked Court out last night. But the words, like the tears, spilled over as if propelled--by or against her will, I could not tell. "When we were out of town last week, he trashed our house. He tried to burn it down, but a friend caught him and stopped him. He destroyed our kitchen and the computers we use for our business. It was the last straw when he poured oil all over the rec room last night and blamed it on ghosts. He was storming out of the house when I called his name. He said, 'don't try to stop me.' I told him I just wanted the key back before he left. The look he gave me as he removed the key from his key ring was one of disbelief and hurt. But it changed to contempt and anger when he threw the key at me."

At this point, her words were literally washed away by tears. I wish I could remember what I said at that point. I wish I could remember what Pastor Roger said – those words would probably be more useful to me in another similar situation. But sadly, the shock of her raw emotion, laden with grief, had its effect on the level of my own self-awareness. There were words of comfort and assurance, I think, though her tears may have washed them away, too. It's hard to tell.

"Where is he now? Is he alive? Did 'die' mean he wanted to kill himself? Will I ever see him again? Will he understand that I had to do it? Will he care? Will he forgive me? Can I ever forgive myself if something happens to him? We have friends who kicked their son out and he died alone in a homeless shelter. Could I live with myself if that happened? Will God watch over Court even as he curses God? This has been going on for almost three years! Will it ever end? Will I ever get my son back? Does God even care about the Harrises!?"

Were there answers to any of those questions – answers that didn't sound like platitudes? None that I could think of. Apparently, Pastor Roger didn't have answers, either,.or maybe he knew that now was not the time to express them. Of course, I don't think it was really knowledge she sought. It was a prayer of the most private kind, offered in a public space. The questions were the pleas – no, demands - of a broken heart, brought to the Lord's house to be answered by the Master. We did the only thing we could do, which was to join her in her requests. With hands on her now quieting shoulders, we prayed. With words more eloquent than mine, but no more heartfelt, Roger, and then I, carried her heart's desires to the Master of this house. We prayed for protection, for comfort, for peace. We asked for mercy and grace to be showered upon the entire family. If I were to write the words of those prayers, they would lay awkwardly upon the page. They might seem like the platitudes we were so anxious to avoid. But prayers are not in the words, especially those prayers of and for a broken heart. Prayers are the breath of God flowing in and through us – a sort of divine CPR. They offer life; they are life; they connect us to the source of life. We concluded with "Amen" - which literally means 'so let it be' – and that pretty much summed it up.

There was a stillness then. The tears abated, though surely, they will return. To be clear, her heart was no less broken, though maybe it was bandaged, at least in part. "Thank you," she said in little more than a whisper. Then with a slight, but sad, smile, she looked at me and said, "You were probably asking about Colin, weren't you?" It took me a moment to realize she was referring to my original question. With a smile reflecting hers, I nodded. "We haven't heard anything new from him. We take that as good news. Thanks for asking, though you may never want to ask again." If I wrote for another 10 pages, I could never convey all that was said in the next few seconds by wrapping my arms around her. Some words are better felt than heard.

Lory left the church just as she entered: alone, physically, at least. I hope her steps are lighter and her day is brighter, if only by a matter of degrees. My morning, which had started so clear and free, is now heavier and a bit darker, and I am grateful for that change. I pray I will carry some measure of the burden for her. I will pray for her often during the day, but I will sleep at night, as I always do. Her heart's cry will echo throughout her day and then engulf her entirely in the middle of the night. This is the unavoidable path of a mother's breaking heart. Many have walked it, as have I, though for different reasons. As well-worn as the trail is, it is desolate and lonely each time; it seems more a labyrinth to the traveler. Even one who has walked a path of the same description cannot tell the current traveler to turn left or right at the next intersection. The only true advice is to look up and follow the Lord's directions. But I know from experience how hard it is to look up when your back is bent with the burdens you carry.

Lord, help me to carry her burden so that she can tilt her head up to follow You. Amen – so let it be.

Missteps and Miracles – Part II — Ken Harris
September 2005 — St. Charles, Illinois

I can't believe she did it! She kicked him out, and in the middle of the night, too! Don't think I'm doing a happy dance here. I'm not. He's my son, too, and I want all the best for him. But he doesn't want the best for himself, and we have been ensnarled in his downward spiral for years now. There is nothing I want more than to welcome him home with open arms – when he can acknowledge this is *my* home. Well, Lory's and mine. At twenty-one years, he has options; the sky should be the limit. But those options do not include destroying my house, my life, my business, or my marriage. And up until last night, he was doing a good job of taking down all four. Maybe I can now start to rebuild them, the last one being the most difficult.

I wish there was something I could do for Lory – some way to comfort her. I tell her she did the right thing, but that isn't what she wants to hear. Honestly, I don't know what she wants, though I'm very talented at discovering the opposite. No one could possibly believe that Court is better off living on the streets. But he needs to be on his own to find his way to that better place – or not. I guess that's the part that is threatening to crush Lory – what happens next, what happens "if?" How do you sleep with that? It's just not a question I choose to contemplate.

I probably should have gone to church with her this morning, for her sake. She won't give up on God any more than she will give up on Court. In fact, the two are absolutely linked in ways I don't understand. She sees no point to the whole situation if God isn't in control; without God, this is just random crap and we have no right to expect anything more. I'm not giving up on God, either, and I think the Court and God issues are linked, too. I'm just starting to think that if God is powerless over Court, He may not be the God for me. In almost three years, I don't see where God has stepped in for us. The most I can say is that Court is still alive, something of a miracle. And, yes, Lory and I are still married. But church wasn't on my radar this morning. She didn't push, and I didn't offer. Lately, that's the highlight of what passes for agreement between us.

I've been working on the hot tub all morning, not that I'm a mechanical wiz. Then again, it doesn't take much to figure out that 120 pounds of water softener salt is going to really mess with the filters and motor. At this point, the best I can do is to remove the parts, so I can drop them off for professional assessment. It feels good to be doing something.

After the holiday tomorrow, I'm going to spend Tuesday getting computers fixed or replaced, ditto with the hot tub, microwave and oven, and now the rec room carpet. Our insurance company is going to love us - again. I'm going to start researching alarm systems this afternoon. It might even help with our insurance rates, which are certainly guaranteed to rise. Regardless, an alarm will help with my peace of mind. That knife could have been in one of us as easily as it was stuck into the door. She may think that Court's reference to "die" refers to himself. But I'm not buying that, and I'm not risking it, either. Standing here, I can see his latest reference to death, still smeared on the patio door in oil – and how his choice of "ink" trails around the rec room and into his bedroom.

Lory is back from church, eyes red-rimmed, as usual, but not currently crying. The first topic of discussion is safe: what to eat for lunch. Since we haven't done a major grocery trip yet, our options are limited. But there are enough random items around to make a salad, which is good since the microwave and oven are currently incapacitated. Working together, we pull items from the fridge and pantry for a concoction to satisfy our stomachs. Gathering the cutting board and tomato, I pull open the knife drawer – which is empty. I catch myself before saying out loud, 'guess it's safe to get the knives out of our bedroom now.' Probably still a bit raw for an attempt at humor. I head upstairs to get the necessary utensils, all the while suppressing a bit of a smile at my inside joke. Instead of small talk, we have tiny-talk during lunch, which is to say, there isn't much conversation to be had. Depositing my dirty dishes in the sink, I head back to the deck to clean up the tools I had used to dismantle the hot tub.

Given the events of the past couple of days, can anyone blame me for the rise in my blood pressure and my fists as they form of their own accord upon seeing Court walk into his bedroom again? I could have jumped through the glass door, and probably would have if Lory hadn't stuck her head out to tell me he was just coming to get some of his clothes. I went in to guard my wife and my house from the vandal/intruder/son. She is trying to talk him into going back to the psych hospital, maybe outpatient care. He looks about as thrilled with that prospect as I am, which is to say that the third time was not a charm, and what good would the fourth time do? Two laundry baskets later, he is out the door getting ready to drive away. Lory piles one more thing into his car: the quilt she had made for his college dorm room a million years ago when the future looked golden. He doesn't seem all that interested in the quilt, but she seems quite insistent that he take it. He will probably need a blanket if he is going to live on the streets. Later, Lory told me that she gave him that quilt, so he would feel her love, her arms holding him, when he pulled it around himself. She is probably reading way too much into that one, but it's a nice sentiment, and given with fewer tears than normal.

Tears – now that is a funny subject. Believe it or not, I have always been the crier in our marriage. Movies make me cry, certain songs can do it, even a sappy human-interest story on the news may bring a tear or two. Lory, on the other hand, never cries about that stuff. She cries when she's mad, which frustrates me no end since I'm generally on the receiving end, and I hate fighting with a crying woman. But otherwise, she has never been a crier – or rather, *had* never been a crier. Now she cries daily, the object of her obsession always being one son or another, and usually, it's son number three. Our office is arranged so that our backs are mostly to each other, but you can get a glimpse of the other's profile with minimal movement. Many times, I have turned to ask her a question and seen the silent tears gathering at her chin and dripping into her lap. Generally, I just turn back to my work. She wants to keep the tears to herself, and I haven't figured out how to effectively comfort her. This is the dance we dance, the roles we have acquired. Movies still make me cry, as do songs and sappy stories. Maybe I even cry more easily for them now – I need a release, too. But her tears outnumber mine ten to one. It has become a way of life for her, so unlike the woman I married.

Anyway, I said Court would probably need a blanket to live on the streets, but that won't be tonight. About an hour after he gathered his earthly belongings in the laundry baskets, he returned to say he would like to go talk to someone at the psych hospital. Lory agreed to drive him down there, and promised not to force him into the hospital if he didn't want to stay. An hour later, she called me to say she was on her way home. After talking with the intake counselor, Court decided not to stay, which is when they found out that Court's decision and Lory's promise could be negated by the counselor's assessment. Court has a new address, at least for the next few days. Psych hold number four – another insurance company to contend with.

Grabbing a broom and a dust pan from the garage, I head back to the deck to clean up the scattered piles of ash. Fortunately, Court is no better at arson than he is at suicide: the house is still standing, and he is still alive, despite too many attempts to count. I guess I should be grateful. But relieved is probably the more accurate word; at least I will be relieved after I get over being mad. I keep bouncing between the two, relief and anger, each time I dig into another restoration project. At least this is the last one for today. I'll ramp up the "mad" again on Tuesday, when dealing with the various insurance companies.

There are half a dozen burn piles scattered around the deck. Some of the piles contain enough of the remains of their former lives to identify, like the Bible Lory gave Court before we left. Additional pieces of charred Scripture are trapped against the house by a slight breeze. I wonder what some of the other piles represent, their previous incarnations no longer apparent. There are chunks of melted, blackened plastic, but mostly just ashes. Eventually, we will tear apart the house looking for something or other, never knowing that I'm sweeping up its remains right now. It is unlikely that Court will remember what he used for kindling, or that he would give us a straight answer, even if he did.

As I sweep the last and largest pile of ash into the dustpan, the broom pushes something solid across the deck. More from curiosity than hopefulness for a survivor of the flames, I pick the item out of the surrounding remnants of fire. The incongruity of the piles of ash and the item in my hand makes me think this could be one of those sappy human-interest news stories. I can almost see the reporters standing beside me, microphone emblazoned with the station logo, while the light on the camera blinks that it is recording. "Fire can be so devastating. Even what is not completely consumed is left permanently marked, contorted, disfigured," the reporter is piling on the adjectives, setting the scene for the viewers. "Imagine resigning yourself to the cleanup process, knowing that all is lost, and finding (dramatic pause and pointing finger) there, in a pile of charred ash, the small wooden figure of the baby Jesus smiling up at you. That is the miracle that awaited Ken Harris when he was cleaning up after a series of arson fires at his house. Ken, what was your reaction when you first saw the hand-carved figure, amid the wreckage?" How many news interviews have I seen where the editors must have struggled for a decent sound-bite? Emotions are too raw, the camera too stark, coherent words too few.

Using my shirt, I wipe soot from the Babe's face. My eyes lock on His. Leaving the broom, I take Jesus to my woodworking shop to clean Him up. It reminds me of when each of my sons was born – that first inventory of 10 fingers and 10 toes. How is it possible that a wooden carving doesn't burn in all this carnage? Among the piles of blackened waste, there is a lone survivor, the Christ Child. It takes a moment or two for me to realize that my tears are joining in the cleaning process. His skin is as pure and unblemished as it always has been. No, wait, there is a small mark on his forehead bearing witness to the trauma. In a way, it seems only fitting that even Jesus couldn't escape completely unscathed, proof of His participation in this weary week.

There is comfort here. I'm not going as far as "miracle;" maybe Court just buried the figure in the ashes. We will probably never know. But something was saved; something was rescued. A piece of wood surviving the flames – maybe. A spark of hope fanned to a flicker of flame – yes. There is something amazing about fire: when the night is darkest, even just the light from a single match shines like a bonfire. It's good to take a break from groping in the dark. And, hey, who thought I would be speaking fondly of fire so soon!

Healing — Lory Harris

September 2005 — St. Charles, Illinois

It started with Labor Day weekend, and "labor" has pretty much described the rest of the week as well. Ironically, Labor Day itself may have been the easiest of the days. That was the day between the initial clean up and the insurance claim games.

Court was safely tucked away in the psych hospital, which he hates, of course. Whoever likes being stuck in a hospital - especially one with locked doors? I used to think that a few days of medical intervention could return our life to what it used to be. I'm not even sure I remember what "used to be" looks like anymore. But I remember the days when I was confident that a prescription or two would right our listing ship. Maybe they still could, but only if he would take them. At least when Court is under lock and key, he has no choice. If he took them long enough, would he see how much better his life would be? Maybe the more important part of the temporary residence is that he can't take the other "meds" he prefers. Is pot his way of dealing with bipolar? Or does it bring on the irrational behavior that has been labeled "bipolar?" I used to think it was the former, but I'm not so sure anymore.

You hear a lot of talk about the stigma of mental illness. It's true and it certainly exists. People aren't sure what to do with it. They make jokes about it, but they are afraid of it. There are dramatic and highly publicized cases that feed that fear – justifiably so. Ironically, though, sometimes when you can pick your own stigma, it's a good choice. Ken and I choose on a case-by-case basis. For example, with the insurance company, we play on the bipolar. If we say our addict son trashed the house, it all comes back to us: we are such pathetic parents that our kid escapes the real world in favor of the psychedelic one. There are simple guidelines to parenting, and if we had followed them, we wouldn't be living through this never-ending nightmare. Kids need to know they are loved (with both words and time) and they need rules (say "no" to drugs, for example). Know their friends, hold them responsible for their actions, have family meals together, take them to church. The truth is we did – all of it! I suppose we didn't do any of it perfectly, which puts us in a league with most parents.

Now we find ourselves struggling through day after day, year after long year, crushed by self-accusations and wondering how much of the blame we should shoulder. So, yeah, sometimes we choose the mental illness label where there is less personal fault than drug addiction. At least with mental illness it's just a bad roll of the genetic dice and not knowingly our fault. Then others can judge us with a modicum of pity – mixed with untouchable status, of course – rather than just pure contempt and superiority.

Am I judging others' reactions harshly? Maybe... I am certainly generalizing. But I'm also speaking from experience. I have been the judgmental superior observer, certain that if other parents did things my way, they, too, would have the perfect family. God has allowed me a steady diet of the rotten fruit born of my condescending attitude. I have deserved it, but I wish it would stop now. Never again could I think my parenting superior to anyone. Maybe I am just judging myself honestly for the first time: I have failed in every conceivable way. In a few short days, my son will be homeless. And I thought we had already hit bottom.

As much as I may not want to spend my evenings at the hospital, I am drawn there like a moth to flame. Ken and I have spent every evening of the past week driving to the daily visitation time with Court. We have the drill down: do not bring food, drink or sharp items. We drop off clothes for him: no belts, hoodies with strings, shoes with laces, or plastic bags. The cigarettes we bring for Court are a peace offering of sorts. Even though we don't approve, they are a small token of reconciliation. The staff will supply the fire for the Camel Lights, as well as the specified time, location and supervision for smoking them.

By now I should know that I can't rescue Court, but my mother's heart won't let me stop trying. So, every evening we arrive, go through security, and wait for our sullen child to shuffle over to greet us. For the next ninety minutes, or as long as we can collectively stand it, we pretend that life is normal. We talk about stuff like sports or other family members or the weather, pretending that we are all a part of that world. Maybe we watch TV together or play a board game. We are marking time, and it is running in reverse. There is no need for Ken and me to converse on the way home. The small talk was all covered at the hospital, such as it was. There is no need for either of us to lie about how much better Court is doing, or when he will be released. Frankly, if they keep him another couple of weeks, it will blissfully forestall Court's inevitable address change. Kicking him out was a long time coming - overdue, I suppose. Even if Ken would consent, I wouldn't rescind the pronouncement. Our son is not invited back home – at least not as a resident.

For me, the highlight of the visits was probably the first night. "I want to show you something," I said, as I pulled my symbol of mercy and grace from my pocket and handed it to Court. The exact look on his face was a bit hard to read, clouded as it was by a pharmaceutical haze attempting to restore sanity, but I thought I saw genuine surprise registered there. He stared down at the small wooden carving as the Babe kept His steady gaze fixed upon my baby boy. "Dad found Him at the bottom of a pile of ashes."

"Wow. It doesn't even have a mark on it. No, wait, there is a little mark on His forehead." He seemed as genuinely surprised by the intact carving as the rest of us were. I couldn't tell if he was relieved, as well, but I wanted him to be, so I inserted it between his words. Someday when all of this is over, someday when I die a natural death and he is still living, someday when normal is not just a setting on my dryer, Court will inherit that crèche set. That Baby Jesus will be in his house. Whether or not he tells his friends and family, he will know that this Christmas visitor survived the flames and the madness of 2005. That is a happy thought, and one I hang onto and will myself to believe when possible. Optimism by degree is better than pessimism by the bucketful.

The doctor called today to give us a day-four-update. Court is responding to the medications but there is still a long way to go. He won't be released for several days at best. He has talked freely with the staff about going to Lazarus House, the homeless shelter here in town. In fact, he tells everyone who will listen that he helped set up the place, along with his brothers, as part of Colin's Boy Scouts Eagle project. That's all true. I had forgotten that Court had helped with that project. Everyone takes this as a good sign. Perhaps most people would think it odd to feel relief at sending their child to a homeless shelter that he had labored to establish half a decade earlier. Sadly, there are some who might understand the modicum of solace it brings.

The director of Lazarus House, Darlene, also volunteers at the jail with me, so we have spoken on many occasions. I like her no-nonsense, no-excuses, in-your-face personality. I've spoken with her often enough to also see her compassion, her soft side. Generally, though, she reminds me more of Colin's drill sergeants in Marine boot camp. If that sergeant had a soft underbelly, I assure you, none of his recruits were scratching it. Maybe Darlene can transform Court the way Colin's taskmasters chiseled him. Most likely, Darlene needs to whip me into shape, too. When I called her to tell her that Court will be one of her guests, she reminds me that once he is there, she will not be able to say anything to me about his stay, even whether he remains with them. They will welcome him as long as he follows their rules and is progressing toward life on his own. They can be a long-term residence, but not a permanent one. I shouldn't be surprised by her candor, but I do feel the slap across the face: well-placed and well-intended – and well-needed, too. I do love that lady, never shying from the truth!

At home, a new microwave heats our coffee and a new oven door contains the heat when in use. Our customers are happy to be receiving their plans again, thanks to two new computers. Bondo and a fresh coat of paint have removed the specter of death from view when we enter our garage. New carpet will be laid next week for us to admire through the clean patio door while we relax in the hot tub. I breathe a sigh of relief with Court safely tucked away for the time being. He is safe, fed, watched over, and receiving the help he needs – or the help we judge he needs. His opinion might be a bit different.

My curio-cabinet holds another Son, tucked safely in His bed, finger and toe inventory complete. Another mother gazes with adoration upon her Son. His eyes hold hers and do not waiver. In them is knowledge of the world that one so young should not bear. He has returned to her and to the love of family, whole, though slightly scarred. I pray that perhaps someday soon, my son will do the same. Perhaps, someday.

A New Address
September 2005

Darlene Marcusson
Lazarus House
St. Charles, Illinois

Lory's call wasn't entirely unexpected; I have counseled her before regarding her son. I cannot recall all the details immediately, but then, the exact story is like so many that details easily blur. At any rate, he would not become a guest at this homeless shelter based on her evaluation of the situation. Court will need to present himself and make his own request. Lazarus House does not turn people away, even in the middle of the night, but we are not a flophouse, either. Those are the distinctions that we will discuss with Court, if he presents himself at our doorstep. Addiction and mental illness both follow a predictable path, which is to say the unexpected is standard.

I wish Lory's second, and more panicked phone call, was less predictable, as well. It, however, was based on neither mental health nor addiction, but rather on insurance company policies. If ever I get a chronic illness, I do hope it will be mental health related. I know it sounds flippant, but it's all too true. As I have told far too many parents over the years, it is the one illness that will be treated "successfully" in five days or less at a psych hospital, regardless of circumstances or severity. Cancer may take months or even years of treatment. But mental illness receives five days of coverage by insurance or by our state Medicaid. So, on the fifth day, insurance companies pronounce that sanity has been successfully restored. Holding a slip of paper entitling the bearer to purchase prescription drugs that they can't afford, and frequently don't even want, the newly "recovered" often find their way to our location.

Late this afternoon, Court did indeed present himself at our doorstep asking for a place to stay. If it was a job interview, the door would have closed on him as quickly as it had opened. The dark growth on his cheeks and chin were a good start to a beard that would make a mountain-man jealous. It was certainly not a fashion statement any more than his ill-fitting ragged clothes. His fingers twitched and twirled a momentarily invisible cigarette. He would, no doubt, spend time on the front stoop with the rest of the smokers. That he was abstaining for the moment was either a sign of respect or desperate hopefulness - or a momentary lack of supply. Most likely the latter, though either of the former could be a good sign.

To be honest, after a cursory glance, his physical appearance was too familiar - too common at this house - to merit closer scrutiny. However, Shakespeare had a point: eyes are the window to the soul. Despite his attempt to keep the blinds drawn, Court's windows allowed a glimpse into both the fear and swagger within. Another of "the least of these" has found his way to our doorstep, and I say the first of many prayers over him and for him and for our staff. *May the divine Windex cut through grime, and may the blinds be lifted to allow the Son-shine to reach the recesses of this young man's soul.* Being a window washer is the calling God has placed upon my life, though without His intervention, I can do nothing. Even with it, I can only play the role He has ordained. And so, we began.

Court's eyes darted in all directions, taking in and evaluating more than his ears, which should have been more actively engaged. That, of course, is to be expected: young suburban male, first day of homelessness. He is desperate, but too cocky to believe this is anything more than a temporary setback, and already calculating how to beat the system. I'm not arrogant enough to think we at Lazarus House can't be duped, but we are experienced enough to have eliminated many, if not most, avenues. And we have the added advantage of an un-chemically-altered thought processes.

"Lazarus House is here to assist you in getting back on your feet. As you adhere to this behavior contract and progress toward the goals you will establish with your case manager, you are welcome to stay here as long as needed." His ears gather enough information to instruct his hand to pick up the pen and sign the contract. The eyes are not focused on the words to which he has agreed. The pen itself, held between two fingers and repeatedly flicked with the thumb, seems to have taken on the role of a now visible, though non-functioning, cigarette. There are more formalities, discussions (largely one-sided), tours, and introductions before I leave Court in the capable hands of Brett, his case manager.

The days are long here, and the nights can be longer. Our guests' demons frequently shun the light of day only to reappear in the evening. Our staff, both paid and volunteer, are dedicated and hardworking. Watching a case manager talking late into the night to calm a fearful or confused guest brings on waves of thankfulness for God's grace and provision. How many times have I watched a volunteer cradle a crying child, allowing the frazzled mother fifteen minutes of time to herself? There are discussions around the table as cards are played, and co-mingled laughter in response to a TV sitcom. There are times when tensions rise, and words start to fly, though these are generally quickly quelled. Our guests know from personal experience that homelessness in a shelter is better than being homeless on the streets. We spend much time on conflict resolution skills, a necessity for all communities, and maybe more so for ours. For many of our guests, this key lacking skill was a contributing cause bringing them to our door. We are patient, but consistent and insistent in these lessons – for their good and for our collective good.

Like all shelters, "tight" is the word: money, supplies, resources, physical space. Our one large gathering room doubles as the men's sleeping quarters. Rows of bunks fill most of the space, leaving room for a couple of large tables, a counter for meal preparation, and a TV in the corner. A bank of lockers lining the back wall holds our guests' worldly possessions. A separate room has been carved from this once larger space to allow an area for our children to play, work on homework, and just to be children. The women's sleeping quarters are in a room down a flight of steps nearer the main entrance. Our current prayer is for more space for our women and children, a space for them to be a family unit. I lean heavily upon the promise in Mark 11:24, "You can pray for anything, and if you believe that you've received it, it will be yours" (NLT). When I look around, I see the embodiment of that promise fulfilled in brick and mortar. I see the efforts of our guests, and remember the faces and stories of those who have come before. Then I believe anew, and humbly bow before His throne to ask again. This house is built on prayer and will collapse without it.

As I gather my purse and keys to head home, the clock simultaneously indicates the start of a new day. Our newest guest, like so many before him, remains sleepless, fingers twitching, again, as his requests for "cold medication" go unanswered. It is a difficult transition, and the staff is not unsympathetic, nor are we ignorant to a non-medical request for chemical alteration. It will be a long night for Court and for many others by extension. Car keys in hand, my spirit pauses before I leave. Believing Mark's words and carrying Court with me, I approach the throne again. Each new guest is unique, and yet each is identical to every other person: we all stand in need of God's grace and mercy.

Father, draw this hurting, confused, lost child to Yourself. May Your image shine through from the core of his being and become a guidepost to Your glory.

Parentage **Ken Harris**
September 2005 **St. Charles, Illinois**

I rose early this morning, before the alarm heralded the start of the day. I could have risen earlier (I wasn't sleeping anyway), but I laid in bed for a while puzzling out how to design the roof on a house I am drafting. I wandered down to my computer somewhere around five, a possible solution having presented itself. Somewhere around 11, after three cups of coffee and some paper and CAD doodling, my early morning ideas were successfully refined. The family who will eventually live in the house won't give a thought to their roof design, that concern having been successfully checked off the list this morning. It has been a long day already, but lunch will be eaten with an air of satisfaction.

In a warped sort of way, it was nice to use brainpower this morning on a 3D geometric problem rather than on third-child problems. The third child issues aren't over – I'm not naïve or delusional enough to believe that. But in Court's physical absence over the past week and a half, I have realized more restful sleep, this morning's early rising notwithstanding. The remnants of Court's rage have been eliminated from sight, though the non-visible wounds will fester longer. The newly installed security system enhances my dreams. Lory wasn't as concerned about the message Court scratched in the door and punctuated with the protruding knife, but "DIE" seemed self-explanatory to me. Her objections to our enhanced security were perfunctory and wouldn't have dissuaded me at any rate. We dutifully set the alarm when we leave and when we sleep. It makes enough noise to wake the dead; apparently, we are much better at remembering to turn it on than turning it off when entering. I'm sure our neighbors are anxious for our learning curve to improve.

I am happily contemplating a BLT complete with a fresh tomato from our garden when the home phone rings. Lory and I both glance at Caller ID. "I'll start lunch," she says, as she sees my mother's name on the screen. My mother and I have a cordial, though not overly close, relationship. In some ways, Court has is closer to his grandmother than I am. She calls on him periodically to help her with her TiVo and other electronic issues. Court likes to mess with that stuff, and she always pays him well. Sometimes I think she invents problems as an excuse to hand him a few bucks. It's hard to know exactly what to do for Court that will constitute help and not enabling. I don't have all the answers, so I'm not judging. Every man for himself, though I would voice my opinion in no uncertain terms in the unlikely event that she let him move in with her. Ironically, Court is exactly the reason for her phone call.

"Court came by my house this morning," she starts. Her tone is casual--almost too casual. My internal alarms are intensifying all my senses with remarkable effectiveness. Naturally, she had me at 'Court,' but as she continues, I marvel at the precision and perceptiveness of my adrenal glands. "He was so sloppily dressed and wild-eyed that I didn't even let him in the house. I just talked to him though the screen door. Well, actually, he just talked at me; I didn't say much."

My mom is a tough bird. She raised three kids on her own after my dad died. I was in my early teens at the time with one sister in junior high and one in elementary school. Being a teacher, Mom ruled over the classroom in much the same fashion as she had parented us, that being by-the-book. It wasn't a pop-culture book full of fluff, either--more like one written in the early 1900s: children were to listen, obey and speak respectfully. On a good day, Court did not fit that mold well, and apparently today was not even close to a 'good' day.

Now, it was Mom's turn to talk and mine to listen. I didn't interrupt as she detailed my son's obvious lack of hygiene as he paced back and forth on her front porch. A trail of cigarette smoke marked an erratic trail in the still morning air – one more reason he would not be allowed entrance to her house. It was the excuse she had used. He wasn't inclined to put the fire out, so she hadn't needed another reason to bar his entrance. Court's rants included a detailed description of the injustices he had suffered throughout his life due to his parentage, culminating with the events of the past few weeks. Mom had a wry chuckle over the difference between Court's diatribe and the version I had shared with her a week earlier. I felt no need to interject in my own defense; Court's tale sounded "tall."

When she came to the true point of her recitation, though, there was nothing to chuckle about, wry or otherwise. Court had gone to her house, hers specifically, to demand a confession of what he regarded as a well-kept family secret, hidden from him since birth. He demanded confirmation that he was not Lory's and my son, but instead had been adopted as an infant. Not receiving her confirmation of this "obvious" charade, he demanded to know if she had witnessed his birth, or if she was just blindly taking our word regarding his true DNA acquisition source.

In the end, their conversation left both parties in a higher state of agitation than when they had started. Court now eyed his grandmother with greater suspicion, having squandered her chance to purge herself of the family's dirty little secret. My mom was now truly frightened by her grandson, after witnessing firsthand the depths of craze that had driven us to install the alarm system for protection from our own biological child. "Mom, if he comes around again, don't open the door. And call the police if necessary." It was the best advice I could offer, and I hoped she would heed it if the time came.

I'm not sure I tasted even a bite of the BLT as Lory and I discussed the call over lunch. My wife's initial reaction to my recounting of the phone call surprised me a bit: she chuckled, laughed out loud, even. "All those hours of labor," she said, "only to find out he isn't our son, after all." But the smile that lingers after her quip holds the undeniable sadness of a freshly wounded heart.

I wish I had some actual solace to offer her. I wish someone would offer meaningful advice to me; something more than 'hang on, the road is about to get really rough.' If there are maps for this path, we haven't found them. I ask directions from the passers-by, who point and describe landmarks to guide by. But the landmarks don't materialize, and each spectator points a different direction, all with the same clueless well-intent. My life, my son, my problem.

Searching for Blessings — Lory Harris
September 2005 — Email sent from St. Charles, Illinois

To my partners in prayer,

Well, no word from Court this morning. He was kicked out of Lazarus House late yesterday - don't know exactly why, though the imagination doesn't have to run too far.

He showed up here last night asking for a ride to St. Joe's (psych unit), which I gave him. He did a running dialog all the way up there. It gave me my smile for the day, though it was indeed a sad smile. Court alternated between pushing me away and drawing closer to me verbally. "This is all your fault – you kicked me out." And then, "I love you! I'm sorry! I don't know what I was thinking. I just want to come home." And then, "You are the worst excuse for a mother I have ever seen! I'm better off without you!"

He is so lost, so hurting. It is a test of my faith just to believe that God could indeed use this for His purposes.

Court wanted out at the main entrance of the hospital and didn't want me to come in with him, so I let him go. He walked into the building and I parked and watched for about 5 minutes to make sure he didn't just walk back out. I hope they checked him in, but the real issue is that if he's not a danger to himself or others, he's not sick enough to need help (what a stupid system). And if he's healthy enough to know he needs help, then he isn't sick enough to merit it. This is the world Court is trapped in, especially without health insurance. We know from experience that the hospital won't confirm or deny that he is or was there. So, until he contacts us, we won't know where he is, or how he is, or even if he is. Guess that means that St. Joe's gets to take his word for what is going on in his life, and Court's a good spin-doctor, though he did ask to go there, so maybe there is hope.

Now we wait. Feels like I've said that before.

I want to pray for peace as directed in Philippians 4:6-7. "Do not be anxious about anything, but in every situation, by prayer and petition, with thanksgiving, present your requests to God" (NIV). The word that jumps out at me there is *thanksgiving*. I am trying to be thankful that:

- God honored me for so many years with a bright, fun, loving child named Court.

- Court has a very strong will to live.

- When he runs, Court always runs to family.

- There is medication that could ease his suffering if only he would take it.

- At least a part of him is willing to take the medication.

- We are self-employed and not in danger of being fired for all this drama, and most of our customers are very understanding of the situation.

- To the best of my knowledge, drugs have not been involved in this latest round, at least to this point.

- There are lots of people in very diverse roles who have taken an active interest in Court's life and well-being.

- God has not abandoned me for an instant of this whole ordeal, nor do I expect that to change in the future.

- Corey loves his brother so deeply that he would ask for a transfer to the Chicago area to help - which he hasn't done, at my insistence.

- The closer Court gets to rock bottom, the closer he gets to bouncing back up and regaining a life that he wants to live.

- God lays it on human hearts to help the "least of these," and right now, I believe Court lands squarely in that category.

- Colin will be home soon, which will ease everyone's mind a bit, and quite possibly ease Court's mind a lot.

Okay, sometimes I need to write out things just to get them straight in my head. Thank you for being my sounding board! And, especially, thank you for praying for my son!

Love and blessings to you all!

Lory

A Mountaintop between Valleys — Lory Harris
September 2005 — St. Charles, Illinois

Today was a good day, a very good day! I had been afraid I would never utter those words again! But I say them now and mean them with my whole heart! Thank you, God! Ken tells me not to get too excited, which might indeed be wise advice. But I've been slogging through the muck of life too long not to take advantage of a break, no matter how brief the respite might be.

We got a call from Court this evening. He's at St. Joe's and back on Depakote, a mood stabilizer. He sounds AWESOME! It has been prescribed to him for the past 18 months, but he only takes it in fits, going off it when he feels better. Maybe this time it will stick! He has an intake interview with Eker Center in Elgin for a place to live when he is released, probably early next week. I really don't know much about it. I guess it's kind of a half-way house for the mentally ill, helping them to get stable on their meds and to find a job. He is nervous that he won't be accepted and will have nowhere to go. He seems to fit their model, so I don't understand his trepidation, though there is a paranoia factor, and I certainly understand that. Right now, I just don't have it in me to doubt that he will get in; God will take care of it. That's what I want to believe, though it has been my experience that God is anything but linear. I map things out from point A to point B. The Lord tends to lead me from A to R to L to W to C and then all the way to Z before finally landing at B – if, indeed, B was ever His endpoint. Still, I pray for a straight line at last. Court, as well as the rest of us, could use the break.

Sometimes when I read the Bible, the words bend and blur and almost drip right off the edge of the page. Of course, it's not the words, it's me. I treat the letters grouped on the page as more of a reading lesson than an inspiration. Five minutes later, I close the book having no idea what the words were, much less how they should guide me. It's a habit, nothing more, though maybe something less – less because I know how much more it should be, and I don't care. I'm just going through the motions, hoping against hope that God will show up. And then He does! He breaks through my malaise with a reverberating shout, waking my body, mind and soul to hope and possibility.

Thank you, Lord! You did that today – even before Court called. I was reading in First Peter, the words being pulled past my eyes like a swiftly moving river. I couldn't see anything clearly, or hold it in my mind to allow for examination. Or maybe it's the other way around: His words stood still as *I* whirled and reeled intent on my dizzy, nonsensical rabbit trails. No doubt that's the way it was. God's Word has been unchanged for millennia. It didn't suddenly start morphing just to confound my addled life.

At some point, as words meandered past my pre-occupied brain, God broke into my world long enough for me to soak up a verse. More specifically, the eighth verse of the fourth chapter of Peter's first letter. "Love covers a multitude of sins" (NLT). Only six words, yet they spoke volumes to me this morning where the previous hundreds had not.

So many times in the past three years, Court has questioned my love for him – *our* love for him, since neither Ken nor I are exempt. It rips our hearts every time, tearing at the fabric of our individual and joint beings. The hurriedly applied patches only serve to stem the blood flow, not to stop it. Still, despite that, we love Court. We both long to welcome him back into the family – the real family that laughs and teases together, comforts and helps each other, gathers for meals, and when possible, lays our heads to sleep under a common roof. Unconsciously, Ken and I alternate shifts in the night, praying, scheming, aching for Court's return. Neither of us can walk into the house without first checking Caller ID: to see if he has called and to make sure no other unwelcome specter has. Court can question it all he wants, but while our love for him might not be perfect, it is complete. I believe he knows there is love here, and he wants it, but in his mental confusion, he doesn't know how to open the door for himself. We love him enough to make him responsible for at least that much.

We have also made mistakes (plenty of them!) over the past three years. Maybe we should have kicked him out earlier, or maybe not at all. Who knows what would have worked "best?" If Court doesn't make it through this, then anything else we could have done would have been the "right" thing. Should we have followed some doctor's advice more closely, or maybe found a different doctor altogether? Should we have spanked him more or punished him less in his formative years? Did we spoil him with things or withhold something that would have focused his intellect for a lifetime pursuit?

In our nighttime meanderings, we have searched for wisdom to guide our steps. But while Ken and I have made an unspoken promise to watch over the night for Court's sake, it seems we have reached agreement on little else, save the one thing we have always agreed upon: we love our son. I guess we can agree we have made mistakes, though we might not agree on what those mistakes were or at whose insistence.

For two thousand years, God has said with unwavering assurance that what He demands of us is love. He promises that love is enough to cover our mistakes, our sins. Who knows what will happen from here. But I refuse to look back and question ourselves, our actions. We did whatever we have done with the best of intentions and the maximum love. Resting my assurance on First Peter 4:8, we have done the big thing right! *We love you, Court!*

Change of Venue — Court Harris
October 2005 — Eker Center
Elgin, Illinois

There is a crack in the ceiling. It doesn't let in water or light, which I guess is good. It doesn't even appear to be the den for a family of spiders, which is even better. Its chief job, as far as I can tell, is to mock me as I lay here on my bed desperately wishing for an address to call my own. The Eker Center is not my home – a way station, maybe, but not a permanent address.

It's hard to believe that I couldn't wait to get here. That might not be accurate; I couldn't wait to get out of St. Joe's Psych Unit. I didn't think it possible, but St. Joe's is even worse than my forced psychological retreat at Linden Oaks two Christmases ago, and then again, a month ago. At least at Linden Oaks we got smoke breaks! St. Joe's is in an actual hospital--and on the 7th floor, at that, where smoking is not allowed. Unhealthy, they say. Inconvenient, I contend. Of course, they have no problem insisting on filling me with a host of pharmaceuticals of their choosing. And when their mixture causes insomnia and high blood pressure, they just supplement my cocktail. Why should they worry about my lungs when they are scrambling my heart and brain!

St. Joe's opinion notwithstanding, a cigarette was my first order of business upon my release. I am basically flat broke, which I haven't allowed to alter my smoking habit in the least. Fortunately, those who are like-minded are a sympathetic and generous lot. Of course, you can't bum cigarettes indefinitely, but Mom has a soft touch and will generally hand over at least a twenty when I see her. And I still have the gas credit card, which is capable of filling more than my car's gas tank.

Upon exiting St. Joe's, my options were a bit limited: here or the streets. Lazarus House told me not to come back until I was stable on my meds. So, crossing that option off my list left scant possibilities. The cold and wet of October will shortly turn into the frigid ice and snow of winter. Eker was at the top of my list of residence options. It was also my only option since my parents steadfastly refuse to let me come home.

Here, we aren't locked up like lab rats as I was at St. Joe's. The Eker doors lock at night, prohibiting a change of venue regardless of the side of the lock you are viewing. But during the day, I may come and go as I please – as long as I please the powers-that-be to their level of satisfaction. I meet with my counselor from time to time, and take my prescriptions as prescribed, at least as far as they know. Of course, there are group sessions, a hallmark of free housing. I walk a thin line by attending enough sessions to merit this bed without drinking too much of their Kool-Aid.

Still staring at the crack, I hear my roommate shuffle in, making indistinguishable muttering noises as he, too, flops on his bed. Whatever words there were to share between us were previously spent as we finished cleaning the dinner dishes. There are 10 live-ins here, bound by the meals we prepare and eat together and the chores that follow – a band of jolly misfits, less the jolly. At least there are only two to a bedroom, unlike Lazarus House where twenty men sleep in one room. It is possible to sleep through the snores of just one other, though occasionally my bunkmate can rattle the rafters all by himself. That might at least partially explain the fractured ceiling.

I need to find a job that pays enough to get my own place before my tilting world capsizes altogether. Eker has contacts with some local employers, matching up our little band of loners with the means to become fully functioning members of society, making way for the next in an endless line of bed-warmers. Eker and I may not always have the same goals for my life, but on this we agree: I need a job. Most of their listings are menial jobs that certainly don't require two years of college. But then, I delivered pizzas for six months and loved it. Of course, that wasn't full-time work, but I would do most anything to get my own place.

I have an interview tomorrow for a janitor's job at a plastics company. Mom would laugh at the thought of me cleaning for 40 hours a week. She has spent a lifetime cleaning up after my brand of clean. But any kind of full-time employment would increase my standing in the drug court's eyes, and they seem to think that all we addicts are capable of is unskilled labor anyway. I've seen Randy's suspicious and disapproving looks in my direction. My parole officer can look all he wants. I've "passed" my drug tests for the past year and a half running; I'm getting close to graduation. Freedom from peeing in a cup three times a week *and* my own place? Now that would be perfect!

Mom and Dad have agreed to pay my security deposit once I have a job that can pay the rent. There is an apartment complex only a couple of miles from our house, well, *their* house. The rates are dirt cheap and it even has a pool. It is the epicenter of any kind of violence that occurs in lily-white, middle-class St. Charles, which still doesn't amount to much. Besides, I survived jail, twice; I can survive Fox River Apartments.

Bring on the mop and bucket! I'm motivated!

Moving On – Part I **Paul Hansen, Supervisor**
Halloween 2005 **Hoffman Plastics Corp**
Elgin, Illinois

It was quite the celebration when Carl retired. For almost eighteen years he had steadfastly, efficiently and flawlessly done his job. There was never a complaint from the office staff, and the bathrooms were spotless. Carl really took pride in what he did, and it showed. He never missed a day and was never late for work. There were smiles all around when he cut that cake. But it was also the worst day of my professional life, I will never have another employee like Carl. The two weeks since have only validated my prognostication.

Aside from having to let an employee go, the thing I like least about my job is filling a position, and right now it's a tough hiring market. Jobs are plentiful, and help is scarce, which can lead to a lot of turnover. Our wages are at or above average and the working conditions are good. I wasn't foolish enough to expect anyone I hired to really replace Carl – in dependability, responsibility, reliability or longevity. But I was hoping for maybe two out of the four.

I took a chance on an eager young kid named Court. He was overqualified with some college under his belt. He wouldn't be happy as a janitor forever, and I didn't expect him to stay there. He would have a foot in the door at a company that promotes from within. It seems he had hit a rough patch in life, and I'm in favor of helping someone in that situation. After all, someone took a chance on me years ago, and subsequently, I had taken a chance on Carl. Some of my best employees are those who didn't seem to fit the job requirements initially.

Court started the week before Carl left, allowing Carl to train his own replacement. The first few days went well enough, as they usually do. Court arrived on time and eager to work, the first order of business being the cleaning of the offices and breakroom before the salaried employees showed up for work. The newbie couldn't believe the mountain of trash that appeared each day in the breakroom. Carl and I had a good laugh about that one. It's just the way it is, but even after all these years, we still marvel at it. It's like the employees collectively clean their home refrigerators and lug everything to the office to provide us with the opportunity to properly dispose of it – daily! The sheer volume of trash is impressive.

From the start, the hardest thing for Court seemed to be break time. He got breaks, of course, never missed one. But what he wanted was a cigarette, which isn't allowed. Because some of our product is destined for the food industry, we must maintain a sterile environment. Smoking is not allowed in the building, and leaving the building during a shift is also not allowed. Access to the building is through a key card system, with every entry recorded. An employee with multiple entries during a day without cause or corresponding justification on their time card is subject to disciplinary action. There are still smokers among us, but we must agree to an eight hour fast from the habit five days a week.

I have six janitors on staff. They each work independently, cleaning their own zone daily. There are also rotating major cleaning projects that we work on in teams of three or four. The new guy is always cut a bit of slack on those projects, at least until he gets the rhythm of his zone-cleaning humming along smoothly and efficiently. Court, though, seemed to enjoy those major projects more. Maybe he is just a more social person. But his zone certainly wasn't living up to Carl's standards – or mine. I needed to address that, which was my self-assigned task when I went looking for Court earlier today.

The zones aren't overwhelming in size, but in a manufacturing facility, they are rather sprawled. Sometimes it requires looking twice when searching for a person who might also be moving around. The two trash containers in the breakroom were only three quarters full, a sure sign that they had been emptied earlier in the day. A cleaning cart near the bathrooms showed no sign of its assigned transporter. Perhaps Court had gone to the storage closet to get supplies or replacement toilet paper or soap, but I didn't find him there, either. On my second round, I saw Greg, a janitor from a neighboring zone. "Have you seen the new guy?" I asked.

"No, did you check by the back door? Sometimes he cracks it for a breath of fresh air, if you know what I mean." I did indeed catch his meaning.

I didn't find Court, but I did find a cigarette butt outside the door sending up ever weakening smoke signals. After another trip around the facility, I make a mental note of the time and deactivate Court's key card. He won't need it anymore. Three weeks: not quite the record in brevity, but certainly no Carl, either. Court got his second paycheck today and, it appears, his last. I head back to my office to arrange for another help wanted ad in the local paper.

Moving On – Part II Court Harris
Halloween 2005 St. Charles, Illinois

It's almost 1:30 when I walk into my apartment. It feels good to be home in time for a late lunch. Mom dropped by a couple of days ago with three bags of groceries. I've already eaten all the good stuff, but there is still a frozen pizza left. After three sons, she knows what we like, and just how little effort we are willing to expend before we head to McDonald's instead. I'm not really in the mood for people, no matter how periphery, especially after stopping at the courthouse on the way home to pee in a cup. I was tempted to skip it, but the last thing I want is Randy showing up at my door. I don't plan on opening my door for any trick-or-treaters, and certainly not for one carrying a badge. I don't think I even need to leave the house again until my next urine deposit in two days.

I cleaned up a little before Mom came over, making the place look halfway presentable. The couch and chair are each clear enough to hold a body and the coffee table only holds a smattering of beer bottles. I take advantage of the clear site line to the TV while lying on the couch waiting for the pizza to cook. I haven't seen much daytime TV recently, not that much seems to have changed in the plot lines. The timer announces the conclusion of lunch preparations just as I am starting to nod off. I consider ignoring it, but the last time I did that, it awakened the smoke alarm. Besides, the smell of the pizza has re-ignited the growl from my stomach.

I've only been in my own apartment for a couple of weeks now. Mom and Dad paid the security deposit, so I only had to come up with half a month's rent to start. They also handed down the couch, chair. TV and coffee table. The bed and empty dresser in the adjoining room came from my former bedroom. I like my little place, and Mom seemed to approve, though I didn't let her into the bedroom. It was worth the effort it took to move a few piles to close that door before she got here. Maybe she will let me come over to the house to do a few loads of laundry. Most of my clothes arrived here needing a bath, something I still haven't remedied. If she had seen the piles, she might have even taken a load or two with her. Amazing but true, she *likes* doing laundry. I'll have to consider that in the future.

Hot pads would have been far more useful for removing the pizza from the oven if I had the slightest idea where they might be. The towel I chose instead just didn't have the same heat protection. A couple of things got knocked over in my hurry to set the pizza on the counter. I see the bills lying on the floor where they fell and leave them, but I pick up my keys and a pen which I am more likely to need later. After wiping a knife on the same hot pad/towel, I cut the pizza and toss the cloth toward my bedroom to join the rest of the laundry fairy hopefuls.

The first piece of pizza disappears before I even sit back down, and along with it goes the outermost layer of skin from the roof of my mouth. A beer sterilizes the area and soothes the pain. Two more triangles of hot tomato and cheese on a crust and another beer join me for some channel surfing. None of the flickering images are holding my attention.

It was apparent from the first day I met Carl that I wasn't going to top his employment reviews or longevity, not that I had anything against Carl. Man, when he cleaned those toilets, they shined! The President of the United States could have used those urinals and combed his hair in the porcelain reflection! Since it seemed unlikely the president would ever be rating my efforts, I saw no need to work to win his approval. I give credit to Carl, though, he really was amazing – compulsively misguided, maybe, but amazing! Personally, when I took the job, I also took the attitude that I might not like it there, but I probably wouldn't like it anywhere else either. Guess now I'll be putting that to the test.

This - my apartment - this is where I like to be. I can eat when I want and what I want. I can fall asleep to the TV or stay awake in silence. The piles of clothes lining my bedroom floor have a meaningful order: mostly clean, serviceable, keeps-people-at-bay, and comes-when-called. When piles number one and two have migrated to three and four, I'll visit the parental units and start the first load of laundry. Mom, in her compulsiveness, will complete the task before I wake from a long nap in front of their TV.

Of course, the question is: how am I going to keep this place? My final paycheck will be enough to satisfy the landlord for the next thirty days, and I can probably stretch that to forty-five days with a smile and a promise of rent to come. I'll be hungry by then, though. I can't count on regular grocery delivery service from Mom. Maybe I can get another job delivering pizza, but I'll have to do that before the gas gauge flashes an irrevocable warning. That gives me two weeks at best.

Looking around, I survey my home-sweet-home. The only thing on the walls is the plastic encased copper wire growing like a vine from my stereo, gathering radio waves and ushering them back to my electronics. The ceiling is pre-stressed concrete (thank you for the education, CB III Designs) covered with textured drywall compound, an ill-fitting disguise doing its part to keep the rent low. The kitchen, which might benefit from a makeover, is sufficient for my brand of gourmet, the remains of which still decorate the counter where I deposited them a short time ago. The carpet is a standard beige, or more accurately, several colors of beige, with a smattering of red and even a bit of green all in highly irregular patterns. I'm happy they didn't replace the carpet before I moved in. It would just be coming off my deposit at the end anyway, since I, too, contributed a couple of patches of color to the emerging abstract design.

Natural light streams in from the large patio door that dominates the exterior wall in the main room. Ordinarily, I might close the shades to create a better napping ambiance, but the effect of warm sunshine and pizza mixed with cold beer seem to have rooted me to my spot. Performing a lazy roll onto my side, I catch a glint of amber plastic on the floor by the coffee table. With barely more movement than I have already expended, I reach for the cylindrical container, which responds with a cautionary rattle like that of a diamondback. Seroquel: the preferred prescription from my latest psychiatric incarceration, supplied compliments of the citizens of the great state of Illinois. I don't have to count them to know that there are 30 nuggets of prescribed sanity inside even though the date on the label indicates there should only be about 10 left.

Now that I think of it, I've been way too hard on Eker. They supplied me with my two biggest blessings: the job that made this apartment possible and the solution to my upcoming money issues. Popping the top, I shake some venom from the rattler into my hand and down it with the last swallow of beer. That was my last beer, so I drown the rest of the poison with the Mountain Dew Mom dropped off. As I watch, the sun slides sideways though the patio door casting vibrant shades of purple and green into my apartment, the perfect end to this day.

Moving On – Part III — Ken Harris

November 2005 — St. Charles, Illinois

I don't know if the emerging pattern is due to age or stress, or maybe the stress of aging, but I find myself rising consistently earlier as the years go by. Even the alarm is still slumbering, not yet ready to start the day's activities. I listen to Lory's regular deep breathing for a while, such a peaceful sound. When we were dating in college, we would frequently fall asleep in each other's dorm rooms, cuddled together on a twin bed, leaving half the mattress unoccupied. Could we reenact those close and comforting times? Dare I risk the cherished memory for a shot at reality? I take my robe and my melancholy, leaving my bride to slumber on.

Grabbing a cup of coffee, I make my way east by southeast down the hallway to my office, which might sound like a strange way to describe this fixed and narrow passage, unless you could see the sight I do through the approaching office windows. If I had to pick my favorite season of the year, it would be Indian summer. Previous frosts have hastened and intensified the fall colors, and the newly revitalized warmth of the season makes for perfect enjoyment of nature's dazzle. This morning's view is a blend of the sunrise between vibrant leaves, blurring the distinction between the two. Red, orange, yellow and gold are sliced vertically by rough black pillars holding their own jewels heavenward to the approaching daylight.

Despite the shortened days and tag along temperatures, my well-being seems to be increasing. I knew we should have kicked Court out a long time ago, and the last two months bear that out. He has a job and an apartment of his own. Okay, we probably have more dollars into that apartment than he does, but it is worth every cent, if just to keep the peace at home. It seems doubtful that we will ever see the rental deposit return to our bank account given the age and gender of the apartment occupant, a sacrifice I am willing to make through only slightly gritted teeth.

As our lives are becoming more predictable, our marriage is settling into a new understanding of our rolls. There is no point to objecting to the groceries Lory drops off with our son. He needs to eat, and she needs to feed him – it's as simple as that. I suspect she needs to lay eyes on him occasionally, too. I can now work without a dramatic vortex assaulting me. The alarm system is still my favorite sleep aid, allowing me the confidence to find rest. It's too early to pronounce Court's transformation a complete success after two months, and not even a calm two months. But maybe we are finally on the right trajectory.

The glow of the Indian summer sunrise makes way to the crisp contrast of blue skies punctuated by the vibrant fragile jewels still clinging to the branches of the only home they have ever known. Freedom can, indeed, be a daunting gift to grant – daunting and necessary.

Ransacked **Court Harris**
November 2005 **St. Charles, Illinois**

Spelled out in two-inch-high red letters in a black box appropriately sized to house them is "00:L." I'm not sure what it means, though the device seems to have some sort of purpose, staring at me from its humble location on the floor. "What do you want?" I croak, my voice sounding raspy and distant. It waits a moment longer and then replies, "I0:L." Already tired of the conversation, I close my eyes again to sleep.

When next I wake, the message has changed to "EE:0I," and then "hE:0I, a new form of computer coding maybe? I cast my glance around the room, hoping for additional clues as to its meaning. Apparently silent-and-insistent is my only companion, though it appears someone else has been here. My clothes are scattered throughout the room. Who (or what) caused the piles to appear is far less obvious than the piles themselves, which now dominate the landscape of my apartment.

Sitting up to have a better look around, my body feels like a shadow might look while moving across undulating ground: tall then short, near then far, flickering in and out as other shadows join and depart in a haphazard dance. I am tempted to lay back down, but my friend urges me on with "S0:II." I need a drink.

The main door to my apartment is slightly ajar, though still held securely: hinges on the left, chain lock on the right. A trail of pizza sauce decorates the space between the two, the pizza crust relaxing on the floor where the trail ends. The kitchen is filled with confetti of irregular shapes and sizes. Looking more closely, some of the confetti has my name on it. Others are full of numbers. Still others appear to belong to establishments like St. Joseph Hospital, Northern Illinois Gas and Sprint. My shadow body comes momentarily close enough to acknowledge that there is some meaning to all this disorder, but other shadows cloud my thoughts before clarity can be attained.

Pushing aside a cabinet door that hangs askew (much like my own thoughts), I find a plastic cup. Not even the sink full of broken dishes can dissuade me. I am thirsty, and water will do. My shadow-hand gains mass as I reach for the faucet handle, filling the glass with lukewarm liquid. I've always heard how good water is for a body. I'll consider that a proven fact. One glass of liquid and I can feel myself solidifying. The second glass goes down almost as quickly with more of the same results.

After filling the glass for a third time, I return to the main room for a more thorough examination. There is no point to stepping over or around the piles of clothes since my legs are not long enough reach the few open patches of carpet. An irregular layer of silt covers the clothes and runs onto the carpet. I could say it looks like the remains of an indoor snow storm, but it reminds me more of nuclear fallout. Acid green dots the landscape, apparently escaped from the bottle of dish soap cowering in the corner. Blood red cascades down another slope - not the color of real blood, thankfully, but more like fake Halloween blood. Someone's prank from last night's celebration, I suppose. Or, more likely, the balance of the container of that beloved hamburger condiment, whose original packaging I find under my foot as I step from hill to valley. For future reference, Rice Krispies emit the same sound when stepped on as when they bathe in milk.

I make my way back to the couch. Coaxing the TV remote from its hiding place between the cushions, I am assaulted by a cheery weatherman expounding on the beauty of this Wednesday afternoon. It looks nice enough when I glance out the slider, but today is Tuesday, my first full day of unemployment. And my first order of business is a nap.

When I awake, the light filtering in through the patio door has lessened. For reasons unknown, the clock is standing on its head in the corner, announcing in big red up-side-down letters what would have been the highly-anticipated end of the work day – 3:57. The sportscaster is droning on about the big Thursday night football match up tomorrow. I must be watching last week's TiVo recording. Today is Tuesday.

Once I get moving, it feels good to be doing something. Opening the back slider, I shake a mixture of cereal, soap and ketchup onto the patio before depositing the piles of clothes into one of my two laundry baskets. In short order, I move on to garbage bags: one for additional clothing that needs to find the inside of a washing machine and the other that holds actual garbage. Some of the clothes, having been sabotaged or slashed beyond usability, top off bag number two. An apparent implement of destruction is found defying gravity in my bathroom. I pull the knife from the drywall and place it in the newly cleared kitchen sink.

In the end, I find two other items of interest: my cell phone, which is remarkably unscathed, and an empty amber cylinder, cracked but intact. Ironically, the content of the latter, once ingested, was neither a highly touted medical savior, nor the releasing one I had hoped for - another psychotropic failure. I should have known.

I catch another Wednesday reference being lobbed from the TV, while friend TiVo is dark and silent, perplexing, even. I pull out my cell phone to arrange for laundry service. "Hi, Mom, what day is this?"

A Fresh Start — Corey Harris

March 2006 — Hermosa Beach, California

This is the day of the year that is near and dear to everyone at the company: profit sharing day. We work all year in anticipation of this reality check and its cashable cousin. You might hate your job 364 days of the year, but not today. Even if you do hate your job, you don't quit on March 14th. That would be financial suicide. Each person's share of the profits can be a substantial portion of their previous year's salary. Even if the check isn't as big as you hoped, no one ever refuses it! On the flip side, those intent on leaving will put in their notice over the next few days, after they have negotiated both their check and terms of employment with a new company.

I've been with Continental Electric for a couple of years, having gone through the management training program. Let's say my eyes have been illuminated to the world of electrical supply. I run my own profit center, meaning I determined the relative financial satisfaction of my employees on this day of anticipation. I have a good idea who will be celebrating at the bar tonight and who will grumble all the way to the bank. If only it was as easy to anticipate the resignation notices. The well-rewarded may have other substantial offers, while the slighted may have already realized their best financial gain. Phase two of the bonus game starts tomorrow. That part I do not control.

The check that I'm really excited about, though, will be paid out some 1700 miles from here. I played a big part in the check being written, but had no input as to the amount. Thanks to some insider information, though, I know the value before the actual payee does. Management has its privileges. The check isn't payable to me, but to my brother.

November seems like a distant speck in the rear-view mirror now and thankfully so. At the same time, it takes a scant ten seconds' recollection to feel that early winter's day panic well up in me again. It grips my gut as strongly now as it did the day Mom called to tell me Court had quit his job and attempted suicide. I guess individually, or even in tandem, those events are not nearly as scarce as they should be in the life-according-to-Court. But this time was different – the shrill scream of desperation still echoes in my consciousness. Previously, what passed for life-ending attempts seemed lame: driving too fast and recklessly, sipping on bleach or bug spray, walking down an interstate highway. Of course, those activities could turn deadly, and I, for one, took them seriously. But the truth is that Court is a smart guy. If he honestly wanted to be dead, he would have done it – effectively, and not by happenstance.

At some point, the whole family got used to his flirtation with death. We never really expected it to turn serious. But taking a month's supply of a prescription drug is taking things up a whole other notch. The part that still brings on the panic for me is that he could have succeeded. We could all have been going about our lives assuming he was doing the same for days after his life had drained away. His actions could have been exposed in the local paper a week after his death while I was still scrambling to get home and make sense of it all. It was a wakeup call for all of us, but it was also a call to action for me.

Continental has locations across the nation, including the Chicago area, but it's still a small enough company that I have some contact with other regions. I didn't exactly arrange the job for Court. He had to make the effort to apply first and drop my name. But once my phone rang, I certainly did pull out the grease bucket, as subtly but effectively as possible. Maybe I really wasn't that subtle, but it certainly was effective. Court got a job in the stock room. I was certain that his fears would subside once he got a good job with genuine future potential.

The four months he has been working at the Chicago office have exceeded not just my expectations, but Court's as well. It's not that Ben, the Chicago manager, calls just to rave about my brother, but he does mention how pleased he is with Court's work. He arrives on time and works late when asked. They needed another licensed driver for deliveries when things get busy or when a driver misses work. Court stepped up and got his CDL, relieving that pressure in the office. He has always been good with computers and happily offers his skills in that department. That profit center has saved a lot of IT dollars by utilizing my brother's talents.

The most accurate and concrete indication of Court's stock at Continental is the check he will receive today. With such a short tenure during the previous year, not quite two months, and not exactly being at the top of the food chain in the office, Court will receive $1500. By rights, he shouldn't have received more than maybe a couple hundred. It's exactly the extra boost that my brother needs! I mean, the money is nice, and I know he can use it, but the recognition and affirmation exceed the dollar amount by a factor of 10 or even 100!

All parties are seeing career potential from my brother at Continental Electric. Court is hoping that plan leads through the stock room to the national IT department, and there are no foreseeable road blocks over the next few years. It's so good to talk to Court and hear the enthusiasm in his voice. He's like a happy puppy basking in the sun with his favorite chew toy: the picture of relaxed contentment after having spent an eternity chasing his own tail. It's the feeling of being on course at long last, a feeling of belonging. Maybe Court wouldn't use those words, but it's the feeling I get from him when I hang up the phone after our talks.

For my part, I was finally able to make up for that disastrous trip he made to see me four Thanksgivings ago in Australia. Soon, even the specter of drug court will be behind him. That turn of the page after his visit to my San Diego home two years ago weighs on him, as it does on me. I still feel guilty about that whole drama, and I am thrilled to have made full amends. I love my brother, and I believe in him. And both feelings will be rewarded today.

Accidental – Part I — Lory Harris
June 2006 — St. Charles, Illinois

No! Just as I was getting lulled into a belief that morning would come and this nightmare would end! Instead, the phone call was too frantic, too one-sided, and well, way too early for a Saturday morning. "Mom, I saw an accident last night. A car got broadsided by a truck. The driver of the car, a kid, was freaking out! I asked him if he was okay, and all he could say was, 'my friend, my friend!' There was no way a passenger could survive the impact, and she didn't. I had to use his phone to call 911, but I was sure they were too late already. I just can't believe it happened! When I close my eyes, all I can see is the crumpled car and the body and the blood."

I can't even remember what I said to Court, and I doubt it mattered. He wasn't really listening, anyway, being so stuck in the surreal events of the night before. Not that I blame him. I wasn't really listening to my fumbling words, either.

Really, God?! Just when things are going smoothly, You let this happen?! I mean, I get it when someone does something to themselves. We aren't puppets on a string that You manipulate for Your desired effect. You let us make our own decisions. I get it! But this is the second time You have dropped my son into a potentially life altering situation from which You could have sheltered him!

First there was hitchhiking in Kentucky. You couldn't have arranged for another car to stop for him – or no car at all?! You couldn't have arranged for Andrew and company to have left a half an hour earlier – or later? Or why couldn't Court have left the ASP center by a different road? I don't blame You that he took off in the middle of the night, but it seems You could have done something about the choice of vehicles responding to his outstretched thumb!

It has been three years now, and he hasn't brought a boyfriend home to meet us, which might mean something. He even brought a girl to Colin's wedding, though he was very specific that she was just a friend. *But, God, if You are so all-powerful, why didn't You at least protect him from that car – from this car? Why add another car to this sordid story?*

Court has a good job with a future, is set to graduate from drug court, and he witnesses this?! I mean, I'm sorry any of it happened. But omnipresence that won't even control traffic seems a waste of capabilities!

How are You going to use this, God? How are You going to protect my son from this? Now what?!

Accidental – Part II — Sean Woodman
June 2006 — Winfield, Illinois

I can't remember exactly what I was dreaming about, but I do remember the peaceful, floating feeling. It was like when you were a kid and you wanted to fly just so you could jump from one fluffy cloud to the next, buoyed by a gentle breeze and energized by the sunshine. Maybe you could even carve the cloud a little and make it into a smiley face, allowing the rest of the world to share in your perfect day. But then there was this buzzing sound: constant, insistent, like a whole colony of killer bees had laid claim to my cloud.

When I opened my eyes, I had crashed back to earth, the bees apparently following. The buzzing continued unabated. Stupid doorbell. Of course, the relative intelligence of the doorbell was greater than the one with the heavy hand employing it at 9:50 on a Saturday morning. I dragged myself to the door if only to stop the annoyance.

It surprised me to see Court standing there. First, I know he knows that Saturday morning doesn't start until noon-thirty. But even more so, because we hadn't really been hanging out lately. Psych ward beginnings notwithstanding, it was just kind of a natural drift, and neither of us fought the opposing currents.

Court walked right in, ignoring the fact that I had obviously just stumbled out of bed to answer the door. He was amped up, pacing and talking a million miles an hour about this horrible accident he saw. Some huge truck had T-boned a car and he watched the whole thing. It took him 10 minutes to describe 5 seconds of screeching tires and twisting metal. Then he went on to describe looking in the car and seeing the body, similarly twisted and lifeless.

The whole time he was here, he paced, apparently distraught and barely holding himself together. I couldn't help but wonder what he was on. Clearly, the whole story was a psychedelic fabrication. Court was always adventurous with his experimenting, and apparently, he had bitten off more than he could handle this time.

I'm not really judging, or maybe I am, but I've been there. I've spent hours, even days, untwisting the real from the seemed-real with varying degrees of success. But I just really wasn't in the mood to take his hand and guide his thought process. Besides, his rambling was putting me to sleep.

Eventually he concluded with some rather sarcastic remarks about friends helping friends in need. I didn't correct that thinking, and didn't hinder his departure, either. Instead, I climbed back into bed, hoping for the return of dreamy dreams. This time, however, the clouds, though silent, were jagged, twisted, and tinged red. I woke myself by 11:30, preferring reality to the seems-too-real, shut-eye alternative.

Crashing — Court Harris
June 2006 — St. Charles, Illinois

When it comes to sleep, I'm anorexic. I mean, eating and sleeping are two things you must do to stay alive, regardless of your aversion to them. The battle against eating might be more "win-able" than the one against sleep. It is possible to complete a hunger strike and successfully arrive at the forgone conclusion.

Sleep is another thing, altogether. If you refuse to sleep, your body will eventually gang up and make you slumber without your consent. In my quest to avoid dreams, I have fallen asleep mid-sentence. Sometimes when I'm driving, I blink and realize I'm miles away from my last glimpse of consciousness. Some would call that a death wish. But I know it for what it is: fear. I fear the reality of dreams: condensed, encapsulated, captured and living behind closed eyes. Once I willed myself to sleep in my car with the intentional and distinct smell of exhaust. A couple of hours later, I returned home with a headache and a near empty gas tank, more exhausted than ever, pardon the pun.

"Sweet dreams," my mom used to say to me. If I dream of puppies, they are pit bulls that rapidly grow into devouring dragons. If I dream of a cool, refreshing pool on a warm day, I lose all buoyancy, watching my life escape bubble by bubble, rising where my body will not. My dreams of flight end as Icarus's did, traveling at break-neck speeds, until, of course, my neck breaks. My idea of sweet dreams is when they reveal only a silent black abyss, unfortunately, mine tend to be 3D and Technicolor with Dolby surround sound.

All week I have dreamed of blue cars painted red, of dump trucks plowing grassy fields, of headstones with taunting inscriptions boasting of their latest conquest. All week, I have avoided the corner of Route 38 and 14th Street. Until today, that is, when I went to stare down the menace that haunts both my waking and sleeping hours.

Last Friday was shaping up to be an awesome day. Work was done for the week and I passed my final Friday drug test before next week's "graduation." As an early present to myself, I decided to skate on an ill-advised edge. Having been assured multiple times that Ecstasy would exit my system prior to Monday's forced proof of chemical cleanliness, I decided to give it a try. Just to thumb my nose at the powers that be, I popped the enhancement into my mouth as I left the courthouse property.

I pulled to a stop in the left-hand turn lane behind another car, feeling the wonder of his glowing red orbs floating just feet above the pavement. Their glow dimmed and size diminished as the car crept steadily away. That was when the world turned sideways. The screech of brakes was the scant forerunner to the deafening crash of metal on metal. I can see it all in slow motion, and yet, even those frames frozen in my mind's eye tell me nothing of the whys that still beg to be answered. Why did he pull out? Why didn't the truck stop? Why did I have to be a witness?

Adrenaline is a more powerful compound than Ecstasy, at least in the short run. But after making the 911 call, I could feel the natural chemical giving way to the manufactured. Civic duty complete, I left the scene, the moaning of sirens approaching, but the flashing lights not yet visible. I called the police station the next morning to give them my contact information, explaining the sudden "illness" that had overtaken me the night before.

Today, I am driving my same car, pulling into the same turn lane, at approximately the same time of day, but everything has changed. To my left there are ruts in the lawn, marking the conclusion of the forward motion of the truck. The scarred earth tells of trauma in the quiet way of nature disturbed, trauma that will heal before the end of the season. The human season of healing will take much longer, if indeed those ruts ever disappear.

Twice I check the color of the turn arrow: green. Three times I stare down the drivers opposite me making sure they remain stationary. An impatient honk of a horn coming from behind me finally moves my foot from the brake to the gas. Rounding the corner, I pull to the curb, put on my hazard lights, and release my irate follower to speed off and continue his life. Cautiously I get out of my car to examine the right side of this road.

I've been here before – this exact location. Last time I was holding a borrowed cell phone, summoning men in blue I did not want to see. Last time there was a frantic driver, a crumpled car and a draining life. This time there are memories, playing in an endless loop. If they have changed in the week, the change has only been to intensify. The gravel shoulder does not bare the marks of the car that came to a sideways halt upon it. There are a couple of pieces of glass winking in the sunshine from the otherwise dull rock, but they might have been there for months or years. They are not specifically identifiable.

This location, though, is no longer anonymous. There are flowers in various states of their return journey to dust, though all still easily recognizable as a memorial to life and a distraught acknowledgement of its abrupt end. They are gathered around a simple white cross. The newly established marker is adorned with balloons fluttering limply in the slight breeze. Bits of school pride, in the form of orange and black ribbon, hang over the crossbar partially obscuring the name of one who would have been my fellow high school alumni - Nicole. She will not walk the stage next year, never move the tassel from right to left.

Nicole is now held between two memorials. The first will be well manicured and marked with a stone bearing witness to her long after the eyes of those who now weep have closed in permanent slumber. The other, this roadside remembrance surrounded by gravel and bits of glass, will mark the passage of time by degrees of visible decay. But at this moment, it is the one that gathers the ache of loss most accurately. Written just below her name in bold black letters, the pain is succinctly summed up, "What the Hell!"

Indeed, Hell, explain yourself!

Pomp and Circumstance **Court Harris**
June 2006 **Geneva High School**
Geneva, Illinois

I graduated from high school with high honors – number 7 out of 700. While the ceremony is generally held outside due to the number of the celebrants, each graduate was given four tickets in case weather forced the ceremony into the gym. It rained that day, so there were only four to cheer me on: my parents and two of my grandparents.

Now, for the second time in four long years, I am participating in graduation, sitting on a high school stage, sans the cap and gown this time. Again, there are four in attendance for me: my parents and Bill and Ann Robinson. I wish there were none. This time, though, there are plenty of empty seats, so I should probably be grateful that only four wait to applaud when my name is announced. Some of my fellow graduates have rows full of admirers; others have no one at all.

This is Bill and Ann's second drug court graduation. Their son went through a similar ceremony a few years back. That is probably why they are here, safe and sympathetic ears for my parents. Every time I see Bill, I can tell he wants to impart words of wisdom on me, and he tries. But after a few halting sentences, he opts for a hand shake and that awkward "guy" embrace with a clap on the back for emphasis – like he's pounding the point home. Ann will give me a hug with her narrow little frame, which I will gingerly return. I'm always afraid I will break her in two with little effort. They are good people and I'm glad they are here, for my parents, at least.

I wish I could skip this charade, as do many of my fellow stage-mates. We will endure, though, if only to cross the last "t," dot the last "i" and put this chapter in our rear-view mirror. Even though I have passed over two years' worth of drug tests with flying colors, I was a late addition to the graduate list. They probably suspect that I am not as clean as my drops indicate--which is true, of course. But they can't figure out how I am scamming the system, either. It makes me smile. We heard again today before we stepped onto the stupid stage that drug court is a one-time-only opportunity. If we are brought before the court again, there will likely be jail and even prison time to pay. They won't be seeing me again. I would rather die – seriously.

On the other hand, there are those who sing the judge's praise at every opportunity. We are forced to listen to their speeches while attempting not to doze off during the ceremony, which is reminiscent of my last graduation. However, unlike the previous one, these "valedictorian" speeches have nothing to do with the best and brightest. They are rambling affairs and grammatically wanting. Looking out at the audience, you can tell the family of the current speaker, their heads bobbing up and down, hanging with rapt attention on every word coming from the dais. With few exceptions, the rest of the audience looks as bored as I feel – zoo primates gazing upon each other with droopy eyes behind invisible bars. The exceptions, though, are all women: middle-aged, white and well-dressed. You can tell this is their children's first serious scrape with the law. They are willing each word and every sentiment of the speaker into their own child's ears and hearts. My own mother, of course, is in this "exceptional" category. My father has the good sense to sleep with his eyes open through this ceremonial BS.

My fellow graduates and I have spent hours together over the past many months, waiting for our weekly opportunity to confer with his judge-ship. Thirty or more addicts gathered by court order to swap stories among ourselves while waiting for a five-minute judicial conversation. Yeah, great plan. There have been some great stories, lots of laughs and a healthy exchange of information. You can tell I haven't spent much time conversing with today's speakers. They were working the program; I was working the system. The rest of us, making an intense study of our fingernails or shoelaces, have developed a tenuous connection that will be completely severed after tonight. There will be no five-year reunion. But if there were, I wonder how many would be both alive and "free" to attend. I won't be leaving my forwarding address to find out.

The droning continues, broken only by polite applause that covers the rustling of paper as orators fade, one to another. My eye rests momentarily on Randy, my parole officer. I suspect it was his objection, apparently overruled, that caused my invitation to this festivity to be so late in coming. Neither of us will miss the other's company. He didn't trust me from the start, which probably doesn't make me anything special in his line of work. But he has spent a lot of time in the last six months trying to prove my unfaithfulness. I won't be shaking his hand before I leave today. I *will* shake the judge's hand, but only because he hands out the diploma.

With some belated mercy, the speaking stops and the roll call commences. There is near constant applause now, though it ebbs and flows in an indiscernible pattern as names are called. My four attending celebrants make their presence known at an appropriate decibel level. I can hear Mom's whistle, endearing, even if it does border on over-the-top. She really should teach me how to do that.

The high school commons area has been decorated with balloons and streamers, which reminds me of a junior high dance. There is punch poured into paper cups and homemade cookies: nothing but the best for this graduating class. The conversation is polite but sparse, there being no bittersweet embraces between lifelong high school friends going their separate ways at the end of an era. In fact, most of us would rather not see the other again. We don't dislike each other; we would just rather fade back into anonymity. Any future interactions will likely be limited to a nod of the head – 'nuf said.

In the end, the speeches done, the Kool-Aid drunk (literally and figuratively), we head for home. I think my feelings are best summed up by the words on the diploma they handed me today. When I removed the ribbon and unwrapped the scroll, I recognized the sentiment. It says, and I quote, absolutely nothing. It's a blank sheet of paper. Yep, that pretty much sums up my experience with the drug court.

SECTION FOUR
PITCH BLACK
June 2006 – October 2006

EVICTION NOTICE

To: Court Harris
Fox Run Apartments #21
St. Charles, Illinois.

You are hereby put on notice that you have violated Section 7B of your lease agreement dated October 17, 2005. The details of your violation are as follows: failure to maintain electrical service to your unit.

Pursuant to state law. YOU MUST EITHER REMEDY YOUR LEASE VIOLATION WITHIN 10 DAYS FROM THE DATE OF THIS NOTICE –OR- VACATE THE PREMISES WITHIN 10 DAYS FROM THE DATE OF THIS NOTICE. If you do not remedy your lease violation or vacate the premises by that time, you are hereby notified that your landlord will take legal action to recover any debt owed, possession of the premises, and damages, including attorney's fees and other costs, if permitted by applicable law.

If you choose to vacate, you must do so by August 24, 2006 at 5:00 p.m.

THIS NOTICE IS BEING ISSUED PURSUANT TO ILLINOIS LAW. NOTHING IN THIS NOTICE SHALL BE CONSTRUED TO WAIVE ANY OF LANDLORD'S RIGHTS OR REMEDIES UNDER STATE OR FEDERAL LAW.

This notice was served on the tenant listed above on August 14, 2006, by Fox River Apartments via hand delivery.

Out of Gas — Lory Harris
July 2006 — St. Charles, Illinois

Just. That might be my favorite four-letter word, or four-letter excuse, anyway. It's just an accident, just a bad day, just money, just adolescence (at the age of 22). Today, it's just a car.

I like the idea of naming cars – "just" for the fun of it. Colin's first truck was named Little Red, which might have been a clever name if it was blue with a red logo. But it was, alas, predictably and completely red. My current car, a VW Beetle, is named Bubu, owing to a series of ill-timed and ill-conceived adolescent adventures that led to its purchase. Ironically, none of those booboos were Court's. I hadn't thought of that before – how backhandedly pleasant. I guess most families with three boys will experience the early demise of a car or two. In our case, we also bid an early farewell to three manual transmissions – one for each son.

For as few driving years as he can boast, Court has certainly had a long history of vehicles. Generally, though, they haven't stuck around long enough to earn a name. First there was the truck that was lost on the side of the road in the Nevada desert. Maybe we should just call it Lost Vegas – an inside and not-so-funny joke.

Next came the Saturn, which we bought used. Apparently, it didn't think it was "just" a car. It wanted to be an airplane, or Court wanted to be a pilot, or both. On a perfectly clear, dry September day, he took it flying, landing with a thud in a ditch, ripping up the undercarriage and totaling the car. It looked to be in perfect shape, except that it refused to move. We could refer to it as Jet Blue. I mean, it was blue. For the scant month that it made its home in our driveway, it proved to be a decent vehicle, though an absolutely inadequate airliner.

The next car was little, rusty-silver, and cheap, the latter being the most important criteria. We bought it for $500 from a friend who warned us it ate oil. Even though Court forgot to feed it, it still had twice the longevity of the Saturn. I don't remember the make or model, but let's call it Plugged Nickel. Seems appropriate.

Between each car, the same marital conversation was played out:

Ken: "Let him buy his own car."

Me: "He has no money and no credit."

Ken: "Then let him walk."

Me: "That just means I'm either Mom's taxi service or Mom's rent-a-car service. I'm either going to be constantly on the run or perpetually stranded. We don't live in a city where public transportation is an option."

And so, each time, we bought another car.

His current vehicle, the Hyundai has been around for two and a half years now, long enough to have earned a name if anyone cared. "Anyone" would be me, and I don't. It's just the Hyundai, or Court's car, or the vehicle that appears in our driveway from time to time, frequently with fresh metallic bruises. Ken and I agreed we didn't want the liability of the car being titled to either of us. Nor did we trust handing our youngest a car free and clear. We settled on titling it to Court, but recording a lien to maintain a modicum of control.

For the past several weeks, Court has been relentless about wanting to sell the car. Perhaps there is some logic to his request, though his rational is far different than ours. Court wants the title so he can sell the car and give money to a friend who "really needs it." I'm sure I couldn't hide the incredulous look on my face when I heard that one. I'm also certain that my disbelief makes no difference to him. It's hard to imagine who might be needier, especially after his apartment was broken into and everything of any value was taken: his TV, TiVo and computer. Also victim to the burglary were the hammered dulcimer Ken made for him and the quilt I made for his high school graduation. I mourn the loss of those two items more than the electronics. I was told the quilt was probably just a convenient way to wrap and carry things off, which does nothing to make me feel better.

Ken and I reason that even if we give him intermittent gas money, Court still can't afford insurance. He doesn't need it to get to work, having quit his job at Continental Electric in a blaze of glorious foolhardiness. Per my youngest, he wasn't appreciated or being promoted fast enough. Sometimes I lay awake at night praying he won't use a ton of metal to hurt himself or someone else. I don't mention my concern to Court, though, not wanting to give or enforce any ideas. Ken and I finally decided to give him the title, lien released, and let the chips fall where he throws them. We won't be buying another car for him. His bike is in our garage and he can use that, or his roller blades, as he chooses.

It's just a car, though Hyundai didn't betray us like Lost Vegas did on so many occasions, taking our son unexpectedly to other area codes and even other time zones. It hasn't run in fear like Jet Blue or Plugged Nickel. Silver Sentinel, that's what I'll name the newly departed. May you receive the rest you so justly deserve.

Dimly Lit — Alex Johnson

July 2006 — St. Charles, Illinois

Cousins are some of my favorite people, and Aunt Lory's boys are some of my favorite cousins. We don't live that close to any of them, which is too bad. But, then, when we see them, it's usually for several days at a time, which is nice! My brother Nick and I are the youngest of the cousins on Mom's side of the family. It's not fair when I can't do some things with Aunt Lory's boys just because they are older. I understand that Nick is still just a little kid at six years old. But I'm nine! Why shouldn't I be able to go to a movie with them or play certain video games or stay up until midnight? My mom is so old fashioned!

Colin, Corey and Court are cool. They are like 10 or 15 years older than I am, but we still like to play around together. Colin is in the Marines and married and has a kid, so not him so much anymore. But Corey and Court are great! I always wanted a big brother, and they are it! They wrestle around with us, give us piggyback rides, and buy us candy that makes Mom roll her eyes. Then they laugh, and we all get away with it!

I couldn't wait to get to Illinois to see Aunt Lory and Uncle Ken. It's too bad that Corey is in California and Colin is in North Carolina. But Court is around, so I was looking forward to seeing him. He has his own apartment now; I thought that would be awesome. We didn't get to see Court until the last day. I guess he was busy. Anyway, we went over to his apartment for lunch.

When we got there, Court was cooking something on the stove. It didn't smell good, and it looked horrible! It was brown and lumpy. He kept dumping things in like ketchup and pickles and even some potato chips. He said he makes one meal and then eats it all week. Fortunately, Dad offered to take us all out to lunch. I don't think he wanted to eat that stuff, either. Court put the whole pan in the fridge, saying he would finish it later.

Dad drove all of us to the restaurant even though it was only about two blocks away. Court was telling us he didn't have a car anymore and he doesn't need one. He just roller blades everywhere. It sounded kind of cool, except if it was raining or something. But he said he didn't care about that; it keeps him in shape. He is strong, but skinny, too. I guess he was hungry because he sure ate a lot! He even stole some of my French fries, but I didn't say anything.

After lunch, Court and Nick and I decided to walk back to his apartment while Mom and Dad waited for the bill. We each got a piggyback ride, too, but not the whole way. Court showed us his bedroom, but we couldn't walk into it without stepping on his junk. You couldn't even see any carpeting. After a couple of minutes, he grabbed his phone and called Aunt Lory. I heard him say that Mom and Dad had left us, and he didn't know what to do. Fortunately, my parents showed up about that time. Court was relieved to see them. So was I.

We cleared stuff off the coach and chairs to sit down for a little bit. Mom did most of the talking. No one else knew exactly what to say. Well, Court seemed to know what to say, or had a lot to say, but I didn't understand most of it. I quit listening.

There was a break in the conversation when I told Mom I had to go to the bathroom. Court pointed to where it was, which I already knew. He told me to be sure to close the door. I already knew that, too! But the light switch didn't work, and when I closed the door I couldn't see anything. I came right back out. Dad said he would help me, but the light switch was useless since there were no light bulbs in the sockets.

Dad asked Court if he had any more bulbs. Court said they kept turning off and on when he was trying to sleep, and it bothered him. He got rid of all of them. Mom piped up and said we had to be going anyway and would stop at a gas station for me.

It was good to see my cousin, and the piggyback ride was fun. But I sure wouldn't want to stay overnight in his apartment and definitely *not* for dinner! We talked about it on the way home. Mom said Court is sick. He just seemed crazy to me.

A Spinach Chaser — Police Officer Kyle Marin

August 2006 — St. Charles, Illinois

I have spent my entire career as a police officer in St. Charles. When I started here twenty-one years ago, it was a much sleepier town, to be sure. No way would I have tried to match stories with a Chicago officer back then. Only 40 miles west of "the city," St. Charles was a different world – or maybe just the distant edge of the same world. It's not like crime skipped us entirely, but we certainly were not featured on the 6 o'clock news – ever.

Though easily delineated on a map, the line between city and suburbs is hard to see. The line between suburbs and countryside is even harder to distinguish. Twenty years ago, St. Charles lay within the blurred line between the latter two. Now we are clearly a suburb. And with that clarity, other changes have ensued: drugs, homelessness, gangs, violence. We have even made the 6 o'clock news on rare occasion, not quite the accomplishment we were seeking. Though I would still lose a game of one-upmanship with a Chicago cop, we have much more in common than we once did.

There is a lot of tedium and boredom in this line of work: traffic traps and stops, fender benders, petty vandalism, and, of course, the endless paperwork that follows each. But at our core, cops are adrenaline junkies. We like the thrill of not knowing exactly what will be waiting for us when we arrive at a call. Even something mundane can turn into something more without notice. The body's chemical reaction is an amazing thing, heightening your senses and reflexes; it's like touching Superman's cape or eating Popeye's spinach! Sometimes the most difficult part is to retain human judgment when super powers are coursing through your body. Superman doesn't seem to struggle with that, but then, he's not human - or maybe it's the tights. Popeye, on the other hand, gets over-the-top physical after a spinach chaser, but I suppose he's not quite human, either.

To stay in this line of work for decades, you must learn to manage your body's natural chemical reaction, or you will burn up in its intensity. Adrenaline has a hair trigger for an "on" switch, but turning it off is a slow process. In the interest of self-preservation, some things that used to cause a rush are now just commonplace – well, at least until they take a turn for the unexpected.

My shift, 3 to 11 p.m., is just starting. After a quick debriefing, I gather my gear and head out the door to my squad car. It is a beautiful summer day. The Fox River, which borders the police station and evenly bisects the town, looks deceptively calm, almost glassy. But, especially this close to the dam, looks can be deceiving. The current can capture even the strongest swimmer. Anything following the water over the dam is trapped in the endless roll of the water below. It can take days for large items to break free of its grasp, and of course, there is no emergency shutoff valve. In my tenure, there have been surprisingly few fatalities at this powerful juncture, perhaps because our major river recreation area is upstream before the current has developed its grip. Even just one such drowning incident will stay with you for a lifetime. I guess that is another side effect of adrenaline: it sears images into your memory for a lifetime of re-processing.

A young man, poorly dressed and wild-eyed, is advancing toward me brandishing a small black square over his head and carrying a navy-blue booklet in the other hand. These are the things you take in at a glance, even before reaching for the can of spinach. His slight and undernourished build doesn't look especially powerful, but if drugs are involved, chemical strength can outperform expectations. I hear internal alarms, bringing all my senses to sudden and focused attention.

"I want her arrested!" he shouts in my direction. "Here is the proof! She broke into my apartment! Get her fingerprints off my wallet and passport. She has no right be break into my home and go through my personal things!"

Officer Jefferson, witnessing the interaction, arrives at my side just as the young man thrusts his wallet in my face. With a quick glance to be sure that a wallet is just a wallet, I look beyond it into the face of the one who possess it. Several days' worth of dark growth covers his lower face, matching the wild dark curls on the top of his head. His eyes are green, but the pupils are far too large in the bright August sunshine. It seems a drug of some sort is interfering with his body's natural desire to protect his retinas. "Who is it you would like us to arrest?" I ask, forcing a calmness to my voice despite my own heightened senses.

"My landlord! She can't just break into my apartment and go through my personal stuff! She even admitted to looking through my wallet!"

Our conversation continues for a short time, Jefferson and I trying to defuse the young man's agitated and singularly-focused complaint. I thought we were making some headway--at least he was allowing us full sentences between his repetitious rant. "We will have to do some investigation before we know if anyone should be arrested," I say by way of placation.

Turning abruptly, he crosses the four or five feet to the river. "Well, when you need them for the fingerprints, they will be right here!" And with that, the wallet sinks into the river. The passport, on the other hand, gathers speed before dropping over the dam to the rolling water below. Worried that our complainant might follow his identification, Officer Jefferson and I flank the young man.

Whether it is drugs or mental illness or both that caused his irrational behavior, a hospital seems a better venue for evaluation than a holding cell. Jefferson calls for an ambulance, which is fortunately housed 100 yards away, just across the street. Arriving in superhero time, the attendant does an excellent job of reducing the agitation level of our self-proclaimed victim, who says his name is Court Harris. We won't be taking a swim to verify that, though.

A quarter of an hour later, I tap the back of the ambulance door as it starts to roll away with its newest guest. Mr. Harris has been safely handed off to more proper authorities. By the end of the required paperwork, my adrenaline levels have returned to near normal. Belatedly, I climb into my squad car and start my rounds, spinach, as always, at the ready.

He's My Son — Ken Harris
August 2006 — St. Charles to Elgin, Illinois

Music is the sound of my life. Sounds cliché, I know, but it's also true. I played the piano, violin, guitar, drums. My mother often said she was afraid I would become a professional musician. She needn't have worried. I was good, but not that good. Still, music is a huge part of my life. I play around at the piano and guitar, and I dabble in the hammered dulcimer. But these days my preferred music is more exclusively an appreciation of the talents of others. Just a few chords, and I am instantly transported to the when and where of the song. I know I'm not unique in that, but it resonates powerfully in and through me. It is the verbal and melodic story of my life.

Music plays constantly in my office and in my car, and when I say "constantly," Lory will agree. When I left full-time outside employment to work in our business, our first hurdle to cross was the sounds in the office. She wanted Christian talk radio; I find that distracting. We finally settled on a new-to-both-of-us CCM radio. We have even become contributors to the station. Still, when I come into the office later than she does, or when I get in her car, it's not unusual for me to enter the world of silence. She says she likes that sound. I turn on the tunes, Simon and Garfunkel notwithstanding.

In the interest of full disclosure, it is true that I don't always hear the ever-present sounds. Take today, for example: Lory and I were going to St. Joseph's psych unit, which is Court's holding tank, again, after drowning his personal identification in the Fox River. It's not necessary for me to think about the drive – it's a virtual straight shot from our door to theirs, and we have made the trip way too many times in my estimation. Honestly, the lyrics hadn't even started when the opening strains of the song moved from my subconscious to the forefront of my mind. A glance at Lory shows that the tears are already making their way down her cheeks. I reach for the radio to change it or silence it. It is one of those times in marriage when you read each other's mind. She turns to me and speaks, "Its okay. It's already too late." Of course, she is right. Even without the radio's electronic assistance, she will hear every word and it will cut her to the core. Mark Schultz utters the next words:

I'm down on my knees again tonight,
I'm hoping this prayer will turn out right.
See, there is a boy that needs Your help.

I've done all that I can do myself.[3]

What right has someone you have never met to lay bare your soul to the world? Mark Schultz is only a guest in my car, and not even specifically or individually invited. Does he realize the force of his words, the truth of his words, the way his words force truth upon us?

His mother is tired,
I'm sure You can understand.
Each night as he sleeps
She goes in to hold his hand,
And she tries
Not to cry
As the tears fill her eyes.

There is Kleenex in the glove box immediately in front of her. She knows that – she put them there. But Lory won't reach for them, not yet, anyway. It might hurt, but the pain is a blessed reminder of where you have been, of what you have endured - a rite of passage, maybe? It's a place I try to avoid. I guess we all do. Yet, when you find yourself mired there involuntarily, it is at that base-level an act of your own will, and it can feel powerful. It's like pulling off a Band-Aid or picking a scab. That little bit of self-inflicted pain declares your independence from the inescapable while paradoxically leaning into it.

Let him grow old,
Live life without this fear.
What would I be
Living without him here?
He's so tired,
And he's scared
Let him know that You're there.

I won't give in to the tears. It would be an easy step to allow them to wet my collar, too. But my self-inflicted bit of pain is to deny my tears and maintain strength for my wife. I will be the rock she can lean into. I may have the same liquid center she does, but at the center it will remain: for the balance of this song and for the rest of the evening as well.

It is a fifteen-minute drive and a three-minute song. I guess I should at least be grateful that it's not the final three minutes of the drive. She will eventually reach for the Kleenex and pull herself together. I will swallow hard. Together we will ring an oddly located doorbell on the

[3] Mark Schultz, "He's My Son," *Mark Schultz*, Word Entertainment (2000).

seventh floor of a hospital, verify our identity and gain admittance to a secure floor whose existence we know too well and would rather not.

In the final predictable stanza, Mark reads my mind again. Just before the music fades, he announces my heart-cry to all who will listen:

Can You hear me?
Can You see him?
Please don't leave him,
He's my son…

Released **Lory Harris**
August 2006 **St. Charles, Illinois**

After a couple of nights of relatively restful sleep, my dark hours have returned to their former gory (pun most definitely intended). Ironically, my opportunity for actual slumber is greatest when Court is at his worst, and therefore, forcefully confined to some authoritative care – hospital or jail. He is out of St. Joe's, again, after the preordained five-day medical vacation that returned him to "full sanity." Well, five days and a fist full of prescriptions that he can't afford and won't fill even if he could. I'm back on the clock from 1 to 3 a.m., arguing my case to an ever-silent deity. Whether I am watching the ceiling or walking the halls, the only reply I receive is the infusion of a steady stream of worry-laced dread.

Per the medical professionals, since he is no longer a danger to himself or to others, Court must be sane. At least, that's how I hear it. Of course, he believes the hospital bracelet has a radio signal in it that lets everyone know he is "diabetic." The Depakote he was prescribed and took under insistent and watchful eyes is a vitamin. Apparently, you need more degrees than I to see the sanity in that line of reasoning, not that Ken or I were consulted in any way. Alas, parenting officially ceases to be recognized on the eighteenth anniversary of the birth of a beloved child.

Thanks to restrictive banking regulations, Court has a little cash in his bank account. They put a hold on the check he received when he sold his car. I suspect the friend who was in such dire need of Court's financial assistance became somewhat less a friend as Court's mania increased. Not that I blame him; Court is hard to be around when he is playing the part of human pinball.

Yesterday I took him to the DMV to get a replacement driver's license. I was amazed at the way he can handle other people. He was quite charming, a glimpse of the son I once knew. But on the way home, he regaled me with stories of being a human lab-rat testing the effectiveness of Seroquel. Reportedly, he is the only test subject until the drug is determined to be safe and effective for the public at large. I waited to cry until after I dropped him off at his apartment.

Darlene Marcusson from Lazarus House has suggested that I petition to become Court's legal guardian. Assuming I can prove that he is unable to care for himself, I would at least have some legal say in his medical care. It's a thought and even a possibility. However, I'm not sure I trust the powers that be to make that decision in my favor and for Court's benefit. If I try for guardianship and am denied, would that cut off the only avenue my son feels he has to someone who really cares about him? If I succeeded, would it be another ineffectual foray into the legal system with the same dubious results?

The four-year anniversary of this relentless nightmare is just a few months away. I went into this kicking and screaming, and expecting four months, tops. How naïve! Unfortunately, four years is a "good start," but not all that impressive among my fellow wanderers. Should I be preparing for four decades - or until by death we part? Whose death it would be is anyone's guess. Can a person survive for decades on an itinerant sleep cycle? Besides, what makes me think I would be the lucky one to die first?

Three thirty a.m. Still wide awake and now past my second bedtime. What difference? It's only a number, and slow moving at that. The clock only moves quickly between second slumber and six a.m. when it will squawk to herald the sun. Just another day to crawl into the future, dragging the reality of the past along with me.

Surprised by Anger — Maureen McKane, LSW, MCSW
August 2006 — St. Charles, Illinois

When a child is being self-destructive, crisis envelopes the whole family – marital bonds especially. Parents in crisis will grab at anything, and in grabbing, will frequently claw and rip at each other, just trying to get a solid hold on something. It's hard to work together when flailing in free fall, though there may be no time where partnership is more needed.

Ken and Lory came to me for couple's counseling in June. We met twice. They gave me their history in a calm orderly fashion, trading off between them with the telling, but agreeing on the details. They wanted advice on how to deal with their son, something that is almost impossible to give, even if I was in the business of dispensing such. The idea, of course, is for them to come to their own conclusions, preferably by consensus.

Lory showed up by herself for our third session. I told her I could meet with her once without Ken, but that the point of couple's counseling would be negated without both partners in attendance. She let me know that it would now be individual counseling; Ken did not feel the need for further mediated discussion. So, one-on-one it became.

It was a story I have heard too many times; sadly, nothing is particularly outstanding. These are things I hear as a counselor, things that are not generally shared with friends or neighbors, and only sparingly with family: a child's destructive behavior is spilling over to other relationships with similar results. Not surprisingly, Lory and Ken's marriage is on shaky grounds, though holding at present. Both are weary, and both want to get back to living a life they recognize. For Ken, that means marching forward with work and activities and plans for the future. Lory might agree with all those goals, but she is standing, firmly planted in a motherly pose, looking back at her son, willing him to move forward. He will not, and she knows it. She cannot go without him, and Ken knows it. Their marriage lies precariously stretched and straddling the two visions of what it means for their tomorrow.

"Life is just too heavy," she says. "Ken and I just argue all the time, and that's assuming we are even talking. Court is out of the hospital – again – with the same results – again. That is, no discernable change in attitude or behavior. To top it all off, there is a woman in my life who is treating me to all the fury she can muster, and we are related, so I can't just walk away." She continues, fleshing out her complaints with stories whose all-too-common details never serve to minimize the actual, individual pain.

"It sounds like you are really angry," I replied when her flow of speech slowed.

A quizzical look crossed her face. "Hurt, yes," she replied, "but I'm not angry."

Sometimes the most direct conversations take place without words. I raise my eyebrows. Her reply, equally soundless, shows her face morph from quizzical, to confusion, to pensive, to the pre-dawn inkling of realization.

In our society, and certainly in her generation, little girls are taught that anger is wrong, un-lady-like. We deny it in ourselves, calling it by many other names: hurt, frustration, depression. Or worse yet, we turn the anger upon ourselves, blaming and shaming ourselves in a hidden game of defiled self-worth. By way of recommendation, I wrote *The Dance of Anger* by Harriet Lerner on a sheet of paper and gave it to Lory. She is motivated and generally self-aware; I think she will learn much from the book, and it will serve as a springboard for our future conversations.

We are approaching our time limit, but she has one final question for the day. Court has been in and out of psych hospitals many times, and with little-to-no lasting sign of change as a result. What can she do to get her son some help that might make a real difference? Being long past the stage of believing in control or even medical miracles, she wasn't looking for a magic bullet.

"What Court really needs is for those who encounter him to see him as a real person, not just another troubled body to be managed. It's your job to make them see him as a fellow human being." I suggested she make a list documenting who Court is and what he has gone through. It will need to be kept up to date, of course, and in an accessible location, but it can be a tangible document of his life and his need for treatment. More than a meandering verbal recitation, it should document everything in one place in a format that can easily be added to his file.

"That makes sense and I can do that," she said as we wrapped up the session, "and I'll read this, too," nodding to the paper with the book's name written on it. We took the time to schedule our next session.

How much difference can a counselor make in an hour? Well, if the timer is stopped at the end, probably not much, to be honest. But our time together is more like the sourdough starter than the finished product. If the client adds the proper ingredients and waits the proper time for the bread to rise, then much can be accomplished as a result of our time. If I had to guess, I would say Lory will be a good bread baker, but only time will tell.

Homeless, Again
August 2006

Court Harris
Lazarus House
St. Charles, Illinois

Now I lay me down to sleep, not even a bag of peanuts by my feet – though there are annoyingly, intermittent, strangling snores coming from that region. I think he said his name is Eric, not that I really care. At least he smells marginally better than my previous house guest, a ferret, whose poor hygiene has forced me out of my own apartment. Officially I still have a home address that is not here at Lazarus House, though that status will likely change in a few hours, if the eviction notice means anything. I don't have next month's rent anyway, so it's just a matter of time.

I've been working hard at getting a job. I've developed quite the rapport with the Nextel employees. It started when I had to contest the late payment charges on my bill, but it has turned into a very good business relationship that I believe will likely lead to my employment. Derek, my main contact, commented several times on how much he liked my latest haircut: short and respectable for the job search, while still retaining a bit of my own individuality. I had it dyed fuchsia with multiple large blonde circles strategically place around my head. I've always been told it is important for an applicant to stand out.

I'm also angling for a job at the St. Charles Historical Museum. The chances for advancement would be much less there, of course, but I am developing an amazing personal relationship with Cathy, who would be my immediate supervisor. Much of the museum showcases local art, past and present. I have brought in several of my pieces for their review, even offering to donate one of them, pen and ink on cardboard. I've never really thought of myself as an artist, nor taken any classes along those lines since they were required in junior high. Even with my limited art supplies, I am pleased with my representation of the world as I see it. Of course, my hair also demonstrates my artistic aesthetic.

I thought I could earn a couple of bucks watching a friend's ferrets for a week. She promised me the ferrets were housebroken when I agreed. They certainly did break the house for habitation; the smell was making me physically ill. That's how I ended up here at Lazarus House, again, favorably comparing fellow guest, Eric, to the ferrets. The win notwithstanding, Eric has little reason to be proud of his olfactory prowess.

I voluntarily went to church with Mom this morning, which I thought would at least earn some points. I even acquiesced when she told me my head looked like a beach ball. The blonde circles are gone, the fuchsia dimmed to the color of Merlot thanks to a healthy dose of brown dye. She also thought I should show a strong chin when applying for jobs, so I'm clean shaven. The two of us spent the afternoon together trying to clean my apartment, so she is aware of the stench I am up against. It was hard to even see what should be cleaned or how clean it might be getting without electricity, the offense that will render me officially homeless by this time tomorrow.

I thought Mom would soften and realize the situation I was up against, maybe let me sleep at the homestead for the night. But both Mom and Dad are holding firm on not allowing me to move back home. All I got was a ride, a hug and an offer to help shampoo the carpets tomorrow if we can borrow some electricity from a neighbor – and if it is still to be my legal address. In some ways, I can't blame them – I did make a mess of the house last time I stayed there. But that was a year ago! You would think they would give their son a second chance after all I've gone through. I even graduated from drug court after they forced that whole undertaking upon me.

Sometimes I wonder who should be the one offering apologies! I could be wasting their money on college, but I'm making my own way in the world instead. One good night's sleep was all I was asking, and they wouldn't even consider it. Sometimes it's hard to be the bigger person.

Specter – Part I

Lory Harris

August 2006

St. Charles, Illinois

It has been such a long week. If only the upcoming weekend had the slimmest chance of being restful; it will just represent more sleepless nights. I was hoping that work would occupy my brain – what cells remain at any rate – rather than worry about Court. How is he getting along at Lazarus House? I long to call and ask, but I am sidelined. The responsibility for his trajectory is Court's alone. Oh, how I wish I could believe that in the middle of the night. I don't really believe it even in the daylight, as evidenced by the endless stream of rescue schemes racing through my consciousness. Even in my sleep-deprived state, I reject every half-baked scenario that forms. I guess I still possess a few brain cells.

What faith I should have - the faith I profess - is held at bay by fear, fault, and self-condemnation. If I was half the mother I thought I was, roughly equal to a quarter of what I portray to the world, my son wouldn't be living three miles away in a homeless shelter. My counselor and friends, alike, tell me it's not my fault; Court is making his own decisions. Indeed, I have always pointed to my sons with pride for their successes while secretly and smugly elevating myself to mother-of-the-year. How can I now jettison responsibility for the ruinous journey Court chooses to travel? What did I do to set his feet so firmly on this perilous, pot-holed path? Certainly, it must be my fault. Was it closely clustered sibling births, or spankings, or childhood requests denied, or inconsistent teenager parenting?

Ken is running errands, leaving me with my silent computer monitor. The stillness is respectful company while my brain races, clamoring in so many directions at once, and going nowhere at all. By moving the mouse, mechanical life would break into my frozen-with-fear world, but even the flick of my wrist seems to require more effort than I possess at present. Instead, I stare out the window, my eyes focused on nothing in particular, looking without seeing. Heat-weary leaves rustle in the breeze, still green but without the shine of spring or the strength of mid-summer. Flowers stand swaying slightly and smiling like a kindergartner waiting for the tooth fairy. They cling haphazardly to their summer glory, knowing their days are numbered, screaming to me more of decay and dying than of the right of regeneration. Winter is coming, or is it already here?

There is movement on our generally quiet road. A specter creeps along the black ribbon of pavement, its body winking through patches of the all-too-soon-to-be-spent foliage. Like ghostly depictions in various media, his clothes - wrinkled, dirty and mismatched - hang so loosely that they seem to be melting. His average frame carries so much less than the appropriate weight. Even the dark start of a beard is unsuccessful in its attempt to fill out his cheeks. As he turns down the driveway, I gather all remaining strength from every corner of my being and move toward the door. Planting my body behind it to deny his entrance, I greet the object of my obsession through a four-inch-wide opening in the door. Having made the journey on foot from Lazarus House, probably rehearsing the whole way, his request is predictable.

"I can't sleep there. Eric snores and the mattresses are so thin. They won't give me the cold medicine I need. I'm sorry for what I said. I don't know what I was thinking. I didn't mean it. I'm sorry. I just need a good night sleep and a shower, so I can look for a job. I'm going to be moving in with a friend next week at the latest. I only need to stay here for a couple of nights..."

It has always worked before – a smile and hearty apology. Of course, the "heart" is in the words only. Maybe he even means what he says in the steady stream of dialog, but only until he gets what he wants. All the apologies and promises will get sucked up in another bout of his drug induced anger and indignation. We both know it, and we both sincerely hope against hope that we are wrong. But then, there is very little hope left in the tank with which to wager.

Oh, to fling the door open and wrap my arms around my youngest child and take his hurt away! There was a time when my hugs and kisses could make everything right. Of all the magical powers of motherhood, that is the one I miss the most. Even just a week ago, I dispensed it liberally. I could chase demons away and make everything go back to days of innocence. But now, there is more naiveté than innocence, and all of it, I fear, is on my side. When did the last of my mothering magic expire? Why did I not guard it more closely?

Promises continue to flow from his lips. I hear without listening as they grow wilder and more desperate. I search his face to find a vestige of my son. As a child, his eyes had been so big and filled with wonder. They captured his world. They captured my heart. There had been a glint in them that reflected the joy in his world. His quick intellect and wit caught fumbling words or incompletely formed thoughts and tossed them back with a laugh. His eyes are still green, of course, but his pupils are so chemically dilated that there isn't much color to be seen, and even what is visible must compete with their bloodshot surroundings. If only there was some echo of magic still working, but I am taunted with only the smallest remnant of the son I so long to welcome into this house, our home, his home.

His pleas and promises dissolve into tirades and jeers, hoping to employ guilt where flattery has failed. Angry words gush from his lips, cutting into my heart with evil precision. There is no rational reason, of course, to listen to his abuse. It is love that bars the door from his entrance – love hoping that I can force him to want a better life for himself. But it is love, too, that keeps the door from closing - love longing for a green flash of recognition. I hear myself screaming my loudest silent cry, going internally hoarse from the effort. But Court continues unaware, refusing to veer from his diatribe posing unsuccessfully as a conversation.

How can so many thoughts be coherently formed, analyzed, and conclusions drawn in the space of so few minutes? Then again, how can he be so far away, and yet I can still see his tar-stained fingers trembling: from anger…from hunger…from chemical longing? His words haven't stopped, but any attempt at logic or civility is long gone. With a quick single finger salute, he turns and walks back down the driveway, still spewing venom as neighbors hang on every word, politely trying not to listen.

Ever so softly, I close the door, collapsing against it, and crying what seem enough tears to quench the very fires of Hell. Apparently, that bit of magic has also expired.

Specter – Part II — Neighbor Marilyn Landon
August 2006 — St. Charles, Illinois

I'm a counselor by trade, but a gardener at heart. Maybe there isn't that much difference between the two. Both strive to add beauty to an otherwise desolate landscape. In either case, I am not the actual beauty, but rather the one with the vision…and the water. Today, my patient and my patience are aligned with the good earth.

By the end of August, all but the most die-hard dirt diggers have hung up their implements, taking a break before the snow shovels become a necessity. That said, I am a part of the hardy minority, still tending to this season's beauty, hoping to end it with a flourish of color-filled sedum and mums.

While working in the front yard, I saw him hiking up the road maybe half an hour ago. His dark hair and lanky body bring to mind the Harris boys. Years ago, I gave this one, whose name I don't recall, a ride to the next bus stop after the big, yellow, school taxi left without him. The years since then have been hard, judging by the look of him. If he hadn't been striding so purposely in the direction of his house, I don't think I would have recognized him.

I don't know the Harrises very well, but it's impossible not to hear that things are not going well at that end of the street. When police cars drive by, it is never the harbinger of good news, though indeed, it is news. Even before the engine cools, the location, if not the purpose, for the visit from law enforcement have become common knowledge among the neighbors. Too often over the past few years, black and white cars have been reported in the Harris driveway. I don't judge the family harshly, having had a professional ringside seat to many such crises. The most I can do at present is respect their privacy, and pray for them, of course.

I had made little progress cleaning the front flowerbed of spent blooms and leggy stalks when I saw him again, retracing his steps. His gate, though still rapid, had changed: less striding and more stomping, I think. The set of his gaze warned against small talk, or even a cheery "hello."

As I turned my attention back to my work, I heard a car approaching, then slowing to stop. My husband can hold a discussion on the value of any car he glimpses: financial, mechanical, and personal. If it belongs in the neighborhood, he can also point out the driveway it frequents. I, on the other hand, can point out its four wheels and its color, seemingly always shades of black, silver or tan. Cars do not garner my interest. However, I know at a glance that the car matching the speed of the heavy-footed young man is his mother's. She drives a blue Mini Cooper, notable in and of itself, and all that much more identifiable by the black and white checkered mirrors and matching racing stripes down the sides. It is one of the few neighbor's cars that I can readily identify – at a glance and at a distance.

"Court, I'll give you a ride back to Lazarus House," I hear her say.

"I don't want anything from you! Leave me alone!" he replied distinctly and without regard for anyone's privacy.

"Just get in. You don't have to walk."

"LORETTA ANN HARRIS IS NOT MY MOTHER! SHE IS HARASSING ME! SOMEONE PLEASE CALL THE POLICE!" Anyone within a block can certainly hear his proclamation, but I am the only one with the front-row seat that can see the pain in her eyes as the blade pierces her heart. After half a moment's hesitation, the Mini Cooper pulls away, fueled by a mixture of gasoline and tears. The disturber of the peace flashes a look of defiance in my direction and returns to his stomping with a shout of victory followed by indistinguishable muttering. I bow my head once more to the spent blooms of summer, but set the pruning shears on the ground beside me. My hands and my mind are suddenly shaking too much to safely employ a sharp object.

Just as I am ready to brave the pruning process again, I hear a car pull to a stop on the road in front of me. It is blue, of course, with checkered racing stripes. She is no longer crying, but her red-rimmed eyes tell of the effort it has taken for her to return to this spot.

"I'm sorry about that. My son has been diagnosed bipolar and is not compliant with his medication. We kicked him out some time ago, and we won't let him move back home." There might have been more to her planned speech, but it is obvious that the Herculean effort of swallowing her tears has rendered her temporarily mute.

"I understand. I'm a counselor. If there is anything I can do," I say by way of affirming that while no further explanation was necessary, it would certainly be welcomed and treated in a compassionate and professional manner. She nodded, mouthing the words "thank you" as the red rims pool with water despite her best efforts. Slowly the checkered racing stripes limp away, heading, I suppose, for a more familiar pit crew.

I pick up the shears, viewing the scraggly object of my morning's project, but my mind is on the Harris household. I want to assure Lory that

I really do understand. It's like these flowers: pruning them makes the whole plant stronger, healthier. It allows resources otherwise going to dying blooms to nourish the roots instead, giving the plant its best chance to survive the winter to come.

But people aren't flowers, and their seasons don't change with predictability. The kind of nursery that grows a son does not offer a replacement guarantee as protection against harsh winters. Setting the shears on the ground again, I realize I am already on my knees, the perfect position for what I need to do next.

Father in heaven, Who orders the seasons, please grant spring, in all its glory, to the Harris family…

A Slamming Door **Email from Court to Lory**

August 2006 **St. Charles, Illinois**

STOP! YOU ARE A HYPOCRITE. WORDS ONLY GO SO FAR WHEN YOUR ACTIONS ALWAYS, ALWAYS, ALWAYS LACK. FOR ONCE, TRY DROPPING YOUR HYPOCRITICAL WASTEFUL AURA OF SUPREMACY.

LEAVE ME ALONE ETERNALLY. YOU WERE A HORRIBLE FAMILY. I AM SO MUCH BETTER OFF JUST CONSIDERING YOU DEAD.

PEACE.

COURTLANDT BRYN

The Guy Next Door — Bill Robinson

September 2006 — St. Charles, Illinois

I consider myself a simple man. On the surface, at least, I'm indistinguishable from the guy next door. I live a good life; I love my wife; I raised a son and a daughter. I work hard and plan for my family's future. But since I've lived next to "the guy next door" my whole life and I've been one just as long, there are some undeniable observations to be made: the mask on the guy next door holds up well to casual conversation even over an extended period, but otherwise, the guy next door doesn't exist.

Take me, for instance. I've worked with machines my whole life. My shop has tools older than I am. When they break, I fix them. When the parts aren't available, I machine them. There is a certain symmetry there, don't you think? My tools aren't stamped with "made in the USA," because they come from a time when that was not a distinction, but the norm. You can see me more clearly now, can't you? Several times a year I unlock the gun case in my basement and head for the mountains--the real ones, not something that passes for mountains in the Midwest flatlands. I tease my wife, Ann, that I will bring home a stuffed moose head for the mantel. But considering we don't have a fireplace, she is probably safe. And, yes, there is a car in my life that hasn't run for almost a decade, but it's not destined for the scrap yard. Doesn't matter if it takes me another decade of tinkering and swearing and mechanical caressing, I will drive it again.

Yard work in the summer is a full day's event and is likely to be celebrated by charring some protein on the grill as the sun dips low in the west. By protein, I mean meat, red meat. And here is the first chink in the mask: no beer. I used to partake, but it has done neither me nor my family any good. I gave it up and see no reason to pick it up again. But that's a whole other story and I can't tell it without Marty. And, well… Like I said, another story.

If my complexion wasn't so ruddy (and sun deepened, at that), you would be able to tell that the oil and grime never completely leave my hands. They cling between the well-defined ridges on the skin there. You could probably read my life line across the room if I held my palm out to you. And on only slightly closer inspection, you can make out the shape of the swirls on my fingertips. But here is chink number two: you assume the calluses on my fingers result from my line of work. Of course, that is a factor. Over the years, my palms have spawned extra layers of skin to protect themselves from actual and potential abuse, a natural and welcome defense. But the calluses on my fingers have been meticulously and purposely crafted, not by the grinding of metal or the heat of friction, but by strings – 4 or 5 or 6 or 12 at a time. If it has strings, I play it. I'm not a machinist; really, I'm a musician with a day job.

It might sound cliché to say my love of music was nurtured at my dad's knee, but it is also accurate. I remember jam sessions in the backyard, also including aunts and uncles and cousins. Sitting in awe, watching them, drinking in the sweet sound: music and song, dotted with laughter. I couldn't wait to turn 6 and join the jam. Music isn't notes on a page. It's color: a dipping, moving, refreshing rainbow of sound. It stirs the soul to feel in Technicolor. I never learned to read music; black notes on a white page are just paper and ink to me. When I write my songs, I must impose on someone else to reduce them to notes on a staff. Bland to the point of lifeless, paper and ink suck the color out of the songs, but at least the shadow remains for future musicians to reconstitute. How's that "guy next door" image holding up now?

Strings: guitar, banjo, string base, violin, piano, hammered dulcimer. You were nodding right along with me 'til the hammered dulcimer, weren't you? Maybe you have never seen one – wooden and trapezoidal, it has 88 strings strung over and through 2 bridges. It is played by striking with, of course, hammers. My hammers are made from corset-stays, tipped with wooden heads. There are at least a couple of tuning patterns: chromatic and diatonic. I tune mine diatonically, called the "Robinson Tuning" - invented, perfected, and espoused by my grandmother.

I'm a big deal in the world of hammered dulcimers, winning more national and international competitions than I can remember. Anymore, I just participate as a guest performer. I've voluntarily stepped aside to let someone else take a turn at top honors, hopefully a protégée of mine! That's how I met Court.

His dad and I make dulcimers together. Ken makes the box; I string, tune and teach. We are keeping the tradition going. I couldn't pass it on to my own son; Marty's interests lay elsewhere at the time. Though, Monica, my daughter, jams with me on occasion. When I met him, Court was a gangly, gregarious, middle-school, math-geek, and athlete. He could never be the "guy next door"; that mask just doesn't begin to cover his many facets. Court reminded me of my Marty at that age – driven but fun-loving, serious but never knowing when to stop the joke. Marty's mask never fit, either.

Maybe it was his mathematic prowess, but Court took to the dulcimer instinctively. I would play, and he would repeat, memorizing a new song nearly every weekly lesson. He liked the fast ones, or more accurately, once learned, would play every song with lightning speed, the corset-stays whipping across the face of the instrument. He was my heir apparent on the competition circuit. And he became something of a second son to me, a grandson, maybe, though there aren't chronologically quite enough years between us for that. I got him on local stages at every opportunity. He was shy enough to stay humble and ham enough to be a performer--a great combination!

Then came high school, and predictably, girls. I could still convince him to take a lesson or so, maybe work on a new song or two. Having raised two children, I knew I would have to ride out those years by staying in touch and available. My competition plans for him might take a backseat for a few years, but I hoped a passion for the music had been ignited and would not be extinguished. I would fan the embers at every opportunity, maintaining our relationship. This (grand)father would wait patiently for as long as needed.

Just before Court left for college, I sat him down for some man-to-man advice: study hard, remember all of us who love you, make us proud. Handing him a hundred-dollar bill, I told him to hide it in his wallet and use it only in case of extreme emergency. Now I wonder how long it took for that emergency to materialize - months? Days? Hours?

When he returned home from college just shy of completing his first semester, his parents' hearts were breaking. You could see it etched in their faces, hear the catch in their voices. They thought they were enduring the worst thing that could happen. I prayed they were right – that this was their "worst." It seemed so like the road I had walked – the beginning of that road, anyway. I wanted to be there for Court and for his parents, but Heaven help me - to walk that road again didn't seem humanly possible.

Trying once more to engage Court with music, I would set lesson times for which he rarely made an appearance. Maybe he said yes to my requests with the best of intentions. But more likely, just like Marty, he knew "yes" would shut me up and forestall the inevitable disappointment and ensuing argument - not that I argued with Court; I'm sure he had enough of that at his house. It's easier to forgive when the drama lives behind someone else's door.

Ann and I would take Ken and Lory to dinner, ending in a night of Pinochle where we could casually discuss the highlights (or more likely, lowlights) of the situation. I think we were their safe ears, experienced and non-judgmental. Those were the nights my dreams caused me to wake confused: was Court living in our house? Or was Marty in theirs? Were they really living at all – either one of them? I wanted to run through the house screaming or beat my fists against the wall until something broke – the drywall, my hand, the overwhelming strangling fear. But I donned my guy-next-door mask, laid still and soundless waiting for sleep or daylight, whichever came first.

There was the day that I found out that Court would be entering the Kane County drug court. Lory was trying to convince anyone who would listen of the merits of this desperate act to get their son the help he needed. Maybe it stands out so clearly in my mind because I had rehearsed and given that same speech some years earlier. Regardless, I went immediately to our medicine cabinet and flushed all non-essential prescription drugs down the toilet. I didn't dream of Marty that night; I just didn't sleep.

Two and a half years later, Ann and I were invited to Court's graduation from drug court. After so many years of Marty-parallels, it was good to feel the optimism of the evening, and to think that history would not repeat itself. The smiles, the handshakes, the congratulations were all genuine and heartfelt. Celebration marked the daylight hours. But in another twist of irony, I found myself staring at the bedroom ceiling that night in a state of mourning. Why had their story ended happily ever after while ours left a dull ache that would never leave? I don't want to call it jealousy, as much a longing. It really was good to see Court back on track, again. Who knew the tracks would be so short…?

Now this new chapter in Court's life – homelessness. I don't blame Ken and Lory for their stance; in fact, quite the opposite. As we once were, they are now, out of options. I know the pain they feel: the sleepless nights, the constant arguments, the blame simmering just below the surface, the hope that rarely pushes its way to the top. I've read the book – I've lived the book - and this is no fairy tale. "Happily ever after" is not penned there. It's just "forever after," and forever is a long time.

There is a chill in the air this September evening, which has been increasing steadily since the sun dropped below the horizon a couple of hours ago. These are the times I escape into the color of music. Starting with something slow and melodic, maybe "Marty's Song," I hear muted blues and greens swirl through the sound waves, simultaneously matching and lifting my mood. I play a waltz next, adding pastels to the mix: pink, yellow and lavender. Now a reel named "Liberty": (Court's go-to song) escapes my fingers. Vivid purples and oranges and greens and blues entwine and carry me forward, hammers flying. Even despite the tenuous connection to a difficult subject, I feel hope rising with each florescent note. Some books, the music insists, are destined to have "happily" penned as the third word from the end.

It's odd, isn't it, that music to me is not sound as much as it is color? Sound is too limiting, too one dimensional, too stark, maybe. Fear, on the other hand, *is* sound. It is the sound of a freight train as a damaging thunder storm approaches, sending you scurrying to the basement. It is the screeching of tires when the right of way should have been yours. It is silence when there should be laughter coming from the backyard. Tonight, it is the doorbell at 10 p.m. It storms through the house chasing away the vibrant colors that had filled it mere seconds before. It shouts in my ear even after the actual sound has faded. The colors have all turned to black.

The doorbell beckons for nothing good at this hour. Time and experience have taught me to expect a uniform facing me when I swing the door open, and to prepare for ensuing recreational gossip for other guys next door. But a glance out the side window does not reveal a squad car in the driveway. For the briefest of moments, I choose to believe I imagined the familiar sound, but a glance at Ann's anxious face vanquishes that hope – that, and the sound of the doorbell repeating its request. Standing on my porch is Court. I've been dreading this meeting, praying I could escape the encounter. With the look of impending doom etched in my face, I wave Ann off to safety at the other end of the house.

In the end, our conversation is short, though it may well reverberate for a lifetime. His request was to live here until he gets back on his feet…or a week or so…or just tonight…or a cup of coffee to warm himself from the crisp fall night. Some might not have the strength to say "no" to him. It is, after all, late evening with temperatures in the 50s. He looks chilled and miserable in a wild-eyed sort of way. But, paradoxically, I don't have the strength to say "yes." I wanted to scream, "How many times have I granted your request, forestalling the inevitable! How can you put me through this again? I sent your mother away to protect her from your manipulating requests. Marty, have you no respect, no compassion!"

In the end, Court gives up more quickly than I expect. I close the door, turn the deadbolt, and slump against the barrier that keeps the world at bay. I feel older and heavier and more tired than I have in a couple of years. Looking out the side window, I watch as the two shuffle down the driveway illuminated by the light of the full moon: the shell of Court and the shadow of Marty, walking in perfect unison.

The touch of Ann's hand brings me back from the black edge. It's her embrace that loosens the tears, and we dampen each other's shoulder well into that dark night. In silence, broken by occasional sobbing gasps for air, we speak of what was, what will never be, and what might become. It is a conversation that can only be shared by those who have buried their child. It is a conversation that I hope against hope Ken and Lory will never join.

Mission Trip Preparations
September 2006

Cathy Kathey
First Baptist Church
Geneva, Illinois

Austria. Its anticipation delays my sleep before finally imbuing my dreams with vivid notes connecting past to future. I am traveling with my cello through the countryside where so much music initially bloomed: Haydn, Mozart, and Strauss, among the more famous. Adventures and friendships come to mind that were experienced during my college years when I had a suitcase full of dreams and little else. In those days, I followed music from hostel to hostel in un-orchestrated travel and survived on staples of bread and beer that filled the evenings and quieted my stomach's lamentations. A couple of years ago, my little sister, Jan, her husband and their children spent a year as missionaries just outside Vienna. How I longed to join her, to show her my Austria even as she experienced her own. It is odd how much more difficult travel is now so many years later. The responsibilities of life and the needs of others overshadow a bank account that would otherwise make travel a possibility.

Later this week, though, Jan and I will travel to Austria together on a two-week mission trip. We will return to the refugee center that was the focus of her previous mission stay. There will be five of us on the team, all from First Baptist: Doug, Mike and Lory rounding out the roster. We have spent the last several months getting to know one another, raising funds and prayerfully preparing for our trip. I already knew Doug from various activities at the church. Mike and Lory know each other, Mike being the husband of Lory's best friend, Merry. Ironically, they each signed up for this, their first mission trip, not knowing the other's intent.

When I consider the scant days left before our departure, it feels like watching a jack-in-the-box at the end of its song. There is the anticipation and expectation, each note of the familiar tune building to the predicted climax. Yet as it draws closer, I find myself bracing for the "surprise" when Jack jumps. I can't wait to go, but I'm not ready to leave, either. My husband and kids are certainly able to fend for themselves for fourteen days, but I feel the responsibility and even desire to make sure things go smoothly while I am away. The laundry still needs to be completed, for their sake, as well as mine. There are errands to run and packing to complete.

Today our team gathered one last time before we meet next at O'Hare in a few days. Each of us will arrive at the airport carrying two suitcases: one with our personal items and the other being filled today with clothing, shoes, medical supplies, and toys for the refugees that are the focus of our trip. Divided into the five duffel bags, protesting zippers notwithstanding, we carefully weigh each bag to insure compliance with the airline standards. The few remaining items will be sent home to fit into our personal bags. There will be no spare ounces in our ten bags when we depart. Luggage on the trip home will require much less lugging!

Packing party complete, we gathered around a table to go over final details, answer any questions, and pray for ourselves, our families and our journey. Going around the table, Jan asked each person how specifically we should pray for them. Of course, we all requested prayers for confidence, or at least willingness, to do what God asks of us in Austria. Jan is feeling the unease of leadership. I have complete confidence in her abilities as she guides the rest of us in the mission so near and dear to her, though I understand her anxious heart. We pray especially for Doug's children who are elementary school-aged, when two weeks away is akin to an eternity. Mike declares his willingness to do whatever it takes, though he would rather not lead prayer time. It's a request we can honor, especially for a first-timer. My concern centers on finding the last needed substitutes to lead my children's music classes. I'm still waiting for one call back. Somehow it will, it must, work out. I just hate coming down to this late date with responsibilities still outstanding.

Lory has been quiet all morning, which doesn't seem all that unusual in the handful of gatherings we have attended together. She has previously shared some information about her youngest son – drug and mental issues - which must be just heartbreaking. I know a month ago she was concerned he would become homeless again. But when it is her turn to share prayer requests, her tear ducts spill forth before the words.

"Last night I received a call from the director of Lazarus House where Court has been for the past week or so. Darlene let me know that when their guests are not stable on their meds, they must at times be asked to leave until they become stable. As she said, it is a 'matter of policy' that she thought I should be aware of." Lory swallows hard and wipes her eyes. "Please pray for Court. We haven't heard anything from him and have no idea where he might be."

The stunned silence in the room is in stark contrast to the clatter of thoughts racing through my head. What would I do if my child was missing? Could I possibly spend the morning packing Band-Aids, Beanie Babies and clothing into suitcases destined for a trip halfway around the world? Would I quietly continue with life even as life itself lay shattered at my feet? Suddenly finding a substitute teacher seems so inconsequential.

Jan speaks first, her leadership skills powerfully demonstrated by her words of compassion. "I'm so sorry. We will pray for Court – and for you and your whole family. If you would like to back out of the trip, we absolutely understand! Besides prayer, how can we help you?"

Lory isn't crying anymore, though her words are spoken softly and with the tremor of tears newly stilled. "Thank you, but I plan to go. I can worry here, or I can worry there. There is nothing more I can do here for Court. He is on his own to choose his own way. We won't go chasing after him, and we wouldn't allow him to move back home even if he asks." Her voice trails off more than it stops, like there is more to say, but words are not adequate to express the depths her soul is traversing.

In two days, we will leave for Austria – five of us, as it stands now. We will travel thousands of miles to work with refugees who have fled their homelands in search of not just a better life, but in many cases, life itself. They have left their homes in the Eastern Bloc countries or Africa. They turned aside from all that is familiar to endure a foreign country and language, poverty, governmental restrictions and societal ostracizing, all the time hoping they won't be forced to return to the very homeland they fled in terror. I can only imagine the horror of it, and yet, my imagination brings only a glimpse of reality. I have no true frame of reference.

But the thought of my own child, lost and alone and beyond my reach – that image wells within me, throwing life into perspective. My imagination does not have to labor to feel the horror of that possibility. It is a punch to the gut that leaves me gasping for air – a hole in my chest where my heart should be. Could I travel half way around the world in such a situation? I think not. But then, I haven't had Lory's years of practice in releasing things that were never really within her grasp. I really believe, though, that any amount of practice would still leave one inadequately prepared.

Father, may Your mercies and grace overwhelm the Harris family. In our weaknesses, may Your strength abound.

Taking Refuge
September 2006

Nana Couffie, Founder
Fellowship of Christian Refugees
Guntramsdorf, Austria

It has been such a long day already, and yet, there is still so much to do. I must plan for the upcoming leadership summit, work on my online classes in religious studies, and study God's word. But above all, I must spend diligent time praying for my family, the ministry God has granted me, and those He has provided to prepare the fields for faith-filled growth here in my adopted country and throughout the world. The clock boasts eleven p.m. and change when I finally sit down at my desk to begin the final tasks of the day. The big toe on my left foot waves a friendly greeting to my discarded shoes; the other nine digits are still secured within my socks. These are my best pair; all my other socks have holes both left and right. Foot covering fit for a king, I muse. Indeed, it has been quite the transformation from royalty to refugee to servant of the King.

I grew up in Africa as a tribal king in Ivory Coast. My life was defined by the best: food, clothing, furnishings, education, opportunities, position and power. In addition to my tribal language, I am fluent in English, German, French and Russian. When I decided to marry, it was a simple affair. I chose a wife, and it was done. There was no dating, no discussion. What woman would not want to be the bride of the king? When a coup forced me to run for my life, Sita came with me, carrying our two-year-old son across the African continent. She prayed to Jesus the entire way, insisting He would provide for us. I scoffed at the notion, needing nothing more than my own strength and cunning to deliver our family to safety.

In some ways, that journey was easier than it was when we arrived at our intended destination. Crisis has a way of reducing life to limited options: left or right, stay or go, hide or fight, live or die. Decisions are made by instinct without the luxury of time to analyze possible outcomes. There is no time for reflection or regret for a previous decision before the next crossroad looms, demanding another choice. Should we trust the kindness of strangers or fear their motive? Will stolen food quiet our hunger or lead to arrest? Each decision is made quickly and irrevocably; each one nudges us along a slightly altered path. There is no time to consider the alternative.

However, at the end of the journey, when the goal is realized, time stops – reverses, even – allowing in-depth analysis of each moment, each decision. Nights are spent wondering what would have been *if only*. The scrutiny is flawed, of course, never knowing where the other path would have led. But even without empirical data, the quest for a better outcome continues unabated.

Once in Austria, we had a roof over our heads, albeit a single room in a former prison-turned-refugee camp. Fortunately, I speak the native tongue of our newly adopted home. The scant food we received was not enough to curb the hunger that was a constant reminder of our plight. Our only possessions were the clothes on our backs and our lives. Too proud to beg and not allowed to work, our prospects for improvement were dismal at best. Sita insisted we go to the Oasis, a mission for refugees, where they would give us food and clothing. Reluctantly, I went, not to quiet my wife, who was still subject to my bidding, but to quiet my son's tears and our rumbling stomachs.

I sat in the back, arms folded, ears closed as tightly as possible, waiting for tea time at the end of a sermon that pointed us to our hosts' God and His Son who, they said, are all loving and giving. Surprisingly, rather than the food that had lured me to this cramped meeting room filled with refugees from so many nationalities, I received sustenance for my soul. The message I heard was spoken in English, translated to German, and then to French, thus reaching my ears three times in quick succession. It was a message of God's gift to my tattered soul. The truth that forgiveness comes only from the shedding of blood was not new to me. That had been a way of life my entire life, the reason for our hasty African departure and the impetus for the refugee status that now holds me captive. But that blood had already been shed on my behalf - that I only needed to claim it to be absolved of my debts – *that* was new. Was forgiveness, acceptance, and a new start possible?

Once again, I stood at a crossroad: left or right, yes or no, accept or reject. Since my decision to accept Christ, I have never paused to examine the antithesis--except to marvel at the grace and mercy of God, who brought this king into the King's presence. Jesus' blood covered me then, and still now, guiding me on paths I could never have imagined or chosen for myself.

Though still a tenuous guest of the Austrian government, God has provided me with the opportunity to minister to other sojourners through the Fellowship of Christian Refugees He led me to establish. This complex, which now houses my family and a small staff of equally unpaid refugees, functions as a guesthouse for missionaries on furlough. Other rooms are used to teach German to refugees, while another is filled with donated computers to teach skills that will be needed once work visas are granted. Everything has been donated or is on loan to us, including the two vans that we use to visit those refugees who have been assigned to rural residences many kilometers from our more urban location.

Along with the group from First Baptist Church of Geneva, Illinois, we visited some of the refugee populations who are not able to access the benefits offered at our location or at the Oasis. We bring hope, companionship, and boxes of winter clothing that will be needed in short order.

I knew some of Lory's story and while in route, I had asked her to speak at the refugee shelter. While I translated to the mostly Russian gathering, she spoke from her heart, telling the assembled that she, too, knows what it is to be a refugee--to be cut off from family while hoping against hope for news. Waking from nightmares only to return to a living nightmare is not limited to political differences or lines on a map. She, too, is a mother, anxious for word from her child after a barren two weeks. Where is he? Is he well? Is he even alive? She sleeps with her phone on silent in deference to others, but clutched tightly in her hand so the vibration will waken her. That is, if she sleeps at all, spending most nights noiselessly wandering the common room of the missionary guesthouse.

Her true hope, though, is not in cellular technology that could possibly connect her with a lost child, but in her God whose will it is to find the lost. Through nearly four years of struggle, He has been her constant, her hope, her heart's protector, and her son's guardian. Before Court was hers, he was God's. He holds her son when she cannot and in ways she never could. The story is not yet complete, the ending unknown. But the Author can be entrusted to bring her hope and love to perfect completion.

I translated her words, but a mother's love is a universal language. In the end, the conversation of the gathered mothers did not need my assistance. They spoke with gestures, tears and embraces. It mattered not that the words originated from different sides of the world. Their meaning was clear: God will be with us, and we will stand united before Him on behalf of those we love.

Now back across the miles to my office, my exposed toe reminds me that not all poverty can be so easily seen. Nor is it necessary to leave the country of one's birth to become a refugee. Walking back to my cramped apartment in the new day's early hours, I pass the guesthouse where our Illinois visitors are staying. I wonder: are they all sleeping? Or is there one who lies awake, one hand clutching her phone while the other reaches to the one true God?

Thank you, Lord that your loving eyes rest on both mother and child, and hold each with tender mercies. May we all, Lord, in our poverty take refuge in You. Amen.

Proof of Life — Ken Harris

September 2006 — St. Charles, Illinois

Lory has been in Austria for a week and a half now. It is the longest we have ever been apart in twenty-eight years of marriage. Despite the seven-hour time difference, our cell phones provide us the ability to talk every day. The conversations aren't long, given international roaming rates, but unless she is wandering the backwoods of Austria, the connection is good.

When she first talked about the mission trip to Austria, I had my reservations. But they were small, nagging ones in the back of my mind, so I left them unvoiced. At the time, Court was fully and successfully employed. We thought we were on level ground again--guilelessly so, it turned out. I was hoping Lory might back out of the trip when Court moved back into Lazarus House. I can't believe she didn't when he was kicked out on the streets a few days before her departure.

When Lory and I agree on something, which used to happen most of the time, we just do it. We were engaged a week after we met and married eight months later. Instant agreement! Six months after the wedding, we also agreed that we had made the biggest mistake of our lives, but equally, that we would not prove all the nay-sayers right. Stubborn, it turns out, does have a place in marriage, if you are stubborn for each other and not only for yourself. Our union has survived almost three decades with such stubbornness. It has served us well.

People who have met the two of us think that I'm the domineering type to Lory's sweet and long-suffering self. But people who truly know us know that I married one stubborn woman. Certainly, she can be "stubborn-for": stubborn for our marriage, stubborn for her beliefs, stubborn for our sons, and especially now, stubborn for Court. That's all well and good. But, believe me, sometimes she is just plain stubborn. If she wants a picture hung, it's not good enough to say I'll do it tomorrow. She wants it done *now*. I can either get a tape measure, hammer and nail and do it right, or look at an off-centered picture for years to come. I have roughly 30 seconds to make my decision before she gathers the tools herself, minus the tape measure. When my wife gets something in her head, there are two options: give in and do it, or roll your eyes and watch her do it herself.

We were in absolute agreement that Court wasn't moving back in with us, even if he showed up at our door. But that still leaves a whole range of "what ifs" to deal with. Halfway around the world, paying by the minute for limited conversation could not be anyone's idea of logical. My wife has left me here to deal with whatever might arise, which could include a whole host of professionals, from medical to legal, who we would rather not meet. At best, she is 24-hours from home should further crises come calling. Yet, with emergency poised on our doorstep, she still boarded the plane.

The phone call I received today, however, was both unexpected and welcomed. Court was calling at a counselor's prodding to let us know he is alive and well in Elgin. Apparently, he walked the 10 miles in the middle of the night to get there after he was asked to leave Lazarus House. He claims to be trying to quit smoking cigarettes (as if that's the cause of all his problems) and he will contact us again when he succeeds. The call was short but left me amazingly refreshed.

I happened to mention Court's call to Bill Robinson when we were talking. He let me know that Court had stopped at his house the night he became homeless, requesting admittance. Bill had turned him down. I can't blame him for that. If he had shown up here, I would have done the same.

When the appointed time came for our global conversation today, the reaction when I told Lory about Court's phone call had the same effect in Austria as it had in St. Charles. The clip to her words was erased by a kind of giddy lightness. Proof of life is an amazing stress reliever.

My wife will be home in two more days. I have a modicum of faith that I will make it without need for a panicked international conversation. Even so, Lory let her selfish-stubborn overrule her stubborn-for. This time it's up to me, I guess, to practice stubborn-for, for both of us.

Passing Notes Electronically — Lory Harris
September 2006 — St. Charles, Illinois

It's a crisp and clear fall morning. Looking out the window, I see a blur of yellow, red and brown. When I allow my eyes to focus on the view, I see a smattering of green, too. There are fewer and fewer unrealistically optimistic leaves left clinging to summer. If green is the color of hope, it is losing the battle.

Half my mind is on Court, of course. It always is. The other half strains to accomplish all other tasks of living: relationships, work, and breathing. Half a brain and half a life - that pretty much sums it up for me.

I haven't laid eyes on my youngest son in over a month now. For the ten miles that separate us, I might as well be back in Austria. The distance is strikingly similar. We have heard from him a couple of times, brief and non-committal. He is getting his life back together and once he has, he will come see us with his head held high. He has quit smoking cigarettes, (which seems important to him but a total non-sequitur to us), and I offer my congratulations, hoping that is what he wants to hear.

There is a bus that takes him to some kind of church for the homeless--Angelo's, he calls it--and then drops him back in Elgin, again. The details are scant, but it seems a hopeful sign. Certainly, the information we receive about his life are selectively offered, but I choose to believe they are representative. Probably unrealistically so, but they rock me to sleep at night as I lean into the charade.

I've sent Court several emails, striving for a balance between light, uplifting conversation and pointing him to God. After enduring this grind for so long, perhaps the only thing I can claim with certainty is that God is the answer and without Him there are not enough Band-Aids to stop the bleeding. Obviously, Court doesn't have a computer, but apparently, he finds one to borrow from time to time. His electronic communication is scant and equally superficial, but not completely void.

My computer screen is currently displaying the second story floor plan of a four-bedroom house. All client requirements have been met within the allotted square footage, if they don't mind standing in the bathtub to brush their teeth. With a long sigh, half of my brain turns back to shaving inches from other areas of the house to supplement the bath. A hushed "ding" emanates as an envelope-shaped icon appears in the bottom corner of the screen. Happy for the distraction, I switch over to my email.

The sender goes by the moniker "G." I have no idea why he has chosen that letter to represent himself, but Court's email address follows it, which is good enough. The message, sent to both Ken and me, is short, but I read it half a dozen times to make sure I didn't skip a word or two that might alter the drastic descent of my heart to my toes.

I retract any and all statements I ever made about being related to either of you in any way, shape, or form. Goodbye forever. I hope your pathetic excuses for lives turn out miserably. Sodom and Gomorrah deserve hailstorms of fire. And, Loretta Ann Packard, you owe me one of your "souls." Amen

Reluctantly, I must acknowledge that his intent and meaning are both clear enough. Why he used the name given to me at birth is an inconsequential mystery. I can feel Ken's eye boring into the back of my head, but when I turn to acknowledge him, he, too, is looking at his email. He closes the screen, grabs his coffee cup and heads to the kitchen for a refill. Wordlessly, I turn back to stare at the screen.

The email is time stamped 10:14 a.m. Not knowing how often he gets to a computer, my mind rushes to a reply, hoping he will get it immediately, but not really knowing what "it" should be. *Please, God, give me the words, and give them to me now.* Did I wait long enough for God to answer my prayer, or am I, as usual, jumping ahead with my ill-conceived, knee-jerk retort? It seems unlikely that mystery will ever be resolved definitively, but with fingers moving quickly over the keyboard, a single heartfelt sentence appears on my screen:

May God Bless and hold you closely on your journey.
Love,
Mom

At 10:18 the computer documents my reply. Will he receive it before he signs off? Will it matter? How much of what he said do I believe? It's not the first time he has vehemently rejected me or other family members. It's the kind of push-me-pull-me that Ken and I have grown to accept as normal in our world, though the impact of the accompanying kick in the stomach never lessens.

It's not his rejection, per se, that will occupy my mind in single digit hours of tonight's darkness. No, it's the fear of the veiled threat that will make my eyes search the ceiling for answers that are never printed there. Will he be content to just disown us? Or will he attempt suicide again? Might that attempt succeed where others have failed?

Ken returns with his coffee and sits down heavily in his chair. "You got the email." I'm not sure if it was a statement or a question, but I nod my head and reply, "We've been here before." I have no tears to offer, just a stomach making a valiant effort at flipping more quickly than my thoughts. Lunch has lost its appeal.

Unfocused, unblinking eyes stare out the window. There is a single green leaf within my vision. With a final desperate act, it throws itself to the wind, hoping to be carried to the land of eternal summer. Chlorophyll still intact, it swirls, gaining altitude momentarily before landing softly among its multi-colored brethren. *But it's still green,* I tell myself, *there must still be hope.*

Down by the River — Court Harris
October 2006 — Elgin, Illinois

I'm not sure who has ordered the 4 a.m. wake-up call, but I know who is delivering it. In the relative warmth of the hot air vent, the river air has been hospitable enough to allow some sleep. That is, until the flashing lights arrived, followed by a quick blast of the siren and humorless men in dark uniforms. "Move along," they intone, as if the comfort offered by the vent was reserved for someone more deserving. Without it, though, the October night air is not warm enough to grant sleep.

I've never really thought of September or October as cold months; in my previous life, they were just "nice fall days." Sometimes, they still are – the days, anyway. Every fifth grader knows why days get shorter this time of year, but it wasn't until now that the inverse has become so pronounced: nights are getting longer and colder, noticeably gathering momentum daily.

I am, shall we say, traveling light. This sweatshirt is not living up to its name. The running shoes Mom bought for me a couple of months ago are not as florescent yellow as they once were, nor are they warm. But I must admit, they are living up to their advertised billing. We are on the run, my shoes and I, most recently from the early morning law-enforcement-evasion-obstacle-course. I could let the cops take me in – I'm not holding, and it would be warm, but any bed they offer would be, well, confining.

I make my way to the homeless highway. Its main branch roughly follows the river though there are many side streets as well: unpaved, unofficial, undocumented access to my adopted world. The path is mostly on public property, I think, though it is punctuated by fences from time to time that force circuitous detours. It's all part of living the life.

One of the first fellow travelers I met was Carl Lewis – no relation to the athlete, I assure you. However, he could probably garner some attention if he changed his name to Wesley Snipes. He's a little older than his famous twin, or maybe that's just a result of the non-Hollywood life he has lived. He should consider wearing dark glasses if he wants to pull off the charade; Carl's eyes are completely void of life. His stories are fascinating, well thought out, and detailed, obviously, the product of an intelligent mind. They are also one sided; he talks whether someone is listening or not. We are well suited, the two of us. His words fill the air and my minimal input serves to spur him on.

I cross paths with a big white guy from time to time. I haven't caught his name, but I call him Mikey, as in Archangel Michael. He is always battling some power, attempting to keep the legions of Hell at bay. His sword, heavy and invisible, is as effective as his celestial cousin's. It's just more proof (as if I needed it) that Christianity is a sham.

Then there was "Q" and his friend, the silent one whose name doesn't stick with me. We kept warm together passing a smoking bowl back and forth. Q's most prized possession, the number of items in his collection being just slightly more numerous than mine, was a bottle of chloroform. Besides bragging rights, I'm not sure what other uses he intends. I didn't ask. He claims to be laying low here in Elgin, avoiding Chicago questions about a car that happened to blow up. Q had a lot to say, most of it grandiose and subject to interpretation. Not wanting to know where the truth started and ended, I moved on when the bowl quit smoking.

A couple of weeks ago, I lent a hand to a fellow traveler named Darren, and was well rewarded for my efforts. I've never seen someone with so pronounced a limp, regardless of age, and Darren wasn't much older than I am. He was carrying a couple bags of groceries, mostly canned goods, and struggling each step of the way. I offered to give him a hand, which he graciously accepted. He said the limp was a result of gang violence, but that still seems impossible to believe. There can't be a gentler heart than his. We arrived at his grandmother's house and he invited me in to hang out and watch TV with him. I have never felt more welcomed. It made me long for a family to call my own. I wouldn't get the same kind of greeting if I showed up on the doorstep of the ones who claim to have loved me my whole life. I'm always on the lookout for Darren in my travels, hoping for another opportunity to assist and to enjoy his company.

Some nights I sleep at an Elgin church that opens its doors to the homeless at night. It may not be the Hilton or have all the comforts of home, but it's the closest I have to an address right now, if you don't count the vent by the river from which I was just evicted. I was headed to the church when I met up with a kid offering heroin. Getting out of the view of judging eyes, we snorted the dragon, though the explosion of bliss and beauty was neither as bright nor as prolonged as on previous occasions. Being of a practical nature, I continued to the church, determined to prolong the high as long as possible by resting in it. Apparently, I fell asleep on the sidewalk. It was dark when I woke to the cold, all traces of my shadow dream world replaced by cold misery. My fellow travelers had not thought it necessary to wake me when the shelter doors opened, nor had they seemed to give me a second thought when they were locked for the night.

I had slept in the gentle warmth of the heater down by the river until I was unceremoniously rousted. Maybe I'll return to the church tonight if a better offer doesn't present itself. At least it's warm there, and easy enough to ignore the obligatory sermons even while feigning interest. I could use a warm meal, running water that is not inhabited by fish, and a good, relatively undisturbed night's sleep. But first, I need to find some coffee and a warm place to drink it.

On Forgiveness – Part I — Email from Court to Lory
October 2006 — Elgin to St. Charles, Illinois

Mom,

I have said and done some terrible things. I don't even know where to begin to apologize for all of that. I am too ashamed of myself and my actions to even consider myself welcome in the presence of you or Dad, again. But, so you know, I am sincerely going to change my life right now. I am giving up smoking entirely, and am getting into a recovery group. I am going to rededicate my life to being a truly good and decent person.

Just looking back, I am so incredibly ashamed of all the things that I have done. This is my biggest weakness: I am too proud. I am truly going to attempt to work on that and be humble. I want to rededicate my life to God, and truly being a good Christian. But, my demons are SO strong. I could really use the love, support, and guidance of my mother right now, if only for a brief moment. I am so tired of being sick and tired, and God has finally gotten to me and said, "STOP!"

In case you were wondering how low I had to sink before I could finally open my eyes and use my brain, I am currently staying, homeless in Elgin. I am seeking employment, and am attempting to join the Navy. I think the structure, and pride in something would really help me get through quitting smoking, and back on my path towards a real life. I truly surrender, and am really going to do my very best to make things work.

If I could have one last request after all the terrible things I have done, it would be your prayer and support in quitting smoking. I am really low right now, and a supportive voice would really help.

Maybe some guidance, too, since all that I can think right now is, "man, I want another cigarette." This is really hard.

Please disregard and forgive anything I sent to you earlier. I was doing a typical Court, and lashing out without thinking because the world wasn't going the way I wanted it to. I want that to change so badly now, and am going to do what I can to make sure that it does. PLEASE HELP, though, if I have not burned my bridge back to all I know and love, utterly and completely.

With love,
Court

On Forgiveness – Part II — Ken Harris

October 2006 — St. Charles, Illinois

Lory and I each got an emailed apology from Court today. Hers was longer and contained more flowers, as expected. Mine was shorter and to the point, again, as expected. He claims he hasn't smoked in the past 24 hours and "isn't turning back." Having smoked for many years in my youth, I think I can guarantee he hasn't had his last cigarette, regardless of the degree of his sincerity. It rarely works that way. While I appreciate the apology, it's not a one-and-done kind of thing. Four years of flipping me off are not erased by an emailed paragraph. I want to see change. This is a start--a positive one--though in the scheme of things, a little too modest.

I almost laughed when he said he wanted to join the Navy. His career would end before it started, just as soon as he peed in the cup. Besides, if quitting smoking is really his goal, then the military would be exactly the wrong direction to turn. I may not want him smoking in front of me, but I agree with Lory: at the rate he's going, he won't live long enough to die of lung cancer.

Looking over our two versions of apology, there is another difference that stands out. Court has asked me if he is forgivable. From Lory, on the other hand, he just seems to expect it. He probably has that right. Absolutely, I'll forgive him. He's my son. But before I jump on that band wagon, I want to kick the tires. I'm just hoping there are tires to kick – that would be the first step.

Of course, Lory responded, though it took her several hours. She said she loved him and wants him in our lives. But she stopped short of saying 'all is forgiven,' asking for more time to think before responding completely to the rest of his email. I thought Court had done a pretty masterful job of pulling at her heart strings: rededicating his life to God, claiming that God has finally gotten ahold of him, asking for prayer, and professing his need for a mother's love and guidance. I had expected her to head to Elgin, scour the streets and bring our prodigal home. Of course, she could have done that any time in the past couple of months and she hasn't.

A few hours after the electronic plea, Court called. We both talked to him briefly, assuring him of our love. Neither of us used the word forgiveness, nor did our son dare to say the word aloud. It's a big word, a weighty one. It's not okay to use it like a broom to sweep the past under the rug. There have been genuine hurts, on both sides, I suppose. One thing I know for sure: there isn't a rug big enough to hide it all. It's going to take time and dedicated effort to clean up this mess. I want to see Court's resolve first – not regarding his nicotine habit, but rather to quit belching smoke and flames when he doesn't get his way.

Maybe this is a beginning of the end, but I've said that before and been made a fool. Let's see where he takes us first.

Caring **Ed Sorenson, PADS Volunteer**
October 2006 **Elgin, Illinois**

I've been volunteering for Public Action to Deliver Shelter (PADS) for a couple of years now. Founded here in Elgin by three clergies many years before I was old enough to acknowledge or care about homelessness, PADS is now well into its second decade of ministry. My wife and I were sitting in church one Sunday when a plea for help was issued from the pulpit for volunteers to help at the overnight shelter every other week or so during the cold months. They especially needed male volunteers. I felt a stabbing pain on my left side and turned to see my wife smiling sweetly at me. She has always had the more tender heart between us - and the sharper elbows.

I went with some trepidation that first night - or ten - but eventually it got into my blood. Maybe I would even say I enjoy it. Well, *enjoyment* would be an imprecise description; *blessing* would be more accurate. I have certainly been blessed, as I hope our guests have. How exactly that happens is still kind of a mystery to me. It is on the days that I most dread my commitment that I end up most aware of God's approval. Self-employed, middle class and white, what do I have in common with those who live on the street? I'm not sure I can answer that question, except to say, "Humanity." And that's enough. I have met some amazing people who send me home in prayerful consideration: *there, but by the grace of God...*

There is, at the same time, a cynicism born of realism that has crept into my thinking. I understand hard times and being down on your luck. But the hallmark of my life has been to buckle down and work harder to make things happen. When I am honest with myself, I only rarely glimpse the "why" that leads people to our church's door to sleep for the night. Mostly I just do my best to love and provide for them while keeping my judgmental side in check.

Of course, I've met those who tried to play me for the fool, as if fronting a twenty to a guest will change his whole life's trajectory. He would be back a night or so later, none the better for the "loan." How many times have I heard them say how unfair employers can be, as if being expected to work for a paycheck is un-American? To my shame, even the word "them" indicates my heart isn't really where God would have it. It is a delicate balance to love "the least of these" without putting yourself on a pedestal, and yet to still love them enough to make them pick themselves up.

The twenty or thirty patrons arriving on our doorstep on any given night are just looking for a warm bed and smile, but if that's all we offer, we would be merely spitting in the wind. We must offer them the things they don't know they need: self-respect, the expectation that things can change, motivation in the process, and knowledge of a God who, once encountered, will not leave us unchanged. *Us* - that is a more appropriate pronoun. God is working at changing me, too.

The church opens its doors at 7:00 p.m. for twelve hours each night to shelter the homeless against the cold. There is a rotating schedule of churches that provide meals that many will have already taken advantage of before coming here to sleep for the night. Every other Thursday, I have the 7-to-11 shift, greeting and checking in the guests. It is a fluke that I am here on a Sunday evening. I would like to be home, preparing for the upcoming week. And by preparing, I mean watching Sunday night football. But when the plea went out for assistance, I discovered my wife's elbows have not dulled a bit in the last couple of years.

The rules laid out for us, volunteers and guests, are cut-and-dried. No drugs, no drinking, no fighting. Mingle with the guests, provide a friendly face and point them to assistance when appropriate. We try not to be too preachy, but God is the one who keeps our doors open, and He will be acknowledged. There is always a prayer before lights out at 10. Fortunately, I'm not often called upon to say those words. Coming up with something fresh and meaningful takes a skill I don't possess.

Each guest must register initially and, thereafter, sign in on a form. This serves several purposes. First, it gives us a headcount and a reliable record of the services rendered. It also gives us a snapshot of each of our guests, allowing us to get to know them better. Finally, it gives us a pattern of their visits. We want to be available and responsive. However, we do not want to become a flophouse where they can repeatedly show up for an evening to dry-out and warm-up before heading back to the streets to commune with their personal demons for another few days. We don't generally turn people away, but there are times when it is appropriate, especially at the beginning of the cold season. September and October functionally set the expectations for the rest of the winter. Since the nights are not as cold as they will be from November on, we try to set the tone for the year. Word gets around – quickly.

On this Sunday night, I'm on check-in duty. I recognize some faces from previous years, and others I've spent time talking with this season. I have the sheets ready when the guests approach. Another familiar face stands in front of me. It is thin, with a dark scruffy beard. He is young and dirty, without distinguishing features. I don't know his name and have only seen him a couple of times. But his last appearance on our doorstep was memorable.

"Court Harris," he tells me by way of introduction. I pull his sheet, but I don't have to study it to know how to respond.

"I'm sorry, Court, but you can't stay there tonight." As I suspected, his sheet showed sporadic attendance.

"You know, it's really cold out there. Freezing to death is a possibility," he countered.

"Yeah, I know." My voice sounds flat and heartless. It lies. Both my head and my heart agree with his assessment and fear for him. But I also know that his real problem isn't the chill in the air. He turns defiantly and walks out the door into the gathering darkness. I wonder if or when he will return.

His attendance sheet tells me he was last here the previous Tuesday night. That isn't entirely true; he was here on Thursday when I opened the doors. After everyone had been checked in, I went out to issue a last call before closing the doors for the night. He was still there, sleeping on the sidewalk. I tried to wake him, his eyes fluttering open before his jaw resumed the slack demeanor of his chemically-induced slumber. An hour later, I stole a glance out the window to make sure he was okay. Apparently, he had awoken and left to find more comfortable sleeping quarters. We never open the doors once they are closed, a hard and fast rule of necessity, and one universally acknowledged and accepted by our guests.

It's almost midnight as I pull into my garage, a weary exhaustion tugging at my eyelids. The morning will bring a long work day; there is so much to be done. I think briefly of going to the office now; it would be Monday by the time I arrived, after all. The best I can expect from my own bed, aside from the warmth it will offer, are dreams of green eyes above a dark scruffy beard, shivering in tandem. I'll scan the police blotter for several days to come, hoping for a glimpse of the young man, and equally hoping to find none.

It's in my blood, now, to care. But caring must be shared on both sides of the divide to be effective. *Care, Mr. Harris, for yourself, about yourself, and about your future. For your own sake, care.*

Midnight Hiking — Court Harris

October 2006 — Chicago, Illinois

I don't remember ever feeling as physically exhausted as I do right now. Even the first week of high school, varsity, soccer practice seems like child's play by comparison. *Ha!* I think, *it was child's play*. In my mind, a sly smile forms at my own joke, but my mouth, being too tired to comply, does not offer the traditional gesture of mirth. The sun is up, bright and clear. I can only hope for solar cell properties to keep me going the final thirteen blocks to my destination.

Standing outside the Elgin church last night, I saw frost forming on the colored glass of the house of God. For all its talk of grace and mercy, they had none for me. If a rock had been available, I would have used it to express my opinion of their deity. And I would have waited patiently for a visit from the men in blue, whose religion lends no room for capriciousness. I intended to use their ridged adherence to rules for my purposes: a warm bed and a semi-permanent address. Finding a suitable projectile a block away, I carried it like a talisman, continuing along my original course. I couple of blocks later, I left it on the sidewalk. The church, now three blocks to my backside, remained safe in its pious indifference.

The Christian-dominated, Republican-voting western suburbs had slammed the door in my face three times now: first by my own parents, then Lazarus House and now PADS. It was apparent I needed to find more enlightened ideology with which to surround myself. The lights of Chicago, glowing steadily above the eastern horizon, drew me on. The brisk walk denied the frost a chance to attach to my exposed extremities.

The streets weren't exactly dark – it's never truly dark in the 'burbs - but as the hours passed, they became largely deserted. My brief stint in the Boy Scouts had taught me enough to assure myself I was still on course despite the various turns necessitated by the realized vision of meandering, suburban, subdivision design. The closer I got to the city and the further from mid-century land-planning, the more grid-like the streets became, and thus, easier to navigate. Knowing the battery indicator on my cell phone was glowing red, I checked my progress against the clock sparingly. When it became apparent that flights into O'Hare were landing behind me, I snuck a glimpse. It was past three a.m., and I had probably travelled about 25 miles.

My righteous indignation having been walked out of me miles before, my determination to place one foot in front of the other was in sync with the battery level on my phone. I was looking for a place to sleep that might offer some relief from the cold when my flagging fortitude was given the boost it needed. The flashing lights I had fantasized at the start of this journey appeared suddenly beside me.

"What are you doing?" His leading question revealing his keen powers of observation, no doubt.

"I'm just walking, sir." No reason to poke the bear.

"Where are you going?"

To Hell, I thought, but I elected to answer with the other truth, "to Chicago."

He considered me for a couple of moments, mentally searching a list of infractions that would take him back to the station with a guest in the back of his car. "You shouldn't be walking here," he finally deduced, "it's not safe."

"Thank you, sir. I'll get out of here as quickly as I can." I wouldn't have accepted a ride to a more secure location even if he had offered, but the rush of warm air when he got back into his car was something close to intoxicating. As my eyes readjusted to the dark that had been temporarily shattered, my feet responded to the wakeup call, walking with renewed resolve.

I wondered, not for the first time on tonight's sojourn, about my mother's reply to my apology. Funny how the more miles I put between us, the more I think of home, or more accurately, the place formerly known as home. Whatever response I had expected from my email did not arrive. It wasn't exactly her words I found lacking, though I had hoped for more. I wanted her electronic insistence that I return home, though that seemed improbable even in my sweetest dreams. Aside from the name of a city that houses 100,000 people, I gave her no indication of where I was. All the same, I wanted her to use her mother-born senses and search until she found me. She had less to go on when I disappeared in Milwaukee, and countless more miles to search when I called from Lincoln, Nebraska. Yet both of those times, she had moved heaven and earth until we were reunited. She didn't find me in Kentucky, even though I was hiding virtually under her nose, but at least she searched. Now she professes her love for me, saying she wants me in her life, but her inaction speaks volumes. As much as I want to believe her, it sounds like one of her bedtime stories of long ago, fanciful and sweet, but with no basis in reality.

The wind calls my attention to the urban version of fall foliage, grey and imbued with printer's ink, skittering along beside me. While the sun offers some long overdue and welcome warmth, I am still hugging my sweatshirt to me in a futile effort to trap my body's heat. Despite having reached anonymity in the land of the tall buildings, I feel as exposed as the emperor in his new suit. At every corner, I expect to see a child tugging on her parent's sleeve and saying, "Look, Mommy, he's naked." And she would be right.

Warm Bed for a Weary Traveler **Lee Mannford, Staff**
October 2006 **Pacific Garden Mission**
Chicago, Illinois

Every night, the Pacific Garden Mission shelters five or six hundred men and women who would otherwise call these south side streets their home. As much as we strive to get to know them all, it just doesn't happen. I'd like to say that no one falls through the cracks, but I'm not nearly that naïve and haven't been since I was somewhere in my single digits. I grew up not far from here to lullabies punctuated with cat calls, sirens and the not infrequent sounds of gunfire. I knew where and what the PGM was early on, but I would have laughed in your face - or hit it - had you dared to suggest I might work here someday. I guess God likes a good joke, because here I am.

The first time I set foot in these doors, I was hungry, cold and defiant. I might not have had much, but the chip on my shoulder was one of my few possessions, and a prized one at that. Over the next eighteen months or so of my sporadic visits, more than one person tried to knock it off. Just as frequently, I was asked to leave for fighting. I kept coming back, though, initially to meet my physical needs and reluctantly sitting through the mandatory come-to-Jesus gatherings. But over time, my fights with other men lessened as I turned my sights on a bigger target: Jesus, Himself.

I would swing wildly away, well into the night, convinced the score cards must be in my favor, exhaustion causing me to sleep and continue my efforts in vivid dreams. Over time I started to feel the weight of that chip pressing down on me. Even without benefit of a mirror, I saw the hideous slouch and pronounced limp it was causing to my soul. I was too deformed to remove the impediment myself, even though I developed a keen longing to be free of it. 'Just get washed clean by the blood of Jesus,' they said. I've taken showers, and I have seen enough blood, but the only place I've seen the two combined is in a horror flick or the aftermath of a gang shooting on a rain slicked night. But then, what did I have to lose?

Turns out the answer was 'just that chip,' and the thinly veiled fear that haunted my dreams. The transformation was sudden, and yet, long-awaited. The sense of relief to stand tall again and to walk without a limp was exhilarating – and foreign. There were times when I longed for the comfort of my former burden. More than once I snatched it back, only to pray again for deliverance. I can spot it in others now with the surety that familiarity breeds. It makes me no better than another; I'm just one beggar telling another where to find food.

When he showed up yesterday, I was working the 3-to-11 shift. There was nothing special about him that caused me to take special note. And if he hadn't called attention to himself later that evening, I'm sure he would have easily blended into the sea of faces. Wild-eyed and gaunt, young Mr. Harris looked cold and hungry, but seemed most interested in a place to sleep. He said he had walked through the night from Elgin to get here, probably about 50 miles, depending on his route. He seemed to be trying a bit too hard to blend in with the brothers, an effort that was severely inhibited by his whiteness; I found it mildly amusing. Jamal lead him through the initial interview, assessing his needs before providing some clean clothes and showing him the shower area.

Court finished in time to join us for the pre-meal worship service. I'm told he sat quietly listening, eyelids drooping. He didn't seem overly anxious for dinner, at least until he received his plate. Jamal reported that he ate ravenously. Maybe he had undertaken the hike he claimed. He certainly had all the earmarks of it.

It was the evening prayers that brought Court's presence back to my attention, though. As is our practice, we broke into smaller groups, asking, though not insisting, that each man offer a prayer before being dismissed to their bunks. After a litany of "God, help me…" and "Jesus, please give me…" Court took a turn. "God, it seems like everyone is asking you for something. But who asks You what You want? Is there something I can do for You? Amen."

I wanted to say, "Yes, there is something He would like of you," but Court was quickly surrounded by several of the men congratulating him on the spirituality of his prayer. Maybe it would be a good topic for the worship session before breakfast the next morning. The men disbursed to their bunks. In theory, I shouldn't have seen Court again until the next evening.

As you can imagine, the logistics of daily caring for so large a group of people can be daunting. Both for keeping order and the accountability needs of our clientele, rules are strictly enforced. The dormitory is reserved for sleeping, and sleeping is accomplished in one of two shifts. The beds are most full at night, of course. After worship and breakfast, their former occupants are expected to be going to jobs, looking for jobs, or otherwise engaged in the business of living. Only those who work night shift jobs are allowed in the dormitory during the day.

I caught my next glimpse of Court among the night shift sleepers as they made their way to their "breakfast" and then on to their evening employment. Distracted by a question from a newer staff member, I lost sight of Court. But as the corresponding line of daytime workers filed in for their worship, dinner and bunk time, I stationed myself at the door. As I suspected, our young Elgin hiker was among them. With so many people swapping positions at the same time, it is easy enough for someone to exit the building and cross into the returning workers line, using PGM as their own private flophouse. We watch for it, of course, but we can't always catch it. I remember stealing multiple sleep shifts once or twice myself, which is probably why I'm so attuned to it.

Putting my arm around Court's shoulder I said, "I know you, and I saw you leaving the dorm with the night shift men. Don't you need to get to work?"

He didn't flinch, but his pupils gave him away, instinctually and unconsciously dilating. "I don't have to go to work tonight," he feigned.

"Well, you've slept through the past two shifts. Time to do something useful. I'll see you in the morning." I watched him turn and leave without further comment.

I hope he does come back tomorrow. I'll have the staff alerted to the possibility and prepared with counseling. But it's 50/50 at best, and probably a bit less. Pride is a powerful master, and shame a tough drink to swallow. I know; I've had my fill of each. There is nothing I would like more than a heartfelt discussion of exactly what God asks of us, and more specifically, of Court.

SECTION FIVE

DARK BEFORE THE DAWN

October 2006 – June 2007

Blue Goose Supermarket
St. Charles, Illinois
10/25/2006

Scott Paper Towels	1.53
Camel filtered pack	4.46
Hershey Chocolate Bar	.50
Paring knife	7.79
TOTAL	$14.28
Cash Tendered	$20.00
Change	$5.72

THANK YOU FOR YOUR PATRONAGE!

Yellow Shoes – Part I — Court Harris
October 2006 — Chicago, Illinois

Of course, the street isn't empty (that might be a physical impossibility in Chicago), but the crowd has thinned considerably. As I stand looking at the mission, a young black man walks by, purposely bumping me with his shoulder, and giving a derisive laugh. "Loser," he shouts without breaking stride or opening his mouth. I watch his backside disappear around the corner. "Tough luck, man," says a voice beside me. I look up to see one of my daytime dormmates. "Been there," he continued, "Just come back in the morning." Unsure of how my voice will sound, I put my hands in my pockets, offer a disimpassioned shrug and head south.

It's not like I intend to employ continual use of the revolving door between food and sleep. I would have been happy to look for a job tomorrow, but my legs are still so sore from the Elgin walk. My body just needs time to recover. Every rule has its exception, right? They should understand that.

Several blocks pass before I stop to wonder where I'm going. Why south? Even though Chicago city limits stop abruptly at the curving line of Lake Michigan, the streets are amazingly geometric. There are occasional diagonal intersections, but it is largely possible to pick a cardinal direction and stay the course. I just spent a night coming from the west; I've exhausted that direction. East would bring me to the Lake in quick order, and I have no interest in going for a swim in freezing waters. And why would anyone head north with winter settling in? So south it is. Kentucky is south; I was happy there once. One foot in front of the other. Just keep moving. Eventually I'll meet I-80 and can hitch a ride.

The streetlights staggered along my route only serve to point out how truly dark it is here: the asphalt, the concrete, houses that have rejected their owners' attempts with a paintbrush. Even the sporadic trees have shown a complete distain for color, either having jettisoned their foliage altogether or clinging tenuously to shriveled brown. The minimal lumens emitted from the corner sentinels serve to create more shadow than light.

Just as I'm about to conclude that I'm part of a charcoal drawing titled *Not in Kansas Anymore*, the facades spring to life in shades of red and blue. "What are you doing here this time of night?" demands the proprietor of the gyrating lights. For all the talk about Chicago lawlessness, you would think they could find an actual crime scene to investigate. "Trying to score some heroin?"

"No, sir, I'm just walking."

He pats me down, locating all my earthly possessions: half a pack of cigarettes, a lighter and a cell phone in need of resuscitation. "Take off your shoes." Sitting on the edge of the squad's backseat, I remove the once-vivid yellow shoes and the formerly white socks that now blend with the shadows. Playing the part of podiatrist, my new-found friend examines my feet, looking for track marks. He won't find any: I'm not a huge fan of needles - arms or feet. I prefer to ingest my chemical-mood-alterations orally. Reluctantly, he draws the same conclusion. "Get out of here. It isn't safe." Returning the minimal protection to my lowest extremities, I continue my southern quest.

I've probably been walking for about four hours, and except for the singular blue and red incident, the scenery hasn't changed. My legs, still tired from my previous trek, are no longer interested in Kentucky. All I can think of are the final words I heard before starting this journey: "Come back in the morning." It feels part request and part imperative. With little more thought than that, I turn on my heels, retracing the near-perfect straight path I just traversed.

There are so few identifiable landmarks with which I can mark my progress: houses in unvaried shades of charcoal and scant trees in stark nakedness. But there are two reliable indicators. First, the numbers on the cross streets are getting smaller, more slowly than hoped, but consistently. And secondly, I've submitted to a follow up visit with my judicially-appointed podiatrist. Apparently, I am still the hottest potential criminal on the south side. The results of the night's second examination, much to his chagrin, are identical.

Socks replaced, I reach for my shoes. A couple of months ago, they were a garish shade of yellow. When I proposed their purchase, Mom thought I was kidding. "No wonder they were on the sale rack," she quipped as we walked out the door with the purchase. With each step I've taken since, imperceptible remnants of yellow have remained, maybe the only testament to my passing. If it was possible to view that trail of yellow from the air, what conclusion would someone draw? What would they think of shoes that have haphazardly wandered through the western suburban neighborhoods, to the heart of Chicago, followed by a linear march through southern asphalt ribbons of questionable reputation, and then backtracked again for good measure? The end of their story, it seems, is at hand, the treads worn completely smooth and the fray of the inner lining starting to poke through.

Slipping them back on my feet, my fingers obediently tie the laces without a trace of conscious thought. With the same kind of automated actions, I stand and continue retracing my steps, hoping to sleep with the night shift again in the morning.

Yellow Shoes – Part II — Colin Harris
October 2006 — St. Charles, Illinois

I've had a job ever since I was 14. My employment experiences are varied: stock boy, gas grill assembler, pizza delivery, dorm resident assistant and LAV (light armored vehicle) driver in the Marines. The job I have now, however, is the quirkiest yet; I work for my parents. The job description is straight forward enough: designing houses to customer specs using CAD. It's the rest of working in a family-owned-and-operated business that can addle the brain. Most hours of the day it works well, but most days there are hours that remind me that eighteen was a good time to have moved out of the homestead. Fortunately, I have a different home to go to at the end of the day. I would never survive if my commute was just down the stairs to my former bedroom.

All three of us boys have worked in the business at some point, though I'm the only one that is giving a serious run at long-term employment and eventual ownership. It has been six months now, a longevity record among my siblings. Onward and upward – or something like that.

I was working on a preliminary floor plan for a customer when the phone rang. Glancing at Caller ID, I see a PACIFIC GARD followed by a Chicago number, not that anyone looking for me would call on the home-line anyway. Mom is at a Bible study, which leaves Dad to answer the ringing intrusion. Mom, Dad and I all work in the same partition-less room and each of us has learned the art of not hearing another's conversation. In fact, I've learned not to hear their radio, either, opting for earbuds that pipe in my preferred music. But some things break though the self-established barriers. "Court? Where are you?" Dad says into the phone. In a totally involuntary act, my eyes catch a glimpse of the ceiling before settling back on my computer screen. The soap-opera-according-to-Court always has that rolling effect on my vision.

Even though I'm the oldest of the three of us, there were stretches of time when I felt like I lived in my younger siblings' shadows. Their grades were better, and they were both jocks, the kinds of things that garner parental attention and exclamation. I spent my time reading and messing with computers – and working. I am also an Eagle Scout, a distinction that I alone carry in this household. My brothers and I each led separate lives, but there was a lot more overlap between the younger two.

"Hang on," I hear Dad continue, and then, "Colin, Court is at a shelter on the south side of Chicago and has been beaten up. I have a customer coming in an hour. Would you be able to go pick him up?"

The previous rolling eyes, notwithstanding, I like the sound of this assignment. Corey, Court and I all have love affairs with our cars. We drive vehicles whose titles have transferred hands a few times, meaning it's not about the biggest and the best. We just love to be behind the wheel, regardless of the where to or why. It's that much better on work time, since I'm being paid my salary plus fifty-cents a mile to do Mom and Dad's bidding. The mileage check makes for a nice monthly "bonus." Ten minutes later, directions and a sandwich in hand, I head into the city.

I do love Court; there is no shadow of me that would say otherwise. But sometimes I would like to give him a shove in the back down the road to Hell he seems so bent on traveling. I suppose that makes my profession of brotherly love sound disingenuous. I assure you, it's not. I would take a bullet for my brother, either one or both. As a Marine, I know what I'm saying, and I mean it – literally.

Court's rejection of reality coincides almost exactly with my time in the military. He entered a psych hospital for the first time as I was finishing my initial training. With an undergrad degree in psychology, I had a better handle on what was happening than either Mom or Dad, not that I tried to educate them on the world of possible outcomes. Ignorantly blissful is a perfectly acceptable honeymoon state. Just like a honeymoon, unfortunately, it is unrealistic and short-lived--though fondly remembered. At that time, I had no experience with honeymoons, but I still stand by my analogy.

I was a 22-year-old, private first class when my boots first landed in Iraq, older than fellow recruits, but equally green as to the business of war. We whiled away our first month in the sandbox practicing in the foreign terrain and perfecting the art of donning chemical weapon suits while waiting for a decision to come down from above. For all the military advances, communication with home was circa World War II. There was no internet in the desert and no phone down on the corner. Honestly, the corner tended to move with the wind, literally here one day and gone the next. Communication with the outside world came either through our commandeering officers, or in the form of letters from home - the latter being the more coveted.

Mom's letters tended to contain much information about and frustration with Court's exploits, anecdotes about Corey, and concern for me. The writing was a bit unbalanced in favor of Court but representative of her life and overwhelmingly welcomed on my side. When I was home after my first deployment I commented once that I couldn't imagine how difficult my post must have been for her. She responded that the distraction Court provided made it easier. She tried to back pedal when she saw my face, but the damage had already been done. Psychological knowledge aside, I risked my life for country while her attention was focused on the one who was throwing his away. I didn't exactly hold that against either Mom or Court, but it didn't sit well, either.

Pulling up to the Pacific Garden Mission, the one who greets me is a shell of the brother I last saw a couple of months earlier. In classic Harris fashion, the length of his hair has made the management of it a losing battle, though it doesn't appear he has even thought to engage the effort. It juts out at impossible angles in some places and corkscrewed in others. High and tight is the only option our hair leaves us; he needs a haircut. I was thin when I graduated from boot camp, though sculpted. Court is bordering on skeletal. His jeans are only able to defy gravity with hardy assistance from a belt. His shoes are the same color as a tennis ball turned highly-favored dog toy.

But it is his eyes that shock me the most. The dark circles under them draw my immediate attention. The orbs themselves are hollow, yet pleading, and they drip on and off the whole way home. For over an hour as we drive, he recounts his last couple months of an existence that makes the inconveniences of my time in Iraq look trifling.

He asks to bum a cigarette, saying he would pay me back when he got some cash. "No need," I tell him. I take one, give him the last three, and I hand him my last $20 to hold him over. Over until what, I wasn't sure. Back at home, he eats some food, showers, dons clean clothes, and takes a short nap, then he and Mom go out.

I love my brother, every bit of his self-tortured being. And I think I understand my Mom's previous back-pedaled statement a little more, too. Families are complex, but worth the fight – and a battle is, indeed, being waged.

Yellow Shoes – Part III — Lory Harris

October 2006 — St. Charles, Illinois

In this age of instant communication, I've missed the one call I have anxiously and repeatedly assailed God's throne to receive. While my cell phone laid in forced silence in my purse, Court called home. An hour after the rest of the family has sprung into the resulting action, I am joyfully being brought up to speed. Once home, I pace the room with all the nervous anticipation of a first-time father. *What's happening? Is everything okay?*

"You know he can't stay here, right?" Given our state of perpetual disagreement, I can't blame Ken for the dictate masquerading as a question. Has he forgotten that I was the one who kicked our youngest out a year ago? I bristle at the implication that I would cave in and change my mind. In truth, I would, if I thought it would bring about a change of heart in our youngest son. Another in a long line of desperate pleas for help, though, does not constitute evidence of such a change. Even if something more concrete was offered today, it would need to be examined and verified before the previous judgment could be vacated.

"I've already talked to Darlene at Lazarus House," I reply as evenly as possible. "She can't guarantee he will be allowed back in, but she will discuss it with Court when he shows up at their door." I feel reasonably confident that Court will have a bed to sleep in tonight. Darlene can be tough as nails, but with the most tender of hearts. I'm not trying to play the friendship card, but I'm not above it, either. If I was, I suppose, I would have let Court handle the transaction on his own.

At long last, with something of a new parent's relief, I saw them: ten fingers and two once-vibrant, now-grubby, yellow shoes. I will take it on faith that the full complement of toes is hidden within. I wrap my arms around my baby boy, whispering *I love you*s and willing his heart to hear mine.

Sandwich, shower and nap complete, Court and I head out for a walk along the river in the general direction of Lazarus House. It is a beautiful day for a walk, crisp and clear with blue skies and the last of the fall foliage reflecting in the waters of the Fox River.

Court tells me how he has been beaten at the south side homeless shelter, but when I ask if he needs to see a doctor, he declines. Whatever injuries he has sustained are not readily apparent on hands and face, his only visible flesh. He is so sorry for all the pain he has caused us, and just wants to come home and make things right, he tells me. And once again, he pledges to quit smoking. He doesn't even have any cigarettes, he claims; he is done. Once again, I wonder about his fixation on that vice. It certainly seems the one least likely to cause immediate health concerns, but I let it pass.

I fumble through the expected dialog: fumble because I want to speak anew from my heart but with advice that is well-worn to my ears and certainly to his, too. "I love you. We want to help, but you must help yourself. In the end, Court, your best help is through God. Turn to Him." They are sentiments often repeated, true and heartfelt, but likely to be received as another repetitive scolding.

Back in the car, I turn the key in the ignition, thankful for the warmth flowing from the vents. We continue our discussion in the idling vehicle. "Mom," he stammers, "if I tell you something, do you promise to let me handle it?"

"Yes, I promise." The words were quickly and easily spoken. Isn't that the point we have been trying to make, that he needs to be responsible for himself? For years, I have wanted him to do things my way, and still, here we are, on our way to Lazarus House for the third time. It is time I tried something new, and by new, I mean turning the wheel over to someone else. I have been trying to drive both my life and Court's, and have been largely ineffective at both. It is time to let God take my life where He will, and time for Court to make that decision for himself, too. I have just made a promise I intend to keep, though the gathering silence coming from the passenger seat makes me wonder at the gravity of the information he is considering sharing.

Just as I am beginning to think I should put the car in gear, Court leans over, unties and removes his right shoe. While no words escape my mouth, my mind is in overdrive. *What is happening here? Is this where he has been beaten and he wants to show me? Does he really need medical care?* But we just walked up and down the river, probably a total of a mile. He didn't seem to be limping. Knowing very few details of his life in the previous two months, maybe one or more of his ten expected digits are no longer present. His every move is slow and deliberate. Slower than slow motion--it is more like watching a freeze-frame movie.

With a final sigh of resignation, he reaches into his grubby yellow shoe and pulls out a wad of paper towels. Carefully unwinding the length of it, he reveals a paring knife and hands it to me. "I was going to kill myself. But I don't want to anymore."

I take the knife from him; it is one from our set at home. "Court, if you want, I'll take you to the hospital instead of Lazarus House. It's up to you." Nothing like turning the wheel over to someone else and then watching the car veer into oncoming traffic.

"No, I'll be okay. I'll go to Lazarus House. I can talk with their counselors there. I love you, Mom."

I hug him to me, never wanting to let him go, and knowing that my grasp is not nearly as secure as my prior illusions have led me to believe.

When I stop in front of Lazarus House, I give him $20, in case he needs to buy something for himself. I don't care if it goes to cigarettes, but I can't stand the thought of him being completely penniless. I give him another hug and a kiss and tell him to call if he wants to talk. "Let's get together tomorrow, ok?"

"Sure, Mom, I'd like that. I'll give you a call."

He is walking up to the door of the shelter as I drive away. Maybe he is looking for the help he needs. Maybe he is turning a corner. The glint of the sun on the knife's blade makes me wonder, though – which corner?

Upping the Ante – Part I / October 2006

Court Harris
Lazarus House
St. Charles, Illinois

I watched Mom drive away last night with hardly a backward glance, leaving me, again, begging for shelter. I'm glad she didn't wait to see me enter, since I wasn't quite ready to ring that doorbell. I had $40 in my pocket, the most money I had held at once in months. I know how I would have used it last month – even last week. But I lacked both transportation and even desire to get high. As soon as I saw Mom's car turn the corner, I headed to the local grocery store. I needed a smoke.

I had held my salvation in my hand, well, my shoe. It was my release, my escape - and I had turned it over to Mom. *Why?* I wondered, though I knew the answer. So many times, I've tried to commit suicide, but always safely, which isn't the oxymoron it seems. Some methods of suicide, though time consuming, seem almost peaceful – an overdose, poison, carbon monoxide. I've tried them all. Such methods give you time to think, reflect, even back out if you want.

If there is one thing I've learned through my attempts, though, it's that the body is very well-built, and it takes effort to destroy it. Sometimes when you drink an ill-advised substance, the body will do its best to reject it, forcefully, if needed. It can make the 24-hour flu seem like a case of the sniffles. Even if you trick the stomach into digestion, there is no guarantee the bowels, liver and bloodstream won't filter out the offending elements.

There are other, more certain methods, of course. I'm old enough to buy a gun, though I would be hard pressed to put that much cash together at one time. But pulling the trigger is something else altogether. That takes complete confidence that in the blink of an eye, things will be better. What if the tales of eternal suffering are true? And if they are, that is most certainly the fate I deserve. Is it fear or cowardice that prevents me? I thought I had finally resolved my doubt – and then, in a fit of "what if," I gave the knife to Mom.

The grocery store is only a couple of blocks away, and the cigarettes are at the front, as usual. But with a small fortune in my pocket, I wandered the aisles in search of something else – a fond memory from childhood, maybe, like Cocoa-Puffs or Pop Tarts or Dove ice cream bars. Maybe I just needed some junk food to garner favor with my new-again bunkmates. Honestly, I was just putting off the inevitable: eventually I would have to ring that doorbell and request admittance. Would they even open the door for me?

I found what I didn't know I was looking for in aisle 9, which boasts an odd conglomeration of non-edibles: storage containers, toothpicks, baby bottles, matches, razors, and…knives. There was one, small enough to reside temporarily in my shoe, and well within my budget. Would I have the nerve to use it? I thought so. At least if I owned it, the option would be available to me.

When I finally dared to return to Lazarus House, I was rewarded with a warm meal and eventually a bed for the night. I don't remember the beds being all that comfortable previously, but then, I've done a lot of sleeping in the great outdoors of late, without the aid of a tent or sleeping bag. I fell asleep almost immediately, waking a few hours later in my usual state of self-defense, my nightmares having followed and been allowed admittance as well.

Even after my heart calmed to a more normal pace, I remained vigilant, eyeing the ceiling and warily listening for my attackers--concealed under cover of night, but ever-present. One might think I am old enough and wise enough to dismiss the surreal demons of the night, chalking them up to "an undigested bit of beef," as Ebenezer Scrooge would say. I contend that just because something is easier to see with eyes closed doesn't mean it disappears when the eyes are open – an adult doppelganger's game of peek-a-boo.

The knife, I mused, would be completely ineffective against the strength of the shadows that haunt me. They are immortal. My previous attempts to slash them seem only to have multiplied their forces. Stupidity is, they say, doing the same thing repeatedly, expecting new results. In a fit of early morning clarity, the answer was clear: do the opposite. Rather than defensive parries with the blade, perhaps I should go on the offensive, instead.

When the wakeup-call was issued, I arose with resolve I have not recently known. I dressed quickly, shoes included, and made my way to the bathroom. Carefully locking the door to keep from being disturbed, I looked myself over very carefully in the mirror. Who had I become, and where would this next transforming step take me?

A knock at the door startled me, and I dropped the knife. With my t-shirt wrapped around my neck, I went to the house phone and dialed the number I have known since my childhood. "Mom, I think I do want to go to the hospital, after all."

Upping the Ante – Part II
October 2006

Lory Harris
Lazarus House
St. Charles, Illinois

I woke early, as usual, but after a good night's sleep, which is so uncharacteristic. Just knowing where Court laid his head last night was enough to ease my mind. I was already dressed and fed by 7:00 when the phone rang. Court's voice replied to my greeting, "Mom, I guess I do want to go to the hospital, after all."

"Okay. I'll be right there." Grabbing my keys, I was out the door in less than thirty seconds. It's only about 2 or 3 miles to the shelter, but I didn't want to give him any chance to change his mind. A series of right hand turns brought me to my destination, unhindered by the morning rush of commuters. I didn't check my watch, but I doubt five minutes had passed since the call.

Ringing the doorbell for admittance, I looked through the door's narrow window for a sign that someone was aware of my presence. Twenty feet away, at the top of a short flight of stairs, I saw a man talking on the phone using animated gestures. I think I recognized him as a member of our church, but I don't know him personally. He was most certainly an overnight volunteer. He glanced my direction, held up one finger telling me to wait, and continued his conversation.

Court came into view, saw me, and descended the stairs to open the door. If the volunteer was animated, my son was the complete opposite. He had the look of a deer in headlights, moving toward me, yes, yet rooted somehow – gliding more than walking. His eyes were wide and unblinking. A navy-blue t-shirt was wrapped around his neck, held in place by his hunched shoulders. He looked like someone burrowing into a scarf to keep the winter wind from blowing down his back, attempting to retain some small measure of warmth.

It's amazing how the ears hear sounds that the brain filters out as unnecessary. But as Court opened the door for me, the sound of approaching sirens finally reached my consciousness. Glancing the block and a half toward Main Street, I saw a firetruck and ambulance turning down the same side street where my car is parked--the same one where I now stand.

It was my turn for my eyes to widen with the dawning of realization. "Court, what did you do?!"

Upping the Ante – Part III — Ken Harris
October 2006 — St. Charles to Geneva, Illinois

It wasn't even 7:30 when the phone rang for a second time, though at least I was expecting this second call. Lory's number popped up on Caller ID, letting me know, I assumed, that they were on the way to St. Joseph's psych unit.

"I'm following the ambulance to Delnor Hospital in Geneva. Court is okay - even I could see that at a glance. But he will be going to a psych hospital after they stitch him up. He tried to slit his throat. It's not deep enough to be life threatening, but it is a gash about 6 inches long."

I set my coffee cup down. Every cell in my body snapped instantly to attention, rendering caffeine a complete redundancy. We are old pros at Court's suicide attempts, but there had been nothing like this!

Colin was just walking in the door for work as I grabbed my keys to head to our local hospital. Our conversation was quick of necessity; I didn't have much information. His face blanched and his pupils widened. "Where did he get the knife?" *Odd question,* I thought, and shrugged in reply. Walking toward the door, I suddenly remembered the history Lory had written out a couple of months earlier, "to make them see Court as a real person" in just such a situation. I grabbed the two-page document and left.

I was shown to a typical ER cubical where Court laid inclined on the gurney and Lory sat beside him on a chair. There was no beehive of medical activity, reinforcing Lory's assessment that Court's attempt was not likely to produce his desired result. Court was tugging at the gauze that was lightly draped around his neck. The wound, starting on his neck below his left ear, was partially visible. It was half an inch deep, I would estimate, but no longer bleeding. From the bits of blood that stained the temporary bandage, it appeared he had stopped cutting just before his Adam's apple.

I've never been one to worry about assigning names to my feelings, which served me well right then, since there are no words to describe that feeling. It was part relief and part anger, part disgust and part love, a sprinkle of fear and a healthy dose of surreal. The doctor had been in to assess the situation and would be back soon to stitch it up, though "soon" was anyone's guess in an emergency room where clocks run capriciously. Not more than a couple minutes later, a nurse stuck her head in asking for either Lory or me to fill out some forms. Just the escape I was looking for; I volunteered immediately.

Following the nurse to a corner desk, I was introduced to the staff social worker who proceeded to explain the hospital's procedures after a suicide attempt. There would be a minimum 72-hour hold for evaluation purposes. However, since this hospital does not have a psych unit, Court would be transferred to St. Joseph in Elgin.

"I'm very familiar," I interrupted. "Court has had three stays at St. Joe's, and yet here he is, again. It isn't working." I pulled out the pages detailing my son's dark history over the past four years and asked her to read it. She skimmed through it, slowing at some sections.

"May I keep these?" she asked. I nodded. "You are right," she acknowledged, "he needs more help than he can receive in a few days. Let's see what we can do." And with that, we rolled up our sleeves, grabbed the scissors and started cutting through red tape.

Without health insurance, any help Court received would be at the expense of the citizens of the state of Illinois. A private hospital was out of the question. Besides, those stays are generally limited to five days, which had proven entirely useless in our experience. The next step in the escalation process is Elgin Mental Health Center. In the state of Illinois, it is also the last step. The only variant after that is duration, not location.

Growing up in this area, I am very familiar with that facility, more affectionately known simply as "Elgin." Parents would say," Stop acting like that or I'll drop you off at Elgin" or, "Elgin called, they are looking for escapees." The grounds are huge and foreboding and have been in various states of disrepair and dilapidation my entire lifetime. Judging by the frequency with which bulldozers gain admittance to the facilities, I would say the "guest" population has dwindled substantially over the decades. I know much more lore than fact about the place, but one fact I know for certain: Elgin is where Illinois houses those not guilty by reason of insanity. No one goes in there and comes out again in less than 72-hours without a staff or visitors badge for passage. Incredulously, here I was, fighting to get my son admitted.

It was at least an hour later when I made my way back to the cubical where little had changed. A nurse was removing the temporary dressing from Court's neck in preparation for the stitches. I called Lory out into the hallway to give her an update. "They agree that another stay at St. Joe's isn't likely to help. It looks like they will take Court at Elgin Mental

Health. It will probably be several hours before everything is squared away, though." Lory looks visibly relieved as we walk back to see Court.

"Hey, Bud," I say, squeezing his leg. "I'm glad you are going to be okay. I need get back to work. I love you and I'll see you soon." He nods and whispers a hoarse 'good-bye.' There is something about the sterile surrounds that make him look impossibly small – less man and more child – my child, my son. And then, with a second glance, he is a stranger with vacant eyes and a gaping neck. Walking back to the car, tears well-up in my eyes. Do I cry for my son, or for his father, or for despair of the desperate hope now set in motion? In the end, I shed enough tears for them all.

Closing a Window — Court Harris
October 2006 — Delnor Hospital
Geneva, Illinois

There is a steady hum in the background: medical personnel move efficiently, quietly, and purposely around their hive. Their low-pitched, near-wordless conversations contrast with the course, whispering screech beating my eardrums from the inside-out. If I had exerted another couple of pounds of pressure, I wouldn't be here now. Well, perhaps my body would have rested here, but I would have vacated it. Sometimes life and death are separated by miles, or years, or seconds, or, in my case, fractions of an inch. I had the means, I had the opportunity, but I also had a doubt, and it played the trump card.

Something has changed, though. My soul didn't run from my body in my feeble attempt to separate the two, but it did glimpse the exit. I can feel its longing to escape in the throbbing of my neck. Like a prisoner peering through a narrow-slit masquerading as a window, glimpsing the denied makes the ache that much more acute. As much as the captive knows it should turn from the unattainable, the longing makes that action impossible. I could have died, I lament, but instead, I draw another breath.

I won't be returning to Lazarus House, not later today, or next week, or next year. This is the third time I have exited their hospitality. They won't offer a fourth, and I won't ask. Ironically, I may resemble their namesake more than most, the Lazarus of New Testament fame having been dragged from death and returned to life. But then, in the Bible story he seemed pleased to find himself living and breathing again; not so for me.

Mom is making small talk, though there isn't much to say, and no one listening, either. A few phrases break through: "not going to St. Joe's again" (Good!), and then "going to Elgin" (What?). I am momentarily confused since St. Joe's is in Elgin. Slowly it dawns on me that "Elgin" is also in Elgin. Can that possibly be what she is saying? How could they? Why would they?

I can feel my world collapsing inward. My soul, hungry as it is for its view of freedom, has retreated to the deepest, darkest crevice of my fractured being. Only the certifiably craziest of the crazies count "Elgin" as a home address. I should have stayed in Chicago. Or, I should have continued walking to Kentucky. No, I should have exerted a few more pounds of pressure this morning…

The doctor comes in bearing a syringe to numb my neck. But it will not be enough to numb the throbbing in my brain. Inconsequential nerve deadening achieved, the man in scrubs picks up the suture. "Wait," I say summoning speech with great effort. "I don't want to be stitched up." The educated eyebrow of the most educated in the room raises. "If you do, I'll sue you," I continue, making certain communication is achieved. His brows now match, both reaching for the ceiling.

"Court, you are welcome to sue him later, but right now, he's going to stitch you up." I sigh in obedience to my mother and lay my head back on the pillow, bearing my neck to the doctor's single fang. With each tug and knot, the window through which my soul stared longingly at freedom, is shuttered. His task complete, the object of my future legal action leaves without further conversation. When Mom attempts conversation, my words are as plentiful as the doctor's were. Eventually, Mom, too, lapses mostly into silence.

It takes several hours before an ambulance is arranged to deposit me at Elgin. I spend the time plotting my escape. In the end, I escape not from, but rather *into*: into myself, into silence, into the world governed by Court, complete with a new necklace, 18 beads long.

Enough Guilt
October 2006

Lory Harris
St. Charles, Illinois

Morning forces itself upon me, nagging at the corners of my mind until I admit defeat and get up. I should have slept well knowing Court was safe and cared for and, hope against hope, on the road back to health. Instead, I stared at the ceiling all night, intent on replaying recent scenes. If yesterday's events were made into a movie, it would have all the requisite individual elements, though I doubt the Academy would be impressed.

There was drama, of course: a man in the prime of his life slitting his own throat, leading to first responders arriving with blaring sirens. The scene lacked the voyeuristic pulsating blood loss, a departure from Hollywood for which I am extremely grateful. Never once during that day did I think my son would die of his injury. But the fear of what his next attempt would bring remained an underlying theme in my early morning review. His previously feeble suicide attempts were suddenly ratcheted up to a level just shy of success.

The pre-ordained miracle was near the beginning of the show rather than the more classically placed conclusion, but amazing none the less. After having taken the time to write out Court's history to reinforce his individuality in just such a situation, its potential use never crossed my mind again. But Ken, who initially scoffed at it as an exercise in futility, remembered and employed the plan. I didn't even know they had social workers in the ER; we hadn't run into one in past suicide attempts. Ken's insistence, though, added weight to those slight pieces of paper and set the machine in motion. Slow and grinding though it was, it moved down a distinctly different path than the well-traveled and ineffective one of previous years.

The intrigue resolved itself quickly enough, which also doesn't make for classically good cinema, though my heart was grateful. The rejection of a St. Joe's five-day-bandage came quickly enough, but the final resolution took hours. It's odd, really. When Court was hospitalized in the state psych hospital in Milwaukee, I fought tooth-and-nail to get him out of what I judged to be a substandard facility. My child needed more than their over-worked, under-staffed and under-funded auspices. Now I was thrilled he was headed to just such a facility. I guess God had painstakingly taken time to prepare me for this new phase of our journey.

Then there was a humorous subplot. The look on the doctor's face when Court threatened a lawsuit was noteworthy of itself. But it was nothing compared to his look when I advocated stitches now and lawsuit later. It got the desired compliance from Court, but I fear the doctor may have had no more sleep last night than I did. Could he not tell that a mother was just trying to calm her crazed child? For the next 3 or 4 hours while we waited for Court's transfer, I tried to catch the doctor to make sure he knew there would be no upcoming legal action. He never came into the room again. Nor did he walk anywhere near it. There was only one additional glimpse of him. He was taking the long route around the nurses' station to avoid our litigious corner of the ER.

I was even granted superhero powers at one point. Growing up, I always envied Superman: to fly, to have super-human strength and x-ray vision. What a trio of talent! If I could only have had one of them, I would have taken flight. Escaping the confines of gravity, turning a narrowly scaled 3D world into the full spectrum of the third dimension, has always sounded idyllic to me. Alas, the superpower granted me was x-ray vision, providing a ringside seat to layers best left hidden. In this case, I had an unhindered view of the gears in Court's head grinding slowly to a halt. His motions slowed, then his emotions, and finally, all movement involving the will stopped completely. He became mute and almost catatonic. We spent the last hour or two of our wait with nothing more than breathing and an occasional shrug of indifference passing between us. I had learned some years ago to join the silence. I'm not a brilliant conversationalist anyway, and I had already used up any marginally meaningful words I might have possessed. Court and I just shared air-space.

Watching the replay on my bedroom ceiling last night, I felt like an actor in a B-movie. It was very serious and compelling to me, but realistically, the audience was destined to be small and unimpressed. The early morning replay should have put me to sleep in quick order, except for one small hidden detail – hidden from everyone else, but looming larger than life for my moonlit-viewing. It was my fault - ALL my fault.

My self-incrimination, continuing through breakfast and into the start of the workday, was disturbed by Colin's arrival for work. "Hey, Mom. How's Court?" There was nothing to report. Visitation is restricted to Wednesdays and weekends. We would see him tomorrow and hopefully gain more information then. Beyond that, all we had been told is that he was "settling in."

My eyes were making a thorough examination of the floor lest my eldest see the guilt in them and call me out. But when I dared to risk a glimpse into his eyes, I saw a familiar fear. His voice was quiet yet thick –

not at all the booming, staccato, Marine-speech we had come to expect since his discharge. "I'm so sorry. It's all my fault. I was just trying to help him out, but I should have known better. I gave him twenty bucks, and he used it to buy the knife. I'm so sorry." His words echoed the plea of my soul. The pain in his eyes matched mine, down to the glint of the tear that was involuntarily forming.

Hugging a Marine can be a difficult task. Their pride and honor keep their backbone as stiff and unyielding as their professional demeanor. But he's also my son, and I needed the embrace at least as much as he did. "I gave him $20, too," I said into his shoulder. "If there is guilt to be had, I guess we will split it. But we did what we did out of love. How can that be wrong?" And with that, both of our souls exhaled.

I guess we could both be branded arrogant fools to think that our small cash gifts were the cause of Court's self-destructive action. He could have found a knife, or an unaware moving car, or an unprotected window on an upper floor. Cash was not the motivating factor. But individually, our love, fear and guilt formed a cord not easily broken. Neither Colin nor I had been able to escape our self-fashioned noose – until we worked together to unbraid the trio. With fear and guilt discarded, all that remained was the love of family. "Happily ever after" is still out of sight in the future, but it's a step closer to the way a movie is supposed to end – with a hug and a degree of hope as the credits roll up the screen.

A Mother's Love
November 2006

Martin Hanson
Kane County Correctional Institute
Geneva, Illinois

I have been battling depression so long that I don't think it can be called a war anymore. It's just the way my life is. At best, I can take an occasional brief vacation. But just like a vacation, it doesn't last long enough. Any temporary escape to fleeting happiness makes the return adjustment even darker by comparison.

Just last week I planned a little getaway. I was traveling light – just my wallet and my car for a trip to the city. I go to Chicago quite often for such day trips, or day "tripping" as my parent's generation might have called it. If you know where to go, there is always a ready supply available. Heroin has two distinct advantages: it's cheap and it provides a mellow, feel-good high without a resounding crash at the end. There are, however, two disadvantages. First, the world to which it returns me is not to my liking, which, of course, is not the drug's fault. But secondly, the insatiable quest for that feeling of well-being takes more and more impetus, meaning the first advantage of heroin no longer applies, and the second is less and less predictable.

My most recent vacation, however, met with great success. My wallet had been fat enough to afford the trip of my dreams - good dreams. That is, until I got back to my hometown and fell asleep while being a law-abiding citizen and obeying a stoplight. I woke to a knocking on my window, a mirthless uniformed attendant issuing my wake-up call. There is nothing like being roused from a dream to a nightmare and then being "offered" a place to sleep. Unfortunately, it was an offer I could not refuse, literally. Now I spend my nights contemplating suicide, and my days making sure I keep that consideration to myself. I don't want to end up in the Risk cellblock, which is nothing short of incarceration raised to the tenth power.

Tonight, a guard came around after dinner asking if anyone wanted to go to the Life Skills class. No one else in my cellblock volunteered. If just to get away from this depressing orange-laden gathering, I raised my hand. I was escorted to a classroom by the officer known as Papa Smurf. Though his skin lacks a blue hue, his round face. white beard, and lacking calloused demeanor makes the description spot on. Even a newcomer knows exactly who he is without need for further explanation.

There were several tables and chairs set up in the room, and a lone dark-haired, middle-aged woman at the front who invited me in. She introduced herself as Lory. A couple of minutes later, Papa Smurf returned with an inmate from a different cellblock, and let us know that would be all for tonight. It was apparent my tangerine-twin and Lory had met before. Their greeting was warm and friendly, something I had previously assumed impossible in these confines. I felt my defenses slip a little as a result.

Lory started the session with prayer, which was a throwback experience for me. It has been a long time since I've talked to the Big Guy. If it was a sermon that came next, it didn't feel like one. "A wise pastor of mine told me," she started, "that God does not bring us through hard situations to just give us our lives back in the end. He wants to make something new from the ashes."

Lory and my partner on this side of the table engaged in a comfortable conversation. "Now that you are here, what comes next?" My head understands that life goes on, but in the past, my eyes have seen how time shifted when I left similar surroundings, like a jagged rip in the universe. It's like jumping on a moving train – the whiplash effects of time inertia are painful. Just how does one keep on living in a holding tank? I couldn't stop the nagging feeling that it was time to stop marking time, which is not the same as moving on. I just need to quit. At the same time, though, I can tell my defenses have slipped another notch or two.

My classmates were subtly trying to include me in the conversation, though I was opting for listening politely. Then Lory asked me a pointed question, "So, Martin, if you don't get your life back, where do you go from here?" I guess there was a part of me that really wanted to talk. I mean that certainly wasn't an inquisition, but I felt myself tumbling down the hill I had been so carefully avoiding.

"All I can think about is *not* being here – suicide," I added to clarify the information I wasn't intending to say in the first place.

Her eyes revealed something, though I couldn't quite make out what it was. Not shock, but not indifference. No, there was an edge of sympathy maybe, and some compassion in a totally matter-of-fact way. "You know not to say that to anyone here, right? Suicide watch is not somewhere you want to go."

I nodded. I would literally rather succeed in my stated endeavor than return there. "I've messed up so many times that it just seems like the best alternative. You know what my greatest fear is?" Her quiet demeanor beckoned me to continue more effectively than words would have. "I don't think my mother can ever love me again." I can't believe I said that out loud! My mom has stuck by me through all these depression and drug-induced years. She is the one thing in my life worth living for, though, just barely. But how many disappointments can she sustain? This time she didn't even answer the phone when I called to tell her I am here.

Lory didn't hesitate even a moment. "Oh, Martin, she loves you! My son is in the hospital right now after a suicide attempt. He slit his throat. What would I have done if he had succeeded? My heart would have died with him. Life has been difficult for him for years, and therefore, for me, but my love for him has never changed. Your mother is no different. She loves you still, now and forever." How I longed to believe her, not just her words, but the way her heart ached for her son, and for me, by extension.

Papa Smurf returned shortly thereafter to take us back and tuck us in for the night. Now, I stare into the incomplete darkness, flanked by snoring compatriots. Even if all the lights were turned out, which they never are, our collective orange glow would still provide a nightlight. When I close my eyes, I see my favorite fantasy: my toes floating a couple of feet above the floor, body tethered by the neck to a pipe above. But as I gently rock and twist, my eyes meet my mother's, her body in a similar pose, held aloft by the same cording. I can't do that to my mother, I just can't. With an act of sheer willpower, I raise the floor until we are both standing, falling into each other's arms.

I love you, Mom, more than I hate living. I'm just trying so hard to remember that.

Belly of the Beast

November 2006

Court Harris
Elgin Mental Health Center
Elgin, Illinois

I've lived in the belly of this monster before, or his twin brother, anyway. His scales are made of linoleum and his nails are fashioned from orange plastic circa 1960. He dresses in thin white cotton, attempting to hide his hideous bulk, though no one is fooled. His eyes are honeycombed, though less insect-like and more chicken wire in appearance. But it's his pharmaceutical fangs that are most feared. They homogenize life, seeking to make us, the captives, into compliant automatons.

Why should I complain? I'm warm, I'm fed, and I'm safe from myself, though none of those are my goal. I scratch absentmindedly at my self-fashioned necklace, my unintended ticket into this behemoth. I wish once more than I had applied just a bit more pressure to that one sweeping motion.

I've been here for a couple of weeks now. Usually by this time, I have played the game they insist upon, pushing the correct buttons like a trained monkey, and voila! The door has swung open granting each of us, my captor and me, freedom from the other.

Here, however, I am not a primate, but rather a number – a number on a prescription bottle, to be precise. I do not receive a sticker for attending meals or group; my presence, my existence goes almost entirely unnoticed. Sleep is optional, both during the day and at night. Here, time has no meaning. If it moves at all, it is in reverse. The only forced compliance comes in a small paper cup twice a day followed by a water chaser. Here, the revered jewels are blue and orange and white, encapsulated or pressed into various shapes, and always stamped with the mark of their particular beast of origin. Here I am merely a repository of those jewels, which they demand I hide, quite literally, deep within my bowels.

Words have no meaning in this place, so I have ceased to employ them. I am tired of trying to fit into a world I don't understand, and I like even less. Silence has always called to me, though the racket of the world tends to drown out its voice. I have sinned too much for judging people to not always hold themselves higher than myself. I am not trying to be forgiven anymore. So, I step down to become as small as I may - small, silent and inconsequential to this universe that spawned me against my will, and now spurns me at its whim.

In my self-fashioned world of silence, other demons are silenced as well. *Suicide* is merely a word, one whose meaning I no longer value or acknowledge. Banished, too, are other worthless words like *love* and *family*. God, however, has become not a word but a quest. Having glimpsed His omnipresence, I long to make His more intimate acquaintance. During Mom's visit tonight, I submitted a written request asking her to assist me in finding a monastery that will aid me in my spiritual desire to maintain a vow of silence. She said she will help once I am released.

I spend my time in prayer and meditation, not just speaking to God, but truly hearing from Him, as well. He has entrusted me with things that the world needs to hear, and they will – eventually. But right now, I don't want to risk being misquoted, so I meditate on the truths revealed. I have literally met Christ and his eight reincarnations face to face. I know the names and events of a few. First was Socrates, then Plato, then Jesus Christ himself, then Buddha, then Confucius, then Shakespeare, then a Salem witch trial victim named Hellen Keller, and a black man no one understands or believes in.

Meaningless as time is, I just saw a calendar that reminded me tomorrow is Mom's birthday, though I will have no occasion to wish her happiness for the day. All such communication must be initiated from the outside-in only. I guess she could call here, though my silence makes phone conversations menial. She said she will be back this weekend, which I do appreciate. Maybe I'll try to make an artistic gift for her in the meantime with such materials as may be entrusted to the mute and the insane.

My evening cup of jewels are spreading their poison throughout my body. It's the Risperdal I hate the most. It makes me so tired that I just want to sleep life away, but so restless that dreams, sweet or otherwise, are just a dream. I walk the halls in wakened sleepiness, or lay in bed in drowsy agitation. The cure for my "depression" is depressing.

Sometimes when I miss the sound of my own voice, I cough just for the reassurance of the existence of friendly company. I miss the rhythm of life, stuck as I am in this beast's rumbling belly. I miss being alive – or even dead, as I hang in solitary suspended animation.

Carry Out Feast
Thanksgiving 2006

Karen Packard
Mother of Lory Harris
St. Charles, Illinois

The calendar marks this as a day for thankfulness, and I do, indeed, have many things to be thankful for. Five times a year I say special thanks on the anniversary of the birth of one of my children. Today, it is for my middle son. My birthday wishes to him were carried through the efforts of Ma Bell. Even across the many miles, we dined on the same menu: turkey, dressing, mashed potatoes and gravy, green beans and pumpkin pie.

I'm thankful, too, for spending the holiday with my daughter Lory and her family. In the hustle and bustle of the preparations, you could almost forget that one of her children was missing from the fray. When we sat to eat, elbow room was at a premium as extended family gathered around an overflowing table of food. A casual observer would not notice that something was amiss. Not notice, that is, until the prayer was offered which included a petition for Court's health and protection. It was a sobering reminder of the grandson we will visit later in the day, though the renewed din of voices and clatter of silverware drown out my own reflections on Court's situation even before the echo of "Amen" had receded.

The dinner conversation was pleasant with a heavy smattering of "please pass the..." interspersed. I'm not sure if it was out of respect, awkwardness, or lack of anything new to say on the subject, but it was not until the meal ended and the cleanup started that Court's absence was mentioned again. Lory took the lead in the second meal preparations. "Don't put away all the stuffing, I need some for the plate we are taking to Court. Where are the potatoes? Should we put the gravy in a separate dish?"

I felt the tug of both anxiety and anticipation at the prospect of visiting my grandson. All parenting is a series of applying previous lessons to new situations, but I have precious few experiences to draw upon when visiting someone I love in a state mental institution. And yet, I can't wait to wrap my arms around him, and to offer my love and whatever hope I may impart.

I glance, again, at my daughter, who so matter-of-factly prepares the meal for later delivery. Her life has revolved around this chaos for what seems an eternity. She is older now, by more years than the calendar indicates. And harder, maybe - or maybe the right word is brittle. She does what she must do, coating herself with those requirements, while simultaneously using them to shield a broken heart. It is a skill mothers have employed throughout time; I have used it myself. But it is one that a mother never wants to see necessitated and engaged by her child.

Soon enough, my husband and I pile into the car with Ken and Lory, a warmed plate of Thanksgiving nutrition perfuming the air. It won't be exactly warm when we present it to Court, but it won't be cold, either. It was the best we could do without the expected benefit of a stove or microwave in the visitation room. The drive was short, as was the conversation. Ken and Lory let us know that from time to time, Court goes into silent mode. It had been a couple of weeks and a couple of prescription modifications since the last episode, so maybe that has been left in the past.

Upon arrival, we signed in and then waited with several other families to be called for our day's second celebration of thankfulness. When our turn was announced, we were instructed to empty our pockets, placing the contents in a locker along with our coats and purses. We were wanded down, and everything that went in with us was inspected. The dinner plate was approved for entrance, as were we. Lory left a bag of items that would be given to Court after further inspection. There were some clothes and a pair of slippers, but also a portable CD player and some CDs that he had recently been approved to possess – a tangible sign of progress, I'm told.

Court seemed concurrently thrilled to see us and upset by our presence. He picked at the food saying how much better it was than Elgin's offerings, but explained that he just wasn't that hungry. The pumpkin pie, though, disappeared in no more than 4 or 5 bites. Between the five of us, conversation was steady during the hour-long visit, but perfunctory. In the end, Court thanked us for the visit, but told us the holiday is a painful and graphic reminder of his caged status. Wanting to cheer him, Ken told him to keep up the good work he was doing, and maybe he would be out for Christmas. It was a valent effort, though it seemed to have little immediate impact.

Bedtime will come early tonight, regardless of whether it is the effect of the day's activity, diet, or borrowed depression. This evening, while the husbands intermittently cheered for and slept through a football game, Lory and I talked in the other room. "The doctors have assigned a dual diagnosis: bipolar and addiction. Of course, we know he has used pot. We aren't aware of any other drugs. But it surprises me how insistent they are on the addiction side. A month of sobriety, even forced, must be good for a body, but they want to release him to a rehab program," Lory explained. Court won't be out for Christmas, and wouldn't be allowed to move home even then. He could walk out of Elgin any time he wanted; he isn't there by court order. Maybe because of his experience with drug court, or maybe because it's cold and he has nowhere else to go, he hasn't raised the question of leaving. I wonder how Ken and Lory would react if he did.

It was bittersweet to see our grandson today: alive but barely living, healthy but confined with an illness. I pray for him daily. Sometimes it seems like an exercise in futility, or maybe it has made the difference between life and death. How could one ever know for sure? Regardless, I won't stop now! *You are loved, Court!*

To Forgive **Lory Harris**
November 2006 **St. Charles, Illinois**

We have very little information regarding the happenings with Court while he is in Elgin. The staff gives us some snippets when we visit, but mostly it's the same song and dance: Court is an adult and we are merely his parents. Frustrating as it is, sometimes I think it's better that way. Too much information is just too much, especially when there is little to be done to alter the situation.

It was a surprise, then, today when the Caller ID alerted us to a call from Elgin Mental Health Center. It crossed quickly through my mind that maybe Court had been allowed to use a phone to call out, but the voice on the other end was clearly not our son's. Instead, one of the staff was letting us know that Court's CDs and player had been taken away from him. Apparently, he had snapped one of the disks in half and was attempting to cut his throat. I was taken completely off-guard. I guess I am playing the part of Pollyanna once again, just when I thought things had been going so well. As often as I don the costume, you would think I could get it right, just once.

Court and I had such a good talk last week about God – a conversation that Court initiated. We talked of God's unfailing love and forgiveness and the grace He extends to us all. *Did I say something wrong? Is this my fault? Did I push too hard or not hard enough?* I'm second guessing every word – or maybe I should second guess the words I didn't say.

I want a do-over! I want to tell my son that I love him no matter what – that God blessed me with a beautiful, loving, intelligent, and sometimes tormented child. I want him to know, really know, that I wouldn't trade him for anyone else's son. Yes, life can be hard, but it's worth the effort. This is my life, my child, my hope, my prayer. I'm not giving up! My journal holds the words I would like to say to him, if I dared:

> *Court, I want you to know that there is forgiveness - my forgiveness and more importantly, God's! Maybe, though, what you really need is to forgive yourself. You are your harshest critic and most vengeful judge. You can't change the past and eradicating the future isn't the answer.*
>
> *You and you alone can change your future into anything you want it to be, and nothing in your past stamps out the world of possible waiting for you. God specializes in taking the broken and brokenhearted, and making them into shining examples. David was an adulterer and a murderer,*

AND a man after God's own heart. Moses was a murderer and a stammer-er, AND a friend of God. And lest you think God's grace is limited to those enshrined in the Bible, Chuck Colson went to prison for deceiving our nation, AND founded Angel Tree and Prison Fellowship. Nana Couffie (my Austrian refugee friend) was a king with total distain for Christians, AND now a follower of that same Christ, and founder and leader of the Fellowship of Christian Refugees.

It's so easy for me to think these thoughts, and in my clearest hours, to believe them, unequivocally. But when the opportunity arises to talk to Court, I find myself shy and doubting – wondering what the magic combination of words is to unlock his heart, to free him from his torment, to show him the world – scarred but still shining. *How do I show him that forgiveness is more than a word he heard in Sunday School? How do I show him how much I love him and make him really believe it? How do I give him God's peace? Indeed, is any of that up to me? Am I a help or a hindrance?* Perhaps I need to practice forgiving myself. Of all the questions, of all the unanswered prayers, maybe what I most want to know is just, *what will tomorrow's prayers look like?*

A New Prescription – Part I
December 2006

Court Harris
Elgin Mental Health Center
Elgin, Illinois

Day 1,264 and counting. There is, apparently, no institutional motivation for the release of inmates from the asylum. (Who ever thought I would be speaking so literally?) The great state of Illinois seems content to have us free-thinkers warehoused, regardless of cost, visited occasionally by those who profess to love us but do not lift a finger to restore us to the land of the living.

We are warm and fed with little required of us. Aside from locked doors and insistence upon our chemical-altering nuggets, the staff will allow us to do as we please: group sessions are non-compulsory, one-on-ones sporadic. Even speech, as I have demonstrated on multiple occasions, is optional. One additional limitation, though, whose bounds I have also tested: you may not hurt yourself. If only that regulation applied to those injuries thrust upon you. In that way, this truly is a jail: if you hurt me, I won't tell the staff. And when I retaliate, you, too, shall keep that information inviolate. While that may sound like freedom, albeit caged, it is certainly a double-edged sword. To gain my actual freedom, I must meet a standard of conformity that, for me, has proven to be illusive, at best.

It occurred to me while enduring my nighttime cocktail of restlessness, that in my century of captivity, I had not yet seen a judge, jury or executioner (well, maybe multiples of the latter) who had imposed a long, painful death by boredom. I was still mulling around these self-revelations when I was called for my periodic meeting with our esteemed host, Dr. Adler.

It would take very few words to describe said doctor: short, balding, spreading, and mirthless. His office was a study of 1960s interior design, complete with faded, dated pictures and stacks of paper that would keep an archeologist happily digging for a lifetime. Aside from the white coat, there is nothing to distinguish him as the giver rather than receiver of his mind-altering nuggets of pharmacology. Come to think of it, perhaps it is the length of one's outer vestments that grants authority: a doctor's jacket, a judge's robe. If I ever get out of here, I'm going to get a jacket that reaches to my knees and regain authority over my own life. I do *not* say these things out loud, which would grant permission to the humorless, self-appointed, authority-over-all-things-Court to intently scribble away on his pad of paper.

The doc started in the usual fashion, urging me to bear my soul with complete candor, something I have ever-so-politely declined to do since the start of my imprisonment. But I had already determined that today's discussion would take a different path. When it was my turn, I asked, "May I leave now? I don't want to stay here any longer."

I wish I could say his demeanor changed even slightly. It did not. For someone who keeps digging to find my emotional core, he certainly keeps his own well sequestered--assuming, of course, that he possesses one. "I don't think you have made enough progress," his reply came without the slightest hitch in his movements. His gaze did not waiver, his pupils not dilating even fractionally. "I think perhaps it is time we try electric shock treatment." Another person might take his cool, even tone to be soothing. I, however, recognized it for the thinly veiled threat it was.

It was at that moment I knew they had broken me. Either I give in or they will permanently fry my brain, leaving me with a lifetime of drooling in my coffee at some diner on the corner of nowhere and oblivion. Illinois is so concerned that I won't scramble my brain properly that they are volunteering to do it for me. Excuse me for saying so, but their offer seems a bit disingenuous.

So here I come, group sessions. See my bobble-head as I ride the train of social correctness along with my fellow prisoners. Here my voice, Dr. Adler, as I bear my soul for your amusement. I wave the white flag, admitting to the world that you have conquered my will to maintain my autonomy. Just don't look behind my back; my fingers are crossed.

A New Prescription – Part II

Lory Harris

December 2006

St. Charles, Illinois

I have settled into a routine with Court housed in Elgin: visits on Wednesday and either Saturday or Sunday, and maybe a phone call in between. I would love to see him get out of there, once there is any kind of sense that he can hold his own. So far, communication with my youngest is haphazard, at best, but much preferred to the times we went months without knowing if he was dead or alive.

The thing is, we might have a great conversation on Wednesday, and when I call to let him know what weekend day we will visit, he may have gone silent. Someone answers the phone and tracks Court down, but all we hear on the other end is breathing. I assume it's my son, but it could be anyone. Then there is the distinctive click that means the conversation has ended, sometimes mid-sentence – mine, that is. On other occasions, the click comes even before I get the chance to say hello. Once I called right back, thinking maybe someone accidentally hung up the phone. There was one ring and a nanosecond connection before the phone was returned to its designated resting area. Communication achieved: don't call again. Having experienced the same phone manners themselves, most of Court's friends have crossed him off their list. I don't blame them, but I long for his friendships even as he pushes them away.

A couple of times, Ken and I have made the journey for a visit, waited, been wanded down, and waited some more. We watched a bit of TV in the meeting room while trying to ignore others' hushed conversations. Eventually, a staff member would let us know that Court was refusing to see us. We drove home, each of us stewing in silence, occasionally punctuated by emotional outbursts that required no reply from the other.

Our son is safe, so that's something, but progress is in fits, and anything but linear. I have a friend whose son was in Elgin for a year before they got the meds right and he could be released. I can't even begin to think about that kind of timetable! But then, who would have thought he would be there for two months already?

I got a call today from a Dr. Adler, the first call we have received from him since Court became his patient. First, he went over Court's medications. They had to add a blood pressure medicine to counteract the effects of the rest of the prescribed collection. His hands shake all the time, also a side effect of the mind-altering concoction, but that should go away when his body adjusts in a month or so. Sometimes, it seems, the cure is worse than the disease, though a quick trip down memory lane still makes the cure preferable in my book. I let the good doctor amble on, not having much to add to the conversation.

The kicker came, though, when he wound his way through the pharmacological maze and arrived at his recommendation: electric shock treatment. Now there was a discussion I could jump into! I was in high school when *One Flew Over the Cuckoo's Nest* was on the silver screen. I remember seeing what happened to Jack Nicholson when his brain was electrified. "There might come a time when we can discuss that option, but that time is not now. Absolutely not!" My reply was abrupt and immediate.

Shaken as I was, my words had deferred slightly to the doctor's education, but in the back of my mind, the discussion ended with, *not my son!* We were desperately content enough to have our son at the mercy of the state of Illinois in order to keep him out of a body bag. But a breathing body needs a brain. Court needs to be reminded that he has a good one, but he doesn't need it scrambled and left to reassemble on its own! The conversation ended shortly thereafter.

There is no way I am going to tell Court about that medical recommendation; he would just see it as a form of intimidation. This much I have learned over the past four years: threats don't work, idle or acted upon. Does my descent even count for anything, being "just the parent" of an adult? Well, I can be a very convincing parent when push comes to shove! He's not there by court order, after all. Court may find the doors locked in Elgin, but if it becomes necessary, I will make sure he is home for Christmas – for better or worse.

Extending Friendship
January 2007

Ryan Ellis
Elgin Mental Health Center
Elgin, Illinois

The cold air fills my lungs, returning me to a world of the familiar as Mrs. Harris and I leave the building. The whole visitation process wasn't that long, an hour and a half total, I would guess, and of course, some of that time was just wait-time. We were probably only with Court for about an hour. Not long at all, though things changed dramatically, my perspective most of all.

I've known Court my whole life. He was born a few weeks after me, not that I specifically remember that. We lived a block apart, and attended the same schools and Sunday School. Our older brothers were friends and so were we. Our lives crossed paths so many times that for large stretches, we were walked side by side.

We ate oranges together at halftime of our first organized soccer games, the oranges among friends being the best part of the match. There were baseball games where we would beat the bat against the dirt, stare down the pitcher and take a mighty swing at the ball which was conveniently resting on the tee in front of us. We climbed trees and tormented girls at recess. We sang together in the church junior choir, with all the predictable enthusiasm, intensity and sincerity of junior high boys. A room full of squirrels would have been more sedate, and probably would have sounded better, too.

In high school, our roads were merged as we both experimented with drugs. My friend, in typical "Court" fashion, went hard and heavy into whatever he decided to do. Frankly, I wasn't that far behind him when I was forced to stop and re-evaluate. In a fit of the best bad luck I have ever had, I was stopped by the police who found my pipe. I pled guilty as a minor to possessing drug paraphernalia. While the punishment handed down by the court was light, the knowledge of what I did to my parents weighed heavily upon me. While I watched Court continue down our former trajectory, I took a hard right, and ran instead toward God.

I brought my memories today, including those from the Appalachian Service Project (ASP) when Court disappeared in 2003. At that point, I had just been learning to lean into my walk with God while Court was running from the same. I watched Mrs. Harris muscle thought that week carried by prayers, mine included, and with the strength she borrowed from above. Later, when Court finally returned home and announced he was gay, a lot of our mutual friends faded away in quick fashion. I didn't care how he defined himself; he was my friend.

I tried to gently share my faith with him: in his dorm, at a bar, on the street. He has always been into music, hip-hop at the time, so I gave him some CDs by a Christian artist named John Reuben. He seemed to really like it. Once Court told me he had a dream that the two of us were singing "Jesus Loves Me" together. I tried to tell him then that God was reaching out to him. Court scoffed at the idea, preferring to compare it to junior high church choir regurgitation, instead.

God has been my gracious and generous teacher over the past several years. Specifically, of late, He has granted me a deeper look into the spirit world of dreams and visions, angels and demons. Drugs, as I am all too aware, are an implement wielded by the underworld. They can look all bright and shiny starting out – tempting and coming just shy of delivering nirvana in the beginning. Then they become demanding, and controlling - Satan's utopian illusion. Their promise of peace and happiness is drowned out by a barrage of demonic laughter. I entered the building at Elgin today with a mission, a mandate, a message for my friend. I prayed to be his mentor, using the divinely granted sword of the Spirit to save my friend. I came armed with a Bible, key verses underlined for Court's benefit.

Taking Ephesians 6 seriously, I put on the belt of truth, the breastplate of righteousness, the helmet of salvation, feet shod in preparation and carrying the shield of faith. I was armed and ready for a spiritual fight, the prize being the soul of my captured friend. There is no greater battle, no greater motivation than that. On the drive to Elgin, I told Mrs. Harris I was going to talk to Court about God. Her response offered neither encouragement nor discouragement. She just sincerely wished me good luck. Now I understand why.

I'm not sure what I expected when Court entered the room, but I was wrong. He seemed drugged, or broken, or both – sedated and so un-Court-like. It was like the light that is Court had been extinguished and what remained was virtually unidentifiable. I tightened my belt and reached up to straighten my helmet. With a firm grasp on my sword, I greeted what remained of my friend. More than ever, I was determined to be God's warrior, to retrieve what the enemy had taken.

I talked to Court of God's love and grace freely given. I read passages to him from the Bible, showing him how I had highlighted them for his future benefit when reading. I prayed for him, laying hands on him, calling upon God's army to defend and protect him. I wasn't being shy or apologetic, but bold and confident in Jesus' name. There was too much on the line to hold anything back. I was all in!

At the end of our time, I watched as he returned to his life-not-living, taking with him the Bible I had so carefully prepared just for him. If seeing his dull eyes had been sobering, watching his hunched shuffle was heartbreaking. Where was the proud, energetic, irreverent and fun-loving peer I had known my whole life?

As the cold hits my face, I reflect on the visit. I had fought with Satan, parrying with him for the ultimate prize. Maybe for a brief shining moment, with God's army standing with me, we had given the under lord all he could handle in the battle for my friend's soul. But it was then that I realized, with a clarity that can only come from God, that I had failed my friend. I was so intent on my battle for him, that I forgot to give him the most important thing: my love and my hope. I had spent my time being an enemy of Satan, but none of it being a friend to Court.

Tomorrow I return to Ohio to resume my studies. I will continue to pray for Court, and I will keep in contact, offering what love and hope I can from afar. But why didn't I give it to him one-on-one when I was there? Why didn't I give him what he really needed – a friend?

Silent Sounds — Ken Harris
February 2007 — St. Charles, Illinois

I wasn't quite a teenager when Simon and Garfunkel released their hit "Sounds of Silence." But like many of my generation, the song shouted of our approaching adulthood. In the aftermath of the '60s, I watched "people talking without speaking" and "hearing without listening." Silence sounded like denial of possibility, marginalization based on chronology, struggle against relentlessly constricting bonds. All these years later, I hear my silent old friend again, but it sounds completely different now.

Lory and I have been married for almost 28 years – mostly good years, some hard years. Hard doesn't necessarily mean bad, though in our recent history, those two adjectives are generally linked. As an adult, the sound of silence is not one of struggle but of weary resignation. It is not marginalization, but the obstinacy of two strong wills resting by leaning against each other – back to back, that is, never face to face.

My buddy Paul Simon warned that "silence like a cancer grows," and in my youth, I heard the call to battle. Mr. Simon likely has a point, but I have seen the opposite as well: angry words flourish, taking on a life of their own. They crush the tender shoots of love and forgiveness that might have stood half a chance with a closed mouth. Silence, at times, can be the salve that heals the soul. There must be a middle ground, but it is illusive at best.

For our part, Lory and I have employed much silence over the past few months, and things seem to be looking up. Granted, our conversation does not always extend much past "Please pass the ketchup" or, "I can't believe it's snowing, again." And it helps that the Court-inflicted drama is being professionally managed by others; it gives our marital words on that subject less vehemence. Maybe we are adjusting to this existence-posing-as-life, or maybe the fight is just getting wrung out of us. But I think there is some more tenderness between us, both in physical touch and scattered throughout our sparse words.

She would like me to go with her to visit Court more often: once a week is enough for me. In truth, once a week is too often for me, but it is a small piece of the middle ground I manage to hold. Sometimes when we go to visit, Court refuses to even see us. Other times, he will see us but refuses to talk or otherwise acknowledge our presence in any meaningful way. There's a sound of silence I would like to choke out of existence. Even during the 'normal' visits, conversation is difficult. Understandably, Court has few topics to bring to the table. You can only talk sports for so long, especially in the dead of winter. Lory and I both made the trip last Wednesday, and she went again today. It's unlikely she will go tomorrow, but I certainly won't.

It's a funny thing that lately our more substantive conversations tend to happen in the dark. Maybe it makes it easier not to see the hurt in each other's eyes, or to betray the vulnerability in our own. But it's also a bit frustrating when I just want to sleep away a chunk of time and my attempts are thwarted by an unstable topic of discussion. It happened again tonight. I saw it coming when I gave her a kiss goodnight. She never sleeps on her back, but there she was, staring up at the ceiling fan. I feared I wouldn't fall asleep fast enough, and I was right.

"Will you go to church with me tomorrow?" That question might sound innocent enough to you, but there is a reason she waited for a dark room to ask. Those are powder keg words, and she knows it.

"Why do you even ask? You know I have no interest. If you want to waste your time at church, go ahead, but leave me out of it!" I'm even a little surprised by the strong edge in my voice. For the past many months, our conversation along these lines has pretty much limited to her telling me she is going to church or Bible study, and me rolling my eyes - the sounds of silence shouting all around us. Look where all her prayers have gotten us: Court is in a state-run mental hospital – he has been for months now! Is this how God treats His friends? I'm sure I am cutting her to the core. Even without the lights, I know her eyes, still fixed on the ceiling fan, are leaking. But I am sliced open, as well, with surgical precision. That may not have been her intent; it probably wasn't. But it feels like an accusation, like Paul Simon's neon light pointing to what she views as my shortcomings. It's not me that has been unfaithful, it's God! She remains quiet throughout my expressed opinion, which I wrap up with the cinching point, "What has God ever done for me?!"

"You want to know what God did for you? I can tell you." There is a quiet calm to her voice, her tone countering my fervor. "When we got married, we changed our vows from 'until death do us part' to 'forever.' We made a promise to each other and to God in front of witnesses. Mine may have been based on my nineteen-year-old idealism, but I meant it.

"Six months ago, I changed my mind. All we were doing was fighting. If it wasn't about Court, it was about money, or work, or even whether the sky is blue or which way was up. I couldn't take it anymore. I lined up place to live and a way to support myself. I was leaving you. The last thing I wanted to do before I told you was to talk with a Christian counselor friend of mine - to get her permission, I suppose. As I sat telling my tale, spinning it, I'm sure, to make it seem like divorce was the only option, I looked up to see her shaking her head. 'No,' she said, 'go home and make it work. If you need to come back and talk to me some more, I'm available. But you do not have Biblical grounds for divorce.'"

Still looking at the ceiling fan, Lory continued. "It's odd, really, that with the shake of her head, I dropped the "d" word from my vocabulary. It's like I finally heard God say to my heart that divorce was not an option; you and I had to make it through. Just like that, I put it aside. So, you want to know what God did for you? He saved our marriage."

Except for the faintly audible gasp that escapes my lips, only the sounds of silence fill the room. But, again, it sounds altogether different. It is a million thoughts vying for attention: shock and relief, disbelief and recognition, fear and gratitude, hope and ... healing. In the dark, I reach for her hand and hold it tightly. I kiss her salty cheek while a song of silence cradles us both.

Change of Venue **Court Harris**
February 2007 **Alexian Rehabilitation Center**
Hoffman Estates, Illinois

The awakening of the hall lights heralds the morning, followed immediately by the simultaneous groans from my roommate and me. I graduated from insane asylum to rehab a week ago, and the daily grind is already well ingrained. The human snooze alarm will be around in another five minutes to make sure we are up. Past that time, sleep is impossible, at least with eyes closed. The knock on the door and command to rise come as predicted. Yesterday's clothing seems serviceable enough, so I put it on to face another day of sameness.

As far as roommates go, Craig is okay. He's a meth head, about my age. His tweaking now appears to be confined to oral hygiene, brushing incessantly as he does, with movements the speed of lightning. You would think he would have a Hollywood smile, but the holes left in his teeth by his chosen vice disqualify him for a leading man's role. Still, he seems to have things pulled together, based on the skewed scale used to rate a fellow rehab detainee.

We shuffle down to breakfast, joined as we go by similar pairs of zombies emerging from their designated nighttime lairs. Our all-inclusive resort does not get five stars for cuisine, or even one, for that matter. Toast, institutional eggs, wafer-thin bacon, and, of course, oatmeal. Point of fact: my breakfast matches the rest of my world - gray, lumpy and viscous. Color-wise, this is worse than jail, which was at least permeated by orange.

Stomachs glued shut, we move on to our structured series of four AA meetings, separated at predictable intervals by smoke breaks and more meals. I've taken up smoking, again, just to give me something worthy of anticipation.

Rehab is kindergarten for adults, adulthood being defined by chronology only. We make no decisions for ourselves, enduring endless repetition of those things that are deemed "good." Each of us is expected to babble on daily about the wrong turns that landed us here, hoping to be granted reverse passage back to a world where living is more than just breathing. Fortunately, I have substantial practice at faking it, thanks to previous practice. I regurgitate the party line, adding a bit of my own spin so it won't be quite as recognizable as the propaganda it is. One week done, three to go. In theory, there is an end in sight, but the light at the end of the tunnel is still defined in shades of black from my vantage point.

The societal point of rehab is clear: a defined place and time for reflection, without our favored pharmacological friends. What is making you engage in this anti-social behavior? Are you compensating for someone or something in your past? Can't you see that running from pain on a treadmill only leaves you exhausted and pained? What is your higher power and how can you connect with it? Rehab is the process of soul searching in a locked down facility, devoid of living, for people who no longer believe the body has a soul.

Our only downtime is at the end of the day, just before our predetermined lights out. Generally, that time is spent smoking in huddled groups, discussing the good times in our past lives, and anticipation for our future. Contrary to the staff's belief, we do think about what comes next, though it generally looks remarkably like our recent past. I'm a rookie, with only one other rehab to my credit. Some guys make regular rounds, especially during the winter. Having effectively missed every single snowflake this season, I'm starting to wonder if I'll ever throw a snowball, again.

Mom and Dad are coming to visit tonight. Usually they look as oatmeal as the rest of my existence. But sometimes, when they walk in, I catch a glimpse of light, a flicker of remembrance. I see my dog, Mocha, chasing a Frisbee, tongue flapping to the side in a doggish grin. I feel the surprise of a water balloon attack on a hot summer day. I hear the nighttime prayers of an innocent heart and anticipate the soft kisses that complete the tucking-in process. I eavesdrop on the giggles of three little boys watching red and white bobbers floating by the dock where fish have been known to congregate.

Sometimes in my dreams I see the impish grin of a dark-haired, green-eyed, little boy. He darts away in a game of hide-and-seek that I don't want to play anymore. I call to him to just come back, but his secreted place is secure. I can't find him.

And when I wake, there is another oatmeal-day to endure.

Halfway to Halfway Home — Lory Harris

March 2007 — Aurora, Illinois

Once again, I spent several hours taking Court to an interview at yet another halfway house. After a 30-minute eastward drive to the rehab facility, I checked my son out, rather like a library book – complete with a short expiration date. He was due back within four hours. We were bound for a house in Aurora, a 30-minute drive west of my original starting point.

Even with scant parking available, we presented ourselves at the prescribed time for Court's visit to his potential new residence. This world of halfway houses is new to me, but I must assume that following the rules, starting with punctuality, is a basic requirement. We walked up a flight of stairs in a building whose glory had faded from memory long before I was even born. Incidentally, that might have been the last time it was painted, too.

A small foyer, likely carved from a once larger space, was dominated by a wooden desk circa 1960. Chairs representing every decade from the '60s through the '80s lined two walls. Four chairs were still available. As directed, Court signed in on a clipboard at the desk while I chose a chair from the '60s. Court claimed the '70s unit next to me a couple of minutes later. Eight other chairs were also performing their assigned task, most of their claimants born in decades similar to the chairs'.

Court nodded to a guy sitting next to him, who responded with, "Hey, Court, I didn't know you were coming here today, too."

"Yeah, I'm supposed to get out next week, but I haven't found a place to go yet." Turning to me, he continued, "Mom, this is Dan. He's in rehab with me." I've never been good at judging ages, and addiction's affects confound my scant abilities, but I would put Dan at much closer to my age than my son's. We exchanged a quick greeting before the guys continued their conversation. Having nothing better to do and nothing of substance to offer, I listened as Dan offered his learned view.

"This is the hardest time of year to get into a halfway house with everyone coming out of winter rehab. In another month or two, more openings will be available. It's too bad I know so much about it." It turns out Dan was in a similar position when this furniture had a decade's less dents and scratches. He was a newly recovering alcoholic at the time, determined to change his ways. And he had changed: he dove into AA, eventually became a sponsor, and shepherded many others through the difficult steps to sobriety. It seems he had been a poster child for the AA process until he succumbed to the siren call of "just one" while at a party with friends. By Dan's own admission, one turned into a number infinitely larger than none. In a whirlwind lasting under two years, he lost not just his sobriety, but his job, his house, and his family, as well.

As his tale wound down, the congregated hopefuls were called into the back for a tour and an interview. As instructed, I kept the now-empty chairs company. Sitting alone in a room I would never consider as possible shelter for myself or the daughter I don't have, I couldn't help but think how odd it is that I pray they will take my son. The pithy motivational posters on the wall look as tired as the peeling paint they cover. The blinds, listing to the right on broken cords, leave the windows sightless. It took little imagination to see the easy access to drugs on the corner outside, or to hear the sirens that make the businessmen of the darkness scatter. *Is this really the place for Court to restart his life? Would it be conducive for him to stay on the prescribed drugs and off the illicit ones?*

If I answer those questions with a "no," then what? Secure as I feel in his continued breath while he is being warehoused, I must admit, he is not living any more there than when he was homeless. At some point, Court must decide what path he takes. His father and I, along with a huge number of like-minded others, have brought him to the trail's head and even given him a shove in the back to indicate the direction he should go. But we can't walk it for him.

I can't take myself seriously when I question whether he should come back home to live. The trail of tears left by the broken tempered-glass oven door, as well as those that gather nightly on my pillow, are still too vivid to allow for serious reconsideration. After all, has Court really changed since that time? Sure, he's had four and a half months of forced sobriety, which had sounded like a good start, until I heard Dan's cautionary tale.

I returned Court to rehab, safe and sound, and before the bewitching hour. He thought the interview had gone well, but there is no opening for a male right now, so it's a waiting game. As with previously visited potential residences, Court's only option for increasing his odds of admittance when an opening arises is to call every day without fail to check for availability. The man with the longest uninterrupted string of inquiries wins. Who knows what kind of head start others already have in this housing derby.

Halfway house, I muse on my way home. I'm hoping it is halfway between forced life-support and real living, a mid-point between just a roof and a real residence. But most fervently, I pray it's a stop that is at least halfway home, as well.

Happy Birthday **Court Harris**
March 2007 **Alexian Rehabilitation Center**
Hoffman Estates, Illinois

Bill Murray has nothing on me; I live a never-ending Groundhog's Day. Of course, I have no freedom to explore and certainly no love interest, but I do endure the same wakeup call every day followed by the exact same set of circumstances with no hope of escape. Oh, one other difference: his calendar was stuck on February 2nd while the date on my calendar changes. I spent Thanksgiving and Christmas in this jail with locks but no bars, and I'm still here. Happy birthday to me.

I've been calling several halfway houses daily, marking time and hoping for an opening. Well, I have suspended the "hoping" part. I'm not the only one here making the calls. I know at least five other guys calling the same numbers – and they have been at it longer than I have. My 30-day rehab is supposed to be up two days from now, but without a forwarding address, I'm stuck here - on Groundhog's Day.

I muddle through the day, collecting birthday wishes from the staff and condolences from my peers. I wonder for the hundred-thousandth time if I can just walk out the doors. Or should I maybe do something to get thrown out? I've seen that effectively employed. But March is still winter in these parts, especially once the sun goes down. If I help myself to an early release, I could count on no help from family. I make another round of pointless phone calls.

Mom and Dad are coming for a visit tonight, of course. It's not really a bright spot in this dismal day, but maybe it will cause the indoor drizzle to let up for a few minutes. Even a birthday gift would be nice, though it will come without ribbons, bows, or wrapping paper. After all, everything coming in to this place must be thoroughly examined for contraband. The animals must be kept safe within their cages. A new pair of jeans would be nice, though. Between a starchy diet and the "good" drugs, I've gained 30 pounds – not to mention high blood-pressure and a palsy-like shake. Good drugs, my ass…

Mom and Dad didn't bring any unwrapped gifts tonight, promising to have them waiting for me when I get out. Then Dad gave Mom a specific spousal glance and Mom responded to it with a slight nod. My stomach did a lurch and headed for my knees. I've seen that exchange before. It means something just changed drastically and it involves me – for better, or more likely, worse.

Dad cleared his throat, another harbinger of dread, expounding on the previous silent marital dialog. "We have an offer for you, though it comes with specific non-negotiable requirements." My stomach hit a dead end at my toenails. "Day after tomorrow, when your thirty days are up, you may move back home with us." As my famous buddy, Groundhog Bill, could tell you, when something desperately coveted, but relentlessly illusive, bursts on the scene, the first reaction is not relief, but disbelief. I know just how he feels. My stomach quit demanding escape, but didn't return to its correct anatomical position, either. I looked from one parental face to the other, seeing matching smiles, paradoxically both sincere and serious.

It took a moment to find my voice, "Wow! That would be awesome! Thank you so much!"

"Hang on," Dad continued. It certainly wasn't a cart blanch offer. Still, it was a good one, conditioned on me continuing to take my prescribed meds, not using any others, and only extending until an opening appeared at a halfway house. In the meantime, I was expected to look for a job, even if it meant I would have to leave that job a month later to move into my new residence. It didn't change my initial emotional outburst, though the words were repeated without the exclamation marks. At the end of the evening, I gave my parents the sincerest hugs I have in ages.

Home. Never in my wildest birthday fantasy had I dared to hope for that. As I lay my head on this familiar but now temporary pillow, a genuine smile tickles the corners of my cheeks. As the lights dim, I have a startling new thought. My parents just took me further in actual rehab than the hundred or so AA meetings I have endured since I arrived here. Maybe I can do this, maybe I want to. Maybe I can live the life everyone else seems to expect of me, after all. An anniversary of the day one was born is as good a day as any to start a new journey.

Happy birthday to me.

Moby Dick — Court Harris
April 2007 — St. Charles, Illinois

I know the numbers by heart. I could even dial them in my sleep, which is kind of what I do every day at 9 a.m. And every day the minimal conversation is the same: I give the voice on the other end my name and birthdate, and presumably, they put a check on a list on their side before replying that there is no room in the inn. Four identical calls within 15 minutes and my second most important daily event is accomplished. Then I shake six capsules out of their various resting places, and wash them down with a glass of OJ. Voila! My daily rent is paid. Putting it that way, it sounds easy. But, in reality, dialing a phone and opening pill bottles is nearly impossible when one is hanging on with white knuckles.

I am grateful to be home. A secret part of me is thankful that the halfway houses have not panned out yet. But it won't last forever, and I feel stuck in limbo, not sure of what to hope for or where to turn. "One day at a time," says AA. Frequently, there are too many waking hours in a day, especially since the sleeping hours are filled with terror that is more tangible than those things I can see, touch, and smell when my eyes are open. I wake several times a night, heart and mind racing, repeating to myself, *It's not real*. But I'm not fooling anyone, least of all myself. It is far, far too real. A wakeful state cannot be maintained indefinitely, though not for lack of effort.

Today, though, holds a bit of promise, or at least possibility. First, I have a job interview at a pool supply warehouse. I'm taking Mom's car to the appointment, which leads to the second bit of good news: Mom and Dad are going car shopping for me. Assuming I ever find an opening at a halfway house, I will need a car to get around, and it most certainly would not be Mom's. I tried to tell them the kind of car I would like, but they waved me off, saying they will get the best car they can for the best price. I'm not in any position to press my point, so I retreated to my basement abode to get ready for the day.

The interview went well, I think. I possess the skills they are looking for: the ability to read, follow directions, and lift heavy items. Except for the reading part, the position could be filled by a housebroken gorilla. Let's hope I'm their primate. When I return home, Mom and Dad are out. I settle in front of the TV, attempting to doze while not sleeping deeply enough to dream. I'm performing that delicate balancing act rather well when Mom and Dad return with the news that they have purchased a car for me. My signature is required since my name will be on the title.

Dad drops Mom and me at the dealership to meet my new ride: a Ford Taurus. My apparently unrealistic and clearly unrealized fantasy of something sporty evaporates, and in its place, is an eight-year-old, white station wagon. "It's a good car, low mileage and within our budget." Her efforts to bolster its image and my spirits are falling flat. I sign the papers, keeping conversation to a minimum for fear I'll say something irrevocable.

When Mom and I get in the car to head home, though, my thoughts burst through my lips despite my best efforts. "I appreciate that you got me a car, but how can I drive this? Anything would have been better than this! I have some pride! How am I supposed to pick up girls in this?" Not eloquent, but succinct.

Mom gave me a long look and then turned back to survey the road. When she spoke, her voice didn't register anger or hurt, it was just very matter-of-fact. "We don't owe you a car. Walk, if you want. Or the car is in your name. Sell it and buy something else. I understand it's not your dream vehicle, but it runs and is in good shape. Given its color and form, I think we should name it Moby Dick." There was a kind of sly smile tugging at her lips, but she was still looking at the road.

She's right, of course. I've owned more than my fair share of motorized transportation in my few years of driving, and have contributed not even a dime to any of them. If I sold this car (undoubtedly for less than they just paid) I would likely be driving around on a motorized skateboard. While a girlfriend has some appeal, I'm not really in the market just now. I opened my mouth to say, "You're right. I'm sorry, and thank you for the car," but what comes out instead is, "Well, Moby Dick was a sperm whale."

She forgives me with her laughter, as I borrow her sly smile - and a stiff upper lip. Just call me Captain Ahab.

Learning to Let Go — Lory Harris
May 2007 — St. Charles, Illinois

Thirteen, fourteen, fifteen, sixteen. It was hardly worth the count; I knew the number would be the same as it has been for each of the past five days since I started counting. The never-dwindling pill count wasn't our first clue, but it is irrefutable confirmation. A couple of weeks ago we noticed a lessening of the shake in his hands, and then a loss of the puffiness in his face. Court isn't taking his meds.

Things had been going so well a month ago, that Ken and I experienced a rare moment of instant marital accord. We told Court he could stop the morning ritualistic calls to halfway houses, making our home his permanent address – provided, of course, that he continued with our rules: take the prescribed and stay away from the street drugs. His job at the pool warehouse seemed to be going well, not that it was his dream job, but he was getting up in the morning and earning a paycheck. At home, he was respectful, helpful, and pleasant to have around.

It's a bit silly for me to continue to count meds. As a married couple, we had discussed the undesirable stability of the contents and decided it was our job to hold our son accountable for his behavior, regardless of pill count. The balance of Court's accomplishments has not changed. His address doesn't seem quite as permanent as it had last month, but it is still holding.

As I recap and replace the container, it occurs to me how well rested I feel. I breath a prayer of thankfulness and wonder. Here we are, poised to jump on a merry-go-round (or is it a tilt-a-whirl?) that has left us spinning out of control so many times in the past. The prescriptions stop, the illicit starts, the anger overtakes our son, and all of us are bound together by centrifugal force like a silly silo, the bottom disappearing once again. Yet, viewing the various carnival rides that signal the seasons of our joint lives, I am at peace. What happens next may take me by surprise, but it will not startle the One who holds my soul.

I'm not sure when I turned the corner, resting at last in God's arms, trusting that wherever life takes me, He will remain my constant. I think He must have brought me here incrementally: not around a corner, but rather, over a long sweeping curve. There was the meal brought by a friend. Not that I couldn't cook for myself, but no beef stew has ever tasted so good or felt so loving and non-judgmental. There were hugs, many of them. But the ones I remember the most were too tight and embarrassingly long. The awkwardness of the embrace showed me acceptance when I could not find in myself. There were surprise birthday guests on a day when celebration was the furthest from my mind--wine, chocolate, balloons, a plastic tiara, and laughter surprised this household that had been far too familiar with tears.

I remember words of encouragement spoken in worn platitudes. But their repetition, tired as they sounded to my ears, provided a salve for my weary soul. There are stacks of cards offering reassurance, many of them making indistinct references to trials I can no longer specifically identify, some sent by people whose faces I can no longer conjure. They were angels God pressed into service to tangibly revive my listing spirit when most needed. There were tears, offered for me and with me, rivers of liquid love washing the grime of blackened days. The cleansing was never entirely complete, but to share the task with another lessened the burden. Midnight wanderings brought me to emails sent hours earlier, but with perfect timing, bringing comfort even as my bed refused.

Then there were the ancient love letters, timelessly recorded and preserved by distant ancestors thousands of years ago. So many times, God's Word jumped from its pages, comforting and accompanying this lonely mother and sojourner. Some of the comfort was specific, for a day or a season only, leaving me wondering what it was that called so specifically to my soul at the time. Other comforts, though, were absorbed into my DNA, claimed often in silent, salty prayers and even repeated in sleep to counteract vivid, abstract visions of the true terror tormenting my son's soul, and mine by extension.

To view a map of my travels along that long sweeping curve would show more of a saw-tooth pattern, as I stepped forward cautiously in faith and then darted back in fear. If the intended path was a hundred miles long, it has taken me a thousand or more to date. The most I can say for myself, at present, is that forward progress is greater than my times of retreat. In momentary clear-headed amazement, I must acknowledge that God never left me alone in my fear, even when I refused to look upon Him. Nor did He run ahead of me as I took tentative steps in His direction. Though with a slightly irreverent sigh, I must also add that being omnipotent as He is, He certainly didn't seem to avoid any potholes, dips, or valleys along the way. Or maybe He did; maybe it would have been worse. I'll have to ask Him someday, if, indeed, it matters once I am face-to-face with His glory.

I could let my mind wander to the what-might-be-again when I think about Court, and indeed, I have done so more than my fair share of times. In fact, I've done it so often that I find myself saying *when* not *if*. My newfound strength of faith is not nearly strong enough to expect this nauseatingly spinning carnival to ever end, or at least not to end well. For now, it is enough to believe with my whole being that God will be there, regardless of where "there" is. That, and faith lets me rest knowing God loves Court more than I do, impossible as that seems. If I, limited in resources and ability, would do anything for my son, how much more will God do? Then again, just what will Court allow God to do for him?

It is the glances between those two questions that prolong the gyrating of my world, snapping my thoughts to-and-fro. Before the dizziness overtakes me, I take another tentative step of faith. I choose to gaze steadily upon the cross. In that most glorious and despicable implement of salvation is the answer to what has been, and the hope for what will be.

Please, God, help me hold on to that regardless of what tomorrow's terrain may bring.

High Wire Act — Court Harris
May 2007 — Wisconsin to Illinois

I have been walking a tightrope over the Grand Canyon for so long. Suspended in the middle, I am uncertain which direction offers the relief I crave. With the tentative steps of a toddler, I put one foot in front of the other, inching my way along the rope. The canyon, I've heard, is beautiful, but I am too focused on both balance and breathing to enjoy the splendor.

My eyes glance briefly past my toes to the swirling waters below, embraced by the canyon walls they carved. The river, in defeating the rock, has become captive to it, never allowed to freely determine its own path again - a surging army imprisoned by its own success.

Bringing my concentration back to my toes and the thin line that separates my here-and-now from what-was-and-might-be, I wonder, would I rather be the river or the rock? The rock, stalwart but scarred, resonates with strength, though the water's relentless assault continues to cut deeper still. The river, self-confident though frenzied, presses on, oblivious to the grave it digs for itself.

With a paid day-off on Monday, it seemed like a good time to get away by myself and consider my options. Moby Dick and I have found our way across the border to the north, wandering and wondering our way around Wisconsin. My travels mirror my mental meandering. Do I continue to walk this tightrope? I can't see the end, leaving me to wonder if this path is worth the death-defying exertion it demands. Do I possess the tenacity to stay the course toward an unknown prize? I could turn around, go back to the start, but that once-upon-a-time story is more fairy tale than reality. Once you have read a story, you can never recapture the original wonder and expectation again. People just want me to be "who I was," but weren't they paying attention? That character was mortally wounded by the dragon many chapters ago. There is no wizard's magic that can undo what has been done.

Tired as I am, my mind is clearer now, the fog of the medical haze having lifted over the past few weeks. I can evaluate the last six months, a lifetime in and of itself, with more clarity. Of all the levels of Hell I have descended into, those were the deepest and darkest, the most unrelenting. There was no occasion for a respite, no glimpse of daylight in the rolling gray murkiness that encased me. The fog was so thick it threatened to drown me with each breath I drew. Indeed, I think its purpose was to force me to grow gills and become a goldfish. It seems my ideal medical outcome was to live life in a bowl, daily swimming to the top to nibble upon doled-out nuggets. If I refused their offerings, they would eventually find me floating belly up and flush me down the toilet. No doubt I have already been replaced with another bug-eyed fish, so indistinguishable that neither the staff at Elgin nor the attendants at rehab have noticed the insignificant DNA change.

So, which will it be? The rocks, grace-filled in their resolute statuary, like the powers-that-be insist upon for my life? Or the river, in its graceful sweeping movement, living on the wild side, pushing past conformity, and risking the extremes of either homelessness or forced lock and key? Stable, trustworthy, and boring verses free-formed, untethered, and illusive but alone? I need some time to think. I need some space to think. I need some thoughts to think.

With slow and measured movements, I lower my center of gravity, mindful that my toes don't slip from the tightrope prematurely. I don't want to crash into the rocks of my life's Grand Canyon, nor do I want to fall headlong into its churning waters. Grasping the wire of my existence firmly with both hands, I lower my body, extending my toes toward the raging waters below. I need to see if the "water" is as cool and refreshing as I remember.

In obedient kinship, it leaps up to tickle my toes, bringing refreshment to my body, brain and soul. It soothes, it caresses, it entices me to loosen my grip and join its primal dance. Though revitalized, I refuse to completely abandon the tightrope. My recent gill-and-fin existence makes me wary of a hasty return to that watery world. In the end, I right myself, again, on the thin wire that spans and separates my options.

No less uncertain than I was when I last crossed the border between Wisconsin and Illinois, I return home. The house is mercifully dark when I arrive. The rocks are sleeping, or so I hoped, though I should have known better. Mom comes down the stairs just as I'm settling onto the couch. "We thought you would be home for dinner. There is some in the fridge if you are hungry. How was your day?"

"Thanks. It was okay. I just needed some time to think." Her eyes lock on mine. I haven't told a lie, but I can't hold her gaze, either.

"You used." There was no air of question in her brief statement.

"No. I thought about it, but I didn't. Honest! I just saw a friend in Wisconsin and the day slipped by before I knew it. Mom, I swear, I didn't use anything!"

She nods and says goodnight before ascending the stairs, but I hear her sigh as she turns the corner. How could she possibly have known?

Over and Back Again – Part I — Court Harris
June 2007 — Geneva, Illinois

It happened again last weekend. On Saturday, I was hanging out with Scott, an AA buddy and sometimes recovering heroin addict. Being without a car – or license – he doesn't mind being seen riding around in the belly of a great white whale. After our weekly date in the church basement (Hello, my name is Court and I'm an addict), we stopped at the grocery store to grab some snacks. I thought at first that Scott wanted something more substantial, like bacon and eggs or something. He opened several egg cartons, using his knuckle to scramble some of the contents right on the spot before rejecting the idea altogether. We bought potato chips, beef jerky and beer, instead.

We made our way back to Scott's apartment, which is, incidentally, in the same complex that had previously requested I take my leave. They certainly didn't use my departure as an excuse to class up the place. The subterranean feel to the hallways evoked visions of post-apocalyptical times: concrete block walls, the stained remnant of what was formerly called carpeting, and light fixtures with alternating usefulness. The place where I now lay my head is certainly homier, but there is something about this drab existence that has appeal.

Groceries open and at the ready, we settled in to watch whatever TV offerings might catch our fancy, which turned out to be *Jurassic Park*. I have seen the movie so many times that I can tell when a line has been edited for the small screen. Six of the twelve beer cans found themselves in the vicinity of the trashcan when Scott filled a bowl with weed. Even before the match was struck, the slightly skunky smell of the herb put two fingers up my nostrils, demanding my full and immediate attention. Taking my host's offering, I drew a restorative breath. I didn't want to be rude, after all.

There's a funny thing about weed: it exaggerates the direction of your lean. For Scott, the words poured out of him faster than the smoke he exhaled. His commentary on dinosaurs was unbelievably detailed, which is a kind way of saying endlessly repetitive. For me, I felt the pounding tremor of the T-Rex's footfalls and heard the roar announcing his unexpected freedom. I saw the intelligent glint in his eye as he took aim at the enemy who had held him captive. If he could, I'm sure my dino-friend would have snacked on Scott just to shut him up. I mumbled something about needing to use the bathroom, but slipped, unnoticed, out the front door instead. When I got home several hours later, the silent house and I enjoyed each other's company. Unfortunately, when I finally drifted off to sleep, T-Rex renewed his mono-syllabic conversation while I ran, dodging tree limbs and gnashing teeth.

I didn't see Mom until she got back from church yesterday morning. "Scott called last night. He said you quit talking and then just disappeared. He was worried and went looking, but couldn't find you." She looked at me with the same reptilian gaze I had seen on Scott's TV. Despite my protest and feeble attempt to present an alternate scenario, we both knew that she knew. "He's a good friend, Court. He cares about you and wants what is best for you." Wouldn't she be surprised by his egg-scrambling-weed-offering brand of friendship? I laid low the rest of the day.

When the alarm went off this morning, I considered giving it my best T-Rex impersonation. The only thing that stopped me was the more impressive display my parents would brandish. Their teeth are longer, sharper and more numerous. I crawled from bed, whistled to Friday's work clothes which were still lazing in the corner where I left them. They gave me a look of tired resignation before rolling over in slumber. Another week and I'll have them trained. Having thrice employed the snooze alarm, I dressed quickly and headed out the door.

The nagging feeling that had been clawing at my consciousness finally ripped through the veil. Mom's naiveté is a vanishing commodity – she knows with certainty I used on at least two occasions. I'm tottering on the edge of a new address, and we both know it. My choices are limited: quit using (a noble though impossible dream), live on the streets (a tried and true disaster), or quit living altogether.

I slid my timecard into the clock at work, which officially started my day's pay, and headed to the back of the warehouse to start pulling items for shipping: a new hot tub for the Smiths, and a robo-pool cleaner for the Henderson's. Johnny wants a floating basketball hoop and Sally wants an inflatable turtle. Maybe it was the absurdity of that fact that I would have to work for three hours just to afford Sally's turtle that finally solidified my decision. I left the child's summer fun in the middle of the aisle and paid a visit to the HR department, instead.

I hadn't noticed how warm the day was getting until I carried my purchase out of Home Depot: a small inflatable boat (quite the bargain at a quarter of the price of a turtle), a five-gallon bucket, a length of rope and a bag of concrete. I cranked up the air and pointed Moby Dick to the other side of town where the Geneva Motel boasts vacancies within their crumbling facade. I shouldn't need their hospitality for more than a few hours, but I paid for two days anyway, using the cash left from Friday's paycheck. Mom and Dad can have my check for my final two hours. It will give them a great start toward a turtle of their own.

Over and Back Again – Part II — Lory Harris
June 2007 — St. Charles to Geneva, Illinois

Just as I was starting to trust the phone, it betrayed me once more. When the Caller ID showed Court's employer, I naturally expected to hear my son's voice in reply to my standard greeting. Instead, it was Patty something-or-other from the HR department. She was asking if Court was home. "Well, no," I replied, "he's there, at work."

"Actually, he quit a couple of hours ago. We have some additional forms for him to sign. Would you please have him give me a call?" Being something of an expert, I can tell you that dread does not come from the top down or the inside out; it surrounds and crushes you with strength and speed that would make a python jealous. I assured Patty I would give my son the message, while simultaneously praying for the opportunity to do just that.

Without benefit of a ring, Court's cell phone went directly to voice mail. It was either turned off or incapacitated. I left a message, giving him Patty's contact information, asking him to call home, and settled in for the wait. Long neglected projects find their way to the top of the list when the phone is threatening my security, as it did today. I cleaned kitchen cabinets and closets while I waited. I was contemplating an afternoon of pulling weeds when I was quite literally saved by the bell. "Mom, I'm at the Geneva Motel, room 3A. Would you come over to see me? I'll tell you all about it when you get here."

It's only a six-mile drive, but for the time it took, I might have been caught on a parade route, wondering when the marching band would show up. There were lights – red – and slow-moving vehicles dawdling in every lane. Finally arriving and parking next to Court's car, I jumped out and knocked on the door marked 3A. All the Geneva Motel held its breath in solidarity with me, waiting for the door to open. Eventually I was forced to exhale, though by autonomic response rather than from relief at the sight of a door swinging on its hinges. Had I wasted Court's last fifteen minutes of life driving to meet him?

Was my shoulder, bolstered by the fear of what-if, strong enough to challenge the door? Or would I need to run to the other end of the complex to get a key? I tested the barrier one more time with the side of my fist, and was rewarded with the sound of a chain-lock sliding across and dropping against the door. As I reached for it, the knob moved of its own accord and then retreated from my hand. Inside that dingy, ill-lit room was the most amazing sight: my son, looking five-years older than he had last night, but whole and beautiful. I wrapped my arms around him in a mama bear hug that said, "I love you!" Silently, I answered my own question. Yes, I really could have broken down the door.

We sat opposite each other, Court on the bed and me on the room's lone chair. It wasn't necessary for me to pull the chair any closer; the size of the room entwined our knees regardless of any preferred placement. Court took the lead, letting the story flow in a way that was likely at least partially rehearsed. "You were right," he started, "I used. I knew you knew, and I knew I was going to end up on the street again. I just couldn't live that way again. I quit my job this morning and got the supplies to kill myself."

His plan, he continued, was to mix some concrete in a five-gallon bucket and tie it to himself. He was going to row out into the middle of the pond behind the motel and go overboard - body, mind and anchor. With enough knots and no knife there would be no turning back. I didn't interrupt as the words continued to tumble out of him, mixed with his apologies, regret and tears. When he finished, he continued to stare at the floor, intent on a stain that was permanently adhered to the host. Did he wonder if his soul bore a similar mark?

"First, Court, I love you, and if you die, you will take a huge part of me with you. Thank you for telling me the truth. I can always tell when you have used because your pupils get so huge – regardless of light. It's a wonder you can see at all." I wasn't sure I should have given him that information, but it's not something he is able to control, either, so maybe it doesn't matter. "Dad and I meant it when we said we would kick you out if you used again. But just as God gives us grace, we will give you grace, too. All of us have sinned, Court. We all screw up, but God forgives us when we truly and honestly ask. That is grace: when you don't get what you really deserve. We will not kick you out this time, though if you continue to use, you will force our hand, and we will ask you to leave. For now, come home."

And with that, he fell into my arms and I into his. He cried like I hadn't seen since he was in high school and we had to put down his dog, Mocha. For all the fear I had felt so recently, there were no tears on my part, only the overwhelming love and peace that comes when a child returns home from a long journey. He was back, at least for the moment, and it was a moment I was content to linger in.

Besides his cell phone and a half-eaten bag of potato chips, there were no belongings to gather up as we left. The planned implements of his demise were still in the back of his car. Court led our six-mile procession home, making it easier for me to keep a constant eye on him. A marching band seemed appropriate now, though there was none to be found. Tomorrow the job hunt starts, again, for my youngest son. But tonight, there will be an AA meeting, a decision that Court made for himself.

SECTION SIX

DAY BREAK

June 2007 – November 2008

First Baptist Church of Geneva
Sunday, November 23, 2008

Call to Worship	Pastor Roger Crites
Hymn	Come, Ye Thankful People, Come
Welcome & Greeting	Pastor Roger Crites
Baptisms	
Anthem	"We Gather Together"
Announcements	Pastor Roger Crites
Offertory	
Chorus	Give Thanks[4]

Give thanks with a grateful heart;
Give thanks to the Holy One;
Give thanks because He's given Jesus Christ, His son.
And now let the weak say, "I am strong;"
Let the poor say, "I am rich,"
Because of what the Lord has done for us.
Give thanks!

Celebrating Thanksgiving	Pastor Roger Crites
A Time of Sharing	
Benediction	

[4] Moen, Don. "Give Thanks, "written by Kenneth Paul Barker, Andy Cloninger, Claire D. Cloninger, & Henry Smith, *Give Thanks*. Warner/Chappell Music, Inc., Capitol Christian Music Group (1978).

Nightlight — Court Harris
July 2007 — St. Charles, Illinois

1:38 a.m. I relish the early morning stillness of home. Being awake to enjoy the solitude is just one of the perks of my job at the local Irish pub. It has also provided me with an income, which might thrill my parents as much as it does me. Besides gas for my transporting behemoth, I have very few actual expenses. My debit card will still fail me occasionally, but not with as great a regularity as the past couple of years.

Restaurant hours are unpredictable to the late side. If I'm scheduled to close, I'm not expected home until well after midnight. And if I get prematurely cut at 9 or 10, it still leaves me with like-minded partiers into the wee hours of the morning, and indefinite expectations of arrival at home. The bigger advantage to me is that Mom had to give into her circadian rhythm and quit checking my eyeballs when I arrive home. I've moved away from the pot, anyway, but my stomach still does a little lurch on those rare occasions when I find her still awake. Mom and Dad don't mind the alcohol, even inviting me to have a beer with them when we dine together. Undoubtedly, they would not be as understanding about the cocaine, though apparently it doesn't give me away the way weed did.

Working at the pub is like going back to high school, except that bellying up to the bar does not result in automatic expulsion. Among the pub staff, there is the goody-goody gang: the ones whose bellies only approach the bar when picking up a customer's order. They go straight home, even when their shift ends earlier than expected. My initial training was done by one of them, a pretty girl named Christine. Our conversations revolved around salad dressing and the day's specials. It still doesn't extend past those topics.

Then there are the wannabees. They try way too had to fit in, but they just don't. In an odd twist of economic fate, Bob is one of them. At least ten years older than most of us, he took to waiting tables when he lost his "real" job. It provides some income and leaves most days open for interviews. He goes home to a wife and kids, but not before first joining the free-agents among us for a brew or two. His attempts to join our guttural guy-talk, which reflects much more of what he thinks we think than his actual views. I guess we are all like that to some extent, but Bob lacks the finesse to pull it off.

Then there are the cool kids. Oh, they know how to party! They just require a better class of compatriots. They are slumming it here, and we all know it. They are moving on as quickly as possible, though some of them, like Gloria, have condescended to this employ for over eighteen months – a lifetime in restaurant years.

That leaves the rest of us. In our teens, we would have been the stoners, I guess. Now we just view ourselves as the normal ones. We aren't hard core druggies, generally working our shifts efficiently before celebrating the crossing of one day into the next. We share tips with each other, our day's earnings and advice – a socialistic experiment with more success on the economic than relational side.

In some ways, it seems like things are looking up for me. Mom and Dad are encouraging me to move forward with life and think about going back to school. But I'm not going back to North Central College, where I went from Dean's List to dropout in one academic year. Both the college and I agreed to a parting of ways, though Mom and Dad don't specifically know about that pact. I really want to study computer programming, so I'm checking into DeVry University. My parents and I agree, though, that the next school will be the last – or at least the last that will see a check with their signature on it.

The biggest problem I have is sleep; it terrifies me. My dreams devour whatever hope I can muster during the day. No matter how much I try to nurture and shield it, darkened eyes hear the sinister laughter as it attacks my fragile hopeful efforts. There are snorts of derisive fire turning the delicate blooms to inky-black ash. Forcing my eyes open brings me from black to black; I wonder, have my two realities become fused? Or, like matter and anti-matter, perhaps I have been obliterated by their joining?

A couple of nights ago, in blackened totality, I was fumbling for some proof of my own life when I stumbled on some Christian hip-hop music, a previously unwrapped gift left on my computer by my friend, Ryan. It brought some light into the room, over and above the light emanating from the computer screen. In its glow, the clouds of Hell seemed slightly less ominous. I reasoned I could not be completely without hope. After all, with everything I have gone through, every level I have descended into, I'm still here.

Sleep is calling to me again in its rough, husky voice. I hate that it will have its way with me, and there is nothing I can do to avoid it. Just as I am about to give into the inevitable, though, something on my bookshelf catches my eyes. I'm not sure why it has remained when so many other mementos have vanished. The binding is black leather emblazoned with gold lettering: *Holy Bible.* I burned the Bible Mom gave me and ripped up the one presented to me by Ryan. But this one, given by the church a decade or so ago, just watched and waited in plain sight, inexplicably avoiding the carnage endured by its twins.

What is the Bible verse written on poster board and held up at football games? John something, I believe. Some lingering memory, long shoved aside, guides me toward the back of the book.

> "In the beginning was the Word, and the Word was with God, and the Word was God. He was with God in the beginning. Through Him all things were made; without Him nothing was made that has been made. In Him was life, and that life was the light of men. The light shines in the darkness, but the darkness does not overcome it." (John 1:1-5, NIV).

I don't understand it, not exactly. But could it be the nightlight I crave during those hours when sleep closes my eyelids and night terrors overtake my being? There, in that dusty book, is not my parent's fairytale, but the documentation of a real man. Like the gold lettering distinguishing itself from the dark leather, something felt real, shining through the darkness.

"Look, the Lamb of God, who takes away the sin of the world!" (John 1:29b, NIV). *A tall order,* I thought as I read, though it was no taller than taking away *my* sin, an impossibly coveted dream.

Eventually I had to give into the sleep my body demanded. As inky blackness swirled around me, pulling me into its grasp, I strained my neck around to catch one final glimpse of the nightlight. There it was, faint but steady: light where none had ever been before.

A New Shirt
August 2007

Pastor Jeff Frazier
First Baptist Church
Geneva, Illinois

There is a holy hush that gathers in a church on Sunday mornings. It is present when the key first turns the lock. As the youth pastor, it was the river's calm before the rapids come into view. But now, as the associate pastor of adult studies, that calm is followed by a grown-up, less frenzied, and less predictable path of worship that includes wonder, grieving, and grappling.

Like the youth, adults will arrive in mass just at, or shortly after the designated start, which makes sense since they tumble out of the same vehicles. The youth whirl in the door laughing and talking with exuberance designed to blend in by hiding their insecurities. Their elders, on the other hand, enter with friendly greetings and reverence, an act that may hide any number of other feelings: fear, anger, loneliness, trepidation and pain, as well as joy and anticipation. It would be hard to say if the youth or the adults wear more masks, but certainly the adults are more likely to have perfected the masquerade.

The absolute tranquility of the early morning Sabbath never lasts long, though it is hard to say exactly when it ends. It is like the difference between sunrise and morning, or the balancing point between high and low tide. At some indistinguishable moment and for no apparent reason, you just suddenly realize the atmosphere has changed, replaced by something altogether different – not worse or unwanted, just different.

The maintenance staff arrives to tend to last minute details, and to be on hand for the unexpected. Children's ministry volunteers bring varying degrees of confidence and preparation to their assigned rooms. Ushers arrive to welcome the worshipers with a friendly greeting and a program. At some point, the holy hush transforms into a holy cacophony, each extreme pointing to the Maker of all things. The exact crossover point along the continuum remains indistinct.

I was standing outside the worship area, greeting those arriving for the service, when I spot a young man walking in with his mother. Fortunately, I'm pretty good at putting names with faces, but I was relying a bit on the Holy Spirit to make that connection for me since it had been years since I had seen him. The face I was looking at was both familiar and entirely foreign.

"Court! It's so good to see you! You look great!"

He looked a little surprised by my statement, but shook my outstretched hand. "Oh, thanks," he said, "I got a new shirt."

"Yeah, that's nice, but that's not it. You just look really good!" His shoulders straightened a little and the smile that crossed his face looked bright and genuine. He thanked me, again. The rest of our conversation was of the see-the-pastor, pre-service variety: Court is working at a local restaurant and will be attending DeVry University starting next month. His mother, Lory, was content to have the conversation center around her son, but there was smile in her eyes, as well.

As nice as his shirt was, it was certainly not a case of the clothes making the man. He could have been wearing a stained and ripped t-shirt. The difference between our last visit at Starbucks and now would still have been stark in contrast. It was the eyes that had altered his appearance. They were no longer hooded and flat with a steady gaze toward death. Instead, the green was bright and open, seeing life and reflecting hope.

I invited him out for another cup of coffee, and sincerely hope we will make it happen. I would love to hear about his journey over the past few years. How has he made the trip from there to here? And what can I do to encourage him along his path? What a blessing to witness first-hand the transformation in one of God's beloved.

The band starts to play in the next room; voices join in praise and worship. I walk down the side aisle to find my designated place in the front row, by the steps to the stage. A couple of songs from now, it will be my turn to relay God's words to those gathered. As for me, I have already seen a sermon this morning. It was written in green.

Among the Stars — Court Harris
October 2007 — St. Charles, Illinois

It's a typical Thursday night. As they routinely do, the restaurant crowds are holding off until tomorrow. Mike and I both had our shifts cut at 8:00 tonight. We have very few tips in our pockets, but a free evening. I don't have class tomorrow, so double the bonus. We head over to Mike's house to while away the evening.

I've lived in Illinois my whole life, and I trust seasons to change when they must. But there is nothing more glorious than a late summer day when it makes a guest appearance in October. The whole day had felt a bit charmed and golden with possibility.

Before we arrived at Mike's house, a seasonally corrected chill was claiming the night. The blue cloudless sky of the day had given way to a starry night that was syphoning off the untimely warmth of the day. My host's parents retreated indoors to conditioned warmth while Mike and I enjoyed solace and solitude in the garage. We snorted a little cocaine and sat back to enjoy the marvels of the diamond-studded backdrop.

That's the thing about coke: you feel an instant burning in your nose and throat, though it's not unpleasant - more like an over injection of euphoria that needs to be shared with the rest of your cells. Like fire-bucket brigades of the past, the body quickly spreads the wealth. Using my finger to connect the dots, the points of light tell familiar stories. Orion, with his bejeweled belt and menacing blade, defends the universe from permanent blackness, whose threat grows daily as the winter approaches. Gemini, the twins, run hand in hand and share secrets of the womb, oblivious to the danger creeping up on them.

As the euphoria reaches my extremities and proceeds to drip from my fingers and toes, returning to the stars themselves, I begin to see the problem. The Big Dipper, once a comforting image from my childhood is now pouring the black ink of my dreams into the sky, inflicting terrors the eyes cannot see. Orion, strong but battle weary, cannot withstand the relentless rush of the darkness being poured on him from above. Nor can I.

The realization of the betrayal makes my landing harsh. Had I been at home by myself, I would have dropped to my knees praying to the Christ that John depicted so eloquently. It is a posture I rely on almost nightly when I attempt to drag my gaze from nightmares to mere night, but it is not the public me I will hold out for inspection and ridicule.

Whoever God is and whatever God does will remain sequestered between the two of us.

Turning slightly, I see that Mike, too, has returned to our starting point. I wonder if he landed with a similar resounding thud. My traveling buddy hands me a beer. I take a long drink before I dare to ask the questions that is heavy on my mind. "Mike, is that what you want for your life?"

His reply does not require time or thought, "No. I want to stop."

"Yeah, me, too."

Having already spoken volumes, we finish our beers mostly in silence. I mumble something about finishing up some homework and take my leave.

Driving north toward home, the Big Dipper beckons me on toward the darkness it continues to vomit. I cannot escape it; it is my destiny. There is but one small glimmer of hope: once, long ago, sitting on our porch, viewing these same stars with my mother by my side, she told me I wasn't bound for Hell. I wonder if I can believe her. I wonder if I should. It doesn't seem possible, but I pray it is so.

There are times when you scale the highest mountain, dragging yourself over the precipice, only to realize that even with the gravity assist, the way down will be as arduous as the ascent was. I have fallen down those mountains, never certain which side I came to rest upon. Lacking the courage to climb again, or to get my bearings, I just muddled on as before.

This time, though, is more like tripping over a line, maybe even a line in the sand. I am sprawled out, elbows and knees scraped, grit in my mouth, but I can see where the line is, and all my previous footprints are on the other side. Something has changed, and that something is me.

The Piano Man
January 2008

Bartender Brian McCaffrey
Claddagh Irish Pub
Geneva, Illinois

Bartenders come in a couple of varieties. There are the ones that are in everyone's business, mostly in a good way. They offer comment and advice on anything and everything. You sit at their bar; they keep your drink and air-space filled. Patrons are integral to the conversation only as far as spurring on the barkeep's natural desire to be the center of attention. These bartenders' fondest desire is to be discovered as a comedian, sportscaster, or color commentator. They are entertaining, if, that is, you are at the bar to be regaled.

My only resemblance to those entertaining cocktail servers is my job title. I'm the Billy Joel, Piano Man, kind of bartender – without the musical instrument, for which you should be very grateful. I'm a listener, contributing to the conversation only to counteract uncomfortable lulls. I keep the drinks filled and the conversations light. Plenty of real estate novelists and Davys who are still in the Navy have told me their stories. I may not remember them all, but something of who they are has become a part of who I am. I could be a therapist, if I could still employ a bar stool and a beer. There would be no couch in my office.

It's not just the patrons that I spend time observing, though. This Irish pub, located in suburban Chicago, has quite the cast of characters. The luck of the Irish comes in two varieties: good and bad. Among the staff, a few days' time will see hook-ups, mix-ups and break-ups. A likes B, but B is pining after C. C won't give B the time of day. A consoles B. B picks himself up and suddenly notices D. B won't notice A until A has hooked up with E. And so, the game goes. I haven't seen any weddings in my twelve-month tenure, but a few move-ins and -outs. The move-outs, thankfully, are always followed by a help wanted advertisement. This pub isn't big enough for their falling-out-of-love drama.

To keep the attention on our paying public, staff are required to take their leave within fifteen minutes of the end of their shift. That gives them just enough time for a beverage and a brief discussion of their day and/or love interest before heading out the door. It was about 9:30 tonight when I caught a glimpse of Court clocking out and removing his server's apron. He made his way to the bar stool at the far end. "The usual?" I asked. He nodded with a smile.

Generally, I don't bother to ask. I know what everyone wants, and I just set it in front of them. Court's "usual" has always been beer, ranging from amber to dark. But a couple of months ago, that changed, and hasn't varied since: O'Doul's. It might sound Irish enough, but the non-alcohol beer would not cut it in the old country.

It's a typical Tuesday night, which is to say that Court could have chosen any one of the bar stools; tips will be light. I put the bottle and a frosted mug in front of my co-worker. We talk a little about his computer programming classes, which he says are going well. He should graduate in a little more than a year. He and his girlfriend, Ashley, are a typical sort of staff hook-up around here. Her ex keeps popping in and out of the picture, causing their relationship to wink in and out as a result.

With a slight nod toward his half empty glass, I asked the question that has been rattling around in my brain for months now: "Why the beverage change?"

Court gives me a shy smile, another change from his previous demeanor, and a shrug. "I quit smoking, too," he confided. "I needed a drastic change in my life, and I finally realized I had to do it for myself. It hasn't been as hard as I thought it would be."

I've heard a lot of New Year's resolutions, not necessarily limited to January, that have often involved the forgoing of alcohol. I make a habit of keeping my remarks to myself a couple of days to weeks later when the commitment has burst like a balloon in a hatpin factory. But Court has made no such proclamations. He just went about doing it. I'm impressed and a bit envious, too, and I told him so.

His "beer" gone, Court stands and extends his hand to me. I shake it, returning a firm grip. "Thanks," he said, "I really appreciate the support!" His fifteen-minute time limit ticking down, he turns to leave. As I watch him wish the hostess a nice evening on this way out the door, a piece of him remains with me. It's the piece that proves that all things really are possible, the piece that gives me hope.

Confessions – Part I
Lory Harris
March 2008
St. Charles, Illinois

Economically speaking, 2008 has picked up right where late 2007 left off – in the doldrums. With Ken, Colin and I all dependent on the income produced by designing houses, whose demand is becoming more and more scarce, it was obvious that we needed an income infusion. Many years ago, I was in the financial field, and it is to that I have returned – part-time for now. I work Monday thru Friday afternoons in a small office, doing whatever needs to be done. Not a glamorous position, but a paycheck, and only six miles from home.

I was doing some filing when the phone rang. Caller ID let me know my husband was trying to reach me even before his voice brought dreaded news, "He's doing it, again, and I'm ready to ring his neck! He's not talking!" I wasn't exactly sure what I could do about it, besides maybe calm some high tensions. But I let my boss know I had to leave and hoped to return shortly.

Frankly, both my heart rate and my thoughts were moving faster than the traffic. Court's first semester grades were straight A's in computer programming and his work at the pub seemed to be going well. He even has a girlfriend. Two or three times a month he joins me at church. Life seemed to be falling back into place. Does his refusal to speak mean Court used again? I had cautiously hoped we were through with that. One word formed in my head as I drove home: *Fool! Will I never learn? Why am I in such a hurry to get home? I have no idea what to say or do to help the situation. Will Court be back out on the streets tonight?* He's already had second-helpings of second-chances. Besides, I can't make a practice of just taking off from work on a whim – mine or Court's. My new employer is sure to be less than thrilled with that. It took a while to find this job, and I don't want to start the process over again, especially in this economy.

The side door was unlocked when I got home, but it took all my effort to push it open against the mounting tension and frustration contained within. "He's in the family room," was the sum total of interaction I received. Court was not the only one carefully rationing his words. Amid the silence, I was expected to say something situation-altering, maybe even life-altering. For perhaps the fifteenth time in as many minutes I started a prayer. *Dear God, I don't know what to say. Help me!* Somehow, *amen* didn't seem to be the next word, but I couldn't think of any others, either. The unfinished heaven-bound request joined the rest of the household in wordless speech.

I sat in the chair across the room from my mute son. "Hey," I said, the dearth of words continuing. Court glanced briefly in my direction, returning his gaze to an in-depth study of his lap. Drawing a deep breath and throwing another *Help me!* heavenward, I dove in. "Court, you can't keep doing this. You can't just stop talking, at least not if you want to keep living here. As a family, we need to talk things out, work them out." Aside from his steady breathing, there was no movement. I could only assume he was hearing me. There was another round of silence as I waited for an improbable response. Even before I said it, I regretted my next question, but it had to be asked – all the cards needed to be on the table. "Court, did you use again?"

He turned to me for the first time, our eyes catching and locking. In them I saw none of the defiance of recent years. Instead, there was softness and, paradoxically, an intense pleading as if he was willing them to say something that his tongue refused. I saw tears pooling along his lower lids as his head drooped again, the burden of holding it erect seeming too taxing. It shook from side to side in deliberate and apparently exhausting communication.

If trust is cash in a bank account, Court's has been bouncing checks for years. Granted, in the past few months he has at least been paying the overdraft charges, but the overall balance is still negative. Unfortunately, this day's silence represented more red ink. So many times, I have been sucked in by his declarations only to have my gullibility spat upon. *Will I believe him, again, and perfect the part of the fool? If I can't trust my son's wordless proclamations, can I trust his eyes? Or am I just willing myself to see my little boy, the one who took his leave half a decade ago?* I wish I could say I agonized over the decision, but the truth is that I have learned little. His eyes held me. Almost certainly, I foolishly believed them.

"Court, I love you and I believe in you. If you need to hear it, I'm happy to say it, again: I forgive you. But what you really need is to forgive yourself. Sometimes that's the harder thing to do."

With that, he looked up at me, again. His tears had lost their battle with gravity as I looked steadily into the pools of green from which they sprung. There was pain clearly written on his face. Though it was mid-afternoon, his newly recovered voice carried the rasp of long hours of non-use. "You don't know what I've done..."

Confessions – Part II — Court Harris
March 2008 — St. Charles, Illinois

The screams reached a fevered pitch: pleading, mingled with moans of hopelessness, circling back to shrieks of agony. Voices mingle, raised in unified terror, though not one hears another, cloistered as they are in their own individual torment. I am surrounded by the damned, my kindred, the company I have chosen, in the realm I fear above all. Franticly grasping at the air which has taken on a quicksand-like quality, my legs flail as they attempt to reach the surface. Which way is up? Which way is out? Where is the light? My eyes register only the depth of the deepest blackness, impossibly aglow with the gloom of fright and pulsating with misery. The sounds escaping my chapped and bleeding lips bear no resemblance to human speech, being only guttural laments of a wasted life. In a momentary flash of clarity, one word forms – one word only. And with my final exhale I rasp: *Jesus.*

Defying the weight of deathly sleep, my eyes snap open, blackness giving way to filtered light. Sitting up quickly, the room spins, tilting madly. The horrible, crushing screams, mine included, echo briefly and then recede into silence. Panicked, heaving gulps of air perform revitalizing lung calisthenics as beads of sweat roll down my face to join their brethren who have already congregated at my t-shirt. Something is still tugging at my legs, threatening to draw me down again. Like a Chinese finger trap, the harder I pull, the firmer the grasp of the sheets around me. In my desperation to be free, I almost pitch myself headlong onto the floor.

The floor – not quicksand, but tile. One leg free and then the other, I drop to my knees on the cool, solid surface. I repeat my previous five-letter speech – *Jesus!* Of all the things I have ever used that word to express, today's meaning is specific and clear: a desperate cry for assistance from the only One who possibly can. The sweat running down my face is joined by rivers from my eyes: salt mixing with salt, fear being washed away by staggering relief.

Jesus, if you will save me from the eternal damnation I deserve, I will take a vow of silence. Never again will my meaningless babble darken this world. Oh God, please! I will silence my voice now and forever. Please, Jesus, please. Amen.

I have no idea how long I remained shivering on aching knees, too grateful and too fearful to change positions. I can hear sounds of life in the house: people walking, muffled conversations, the smell of cooking food reminding me of my hunger. When at last I rise, I take my protesting joints to the shower to drown any foul blackness that clings to my body.

Making my way upstairs, I am performing a careful examination of the refrigerator when Dad joins me in the kitchen. "How was work last night?" Nothing remarkable, so I shrug in response. His eyes register brief surprise and then narrow a bit. "Do you work tonight?" I shake my head no. "What is going on here?" His tone has shifted considerably. I shrug, again. Even with his head now turned away as he retreats to his office, there is the gruff exclamation like one who has been sucker-punched in the gut, followed by his crystal-clear words, "I'm not playing this game, again!"

Colin can see both Dad and me from his desk. Looking between the two of us, he sighs in resignation, gets up from his chair and stomps in my direction. "Court, what are you doing? You can't keep doing this to Mom and Dad! Do you want to get kicked out?" There is no way to explain with shrugs and nods, and to relive the night's terror by speaking it out loud is more frightening than the streets. Leaving Colin standing by the fridge, I opt for mindless mid-afternoon television viewing in the family room.

Halfway through Judge Judy, Mom shows up – an emissary of peace and compromise, as always. If I wasn't such a hopeless cause, she might even be an advocate, but that's not likely now.

She says she forgives me, but she can't forgive what she doesn't know. She tells me to forgive myself. That isn't even possible. I want to maintain my silence, my bargain with God, a last-ditch effort to save my very soul. I am screaming at her to make her understand the words that drip from my eyes. As I stare at my hands, I see the blackness covering them, again. I washed the outside, but internal darkness is oozing out my pores, steadily and completely returning my true color. Would she still love me, still forgive me, if she knew the truth? Despite my best efforts, the words come vomiting out of me, laying bare my wretchedness. "You don't know what I've done…"

Confessions – Part III **Lory Harris**
March 2008 **St. Charles, Illinois**

As I had promised my boss with the best of intentions, I'm on my way back to work. It has only been about an hour, or a lifetime; the time clock will let me know for sure. I wonder if I can remember the alphabet well enough to continue filing. Or maybe I should do something more basic, like clean the coffee pot – except that we don't even have one since no one in our office uses that caffeine delivery system. I mechanically follow as the car ahead of me moves forward when the light turns from red to green. If I had been first in line, I likely would have waited until the honks from behind me reminded me how to drive.

"One night while you were sleeping upstairs," my son had confessed, "I was so mad at you and Dad. I went up to the garage to get some gasoline, but the container was empty. I found some chainsaw oil instead and brought it down to the basement and trailed it across the carpet. Standing at the exterior door, I lit a match, intending to watch the trail of flame as it ran into the house. But it wouldn't light."

He was watching me intently as the words burrowed into my heart. I have no idea what my face revealed or how he might be reading that neon signpost. My son's pleading eyes disappeared, replaced with the memory of our return from Massachusetts to a shattered house and dreams to match. I heard, again, that midnight creak of the floorboards as Court approached our bedroom to alert us to the destruction caused by "ghosts" in our basement. A meandering trail of oil soaked the lower level carpeting ending at the door, where the single word 'die' had been sprawled on the glass with the viscous substance.

Silenced, myself, by the stunning confession, I had to acknowledge the truth of his admission as the three-year-old puzzle pieces tumbled into place. My own green eyes, now wide with recognition, locked onto his as they puddled and spilled over with remorse. "I kicked you out of the house," I said, completing the story of that pivotal day. An unnatural sense of calm and wonder settled over me.

All those years before, Ken had seen what I couldn't, or wouldn't. He had correctly interpreted the word "die," initially carved into the service door and then smeared in oil on the patio door. Had he saved our lives by insisting we sleep with all our kitchen knives tucked under our bed? For months prior to that "ghostly" day, I had been resisting Ken's directive to kick Court out of the house. That night, of all nights, with weariness that included not an ounce of contemplation, I had asked my son to return the house key and leave. For all these years since, I have flogged myself, fearing I had made a hasty decision that damned my son to the life that followed. Perhaps it was that same action, having been delayed beyond reason and nearly to the point disaster, that had saved our lives.

"I still love you, I still forgive you, and you still need to forgive yourself. God protected us then, Court. He protected Dad and me from the flames, and He protected you from yourself. He hasn't stopped. Think of all the times for the past few years when what could have happened, didn't. You still possess every bit of potential you ever had, and God still wants to use it."

As I pull into my parking spot at work, I muse that there was so much more to that conversation, mostly from my side, and I don't remember a word of it. However, Court's words, or their meaning at least, are seared into my consciousness – not in an evil way, but a redemptive one. Maybe now he can walk through that door, shutting and locking it behind him. That little shanty may still stand as a reminder, but it no longer needs to be his residence.

Even as I rewrite my own history to include Court's attempt on my life three years prior, I praise God for the holy revision. Does chain oil not burn? I have never had reason to contemplate that, but I would have thought so. Having still been in lawn mowing season at the time, the gas container was empty only because Court had used it trying to set the deck on fire, when we were out of town. We had not refill it yet. Otherwise, no doubt, the match would have done its job most efficiently.

"I forgive you," I had said, and I meant it. But was I being too quick with the healing process? My newly discovered three-year-old reality bursts into the present day. Is he clean now, or was it drugs that rendered him 'speechless' this afternoon? Is this really the end, or even the beginning of the end? Are there more revelations to come? He had to tell me, of course; confession is the only way to purge oneself of that kind of darkness.

So many years ago, when this still-unfolding scenario was new, I had stubbornly refused to loosen my grip on the trust my son had garnered over his lifetime. On that now infamous night, I had finally and reluctantly let it go, no longer strong enough to maintain my hold. Then, about a year ago, I had bent down for a closer look at the trust still laying trampled at my feet. I had poked and prodded, trying to ascertain if it was as docile as it appeared, or if it would turn and snap at me if I picked it up. Slowly, cautiously, I had been gathering trust to my heart again, stroking its fur, scratching behind its ears. Today, it growled at me--or maybe it was just an echo of a growl, I can't tell. I haven't dropped it altogether, but I am now holding trust at arm's length, returning to the weary wait-and-see game.

In my heart of hearts, I know I do forgive him. And I know there is no trust where there is no truth. Yet this morning, I was happier in my ignorance than I am now in my shocked enlightenment. But, then, if God can arrange for fireless oil, perhaps I can pick through the wreckage once again in search of trust. At least this wreckage, thank God, isn't charred.

Sunrise — Court Harris

May 2008 — St. Charles, Illinois

I know I'll sleep well tonight, just to make up for last night, if nothing else. The wee hours of the morning saw me putting final touches on my major presentation for school today until my eyes absolutely refused to comply. We hit upon a compromise, my body and I, an agreement that my body tried to renege upon when the alarm burst into the morning darkness at 5:00. I acquiesced to one round of the snooze alarm before I went in search of coffee.

Making my way back to my computer, books and meandering trails of notes, I glanced out the window. Maybe it would be more accurate to say the outside was looking in on me. At any rate, with my hand poised to brighten the room artificially, I paused, transfixed by the beckoning view. Where blackness had prevailed, it was being relentlessly vanquished by the sun's blazing new morning glory. The night sky's former pinholes of light were winking away in deference to the Earth's superior and personal companion with flames of red, orange and yellow. Clouds, formerly black and foreboding, shed their gloomy mantel, catching and magnifying the splendor of the coming day.

Of course, I've seen sunrises before, and I suppose, meteorologically speaking, this one was not particularly remarkable. But, just a few minutes ago, I had been stumbling in the dark, hungering for the revitalization of caffeine and shunning the logical assistance of the incandescent bulb above. With only the slight wiggle of a single finger, I could have forced piercing light upon my body. It could have changed that fast; yet I had refused. Here, despite my initial reluctance, light had come: slowly, steadily, radiating beauty that even Edison could not have hoped to duplicate. The sunrise only lasted a few minutes; my coffee is still warm. But compared to the flip of a switch, it had lasted an eternity, and the journey had been worth every second.

Moving aside last night's empty coffee cup, I offer the coaster to its younger, warmer, caffeinated brother. With a flick of the wrist, my computer roars back to life; Thomas Edison is returned to hero status. I pick up last night's papers and start to review, reading the first paragraph three times before admitting that my train of thought is on a different track altogether.

I've heard enough stories of "lightbulb" moments, when everything comes together in the twitch of a finger and life is miraculously changed. Fairy tales of those types were often told at AA, though I never believed them. But I've heard them recently at Come Thirsty, a group of twenty-something-singles at the church, gathering for friendship, fellowship and food. We aren't Bible scholars and we certainly aren't chefs, but we are all thirsty for the Holy Spirit's refreshment. It is there that I trust the stories of instant transformation, and witness the lives changed as a result. But they are just not my story.

Christ, to me, is like sobriety. In fact, the two are synonymous. I held onto both, white knuckles straining from the struggle, willing myself to want what I was physically able to attain only in fits and starts. Falling as I inevitably would, it was up to me to claw myself back to Christ and the sobriety He demanded. The tighter my grasp, the further I fell when it inevitably failed me, and the sterner my Savior's face became. That was the night my soul found me staring into the blackness, confident that the sun would never offer its warmth and light to me, again.

Then came the sunrise, though exactly when I cannot say. I had long previously rejected the possibility of a light switch chasing away the darkness – the switch or the bulb were fickle at best, lighting only my knuckles to the ghostly color of my unsustainable effort. And then, as I was falling once again, headlong into the darkness, I experienced the first reds of sunrise catching and holding me. I flexed my fingers, marveling as a pink-tinge flowed from wrist to hand to fingertips. No longer was I struggling to hold onto Christ and the sobriety He demanded. Instead, wonder of wonders, He was holding onto me. His face was not stern, nor was it entwined with sobriety's taunting obscenity. His eyes held mine tenderly, freely offering the grace and mercy I did not deserve.

Always before I had fixated on a broken world: broken glass, broken hearts, broken lives. I reached for a god to help *me* fix the world. That god has failed me time and time again, leaving my world more shattered and blood-soaked than before. But in this new dawn, it was, well, dawning on me that a Court-sized god had always been doomed to failure. I need a deity bigger than me, bigger than this woeful world. I needed a God big enough to love the world with all its humanly induced flaws, big enough to love it because He was big enough to have created it in the first place. I needed Jesus, and with that admission, He ran to catch me, to rescue me from my self-centered and self-created disaster.

A presentation is calling; the time is now. Grabbing a piece of paper, I begin to write, not of programming and web page designs, but of gratitude for God's gift of my life:

Too often I look right past an empty cross and forget how very much my life has cost You. I wipe away the crimson stains from the cross and dull the nails that should serve as a constant reminder of how very much pain You bore for my existence. God, I need You more and more each day that passes. I owe You more each hour gone by, whether it be gratitude or the deeds that, all in all, my faith tends to lack. God, I battle between Your heavenly grace and my pride. It is an unbearable weight that I cannot carry alone or even at all. God, take my world apart if that is what it takes, take it all apart. Help me serve the ones that I despise. Help me speak Your Word, a word that I cannot even pretend to deny. God, help me not to just watch a world that You once proclaimed "good" fall to dust and look away from You. God, I am on my knees and I pray that You take my world apart; take my world apart; I pray, oh Lord, I pray. Take my world apart. Amen.

Overdue Thanks **Court Harris**
July 2008 **Claddagh Irish Pub**
Geneva, Illinois

It's a normal Wednesday night at work, steady but certainly not overwhelming. I'm here until close, but much of the dinner staff has already been cut for the day; my tip count is looking up. The hostess lets me know she just sat table 15 in my section. Heading over to offer my assistance, I do a little stutter step as a bolt of recognition passes through me.

The kid's back is to me; a dark pony tail is trailing down the grey t-shirt. Facing me, his father's head is bent slightly over the menu. Certainly, his eyes are open, but from my angle, I can't tell. He looks like he's praying, but maybe it only seems that way because I have seen him model that position so often.

"Hi! My name is Court and I'll be your server." Looking up at me, Angelo nods a greeting. There is no spark of recognition in his eyes. His son, Joshua, has gotten bigger in the last couple of years, as boys do in their early teens, but his trademark ponytail hasn't changed. He, too, appears more interested in dinner than in the stranger who will serve it. I wonder if my appearance has changed that much, or if I am just indistinguishable from the hundreds of others just like me they have seen over the years. I take their drink order and leave the table. I'm kind of relieved they don't remember me. It's generally not a good thing when someone from that part of my life does.

Angelo is not a feel-good kind of guy. But then, you can't be when you are dealing with the homeless. They will play you and take you for anything they can get, if you aren't tough as nails. Weekly, he sent one of his volunteers to drive the streets of Elgin in a bus that had done its penance with school children, and was now stuck in purgatory with the homeless. We would be rounded up and taken to Angelo's place, which wasn't much to look at, but there was always warm coffee and something to eat before prayers and a sermon. The congregants would likely have been frowned upon in a more traditional setting.

There was usually some time either before or after the service to just hang out. That's when I got to know Joshua. He reminded me of the kid I had met on Kentucky's back roads: kind-hearted and appropriately naïve, which was surprising with so many of us crossing his doorstep. Josh and I bonded over sci-fi. There's nothing like engaging a geeky, pre-teen boy on that topic, his imagination still pliable enough to suspend logic and explore a universe of possibilities. I was more than twice Josh's age, but he was a good friend in a lopsided kind of way. When we talked of stars and dust and magical technological advances yet to come, I got to shed years and return to innocence. It felt good. All too soon, the bus would take me back home, which is to say to some designated street corner back in Elgin. Home, at that time, was wherever my feet took me.

I want to say something to them, but the words don't form coherently when I take their order, seem trite when I bring them their food, and feel awkward while they are eating. I'm still new to this Christian thing and not sure I want to be branded as an outcast.

But I swear I can hear God whispering to my heart to say *something*. So, when I bring the check to the table, I bring a long overdue thank you with it. I tell Angelo and Josh that I had been a guest at their place. They were a step along the road that ultimately brought me back to God. I thank them for their compassion, for living their faith with and for the homeless. We all shake hands before they leave.

It's odd, really, that I worry what people will think of me as a Christian. I never worried about popular opinion when I truly was a social outcast. Of course, at that time, no one could have thought less of me than I already did, so making a good impression was a moot point.

I hope Angelo feels blessed, or affirmed at least. But like I said, he's tough as nails, and that's a good thing. His son certainly leads a less-than-conventional life, but I hope he follows his father's example of faith. Angelo is a good man who lives for the least of these. I know; I was.

Transformations **Court Harris**
September 2008 **St. Charles, Illinois**

It probably originated from one of those trite and trivial Facebook conversation starters – or what passes for conversation in the virtual world: if you could choose, how would you like to die? As someone who has spent so much time obsessing about such things for so many years, it took me completely by surprise when my co-worker, Brian, threw it out there as bartender-banter. The truly amazing part, though, is that I had an answer, without a moment's hesitation: I would like to be a martyr for Jesus Christ. He was shocked by an unexpected answer, but not as surprised as I by the stark truth of my soul's declaration.

How did I transform from a soulless zombie wanting to leave my purposeless existence, to a hope-filled disciple willing to die for the only thing worth living for? Just a couple of months ago, I was reticent to even say the name "Jesus" out loud, afraid of branding myself with a label that would make me a societal outcast. Now I'm willing to die, would be honored to die, for that name. It is a name that I have used far too many times to marginalize, defame, and destroy my fellow man. But it is that same name, spoken in desperation, that has made me whole again. Despite all my years of jeers, all my rants and taunts, Jesus rescued me. Me. Who am I to deserve such grace?

The pretty girl who trained me at the Claddagh, Christine, the one to whom the discussion of the daily special was our most meaningful conversation, is now my girlfriend. Our relationship is growing and deepening as we attend several Christian groups together. Friendships formed there spur us along our Christian walk. Her father is one of my Christian mentors, showing me what it means to be a man after God's own heart. Pastor Jeff and I also continue to meet when it can be arranged, our discussions diving deeper into matters of the eternal.

My parents and brothers, battle wounds healing, are a family again. We can never go back to who we were, nor would I want to; I am a new creation. But there are times when I see clearly how my actions have affected them, and I cringe. I wish I could expunge their memories of the pain I inflicted and flaunted for so many years. The venom I spat upon the ones I love has left ugly scars, burn marks that may fade, but will never disappear. They serve as a reminder of who I was and how I have been redeemed.

At times, I will casually inquire of missing items: the picture of Corey surfing in Australia or the quilt Mom made for my high school graduation. They look at me oddly, checking to see if I'm joking, before telling me the tale of how those items and so many others vanished in fits of my own rage. I'm learning not to ask anymore. It's enough that I am still here, that we are still here, that we are still family.

Last Sunday, the church announced upcoming baptism classes in preparation for the November ritual. In the United Methodist tradition into which I was born, I was baptized as an infant by my grandfather. Of course, I don't remember it, the event being of more importance to my parents than to me at the time. The Baptist church we now attend practices believer baptism. There in the pew, I felt the tug of the Spirit telling me I am a new person; I have been born again. I want to be baptized again, this time as an act of my own will, as a declaration of my faith. I asked Mom if she would be interested in joining me in being re-baptized. She agreed immediately.

Just as the water sprinkled on me so long ago was symbolic, not transformative, the water that will surround me in November will not wash me clean. I've already been washed in my Savior's blood and bleached whiter than snow. Who would have thought I would be so excited for the opportunity to brag publicly on the mercy God continually extends to me? That's what a second chance, a new life, will do for you!

Mercy **Lory Harris**
November 2008 **St. Charles, Illinois**

I will be baptized tomorrow – for the second time. When Court asked if I would join him there was no doubt I would – I am honored! Still, I had to wrestle privately with the concept. I value my first baptism, though I don't even vaguely remember it. But I imagine it: my parents standing up in front of the church with their first daughter, Dad relinquishing the pastor's position to his boss, the same man who would lead the pre-marital counseling for Ken and me a couple of decades later. It has always been important to me, and frankly life altering, that my parents took that first step on my behalf – that and so many more steps along the way to nurture my spiritual growth.

I don't want to be disloyal or ungrateful to my parents. Though as a parent, myself, there was no doubt that I must support my son on his journey, especially this journey! My friend Pam, herself both sprinkled and dunked, brought the internal discussion to a close with a question: If you have a chance to stand before a couple of hundred people and brag on God, why wouldn't you? Bring on the brag!

We have been encouraged, or more accurately, directed, to write out what we will say before our dip tomorrow. The written word and I are good friends, though the thought of speaking them tomorrow causes me angst. With so many baptismal candidates, my words must be whittled down into condensed God-brags. How does one sum up a lifetime of blessings in so few words? Each word must convey a thousand. Who am I kidding? My words, at best, will be one for one. It is the Spirit's job to cause them to swell and grow in the hearts of the listener.

My printer spits out the final draft:

> *As a young child, I accepted Christ at a revival meeting. I still remember thinking, "Who would not want that?" when the pastor described the gift of salvation. For the next 30 some years, I walked with Christ – sometimes closer, sometimes further away. But it was a pretty easy journey and I thought I had God all figured out.*
>
> *About six years ago, my life fell apart, and for the next five years or so, my heart was broken into so many pieces that I can't believe it kept beating. I cried more tears than I thought a body could produce. I cried to God and I yelled at Him. At times, I accused and cursed Him. And I found out that I really didn't know God so well after all. He is so much bigger than the pigeon hole I had tried to put Him into. I learned that*

God is not tame, but He is good. His actions are not predictable, but His grace is always present. His mercy arrives in abundance just when you think there is no hope at all.

I thank God for those years. He grew me up, He cleaned me up, and He gave me wings. I would relive every moment of those painful years again – a thousand times over – just to get to where I am now – this moment, right here. I'm anxious to see where He takes me. With anticipation and some fear, I wait to see what is next.

I've read and re-read the words so many times I could recite them without a glance, though I won't try that tomorrow. I would rather stare at black ink swimming on a white page than the hundreds of eyes staring back at my exposed soul. It is imperative to get this right – though over these years, I should have learned that "right" is not always immediately apparent.

Still, the words, reduced and distilled, tell the truth; they tell on me and they tell of the Holy One. When I think of the unfathomable gift of mercy and grace that has brought me to the point of joining my son in baptism, my soul sings in registers too high to be recorded and in a foreign language not of this earth. *Why me? Why have I received so priceless a gift when other mothers bury their sons and daughters?* It has been over a year since Court has displayed any of the graphic signs of being bipolar, and longer than that since he unilaterally stopped taking any medications. My confidence in an initial medical misdiagnosis grows daily. He was an addict, pure and simple.

Perhaps God took me to the brink of my limits - well beyond, by my perception - and then pulled me back. Or maybe, more likely, God just isn't done with me yet. There will be another precipice to dangle over, though who can say what the next one will look like?

I would relive those years "a thousand times over," I have declared, with all sincerity! These last few years have been the most precious of my life. I would not give them up for anything, their lessons being of more value than gold. Yet, I know the proclamation is only a half-truth. Were it up to me, I would run screaming in the opposite direction rather than start over. The pain is too real, my soul rubbed too raw, the anguish still too stark. Even knowing where God has brought me, I could not even once repeat those years by an act of my own will. I'm not brave enough, not strong enough, to choose that path again. God would have to choose it for me, push me forward against my will, just as He did the first time.

If I suddenly found myself there, again, what would I change? Everything! Even standing on this side, knowing the overwhelming blessing of seeing my child redeemed and walking with the Lord, in hypothetical round number two, I would do everything differently. Maybe I could make the trip more efficiently, carry my son with more strength or more compassion, or both. I would alter every step, but would it change anything? Someday, when I stand face to face with Jesus, I will ask Him where I was right and where I failed. Or perhaps when "someday" comes, I'll know that standing so near to Jesus is all that matters. The questions that plague me now will fade into dusty insignificance in the radiance of His glory.

Father God, I want to mean "a thousand times." I will myself to believe You a thousand times over. Jesus, if You will walk with me, carry me when necessary, comfort this frightened, confused toddler despite my tirades, then I will do my best to trust You when the road leads me where I fear to go. Amen.

And Grace **Court Harris**
November 2008 **First Baptist Church**
Geneva, Illinois

Not ordered by alphabet or age or length of attendance, Mom and I find ourselves placed at the end of the line of those to be baptized. There are probably a dozen people ahead of us, all barefoot and dressed in white robes. I wonder how many souls have worn this mantle before me. Were they as nervous as I am? Public speaking is high on the list of things people dread, which would be enough to churn my stomach, but there is more.

To most of the congregation, I will be just another soggy person. Some out there know more of my story than I will reveal today in my few words. Some know nothing yet and may not really care about my offerings. They may be happy for me and I hope they give God the praise, but by the end of their noontime meal, I will be all but forgotten. I will talk to all of them, but there are some with eyes and ears inclined my direction to whom I really want to speak. There are my parents, certainly, Mom standing beside me in anxious white and Dad watching from the pews. There are my friends from Come Thirsty who know large sections of my story and rally around me still. Christine, who has the most information of anyone who didn't walk the path with me, is seated with her parents, who have no idea the depths of the grace to which I will bear witness.

Our robed compatriots move slowly up the back steps, waiting their turn, alternately listening to those ahead and re-reading their own story. I realize their testimony is exiting my consciousness as quickly as it enters; by lunchtime I probably won't even remember exactly what I said. Good thing I hold it in my hands.

Mom and I reach the top step after the lady in front of us steps down into the five-by-five-foot pool. Pastor Jeff stands in the water, smiling, listening, and nodding when appropriate. He's a big man. It's not necessary to ask if he played football in college; that is a foregone conclusion. He wrestled, too, heavy-weight, no doubt. Those are the typical first impressions, but his soul is tender and witty and tuned to God. There is no one I would rather have push me under the water.

Another dripping, forgiven sinner is making her way up the steps on the far side. Mom and I catch each other's eye, take a deep breath, share a nervous smile and step down into the pool. Together we wade the couple of steps to the front ledge were a microphone awaits us.

As predetermined, Mom starts. I know she is nervous: her paper flutters slightly where there is no breeze, but her voice is steady and clear. She let me read her page a couple of days ago, while I was still trying to squeeze out words of my own. However, she hasn't seen what I will say. I don't think she wanted to sway my words. After much prayer, I hope that it is the Spirit who did the swaying, as indeed He has moved my heart.

Mom finishes, relinquishing the microphone to me, and steps over to Jeff. "Lory, buried with Christ and raised to walk in newness of life." With his hand on her back and a handkerchief covering her mouth and nose, I watch my mother disappear briefly beneath the surface. Reappearing with water running from her hair, she whispers, "thank you," to Jeff and then stands to his left, waiting for me. We will leave these waters as we entered: together.

My turn. I glance briefly at the congregation in front of me. This is right; this is where I should be. Regardless of the effect my words have on anyone, I am so grateful to have lived long enough for this opportunity.

"I was raised in a loving, Christian home, and was always surrounded by the blessings that God bestows on a family. I always believed in Christ and prayed to Him daily, and in middle school, while attending Camp Timber Lee in Wisconsin, Christ took a more personal role in my life. Through a couple of very specific songs and a moving speech from a visiting pastor, I was broken to tears for hours and accepted Christ as my personal savior. The immediate road afterwards was full of faith and praise.

"Unfortunately, when I was in high school, I began to fall into the ways of the world and away from Christ. I made the mistake of taking specific verses of Scripture out of context and to heart excessively while ignoring the rest of it. In my own mind, I was testing my faith by ignoring it completely and throwing the burden upon Christ's shoulders to come and hunt me down…or else.

"Through my arrogance and self-love, I managed to tear holes in the fabric of my family and couldn't see past my own pride. The more that Christ tapped on my shoulder to be let back in, the less I listened. After a couple of destructive years, I found myself homeless on the streets of Elgin, breaking bread with convicted felons on the run from justice, drug dealers, gang bangers, the mentally ill, and my ever-present, consuming pride.

"On one particularly cold night, Christ removed the blinders of pride and sin from my eyes and I was able to look back and wince at the destruction I'd left behind. I was able to realize that I had been steadily and proudly walking towards the world and Satan, and ignoring the taps of my Savior on my back.

"Through the grace of God Almighty and the love of my incredible father and mother, I was able to escape a fate that I made for myself and deserved to suffer. God never left me, as far as I tried to run, and today I've rededicated myself to Christ's kingdom and hold Him closely. Today, Christ's love, prayer and Scripture have taken a root in my heart, and though I still struggle with pride, a loving God reigns in my soul. Through our relationship, Christ tames my pride and holds the focus of my heart. I thank God daily for His gift of transformative grace and my inability to out-sin or out-run it. And, today, I stand an adult that my middle-school self would have envisioned and smiled upon."

Epilogue

Two years later, Court and Christine were married. Now their growing family fills a house that knows no silence, but plenty of joy.

Lory remains in Illinois with her husband, Ken. Three days a week, her "Clark Kent" role is in the field of finance. The remaining eight days a week, she wears her grandma cape – red, of course - for all the mini loves of her life.

You may follow Lory's blog at loryharris.com.

Ken, Lory and Court Harris

Acknowledgments

If I were to thank all the people who carried me along the paths of both living through and writing this book, the page count would resemble *War and Peace,* though without the literary longevity. I am humbled and offer my sincere group thanks to all in deference to the page count.

To my fellow travelers, either through my journey or your own of a similar variety - I hope you see yourself within these pages, and feel as blessed as I do by your companionship. I hope you catch the hope, not from me, but from the Author of all. In stillness, may you feel His loving arms wrap around you.

To Stephanie Rische – without your faith, guidance and encouragement, this book would have been thin, indeed, and privately held. Thank you for your belief and enthusiasm. I am so grateful that God happened you into my life!

To Merry Luehr – God knew how much I would need you when He engineered our acquaintance. I could not have lived through the years represented in this book without you. Nor would I now be enjoying life on this side nearly as much. Thank you for keeping me real, honest and on the right track – and thank you for being twelve-years-old with me when necessary.

To my family – thank you for letting me publicly remove any doubt regarding the fallacy of our perfect family image. Of course, Colin and Corey, you have been well aware of our familial warts since you could signify your age using the fingers on just one hand. Ken, my love, we have walked together for almost four decades – at times side by side, or face to face, or back to back. But we are together, and gratefully, purposely, lovingly so. When all is said and done, I am blessed beyond measure when our family gathers, in growing numbers, to laugh and tease and love each other beyond measure.

And finally, to Court – my baby boy who grew into a man of God. Thank you for your willingness to contribute to the authenticity and color of this story by sharing your recollections. How many times did we surprise each other as we discussed common events viewed from opposite sides of the fence? Words refuse to form that adequately express my love, awe and appreciation for your willingness to be so transparent, resulting in the light of Christ shining through you for all to see.

Thank you, God, for unwanted lessons – slowly, painfully learned and eternally treasured. I truly am the most blessed person I know.

About the Author

Lory Harris stands in awe of mercy and grace every time she remembers the years recounted here, which is just about daily. She sees it in her sons' eyes, her husband's embrace, and her grandloves' sloppy kisses. She hears it in the echo of the past and in dreams for the future. Some things stick with you for a long time; some things just should.

Her current lexicon meanderings tend to center around the next generations, and frequently sprout up in her blog, *Snip(pet)s and Snails and Grandboy Tales,* which tells stories of love and laughter, and sometimes tears. Life is, as it always has been, an unpredictable mixture of happy and sad. Please join the celebration, joyful or soggy, at LoryHarris.com.

Made in the USA
Lexington, KY
04 November 2017